W9-DIU-211

DETROIT AND ITS BANKS

Arthur M. Woodford

DETROIT AND ITS BANKS

The Story of Detroit Bank & Trust

Published for The Detroit Bank & Trust Company
by Wayne State University Press   Detroit   1974

A Savoyard Book

Library of Congress Cataloging in Publication Data

Woodford, Arthur M   1940–
   Detroit and its banks.

   (A Savoyard book)
   Bibliography: p.
   1. Detroit Bank and Trust Company—History.
I. Title.
HG2613.D64D518 1974 · 332.2'1'0977434   74-3455
ISBN 0-8143-1521-6

contents

List of Illustrations   7
Preface   9

1 Land of the Beaver
French Village   13
Under the Union Jack   20
The Americans Arrive   27

2 Era of the Wildcats
Cut Money and Shinplasters   35
Mercantile Center   41
"An Act to Organize and Regulate . . ."   48
Panic of 1837   56

3 Detroit Savings Fund Institute
Detroit in 1849   63
"A Bank for the Industrious and Prudent"   69
Panic of 1857   81
Civil War   87

4 Detroit Savings Bank
Mining, Railroads, and Consumer Goods   94
Tradesmen, Mechanics, and Laborers   103
Panic, Depression, and Recovery   114

5 The Age of the Motorcar
"At an Even Rate of Speed"   124
Branching Out   131
World War I   136
The Twenties   144

Governor Comstock's Proclamation
Mergers and Consolidations   152
"Shout It from the Housetops"   159
A National Holiday   168

Mr. Dodge at the Helm
The Recovery Road   179
A New Battle Front   189
To Berlin, Tokyo, and Washington   198

A New Direction
A Billion Dollar Bank   209
Branches, Branches Everywhere   215
Fort at Washington   222
Tomorrow   232

Appendices

Appendix A—"An Act to Incorporate
             the Detroit Savings Fund
             Institute." March 5, 1849.   237
Appendix B—"By-Laws and Regula-
             tions." May 9, 1849.   239
Appendix C—Detroit Savings Bank. "Ar-
             ticles of Association."
             July, 1871.   242
Appendix D—Detroit Bank and Trust
             merger history, March
             1849—March 1974.   246
Appendix E—Chairmen of the Board.   248
Appendix F—Presidents.   248
Appendix G—Directors.   248
Appendix H—Detroit Bank and Trust.
             Branches. 1974.   251
Appendix I—Detroit Bank and Trust.
             List of Officers and De-
             partments. 1974.   253

Notes   259
Bibliography   274
Index   281

list of illustrations

Illustrations 1–23 follow p. 37 in text.

1. Variations of the beaver hat.
2. A French *voyageur*.
3. A fur trade canoe.
4. *Voyageurs* portaging their canoe.
5. Indian wampum.
6. Indians bartering for goods.
7. Interior of a fur trading store.
8. Fort Lernoult.
9. United States colonial currency, 1775.
10 and 11. United States three, seven, and eight dollar bills (shin-plasters), 1780.
12. Detroit in 1794.
13. Bank of Detroit note, 1806.
14. British proclamation signed by General Procter at Detroit, 1813.
15. Bank of Michigan note, 1839.
16. Detroit in 1837.
17. City of Detroit due bill, 1837–40.
18. Detroit City Bank note, 1837.
19 and 20. Michigan wildcat bank notes.
21. Detroit and St. Joseph Rail Road Bank note, 1840.
22. Morris Canal & Banking Company note, 1841.
23. Mariners' Church.

Illustrations 24–43 follow p. 95 in text.

24. Elon Farnsworth.
25. Detroit in 1855.
26. Citizens' meeting, 1861.
27. Seymour Finney's livery barn.
28. Bank Chambers, 1881.
29. Detroit Savings Bank staff, 1881.
30. Alexander H. Adams.
31. Detroit in 1887.
32. Sidney D. Miller.
33. Main banking room, Bank Chambers, 1890.

34. King's and Detroit's first automobile, 1896.
35. Henry Ford and his quadricycle.
36. Olds Motor Works.
37. Detroit Savings Bank, branch no. 1.
38. Penobscot Building, main office of the Detroit Savings Bank, 1906–21.
39. DeWitt C. Delamater.
40. Second Liberty Loan Drive, 1918.
41. Detroit Trust Company Building, 1926.
42. Main office, Detroit Savings Bank and The Detroit Bank, 1921–63.
43. George S. Baker.

Illustrations 44–63 follow p. 211 in text.

44. *Detroit Times,* Tuesday, February 14, 1933.
45. Detroit Savings Bank reopening announcement, March 14, 1933.
46. Walter L. Dunham.
47. City of Detroit scrip, 1933.
48. Joseph M. Dodge.
49. Raymond T. Perring.
50. Charles H. Hewitt.
51. Joseph M. Dodge receiving the Grand Cordon of the First Class Order of the Rising Sun.
52. William B. Hall and Dr. Arnold Pilling at Fort Lernoult excavation.
53. Remodeling of old Detroit Trust Company Building, in 1964.
54. C. Boyd Stockmeyer.
55. Detroit Bank and Trust main office, 1964.
56. Detroit Bank and Trust, branch no. 84.
57–60. The Indian head logo of The Detroit Bank, and The Detroit Bank and Trust Company.
61–63. Maps of Detroit and its banks, 1849, 1929, and 1974.

My earliest recollection of Detroit Bank and Trust was as a very small boy who went with his mother while she did the family banking at the then Detroit Bank branch office on Hamilton and Collingwood. Of far more interest than the bank, though, was the National Guard Armory behind the branch. During the closing days of World War II, the Armory was filled with soldiers, trucks, jeeps, and tanks—all much more exciting than a bank. Later with my schoolmates from Doty Elementary School, I went to the same branch office to meet a real live American Indian. I shook hands with Chief Blue Cloud during the bank's 100th anniversary celebration. It took a week before my mother was able to convince me that I really should wash that hand.

Many years later, I was to learn that The Detroit Bank and Trust Company was founded in 1849 as the Detroit Savings Fund Institute. At the time the Institute first opened for business, the mood of the community was anything but friendly toward banks. I uncovered a sample of this feeling in an anonymous poem (written in 1849) from the files of the Burton Historical Collection:

> Come eastern friend, if you'll attend
> Unto the counsel of a friend,
> I think it would be your best plan
> To stay away from Michigan.
>
> The sawmills, they are dangerous things,
> Are running fast and slabs they fling;
> They kill you or cut off your hand
> And leave you a beggar in Michigan.
>
> Each Saturday night you want your pay,
> Expect your money right away,

But a written order is put in your hand.
That's the way you're paid in Michigan.

The doctors they are young in skill;
They do no good, but put in their bill;
They tell you they do all they can,
And let you die in Michigan.

The people they are getting sad
Because their money is all bad;
The banks all broke, but two or three,
And they'll soon die with "cholerie."

The swamps they are all filled with brakes,*
And are alive with rattlesnakes.
They lie and watch; do all they can
To bite the folks in Michigan.

There are a few nice boys, 'tis true,
But O, alas, what can they do?
For if one wants a pretty wife
She can't be found to save his life.

There are nice girls, I'll own it's true.
But, deary me, what can they do?
For if they want a pretty man
They have to leave their Michigan.

This, then, was the atmosphere in which The Detroit Bank and Trust Company was established. The fact that it has survived and grown to one of this nation's greatest banking institutions is a testimony to the integrity of the men who founded the Detroit Savings Fund Institute.

No book of this kind can be considered complete without the author's acknowledgement of the help of the many people who gave freely of their time, advice, materials, and specialized knowledge. Without them, the end product would be much less than it is.

First, thanks to Mrs. Bernice Sprenger, chief of the Burton Historical Collection, Detroit Public Library, her first assistant, Mrs. Alice Dalligan, and to the curator of manuscripts, Joseph F. Oldenburg. They were most helpful in digging out a wealth of information, making suggestions, and assisting with the selection of illustrations. Their knowledge of available material, and their unfailing promptness in responding to de-

* Brake—a place overgrown with bushes, shrubs, brambles, or cane; a thicket. Any large or coarse fern.

mands for it, has earned them an admirable reputation as scholarly assistants.

Other members of the Detroit Public Library staff that I would like to especially thank include James Bradley, chief of the Automotive History Collection, who was most helpful in providing statistical information and resource material for the sections of this book dealing with the automobile. Thomas Mulford of the Business and Finance Department assisted in gathering materials on Detroit's current banking scene: and Richard Maciejewski of the Sociology and Economics Department assisted in locating information from census reports and other government publications.

Thanks also to Dr. Robert Warner and his staff at the Michigan Historical Collections, University of Michigan, Ann Arbor, and to Solon Weeks, director, and Miss Margot Pearsall, assistant director, Detroit Historical Museum.

In addition, I must express my profound gratitude to the staff of Detroit Bank and Trust. Their enthusiasm, always a sustaining ingredient, was matched only by their cooperation in making available everything I asked for, and in giving me free use of the bank's records and facilities. It was a pleasure to work with Raymond T. Perring, chairman of the board. Not only did he take time from his very busy schedule to talk with me about the bank and its history, but he also read the manuscript in rough form. As a result, he made several extremely helpful suggestions and, in more than one instance, saved me from grievous error.

I am grateful, too, to former cashier Harold P. Carr and his secretary Miss Anne Nielan. Miss Nielan was always most cheerful in providing the minutes of the board of directors, in locating annual reports, and in gathering other needed materials. Eugene A. Miller, vice-president and controller, deserves a special thanks for patiently explaining banking terms, figures from bank statements, etc. He was always willing to answer my frequent and hurried telephone requests. Also thanks to retired vice-president Arthur G. Reeves who invited me into his home to use his private library and to read and use several of his unpublished papers on the history of banking. A very special word is due Darwin D. Martin, Jr., assistant vice-president, Public Relations, whose assistance, frequently at the sacrifice of his own time and convenience, helped me over some of the most troublesome parts of this undertaking.

Other members of the bank's staff, the value of whose help must not be measured by the brevity of this expression of thanks, include: C. Boyd Stockmeyer, president; Rodkey Craighead, executive vice-president; Jack L. Talbot, senior vice-president and his Branch Offices Administration staff; Charles J. Snell, vice-president, Marketing; Frederick C. Hertel, vice-president, International Banking; Walter B. Fisher, vice-president, Holding Company; and William F. Piper, former manager, and Donald F. Rodgers, sub-manager, operations, London, England branch office. Messrs. Piper and Rodgers were most helpful in discussing their operation during my visit to their great city.

Finally, special thanks to Joseph Klima, Detroit Institute of Arts, for his assistance in the preparation of the illustrations; Ronald G. Williams, Treasurer's Office, City of Detroit; Miss Sue Cherry, Money Museum, National Bank of Detroit; Oliver Marcks, former vice-president of the Equitable Trust Company; and Malcolm C. Taylor, former deputy commissioner, Michigan State Banking Commission.

Lastly, thanks to my friend George W. Southworth who read the manuscript, and on many a lunch hour sat with me over a cup of coffee discussing the history of Detroit and its banks.

1

Land of the Beaver

FRENCH VILLAGE

The City of Detroit was founded in 1701 as a French outpost to control the rich fur trade in what is now Michigan and the Old Northwest, and to prevent the British from encroaching upon the area. To understand the crucial importance of the fur trade in determining the destiny of Detroit and its commercial and financial life, it is necessary to realize that the commerce of early modern times, unlike that of the twentieth century industrial world, was largely in luxury commodities. The trade in foodstuffs, textiles, and other necessities was less important because such a major proportion of the population of Europe produced and processed the necessities of life for themselves. While the trade in peltry is no small business today, it in no way exerts the powerful influence that it did in the seventeenth and eighteenth centuries. Furs were worn by the French aristocrats and the members of the wealthy middle class. Since France had become the fashion center of Europe under Louis XIV, the wearing of furs spread to other European countries. Of special importance in creating a demand for furs was the vogue of the broad-brimmed beaver hat in the seventeenth century. For a long time Europe had been able to meet the demand for furs; yet, as time went on, the harvest of peltries ran short. Poland, which had been a chief source of beaver for the

13

French market, became "trapped out"; so France turned to the new world and Canada.

France was not alone; other European powers also sent explorers across the Atlantic. Spain claimed Central and South America, and England claimed what became the United States seaboard. Each colonizing power demanded a profit from its colonies. Spain acquired the gold and silver of Mexico and Peru; England prospered by shipping tobacco out of Virginia, and codfish and naval stores out of New England. Canada produced neither gold nor silver nor much tobacco, but it was rich in fur.

France's claim to Canada was established in 1535 when Jacques Cartier discovered the St. Lawrence River and sailed up it to the site of Montreal. In 1608 Samuel de Champlain arrived as governor and about that time the period of settlement began. Many immigrants found the fur trade much more lucrative than the drudgery of farming. This spurred the fur trade even more. To control it, as well as to offer protection against the Iroquois, a string of outposts was established. Some of these were where the missionaries had already set up missions. Years before Detroit was founded, several of these forts or trading posts were flourishing in Michigan. They were at Sault Ste. Marie as early as 1668; Fort de Buade at St. Ignace in 1686; Fort St. Joseph, where Port Huron is now located, in 1686; and others at or near modern St. Joseph (1679) and Niles (1691).

The head of a typical French trading post was called the *bourgeois.* Under him was a small army of traders sent to secure the peltry. His duty was to secure food, traps, and blankets for them, supply them with articles to trade, see that the furs they brought in were properly cured and stored, and make arrangements for shipping the furs to the East.

Two groups of men were indispensable to the *bourgeois* in carrying on the fur trade. The first, called *coureurs de bois* went out into the forests, hunted and trapped, lived with the Indians, and bargained with them for furs. Sturdy, rough, and independent, they could endure unbelievable hardships. Frequently their only protection from the weather was a rude bower of evergreen branches; their only food, corn and bear fat. The corn was prepared by boiling it in strong lye, the hulls were then removed and the kernels mashed and dried. The ordinary allowance was a bushel of corn and two pounds of grease per man, per month. Leaving the outposts in the fall, they spent the winter in the woods, then came out again in the spring with canoe loads of furs. They often lived among the Indians for

14

years and took Indian wives. The *coureurs de bois* (the name was given to both French and French-Indians) had no particular allegiance to the French authorities and as often as not traded with the English at Albany.

The other group, the *voyageurs,* were the boatmen. Seemingly tireless at the paddles of a canoe, they would drive their frail craft upstream for hours on end, keeping time with their strokes to the lilt of a lively song. The largest canoes were of birch bark, 33 feet long and 4½ feet wide. They could carry a load of 4 tons, including the weight of 8 paddlemen. When a rocky reach of water blocked their way, they unloaded the canoe, swung a 90-pound pack of furs or merchandise onto their backs, and trotted along the portage path to a place where the canoe could be launched again.[1]

While both *coureurs de bois* and *voyageurs* were essential to the fur trade, they were nuisances in the settlements. Drinking, brawling, swaggering along the streets, always ready for a fight, they frightened the peaceful *habitants,* who were greatly relieved when they set out again for the north country in the fall.

The fundamental difficulty with the fur trade was that it was simply a gamble. It could not be otherwise, considering the methods of doing business. The merchants in Montreal dominated the industry. They imported goods from Europe, usually on a commission basis, and shipped them to the *bourgeois* at the trading posts at an advance on the cost. These consignments were sent at the expense of the consignee, who also had to accept the risk of loss during transportation. It was reckoned that one canoe load of Indian goods would buy four canoe loads of furs. Sometimes the profits were fabulous, as much as 1,000 percent on the investment in trade goods. In other years so many skins were taken to Montreal and Quebec that the prices were ruinous; yet the search for furs continued.[2]

The growth of the fur trade in Canada was carried out under the effective administration of Louis de Buade, Comte de Frontenac, the governor of New France. While endeavoring to keep tight control of the fur trade, Frontenac ran into trouble. The clergy, particularly the Jesuits, frowned upon Frontenac's system, regarding the trading posts as dens of licentiousness and depravity, which in truth they frequently were. Brandy was a chief trade item and the Indians could not get enough of it. Far too often the Indians exchanged all of their furs for brandy; and after a wild celebration which might last for several days, they would have nothing to show for a winter's trapping

15

in the woods. The difficulties between the Jesuits and Frontenac led to the latter's recall in 1682. However, matters did not greatly improve during his absence. Since he was a favorite at the court of Louis XIV and had great influence there, he was sent back to New France in 1689.

Upon Frontenac's return, the situation continued to deteriorate, and in 1696 the government decreed that all furs had to be delivered by the Indians to Montreal. The forts strung around the Great Lakes were ordered closed and abandoned. Only the Jesuits henceforth were to be permitted to maintain mission settlements in Indian country.

Unfortunately for the French, their plan was not at all successful as the Indians turned to trade with the English. It quickly became apparent to Frontenac that a new start in the West was essential if the region was to be rescued from British domination. So, in 1698, he sent a favorite lieutenant back to France to present a plan to Louis XIV and his ministers to remedy the situation. Frontenac's lieutenant was Antoine de la Mothe Cadillac, who had been commandant at the key post of Fort de Buade at St. Ignace before it was closed down.

Cadillac's plan in simplest terms called for colonizing the West on a permanent basis. He realized that Michilimackinac was not the place to start because the northern region was too cold and too barren. A better place, he insisted, could be found lower down the lakes, a place like *le Détroit*, the strait connecting Lake Erie with the upper lakes, where the land was fertile, where the waters narrowed and a defense could be made against British intrusion. There Cadillac recommended a fortified town be built, a place at which the Indians could be induced to establish their villages. If this model settlement should work out satisfactorily, others would be constructed. Cadillac specifically had in mind a place at the mouth of the Mississippi, and another part way up that river. He was never able to build them, but his plan was used by others, resulting in present-day New Orleans and St. Louis.

Basically Cadillac's plan was this: if Louis XIV would give him a generous piece of land on the Detroit River with seignorial rights, together with a trade monopoly, Cadillac would hire soldiers for the garrison and furnish civilians for farming and trading, all at his own expense. The farmers would make the post self-sustaining, the traders and Indians he expected to attract would make it financially stable, and the soldiers would maintain French sovereignty in the entire region.[3] The king and his chief counselor, Count Pontchartrain whose jurisdiction extended over the colonies, were quite enthusiastic over the plan and early in 1701 Cadillac returned to Canada with the king's approval.

Cadillac immediately set about obtaining provisions and supplies for his expedition and in early July the flotilla of canoes pushed off from Montreal. Because a peace treaty was being negotiated with the Iroquois, Cadillac thought it best not to travel the easy route up the St. Lawrence and through Lakes Ontario and Erie. Instead, he chose the old wilderness road of the *voyageurs* up the Ottawa River, through Lake Nipissing, and down the French River to Georgian Bay. Although this entailed some back-breaking portages, it was a far safer route. Once in Georgian Bay and out into Lake Huron, the expedition followed the eastern shore south to the entrance of the Detroit River. They passed the present site of Detroit and, on the night of July 23, camped on Grosse Ile, which was seriously considered for a location of the settlement. Because of the width of the river there close to the head of Lake Erie, Cadillac had second thoughts.

The following day the expedition, which consisted of 100 uniformed soldiers and *voyageurs* in 25 large canoes, headed back up the river. Cadillac and his men turned their canoes from mid-stream and drew them up onto the narrow sandy beach. They climbed the 20-foot bluff and surveyed the terrain. The site Cadillac had chosen for his settlement was at a point where the river was at its narrowest and where the high banks made it the most defensible. As far as can be determined, the landing point was at the foot of present-day Shelby Street a few feet below Jefferson Avenue. [If one were to seek the spot today, he would find it where the Veterans Memorial Building stands.]

Cadillac at once paced off the limits of his planned village between the Detroit River and the small Savoyard River to the rear, marked the corners of his stockade, and within two hours his ax-men were in the nearby woods felling timber for construction.

The next few weeks were devoted to clearing the land and building the fort. The stockade consisted of a wall of twenty-foot logs, four feet of which was embedded in the earth. A bastion or blockhouse was set at each corner and a moat was dug outside. At least two gates provided access, one on the river side wide enough to permit large loads to be brought in, and another in the east wall.

17

There was really only one street—Ste. Anne—which paralleled the river along the top of the bluff. It was twenty-two feet wide. Another shorter street above Ste. Anne and two north-south streets, more properly alleys or lanes, were the only other roads in the village. The first building erected was the church. It has been said that it was completed in two days and that the first Mass was sung on the feast of Ste. Anne in whose honor it was dedicated and for whom it was named.* Next, lots were marked out and houses were built. The ordinary houses were made of small oak logs or posts set perpendicularly into the ground like the stockade, chinked with grass or mud, and roofed with bark slabs. Shortly after this a large warehouse was built for storage of public property and furs, and for use as a trade store. The whole village—stockade, streets, and buildings—occupied an area which today consists of about one city block, bounded roughly by Griswold, Jefferson, Shelby and Larned.

In September 1701 Madame Cadillac and Madame Tonty, the wife of Alphonse de Tonty, who was second in command, arrived at Detroit. There had been no women in the original expedition, and Cadillac wanted to convince the Indians that Detroit was intended to be a permanent settlement. In October 1701 ground was broken adjacent to the fort and about fifteen acres of winter wheat were sown. There was a crop the following July, although it was said to have been rather poor. Nevertheless, it demonstrated that the land could be cultivated and that the village could be made reasonably self-sufficient. From the standpoint of trade, matters went well from the beginning. A band of Hurons set up a village near the foot of present-day Third Street; the Ottawas settled across the river near the foot of Belle Isle; and the Potawatomis and Miamis set up their villages a short distance downriver. Before long Cadillac reported 2,000 Indians in the area, and in the spring distant tribes from as far away as Lake Superior and the Illinois country came in to trade their furs. The pelts that were shipped from *Fort Ponchartrain du Détroit* included bear, elk, deer, marten, raccoon, mink, lynx, muskrat, opossum, wolf, fox and beaver.[4] Thus within a very short time Detroit was established as the center of the Great Lakes fur trade.[5]

Much to his disappointment, Cadillac never was given seigneury at Detroit. However, he did possess certain feudal rights and among

* The present-day Ste. Anne's Church is located on the corner of Howard and Ste. Anne on Detroit's near west side not far from the Ambassador Bridge. Ste. Anne's is the second oldest continuous parish in the United States, the oldest being a parish in St. Augustine, Florida.[6]

18

them was the granting of land to the *habitants*. At first these grants consisted of house lots inside the stockade; the farmers worked the public domain outside the palisade walls. Beginning about 1707, he awarded farms to *habitants* on both sides of the river. These farm grants, known as the private claims in today's land abstracts, consisted of river frontages of from one to four or five arpents (an arpent was about 200 linear feet), and in some cases extended back two or three miles. The rear line of most of the original grants that are now within the city of Detroit is somewhere in the vicinity of Holden and Harper avenues. They became known as ribbon farms because of their long narrow shape, and their boundaries are marked in modern Detroit by streets which bear the names of the original grantees, such as Beaubien, Riopelle, St. Aubin, Chene, Campau, and Livernois.

For the next few years, Cadillac's little settlement prospered. In 1710 he was appointed governor of Louisiana Territory and in 1711 he left Detroit never to return. After a brief visit to France he came back to America to his new post with headquarters at Mobile. In 1720 he returned to France for good and was given the governorship of Castelsarrasin, a small town near his birthplace. He filled that position until his death on October 15, 1730.

For nearly sixty years after Cadillac's founding of Detroit, it was a completely French town, socially as well as governmentally. And except for the siege of the fort by the Fox Indians in 1712, and other occasional Indian troubles, life in the town was quiet and uneventful. The French settlers were not a particularly progressive people. Conservative by habit, they were content to live in a semi-feudal society, living off their fur trade and their small farms. There were no attempts at or interest in developing even the most primitive industrial enterprise.

The fertile soil yielded good crops of wheat, oats, and some corn. Most of what was raised was consumed by the family with the surplus being sold or given for the support of the town, the garrison, and the church. Almost all of the farms had cattle, pigs, and chickens, while the nearby forest supplied the family table with venison, birds, and muskrat; and the river at the front door was a never-failing source of sturgeon and whitefish. Each farm had its orchard of apple, peach, and pear trees. The apple crop made a superior cider, the peaches produced an excellent brandy, and there were both wild and cultivated grapes and berries aplenty, so that the wine crocks were always full.

The houses of the *habitants* became a little more livable as time went on, although they were never pretentious. The early rough pole structures eventually were clapboarded over; lofts or second floors, lighted by dormer windows, became common. Many of the houses were whitewashed and their Dutch doors were frequently painted apple-green. Their yards, enclosed by picket fences, contained the usual bake ovens and wells with long sweeps. Similar houses can still be seen along the St. Lawrence.

The *habitants* raised large families, and their sons and daughters married at an early age. While they were devoted to their church, they were also a merry lot, with their songs and dances. In warmer weather there was cart racing, in the winter months horse racing and sleigh riding up and down the frozen river were the most common sports. Schools were not regularly kept, and most of the *habitants* were illiterate. Newspapers were unheard of and unneeded. When the occasional traveler brought news of the outside world or an official announcement was to be made, the towncrier called it out from the porch of Ste. Anne's after Sunday morning Mass. Politics in the modern sense of the word was absent as there were no democratic institutions. All in all it was an isolated, and in a sense, idyllic life that Detroiters lived in this period.

But there were clouds upon the horizon. Within a few short years France and England were once again at war.

UNDER THE UNION JACK

In 1760, after fifty-nine years of French rule, Detroit became a British possession. This occurred as a result of the French and Indian War. While an offshoot of a long European power struggle, the conflict was almost entirely a North American war. In simplest terms, it grew out of the covetousness of the English seaboard colonies for the vast rich Ohio River and Great Lakes basins which were French property.

The fighting lasted from 1754 until 1760, but Detroit never came under direct attack from the British. The issue was settled elsewhere, on the Plains of Abraham just outside of Quebec. On September 13, 1759, General James Wolfe scaled the high bluff that appeared to make the city impregnable and decisively defeated the defenders. Only Montreal was left and it was surrendered to General Jeffrey Amherst on September 8, 1760. Detroit and all the remaining French possessions were included in the capitulation.

Detroit was still more of an area than a village when the British arrived. The entire population up and down both sides of the river was about 2,000, exclusive of the garrison. Perhaps 500 people lived in the village or adjacent to it. There were about 300 buildings in the stockade and adjoining fields. The fort itself was considerably larger than the one Cadillac had built; its dimensions were about 100 yards north and south by 200 yards east and west. There were bastions or blockhouses at the corners and over the main gates. These towers were armed with cannon of varying size. Inside the stockade, the streets were much as they had been—some of them had been extended beyond the walls, so the village actually included more than just the fort. In fact, more people lived outside the walls than inside.

Early in the spring of 1761, English traders began to arrive at Detroit. This afforded the Indians an opportunity to dispose of their winter's catch of furs and to trade for needed goods. In order to satisfy the wants of the Indians, the traders had to stock a large variety of items. Articles most frequently in demand were: strouds (blankets) of blue, black, and scarlet; cotton and heavy napped woolen cloth for stockings; worsted and yarn hose; flowered serges of a variety of colors; calicos and calamancos (a glossy woolen fabric) for gowns; ribbons of all sorts; linen for shirts and readymade shirts; threads, needles, and awls; clasp knives and scalping knives; vermilion and verdigris for body painting; jew's harps and hawk bells, stone and plain rings; silver gorgets and trinkets; small beads, brass wire, horn combs, scissors, razors, and hand mirrors; brass and tin kettles; tobacco, pipes, and snuff boxes; tomahawks and small hatchets; black and white wampum; red leather trunks, pewter spoons, and gilt cups; powder, flints, lead, duck shot, and muskets; beaver and fox traps; iron fish spears; and of course rum.[7]

Unfortunately, the traders proved to be unscrupulous and hard bargainers and the Indian soon began to complain to Captain Campbell, the British Commandant, of the prices they had to pay. The Indians who at first had welcomed the British takeover of Detroit were quickly becoming disillusioned.

To get a firsthand view of the trade problems and to hold private conferences with the Indians in the area, British Superintendent of Indian Affairs Sir William Johnson arrived at Detroit in September 1761. His first task was to establish official regulations to govern the fur trade. While Johnson was to determine these regulations, it was to be the responsibility of Captain Campbell and his officers to see to it that they were not broken.

Included in the new regulations was a list of prices for furs. Not only was the cost of trade goods in pelts important to the Indians, but the relative value of particular kinds of fur as well. All prices were to be quoted in terms of beavers or bucks—a buck being a buckskin, the hide of one large prime male deer. Johnson decreed that one beaver was worth one good buckskin or one small buckskin and one doeskin. One small beaver was worth one marten or two raccoons while one large beaver might be worth as much as six raccoons.

Johnson also felt that since the traders at Oswego, on Lake Ontario, made a 50 percent profit, which he thought reasonable for the expense and risk of transporting goods there, the traders at Detroit ought to be allowed somewhat more in proportion to the greater distance. Thus, with the beaver or the buck [from which evolved our slang term for a dollar] as the basic medium of exchange, a whole list of prices was set on various commodities: a large blanket could be purchased for three beavers, and a small striped blanket for two beavers. An ordinary man's shirt was given a valuation of one beaver, and a ruffled shirt was sold for two beavers. A pound of gunpowder sold for one beaver as did four bars of lead from which musket balls were made. Of course a musket was the most expensive item selling for anywhere from ten to twenty beaverskins.[8]

Prices were also set for the two items that were most frequently asked for by the Indians—tobacco and rum. Usually these were given as presents but when sold, the tobacco fetched one beaverskin per foot; the rum diluted with water, two beavers per jug. The tobacco was commonly twisted in the form of a rope, and the quantity of a given portion was indicated by its length. The degree to which the rum was diluted depended primarily on the honesty of the trader and how badly the Indian wanted a bottle of the firewater.[9]

Throughout the month of September, Johnson held his conferences with the Indians, trying to assure them of the friendship of their new British father, King George III. The conferences ended with a great council meeting. To emphasize his sincerity, Johnson presented to the Indians a belt of wampum, a large quantity of gifts, and had an ox roasted for the feast. After the council was completed, Johnson left Detroit and returned East.

Yet, even with Johnson's assurances of British friendship, the natives grew more wary. The underlying causes of dissatisfaction still remained: the frosty arrogance of the British officers at the fort; the dishonesty of the traders; the continued rationing of rum; and the fear of the advancing tide of frontier settlement. The final blow came when General Amherst issued orders limiting the distribution of ammunition, and the Indians easily believed the rumor that the British were trying to starve them to death.

In the spring of 1763, the gathering tempest broke. Under a plan of confederation developed by the Ottawa Chief Pontiac, the British forts from Niagara and Fort Pitt to Mackinac and St. Joseph were simultaneously attacked. For himself, Pontiac reserved the principal fort—Detroit. One by one the posts were taken—soon every fort west of Niagara except Detroit was wiped out. Sandusky, St. Joseph, Fort Miamis, Presque Isle, and Mackinac were all captured and their garrisons either massacred or held prisoner.

At Detroit, the vigilance of Major Gladwin (who had arrived in Detroit as commandant in September 1761) defeated an attempted surprise attack, and his strong leadership maintained the defense against heavy odds during many desperate weeks.

The siege at Detroit continued through the summer months but as autumn approached the Ottawas were deserted by their Indian allies. Finally, on October 31, 1763, Pontiac sent a message to Gladwin offering to make peace. Without waiting for an official reply, Pontiac and his followers left Detroit for their home on the Maumee River. The siege was at an end and of all the western posts, only Detroit had survived.

Following Pontiac's War, life in Detroit settled down to a peaceful and normal pattern which more or less continued for about a dozen years. But the peaceful days did not last. In 1775 Britain's Atlantic seaboard colonies rose up in armed rebellion.

Detroit played a key, although not a decisive, role in the American Revolution. Chiefly it served as a base from which expeditions were sent to harass the American settlements in Kentucky, western Pennsylvania, and New York. These marauding parties, composed of Indians led by white partisan raiders, caused great havoc on the frontier. It has been estimated that more than two thousand men, women, and children were killed and scalped by Detroit-based Indian war parties.[10]

Behind all this border fury was Henry Hamilton, who had arrived in Detroit on November 9, 1775, to assume the duties of lieutenant-governor. Although he was an army man, his duties as lieutenant-governor were more those of a civil administrator. He determined overall policy, but he did not command the garrison which for most of the war was in the capable hands of Captain Richard B. Lernoult. Because of Hamilton's part in planning and directing raids, particularly against Kentucky, the Americans hung the label of "Hamilton the Hair-Buyer" on him. There is no real evidence that he paid for scalps; on the contrary, he frequently cautioned departing war parties not to make war against women and children.[11]

In order to check the raiding parties from Detroit and hopefully to capture the fort, the Americans organized an offensive in 1778 under Colonel George Rogers Clark. With a force of Virginia and Kentucky frontiersmen, he captured the distant posts of Kaskaskia and Cahokia and appeared ready to advance upon Detroit. Alarmed by the threat, Lieutenant-Governor Hamilton gathered a small force of rangers and regulars and went to Vincennes, Indiana, to block Clark's advance. Clark, however, made an epic march across the flooded plains of southern Illinois and Indiana, and surprised Vincennes. Hamilton, outnumbered and unprepared, surrendered.

Clark's planned advance toward Detroit was stalled by lack of manpower; meanwhile, a new threat was posed. Daniel Brodhead with a small army of Pennsylvanians marched from Pittsburgh into Ohio and built a fort about 90 miles south of Sandusky. To Captain Lernoult, an attack against Detroit appeared certain and imminent. Surveying his facilities for defense, Lernoult found much to be desired. The town was a tinderbox with its wooden buildings; and it was obvious the old stockade could not withstand an attack by a properly armed enemy. From the height of land several hundred yards north of the town, enemy cannon could easily control the defenses and force a quick surrender. Lernoult decided that a new fort must be built as soon as possible on the strategic hill if Detroit were to be held by the British.

In the absence of the regular engineering officer, Lernoult picked Captain Henry Bird to design and construct the new fort. One late afternoon in November 1778, Bird paced off the outline of a new defense works, and the next day construction began. The new fort was placed on the rising ground north of town. It covered an area of about three acres, its center being in what is now the intersection of Fort and Shelby streets.

During the winter of 1778–79, Lernoult and Bird drove their men relentlessly. Lernoult also enlisted civilians from Detroit to help on the project, ordering all able-bodied men to work three days out of nine. The British citizens, mostly merchants, willingly consented to these demands, while the French settlers had to be coerced. Finally, in April 1779, the work, named Fort Lernoult in honor of the captain, was ready for action.

The completed fort had earthen ramparts eleven feet high, twenty-six feet thick at the base, and twelve feet wide at the top of the parapet. The land surrounding the new fort was cleared so that the enemy would have no cover during an attack. There was only one gate, on the south or town side. It was protected by a blockhouse tower and a drawbridge. Lernoult stripped the old fort and the naval vessels on the river of their guns and requisitioned more from Quebec. Inside the fort a number of buildings were put up and a well was dug to insure a supply of fresh water. Finally, pickets were erected to extend from the corners of the new fort down to the east-west walls of the town.

When construction was completed, the garrison moved into the fort and prepared for an attack. Captain Lernoult waited to hear of the movements of the American forces—the threatened attack never came. The Americans were never able to muster a force sufficient for such a campaign.[12]

The fort continued to be called Fort Lernoult as long as the British occupied Detroit. When the Americans took over, it was renamed Fort Detroit, and was so known until after the War of 1812 when it became Fort Shelby in honor of the governor of Kentucky who led an army of Kentuckians to the relief of Detroit. In 1827, no longer needed, the fort was dismantled; the earth from the ramparts was used to fill in the land below Jefferson Avenue, and the ground where the fort had stood was subdivided. [It now comprises the heart of Detroit's financial district.]

The Revolutionary War ended in 1781 with the surrender of Yorktown, and yet it did not end for Detroit. A formal peace treaty was signed in 1783, assigning all of the Northwest Territory between the Ohio and Mississippi rivers and the Great Lakes to the United States. This, of course, included Michigan and Detroit. To assert its sovereignty over the areas as well as to provide for its orderly development, Congress adopted the Ordinance of 1787, better known as the Northwest Ordinance. A notable charter, the ordinance provided for the territory's division into five states when the population warranted and laid down certain ground rules for a territorial form of government until the time for admission to the Union arrived.

But the transition was slow as far as Detroit was concerned. The British were loath to give Detroit up. Under pressure from local and

Montreal merchants who did not want to lose the rich Indian trade, British occupation continued. The excuse was that the United States had not yet fulfilled all its 1783 treaty obligations. Consequently Detroit existed in a sort of political limbo. Although legally it was a United States possession, the British continued to occupy it with troops and to govern it after a fashion. It continued to be the chief western base for the British Indian Department, and the British gave huge amounts of money in the forms of gifts and subsidies in an effort to maintain control over the Midwest tribes. War parties still harassed Ohio and Indiana, and the authorities at Detroit just turned their backs on what was happening. Merchants complained because what amounted to military government was bad for business. A lack of civil courts made the collection of debts difficult. At this time nearly all Detroit business and property was owned by seventeen individual merchants or partnerships.[13] To placate them, a semblance of civil law was established; and in 1791, when Upper Canada, now Ontario, was separated from Quebec, Detroit, an American city, anomalously elected two representatives to the Canadian provincial council of parliament.

Obviously it was a situation the United States could not long tolerate. President George Washington sent an army into the Ohio country to subdue the Indians once and for all. After a couple of abortive campaigns, General "Mad Anthony" Wayne defeated the confederated tribes in 1794 at the Battle of Fallen Timbers near present-day Toledo. This victory placed a well-trained and effective American army on the doorstep of Detroit. The British position was untenable, and when Chief Justice John Jay negotiated a peace and commercial treaty with the British government in November 1794, he had no difficulty in securing an article that provided for the evacuation of Detroit. In the spring of 1796 the garrison of Detroit was withdrawn across the river, and the new British base Fort Malden was established at Amherstburg at the mouth of the Detroit River. Only a small detail of British troops remained at Detroit.

On July 11, 1796, a detachment of sixty-five American troops under the command of Captain Moses Porter arrived at Detroit. The fort was turned over to them and the Stars and Stripes were hoisted. Detroit became an American town at last.

THE AMERICANS ARRIVE

Following the arrival of the Americans, the major mercantile interest in Detroit continued to be furs. One of the first tasks facing the Americans was the establishment of a policy for the management of the trade. The French and British had found the regulation of the trade to be an almost impossible task. The French attempted to place the traffic in peltries in the hands of a few, a fur-trading aristocracy, and piled decree upon decree to control it. The result was corruption, illegal trade, and defiance of the laws which many considered unjust and unfair. Under the British, licenses were issued to almost anyone merely for the asking. This policy ended in disaster with dishonest traders using every means to get the advantage over their competitors. Only the sharpest and most ruthless of these independent traders survived.

The American plan for controlling the trade was to establish a series of trading posts or factories. Agents were to be appointed to operate the factories where quality goods would be sold to the Indians at low prices in the hope that this sort of competition would compel the independent traders to change their practices. In this manner the government hoped to win the friendship of the Indians as well as control the fur trade. The first factory at Detroit was opened in 1802. After the fire of 1805, it was moved to Mackinac and independent traders such as John Askin, William Macomb, James Abbott, and John May·retained control of the trade in the Detroit area. Generally, the factories were not successful and the system was abolished in 1822.[14]

Besides their interest in the fur trade, the merchants in Detroit also carried on a considerable local trade. When they went shopping, the townspeople had a wide variety of items from which to choose: foodstuffs, spices, wines, rum, household goods, yard goods, clothing, shoes, boots, cooking utensils, and homemade remedies. In addition they could purchase or order building supplies, carpenter's tools, farm implements, hunting knives, fishing gear, traps, guns, powder, and shot. They could also bargain for horses, cattle, oxen, sheep, goats, or even a hive of bees.[15]

At this time, since specie was scarce and there was no bank in Detroit, the merchants often acted as bankers for their customers. Many customers paid their debts by the delivery of goods or by working for the merchants. Others sold their products through the merchants, who credited the amount to the maker and charged the cost to the purchaser. These services were provided for the convenience of customers, apparently gratis. Interest, however, was charged on debts at the rate of six percent.[16]

As a matter of fact, specie, or cash, had always been scarce in Detroit. The earliest money circulated in Detroit was called "card money." It was issued by the French to pay the soldiers and consisted of ordinary playing cards cut into four pieces and signed by the governor. This money was in use in Detroit as early as 1717.[17]

The Indians, of course, had long carried on their trade by barter and by the use of the black and white shell bead currency, wampum. The black beads were made of the inside shell of clams or mussels and were rarer and therefore more valuable than the white beads from conch shells. Usually, the ratio of white to black shells was two to one. These beads, about half an inch long, were strung on leather thongs and in addition to being used as currency, were sometimes worked into belts to be exchanged as tokens of friendship. Along with wampum, Pontiac is said to have issued pieces of birch bark as money upon which the figure of an otter had been crudely drawn. Tradition also says that he faithfully redeemed them.[18]

Under French rule the merchants kept their accounts in French currency; soon after 1760, the English system of pounds, shillings, and pence displaced the franc, livre, and sol. By 1800, the merchants reckoned their accounts in New York, or for short, York currency. In 1796 the York shilling was worth twelve and one-half cents, half the value of the sterling shilling, and eight York shillings were equivalent to one dollar. This was the Spanish dollar, which had for a long time served as a standard of value and which the United States used as the basis of its monetary system.[19]

Even though silver and gold coins of France, Great Britain, Spain, and Portugal came into town in trade, and coins and bank notes were put into circulation by the soldiers at the fort, most of it was drawn off to pay debts due eastern creditors. Consequently, many Detroit merchants issued their own currency in the form of notes or due bills based on the value of the goods of the issuer and, of course, on his reputation. These notes did not circulate outside the community or, at least, beyond the region in which the signer was known. As they were brought in from time to time by customers, they were destroyed and new ones were issued. This practice continued well into the nineteenth century.[20]

By 1805 the population of the area had increased to a point where Michigan was set off as a separate territory and provision was made for its government by a board of appointed officers known as the Governor and Judges. President Jefferson appointed the Revolutionary War veteran William Hull of Massachusetts as governor and Stanley Griswold of New Hampshire as secretary. The judges were Augustus Brevoort Woodward, a native of New York who at the time of his appointment was living in Washington, D.C., Samuel Huntington of Ohio, and Frederick Bates of Virginia, who had been serving as Detroit's first postmaster since 1802. Huntington declined the appointment and John Griffin of Virginia was made his replacement.

In 1802, prior to these developments, Detroit was incorporated and a slate of municipal officers, including a board of five trustees, a secretary, an assessor, a tax collector, and a marshall were elected. The first meeting of the trustees was held in February 1802, and one of their first official acts was to adopt better ordinances for fire protection. The old tinder dry frame houses crowded on top of each other and made the town a veritable fire trap.

June 11, 1805, dawned like most other early summer days in Detroit. It was a market day and a Catholic feast day. The French farmers came to town early to attend Mass at Ste. Anne's before spreading out their produce for sale on the commons just outside the east wall of the stockade. Elsewhere the town was bustling as usual with the people going about their business. Then, suddenly, there was the dread cry, "Fire." Just how it started no one knows exactly. It has long been believed it began in the stable of John Harvey, the town baker, whose establishment was near the west end of the village. Some said that either Harvey or one of his employees knocked a live coal out of his pipe, setting fire to a pile of straw. In a matter of seconds the blaze engulfed the building and spread rapidly to adjoining structures. The alarm was sounded and men rushed to form bucket brigades. Soldiers hurried down from the fort to lend a hand and the town's only fire engine was brought into action. One engine could make little headway against what was by then a roaring inferno.

The flames raced down Ste. Anne Street (Jefferson Avenue) devouring John Dodemead's tavern, the stores of the merchants, the church, the Council House, and the government fur factory. On an almost windless day, the fire still created enough draft to sweep across town in all directions.

In less than three hours nothing remained of Detroit except a warehouse near the river, a blockhouse, and a few fire-blackened chimneys, pointing like accusing fingers at the sky. Everything else was gone. From the fort which remained untouched, observers gazed on a scene of indescribable desolation. People took refuge wherever they could find it: in the farm houses up and down the river, in the fort, and in tents and hastily constructed bowers of branches on the common.

The fire of 1805 proved to be a blessing in disguise. As a result of the disaster, Detroit was rebuilt in the semblance of a modern city with more spacious lots, wider streets, and open areas for parks and public buildings. Of course this did not happen all at once, but a plan was prepared as a starting point. The town that was destroyed contained about three hundred buildings, including sheds, stores, outhouses, barns, and sties. The population was an estimated 500 people, not counting the soldiers in the fort. There were probably not more than 100 dwelling places and the entire town, exclusive of government structures, was owned by 69 proprietors.

The idea of reestablishing the village within its former crowded and confined limits was rejected. Instead, the Governor and Judges persuaded Congress to donate the commons west of the Brush farm and extending north three miles, plus an additional parcel known as the Ten Thousand Acre Tract so that the area of the city could be expanded. A surveyor was hired and the land was measured off along the river and for a short distance back from the shore line, and laid out in lots.

Detroit was rebuilt slowly after the fire and solidly. New streets conforming to the Woodward Plan* were opened, and some of the old streets were widened and renamed. For example, Ste. Anne Street became Jefferson Avenue. The heart of the town centered between the river and Larned. The principal north-south streets were Wayne [now Washington Boulevard], Shelby, Griswold, Woodward, Bates and Randolph. Residential building on these streets extended to about Lafayette, only a few families settled north of Campus Martius. West of Griswold, building was discouraged by the federal government which wanted to keep a clear field of fire for the fort.

* Judge Woodward was the architect of Detroit's rebuilding. While living in Washington he had observed Major Charles L'Enfant's plans. The Woodward Plan consisted of a series of wide boulevards and avenues which would radiate from circular plazas or circuses. Although the plan was abandoned in 1818, remnants of it may still be seen in the central part of downtown. Woodward had actually planned Washington Boulevard to be the main street; the location of the fort prevented its extension south to the river. The avenue that eventually did become the main street was named Woodward not in his honor, the judge coyly observed, but because it ran "towards the wood, or wood ward." [21]

30

Judge Woodward's Bank

During the winter of 1805-6 Governor Hull traveled in the East and while there met a group of Boston financiers. To these men, a bank of original issue in the Great Lakes area would have been very useful, provided they could control it. They convinced Hull that such a bank would facilitate the carrying on of the fur trade and aid in the development of Detroit and the Michigan Territory.

The establishment of a full-fledged banking institution was hardly justified in a village where local trade was still carried on largely by barter, where mercantile business was carried on largely through credit arrangements with eastern banks and merchants, and where there was almost no circulating specie. Yet the idea sounded good to Hull and, not overlooking the possibility of personal gain, he was easily persuaded to lend his influence to the project.

When Hull wrote to Judge Woodward about the formation of a bank, the judge was very enthusiastic. He saw a bank for Detroit as entirely logical. He easily convinced himself that it would concentrate in Detroit the fur trade for which Michigan was competing with the Canadians. With the encouragement of Hull and Woodward, in the spring of 1806, the Boston bankers submitted a petition for the establishment of a bank. In September of that year the Governor and Judges issued a charter creating the Bank of Detroit. The act by which it was granted was forwarded to Washington for the approval of Congress.

Without waiting for congressional approval of the act, a two-story brick building was erected on the northwest corner of Jefferson Avenue and Randolph Street, and the bank was opened for business. William Flanagan of Boston was sent to Detroit to take charge of the bank and act as cashier. As a matter of policy, the promoters picked a local man for president. Their choice was Judge Woodward who was quite willing to add the prestige of heading a financial institution to his many other accomplishments.

The Bank of Detroit was first capitalized at $100,000 of which only $19,000 was paid in. Twenty-four Detroiters were subscribers, including Woodward who, as president, bought one qualifying share on which he paid an initial—and only—installment of two dollars. The Territory of Michigan itself subscribed to ten shares, but the controlling interest, as could be expected, remained in Boston. The charter had a life of thirty years.

Neither the term of the charter nor the capitalization satisfied Judge Woodward. He preferred things on a much grander scale.

Therefore, in his enthusiasm for the project, Woodward induced his colleagues to extend the charter to 101 years and increase the capital to one million dollars.

Shortly after the bank began operations, the real purpose of the syndicate became clear. It was not to encourage the fur trade or to improve the conditions of Detroit, but to circulate paper money in the East—so far away from the point of issue that it would be difficult to determine the discount rate or present it for redemption. Within a few weeks, $165,000 worth of scrip had been printed and put in circulation in the East by Boston promoters. It was peddled at a discount of from 10 to 25 percent. With this scrip disposed of, the printing presses began turning out more, until within a few months the eastern seaboard was flooded with a total of $1,500,000 of virtually worthless paper money.

Of course this had been obtained by the promoters in the first place as a loan or series of loans, backed only by notes and without any discernible collateral. Having thus milked the institution, the original backers proceeded to dispose of their stock. Gradually the scrip began to drift back to Detroit and was presented for payment. At first there were no problems. Within a short time, though, the supply of specie was exhausted and further payments were refused.

Governor Hull realized he and the others had been duped. The situation became critical first, when Hull received an ominous order from Secretary of State James Madison to forward to Washington copies of the territorial law "respecting the erection of a bank" and second, when the secretary of war cautioned the commandant at the fort against paying the Detroit garrison in notes of the bank. The crushing blow came, however, when Congress annulled the act of incorporation on March 3, 1807.

The bank officials tried to continue operating the bank as a private institution but in December 1808, the officers of the territory passed a law prohibiting the issuance of bills by private banks. In 1809, an unsuccessful attempt was made to repeal the law and Detroit's first banking institution was forced out of existence.[22]

The ill feelings created by the Bank of Detroit persisted for many years. In fact, a second bank was not to open its doors in Detroit until 1819. To some extent, the fiasco was responsible for the slow economic and social development of the territory. Remembering the worthless scrip that had been foisted on them, eastern capitalists and eastern settlers bypassed Detroit during a decade when Detroit and Michigan could have advantageously used both capital and settlers.

Even though Detroit's first banking venture ended in disaster, it did not seriously affect business in the town, and the fur trade continued to prosper. Unfortunately, in most cases it prospered at the expense of the Indians. Many independent traders continued their dishonest practices and the government factories were little better.

The dissatisfaction with the government's fur trading policies and the unhappiness because of settler encroachment on their hunting lands caused the Indians to look to the British for aid and comfort. These Indian problems continued to grow and, while not the only causes, were major contributing factors to a conflict that many had seen as inevitable—the War of 1812.

The War of 1812 marked a period of real suffering for the people of Detroit. In June 1812 Governor Hull reluctantly accepted command of the Army of the Northwest and gathered together a force of 2500 U.S. Army regulars, Ohio volunteers, and local militia. After an abortive attack on Fort Malden, Hull retreated to Detroit and prepared for an attack. He did not have to wait long. On August 13 General Isaac Brock, commander of British forces in Upper Canada, sent Hull a demand for surrender. When the demand was rejected by Hull, Brock began a cannon bombardment of Detroit from the Canadian shore. Realizing that his supply lines were cut off and fearing Indian atrocities if he put up a fight, Hull decided to surrender. Altogether it was one of the most dreary military fiascos ever suffered by American troops. It was made more so by the fact that with a numerically superior and well-armed force at Hull's command, not a single shot was fired in defense of Detroit.

The British occupation that followed Hull's surrender lasted just over one year. During that time the people of Detroit were forced to live under semi-martial law. Business, already badly disjointed by the war, suffered even more by the lack of civil law. The Indians were allowed free access to the town and most merchants had their stores broken into and their merchandise carted away. The British commandant, General Procter, refused to prevent this plundering. The Indians were fickle allies at best and he dared not risk offending them.

Following an American naval victory on Lake Erie on September 10, 1813, American troops invaded Upper Canada. Under the command of General William Henry Harrison, the Americans captured Fort Malden, and on September 29, reoccupied Detroit. Although the war was to continue for another year, Detroit was never again seriously threatened.

33

Detroit and Its Banks

The year 1814, however, marked a low point in Detroit's history. Even though a large number of troops were stationed in town, the citizens lived in constant fear of another attack by the British and their Indian allies. During the winter of 1813–14, an epidemic swept through the town and several hundred persons died. No one was certain what the disease was and it was simply called a plague. Another problem was that the war had interrupted the planting of crops and the townspeople and soldiers were constantly hungry. It was difficult to get supplies from the East, particularly during the winter, and everyone was forced to tighten his belt.

The War of 1812 came to an end with the signing of the Treaty of Ghent on December 24, 1814. The following February, word reached Detroit that the peace pact had been ratified by Congress. To celebrate the ending of the war, the leading citizens of the town gathered at the Steamboat Hotel and threw an all night party billed as The Grand Pacification Ball. To show that there were no hard feelings, the Detroiters invited the British officers from Fort Malden.

Following the War of 1812, the fur trade again became Detroit's major industry although it did not last for long. In 1820, eight or ten merchants were still engaged, directly or indirectly, in the fur trade and $325,000 worth of furs were exported from Detroit during 1829. After 1830 the trade declined rapidly and by 1840 it was no longer a major factor in Detroit's commercial life.[23] By this time the supply of fur-bearing animals was becoming exhausted in Michigan, and the incoming settlers were pushing out the Indians and destroying the forests. The era of the fur trade in Detroit had come to an end.

Era of the Wildcats

CUT MONEY AND SHINPLASTERS

The years immediately following the War of 1812 were difficult ones for Detroiters. A number of very serious problems faced the townsfolk of this small frontier community. During the war, the cost of living had skyrocketed; and following the war, higher prices were paid for food in the Detroit area than in any other market in the United States. Wheat and corn sold for $2.00 a bushel, oats $1.00 and potatoes $1.25 a bushel. Flour was selling for $12.00 to $13.00 per barrel and pork from $26.00 to $30.00 per barrel. Cattle raising had been almost wiped out by the war and for several years most of the beef, which sold for $6.00 per hundred weight, had to be imported from Ohio. In 1814 James Witherell wrote to his wife that a man's suit could not be purchased in Detroit for less than $150. This was at a time when a common laborer was paid $1.00 a day in wages and masons and carpenters earned $2.25 to $2.50 a day.[1]

Of the difficulties facing Detroit, none was greater than the continued scarcity of specie. The disruption of the fur trade during the war had left the town without an export staple to balance the importation of foodstuffs and manufactured goods. The relatively small amount of capital that had been available was consumed by the war so that any specie that now entered the town had to be used to pay for the imports.

To meet this money shortage, the townspeople resorted to the use of a variety of substitute currencies and paper bank notes. Bank notes were the most practicable medium of exchange and the majority of paper money in Detroit at this time was from banks in Ohio, with some from as far away as Kentucky and western Pennsylvania. Confidence in these banks fluctuated with the public's ability to redeem their bills in specie. The financial backing of many was open to conjecture, and their solvency was frequently questioned. Since communication was slow and difficult, and since a bill had to be presented at its source for redemption in specie, the holders of bills who were most distant from the place of issue stood the least chance of having them honored should the bank get into difficulty. As a rule, the farther west currency traveled from its source, the more it decreased in value.[2]

Ohio bankpaper was discounted in Detroit at varying rates. Notes of chartered banks passed freely at a small discount, while those of unchartered banks were discounted at a somewhat higher rate. The reason that the bills of the Ohio banks passed so readily was probably due to the fact that much of the meat and flour imported into Detroit came from Ohio and could be paid for with Ohio paper.

Early in 1818, Detroit was faced with a financial crisis when many of the unchartered banks in Ohio failed. When the federal government demanded payment in specie from these banks, those that could not pay were forced to close their doors. As a result, thousands of worthless notes were left in the hands of individuals throughout the Territory of Michigan. In addition, many of the chartered banks were on very shaky ground. The situation in Detroit bordered on the chaotic. The *Detroit Gazette* begged anyone possessing "competent knowledge" to volunteer information concerning the various Ohio banks. Shortly thereafter, for the benefit of its readers, the paper classified the banks as "good," "decent," "middling," or "good for nothing."[3] At a citizens' meeting early in December 1819, a committee was appointed to investigate the paying ability of the Ohio banks and publish guidelines for acceptance of their bills. Local merchants expressed their determination to accept only those notes recommended by the committee. Fortunately this action was effective in curbing the circulation of suspect bank notes.[4]

The most prevalent type of substitute currency in circulation at this time was the individual due bill similar to the type used before the war. Within a few years, the use of due bills, or "shinplasters" * as they were then called, became so widespread that in addition to the merchants, many innkeepers, mechanics, hucksters, clergymen, and even public officials began printing their own bills. Judge Woodward, for example, had some of his notes in circulation for sums as small as one and two cents.[5]

Another Detroiter who issued his own "shinplasters" was Father Gabriel Richard, the rector of Ste. Anne's Church. Father Richard was supervising the construction of a new church and used his bills to pay the workmen. The notes were printed for him in the office of the *Detroit Gazette*. One of the printers, a man named Cooper, surreptitiously appropriated the type, ran off a large number of bills and counterfeited Richard's signature on them. He then proceeded to flood the countryside with them. Printer Cooper escaped punishment by enlisting in the army and being transferred before his crime was discovered. Father Richard set about to redeem the worthless money, pledging as security a piece of property near the church "worth ten times more than the whole amount of the bills now in circulation." It is reported that he eventually redeemed almost all of these counterfeit notes.[6]

In September 1817, it was suggested that a city corporation be formed to be the sole authorized issuer of small bills for marketing purposes. Nothing came of the plan and individual due bills continued to be issued at an ever increasing rate. By 1819, the counterfeiting and misuse of "shinplasters" had become so serious that a citizens committee met and adopted the following resolution:

> Resolved, that the issuing of small change notes, by individuals who do not redeem them at sight, is an evil which we pledge ourselves to endeavor to correct.
>
> Resolved, that any person issuing small bills after the first day of March next shall give security to the public for the faithful and punctual redemption of said bills.
>
> Resolved, as the sense of this meeting, that we will not circulate or

---

* The name shinplaster was derived from the use of small pieces of brown paper by hunters, trappers, and early settlers to protect bruises and sores on their shins. Usually, the papers were "medicated" with vinegar, tar, tobacco juice, or the like to make them stick. From this came the name humorously applied to paper money frequently issued without financial security.[7]

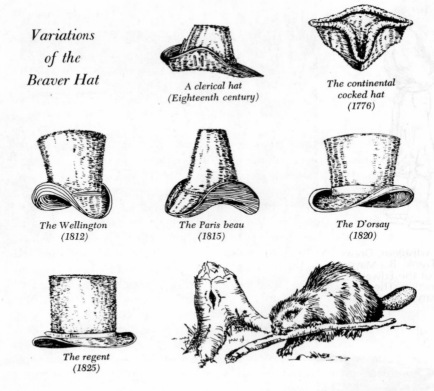

Variations of the Beaver Hat

A clerical hat
(Eighteenth century)

The continental
cocked hat
(1776)

The Wellington
(1812)

The Paris beau
(1815)

The D'orsay
(1820)

The regent
(1825)

Variations of the famous beaver hat. Drawing by Rhoda R. Gilman. Reprinted by permission from North American Fur Trade Conference, *Aspects of the Fur Trade* (St. Paul, 1967), p. 39.

A fur trade canoe on the Mattawa River, Ontario, pictured by Frances Hopkins. Reprinted from G.M. Grant, *Ocean to Ocean: Sanford Fleming's Expedition Through Canada in 1872* (London, 1873).

A French *voyageur*. Drawing by Frank B. Mayer. Courtesy of the Edward E. Ayer Collection, The Newberry Library, Chicago.

Voyageurs portaging their canoe. Drawing by William T. Woodward. Reprinted by permission from Fred C. Hamil, *When Beaver Was King* (Detroit, 1951), p. 13.

Indian wampum—a belt. Courtesy of the Money Museum, National Bank of Detroit.

Indians bartering for goods. Drawing by William T. Woodward. Reprinted by permission from Fred C. Hamil, *When Beaver Was King* (Detroit, 1951), p. 20.

The interior of a fur trading store. Drawing by William T. Woodward. Reprinted by permission from Fred C. Hamil, *When Beaver Was King* (Detroit, 1951), p. 10.

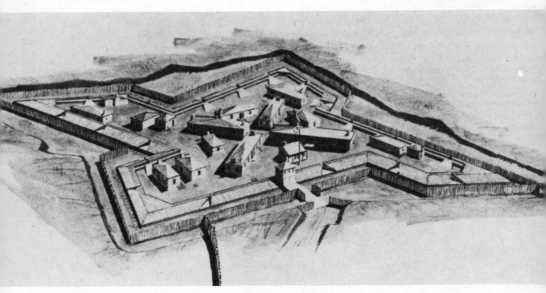

Fort Lernoult. Reprinted by permission from Philip P. Mason, *Detroit, Fort Lernoult, and the American Revolution* (Detroit, 1964).

United States colonial currency—continental currency, Philadelphia, 1775. Courtesy of the Burton Historical Collection, Detroit Public Library.

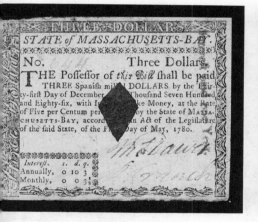

United States three dollar bill, 1780. Courtesy of the Burton Historical Collection, Detroit Public Library.

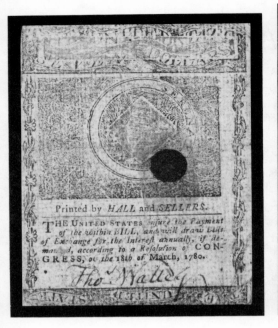

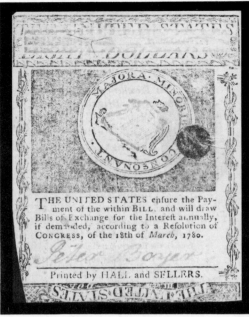

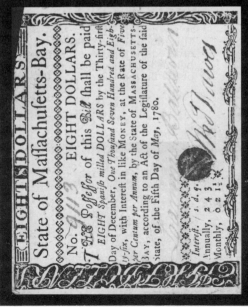

United States seven and eight dollar bills, 1780. Also known by the more common name of "shinplasters". Courtesy of the Burton Historical Collection, Detroit Public Library.

A PROCLAMATION.

By His Excellency HENRY PROCTER Efqr. *Governor of the Territory of Michigan & Brigadier General Commanding His* MAJESTY'S FORCES *therein,* &c. &c. &c.

WHEREAS in the Prefent fcarcely of fpecie within the faid Territory, it would tend greatly as well to promote his Majefty's fervice, as to facilitate the inhabitants in their ordinary concerns by rendering the circulating medium more plenty, if his MAJESTY's ARMY BILLS and COMMISSARIAT BILLS were made current within the faid Territory : NOW THEREFORE, I the faid HENRY PROCTER, Efqr Do hereby order & direct that the above mentioned ARMY BILLS and COMMISSARIAT BILLS fhall be, from the date of this PROCLAMATION, a legal tender in the payment of all debts, & that the fame, shall, in every refpect, be as current within the faid Territory as Gold & Silver Coins are now current therein. And any perfon or perfons refufing to receive the fame in payment of debts or otherwife shall be fubject to a penalty of TWO HUNDRED DOLLARS, which penalty shall be recovered before the perfon or perfons appointed or to be appointed for fuch purpofes, on the OATH of one credible witnefs, being fome other than the informer.

GIVEN under my hand at Detroit this 25th day of March, in the year of our Lord 1813, & in the 53d. year of His MAJESTY'S REIGN.

HENRY PROCTER,
BRIG. GENERAL
Coms.

This proclamation, which was issued by General Henry Procter in 1813, ordered the citizens of Detroit to accept British army and commissariat bills as legal tender during the British occupation of the city. Courtesy of the Burton Historical Collection, Detroit Public Library.

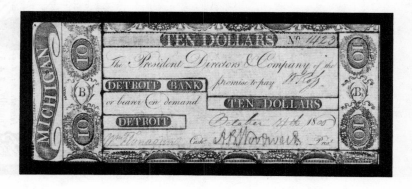

Bank of Detroit note, 1806. Courtesy of the Burton Historical Collection, Detroit Public Library.

Bank of Michigan note, 1839. Courtesy of the Burton Historical Collection, Detroit Public Library.

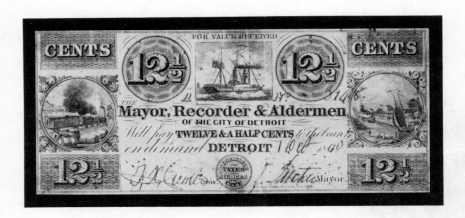

City of Detroit due bill, 1837–40. Courtesy of the Burton Historical Collection, Detroit Public Library.

Detroit in 1794. The earliest known authentic dated view of Detroit. Courtesy of the Burton Historical Collection, Detroit Public Library.

Detroit in 1837, the year Michigan's first general banking law was passed. Courtesy of the Detroit Institute of Arts.

Detroit City Bank note, 1837. This bank was Detroit's only wildcat
bank. Courtesy of the Burton Historical Collection, Detroit Public
Library.

Michigan wildcat bank note. Exchange Bank of Shiawassee, 1837.
Courtesy of the Burton Historical Collection, Detroit Public Library.

Michigan wildcat bank note. Jackson County Bank, 1837. Courtesy of the Burton Historical Collection, Detroit Public Library.

Detroit and St. Joseph Rail Road Bank note, 1840. Courtesy of the Burton Historical Collection, Detroit Public Library.

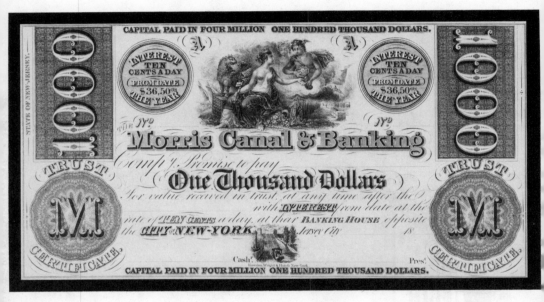

Morris Canal & Banking Company note, 1841. The Morris Canal & Banking Company was the bond agent for Michigan's infamous $5,000,000 internal improvement loan. Courtesy of the Burton Historical Collection, Detroit Public Library.

Mariners' Church, erected in 1849, Woodward Avenue and Wood-bridge Street. This photograph of the church was taken in the mid-1870s. The Detroit Savings Fund Institute first opened for business in rented quarters at the rear of the church on the corner of Woodbridge and Griswold streets. Courtesy of the Burton Historical Collection, Detroit Public Library.

give currency to the bills of any individual after the first day of March next, who shall fail to redeem them within three days from their presentation for payment.

[*Detroit Gazette*, February 5, 1819]

Several of the citizens who signed the resolution redeemed their notes immediately and while this resulted in the decline of the use of due bills, some continued in circulation until 1822. Late in that year, a group of 97 influential merchants and businessmen pledged that they would no longer pass these bills nor accept them in trade. This concerted effort finally ended the use of individual due bills as substitute currency.[8]

A second form of substitute money current in Detroit at this time was government scrip. This scrip was first issued by the Governor and Judges in 1819. The bills were printed in values of two, three, five, ten, and twenty dollars. The scrip bore interest at the rate of six percent and was to be redeemed out of the proceeds of the sale of lands in the Ten Thousand Acre Tract, but the land sold at such a low price that it depreciated in value. In addition, Wayne County was having a difficult time collecting its taxes so that the scrip depreciated to such an extent until, in 1821, it passed at a discount of from ten to twenty-five percent. By 1826, when the issuing of scrip was finally discontinued, $22,500 of the bills had been issued.[9]

As specie began to return to circulation, a new problem confronted Detroiters. That was the problem of money cutting. Whenever a shopowner needed to make change for a silver dollar and had no small coins at hand, he would merely cut the dollar into eight equal triangular pieces or "bits." Each "bit" could then be circulated as a York shilling, the equivalent of 12½ cents. Two of these "bits" were equivalent to 25 cents or a quarter-of-a-dollar. Sometimes, however, a dollar would be cut into nine or even ten equal parts and the difficulty of distinguishing between an eighth part and a ninth or tenth part of a dollar enabled a few dishonest characters to make a profit for themselves.

By 1820 there was so much of this cut money in circulation that the *Detroit Gazette* called it a "grievous nuisance," and almost a year passed before any real attempt was made to outlaw it. In August 1821, "at a very numerous meeting of the citizens of Detroit," a resolution was adopted whereby cut money would no longer be accepted as valid currency.[10] The signers pledged themselves to do everything in their power to discontinue its circulation. This pretty much put an end to money cutting in the city and thereafter the pieces were sold only by weight, many pieces being converted into ornaments for the Indian trade.

The federal government was in large part responsible for the seriousness of the currency problem in Detroit. Federal disbursements for the support and pay of the troops in the garrison comprised the major source of the much needed currency. Ordinarily, the troops were paid in Ohio money, and since there were about 1500 soldiers at Detroit, a considerable amount should have been placed in circulation. At one point, however, the soldiers had not been paid for more than a year, and the loss of this income aggravated the money shortage and worked a real hardship on the merchants. Credit was refused the unpaid troops because it was feared that they might be transferred to another post before they could pay their bills. Merchants found themselves with large stocks of goods on their shelves which they had purchased on credit, and no available means of paying for them.

Later, even when business improved, Detroit merchants found it difficult to make payments to their creditors. No local bank existed to facilitate financial transactions, and exchange acceptable in the seaboard cities was extremely difficult to obtain. Ohio bank bills and drafts were subject to such large discounts in the East that the local merchants could ill afford to use them in payment for their imports. Occasionally, they managed to purchase drafts on eastern banks or upon individuals residing in the East; sometimes they would have the good fortune to obtain British Army bills which commanded a premium in New York and other eastern cities. For want of an acceptable means of exchange, there were times when the merchants were unable to make payments on their obligations, even though they had sufficient money on hand in the form of due bills and Ohio currency.[11]

Detroit's Second Bank—the Bank of Michigan

What Detroit needed was a bank. Thus, it was in this atmosphere of "shinplasters," due bills, cut money, scrip, and questionable bank notes, that Detroit's second banking institution was chartered.

On December 19, 1817, the territorial legislative council granted a charter for the establishment of the Bank of Michigan. The bank was incorporated in June of the following year when its stock was placed on the market and a board of directors elected from the stockholders. John R. Williams was chosen president, and James McCloskey cashier. The bank's capital was limited to $100,000 worth with shares of stock selling at $100 each, ten dollars of which was demanded in specie at the time of purchase. No bills were to be issued until $10,000 in specie had been accumulated. By January 1819, $12,000 in specie had been paid-in, the first bills were issued, and on January 2, the bank opened its doors for business in the old Bank of Detroit Building.[12]

From the first day of business, when over $400 was deposited, the bank was operated in a conservative manner. It soon won public confidence. The territory proved to be a ripe field for banking operations, and at the end of the first year the bank appeared to be safely launched on a prosperous career. As an indication of its soundness, the secretary of the treasury directed the receiver of public money in Detroit to accept its bills. In January 1822, the bank declared a dividend for the last half of 1821 of four percent on the paid-in capital. This was followed by dividends of six percent in 1822, and seven percent in 1823. At no time during these years was there any doubt of the bank's ability to redeem its notes in specie. In fact, there probably was never a time that its circulation exceeded its specie backing.

Within a year after their issuance, the bank's notes were accepted for payment of debts as far away as Chillicothe, Ohio, and by 1823, they were being exchanged with a bank in Geneva, New York. However, there were still a few problems. In the East, there remained memories of the Bank of Detroit and the losses sustained when it failed to redeem the thousands of bills it placed in circulation. As late as 1825, Boston merchants attempted to curb the passage of the notes of the bank, intimating that the public could again be defrauded. In the fall of 1825, because of the bank's conservative operation, Bank of Michigan bills were redeemed at a very small discount at Albany; and in the spring of 1826, many New York merchants began to accept them at par on all of their accounts.[13]

While the conservative policy maintained by the management assured the integrity of the bank, it was incompatible with the growing commercial activity of the city. With its limited capital, the bank was unable to satisfy the rising demand for credit. In early 1824, the controlling interest of the bank was acquired by a group of eastern financiers headed by Henry Dwight of Geneva, New York. Within a short time, these men increased the bank's paid-in capital to $60,000. Because of differences with the new stockholders, John R.

Williams resigned as president, and Eurotas P. Hastings was elected in his place, with Charles C. Trowbridge as cashier.[14]

Remembering the old Bank of Detroit, many of the local citizens were uneasy now that the major stockholders were again outsiders. Despite their fears, the bank was blessed with continued good management, and its increase in capital enabled it to render excellent service to the commercial interests of the growing city.

In addition to providing the city with a sound currency, the Bank of Michigan furnished Detroit merchants with facilities for making eastern remittances, and the bank soon became the clearing house for eastern exchange. With the increase in population in the territory and the resultant growth in city trade and commerce, eastern exchange became more abundant in Detroit; and with its growth of capital, the Bank of Michigan was able to eliminate most of the difficulties local merchants had formerly experienced in making payments to their eastern creditors.

Thus, by 1830, the Bank of Michigan was on a sound financial footing. In 1831 its charter was renewed for 25 years and the bank moved to larger quarters in a building on the south side of Jefferson near Woodward. Further expansion came in 1834 when the bank was authorized to establish a branch at Bronson [now called Kalamazoo] and to increase its capital by $350,000.[15]

It is true that the Bank of Michigan had been in existence for only a few short years, but in that time it had grown and prospered. In those same years, the city of Detroit had also grown and prospered.

MERCANTILE CENTER

The prosperity that Detroit experienced during the 1820s and 1830s can largely be attributed to one man—Lewis Cass. A man of extraordinary talents, he probably had a greater influence on the growth and development of Detroit and Michigan than did any other single individual.

Born in New Hampshire in 1782, Cass moved to Ohio as a young man and began to study law. He appeared first in Detroit as a colonel of Ohio Volunteers in 1812. After the capitulation of Detroit, Cass was sent back to Ohio on parole. Later he was exchanged, and returned to Detroit in 1813 with General Harrison's army.

Cass served as governor of the Territory of Michigan from 1813 until 1831. When he finally relinquished the position, after eighteen highly successful and progressive years, he went on to become secretary of war, minister to France, United States senator from Michigan, presidential nominee of the Democratic Party in 1848, and finally secretary of state on the eve of the outbreak of the Civil War.

At the end of the War of 1812, Detroit had a population of 850 persons, and that of the Michigan Territory was less than 5,000. It was obvious to Governor Cass that what was most needed were settlers. Immediately after the war, with the Indian danger no longer serious, a great westward migration began. Citizen-soldiers from the eastern states had their first look at the West during the war and liked what they saw. Congress set aside vast tracts in the Old Northwest as bounty lands for ex-soldiers. But the rush of settlers by-passed Michigan. Instead they poured into Ohio, Indiana and Illinois. One reason was the bad name that Detroit and Michigan gained from the adverse report of government surveyors, one of whom declared in 1817 that Michigan was "an interminable swamp." He and others circulated the story that not one acre in ten thousand was fit for cultivation. Fur trading companies, particularly the American Fur Company of which John Jacob Astor was the proprietor, encouraged and helped circulate these false reports. The fur men preferred beaver to settlers in Michigan. Still another reason for the lack of public enthusiasm for Michigan was its inaccessibility. To reach Detroit one had to haul a wagon across Ohio, an arduous pull which included traversing the Black Swamp,* or across Canada, in the early postwar days regarded by many as hostile territory. The only other way was by slow, uncertain, and expensive passage from Buffalo or some other lake port on a sailing vessel.

Thus throughout the East, Michigan was given an undeservedly bad image. Governor Cass realized this and set out to change it. A capable writer himself, he wrote articles for major eastern publications and urged residents of the territory to write letters back home to friends and relatives telling of the many outstanding features of the territory. Visitors and tourists were invited to come and see for themselves. One who made the trip was the noted geographer, Dr.

---

* The Black Swamp, comprising about 4,000 square miles in area, was located at the southwest end of Lake Erie. It extended westward from Sandusky Bay to the lower course of the Maumee. Heavily timbered and with an underlying clay formation impervious to water, the Swamp resembled a shallow, muck-bottomed lake during much of the year. Only in extreme cold weather could it be traversed with relative ease, and all who encountered it retained lifelong memories of its horrors.[16]

Jedediah Morse. He was the cartographer who had written "interminable swamp" across his maps of Michigan, a place he never saw
until 1820. After his visit, he returned East with a very different
opinion.

In 1817 President James Monroe was persuaded to visit Detroit,
and other distinguished citizens came from time to time. Their visits
received considerable publicity in the East and helped change the
bad image of Michigan. To further dispel the derogatory reports, Cass
organized exploring parties that penetrated the interior. Some of the
places visited were no more than 20 or 25 miles from Detroit, yet no
white man had ever seen them before. While some of these trips
were no more than four and five days in length, others were
large-scale expeditions financed by the federal government, such as
that of 1820 on which Cass led a group of scientists into the Upper
Peninsula and to what is now Minnesota in search of the source of
the Mississippi River.

There were also three national events that influenced this
situation and were major elements in determining Detroit's growth
from frontier outpost to mercantile center. The first of these events
was the development of the steamboat. In 1811 Robert Fulton sailed
his steamboat *Clermont* up the Hudson River from New York and
almost immediately people began to think in terms of steam
navigation. At Black Rock, near Buffalo, shipbuilders laid the keel of a
one hundred thirty-five foot side-wheeler which was launched May
28, 1818, and named *Walk-in-the-Water*. As the first steamboat on the
upper Great Lakes, she excited much enthusiasm in the West. Her
maiden voyage was to be to Detroit and the city prepared for her
arrival by building a new wharf at the foot of Bates Street.

Walk-in-the-Water sailed from Buffalo on August 23, 1818. Her
skipper was Captain Job Fish and she carried 29 passengers. After a
number of stops along the way, she arrived at Detroit on the morning
of August 27. Among her passengers was Mrs. Julia Anderson who,
with her sister Charlotte Taylor, would later donate the land on
which Mariners' Church was built.

Walk-in-the-Water continued in operation for three years. The
fare between Buffalo and Detroit was $18 first class and $7 steerage.
She was capable of accommodating 100 passengers and was soon on
a biweekly schedule which continued until 1821, when she
foundered in a gale on the Canadian shore near Buffalo. But she set
the pattern for what was to come, for before long many more
steamships were built. Among the most well-known in the 1820s and

43

1830s were the *Charles Townsend, Superior, Henry Clay, William Penn, Niagara, Peacock,* and *Enterprise.* By 1831 Detroit could expect daily arrivals during the navigation season. In 1827 Detroit built its first steamboat, the small steam ferry, *Argo.* In 1833 Oliver Newberry, an enterprising Detroiter, launched the steamship *Michigan.* Weighing 472 tons, she was acclaimed as the largest and finest steamer on the lakes.[17]

The second factor affecting Detroit's growth was the offering of public lands in Michigan for sale to would-be settlers. One of the first things Lewis Cass had done as governor was to negotiate treaties with the Indians by which they ceded virtually all of what is now the two peninsulas of Michigan to the United States Government. A federal land office had been opened in Detroit as early as 1804 although it was not very active. Until Cass negotiated these treaties, there simply was not much land to sell. By 1820, after the surveys were begun and the first treaties effected, the story was different. In that same year, Congress repealed the old land act and passed a new one which provided for auctions as before, but permitted individuals after the auction to purchase a minimum of 80 acres for cash at $1.25 an acre. At that rate a man with $100 could purchase for himself a family-size farm. Sales at the Detroit land office mounted during the early 1820s to 92,332 acres in 1825. Business became so brisk that in 1826 the land office was moved to the basement of the Bank of Michigan Building (the old Bank of Detroit Building) at the northwest corner of Jefferson and Randolph. On some days, hundreds of men queued up along Jefferson Avenue waiting to file their claims.

After a slight recession in the late twenties, the situation improved in 1831 when 217,943 acres of land were sold. "Michigan fever," an overwhelming desire to settle in Michigan, had finally infected thousands of people in the East. In 1833 the quantity of land purchased in the whole territory was 44,780 acres, and in 1836 more than four million acres, the largest amount in any state or territory that year.[18] Money was plentiful—everyone expected to get rich. This high tide of inflation was soon to end in the Panic of 1837.

The third link in the chain of events which shaped Detroit's economic future was the Erie Canal, or more properly the New York State Barge Canal. Planned by New York's Governor DeWitt Clinton as a waterway to connect the eastern seaboard and the Great Lakes, construction began in 1817. When completed in 1825, the canal stretched 363 miles across New York State, running through the Mohawk Valley and skirting the Finger Lakes. With its eastern terminus at the Hudson River between Albany and Troy, and its western outlet near Buffalo, the canal averaged a width of 40 feet and a depth of 4 feet. It cost the then staggering sum of $20,000 a mile to dig but it was a financial success almost from the beginning. Within three years, the tolls collected more than paid for the cost of construction.[19] It opened officially on October 25, 1825, with impressive ceremonies; and though October is late in the season for navigation on the Great Lakes, traffic nevertheless started with a rush. Big cumbersome barges, capable of hauling heavy loads and many passengers, were pulled across New York by horses at the rate of "a cent and a half a mile; a mile and a half an hour."[20] At Buffalo the westward bound passengers or cargo could be placed aboard one of the new lake steamers and be in Detroit in a matter of hours. Hailing the canal's opening, the *Detroit Gazette* pointed out: "We can now go from Detroit to New York in five and a half days. Before the war, it took at least two months more."[21]

The combination of better transportation and abundantly cheap land worked wonders for Michigan and established for all time Detroit's position as the metropolis of the territory and state. The steamboat and Erie Canal tapped a large and restless population in New England and in eastern and central New York. As these people came West by the thousands in one of the most significant migrations in history, they brought with them their Yankee characteristics and colloquialisms, and their independence of mind. Along with their household belongings and farm implements which the new transportation facilities permitted them to carry, they also brought the virtues of morality, religion, and thrift.

Detroit was the funnel through which the settlers heading for the interior of Michigan passed; and during the 1820s and 1830s the reception of new arrivals was the city's most important business. Detroit was the port of debarkation for thousands, most of whom paused only long enough to refresh themselves and get a line on some good land before pushing on to the interior.

On a single May day in 1836 more than 2400 settlers poured into Detroit, and the arrival of from 7 to 10 steamboats daily was not uncommon. Observing this hustle and bustle, Charles C. Trowbridge wrote to Lewis Cass who was then in Paris:

> The opening of navigation has brought us immense crowds of old fashioned immigrants with their wives and babies and wagons and spinning wheels, and a hundred dollars to buy an eighty acre lot for each of the boys. I never saw more crowded boats. Yesterday (May 28,

45

1837) our arrivals were eight steamboats, one ship, three large brigs, and nineteen schooners. The day before, seven steamboats arrived.[22]

Detroit's growth, at first not spectacular, was nonetheless steady. In 1819, the population was only 1,110 not much more than at the end of the war. By 1830, it had doubled to 2,222, and from then on it began to boom. In 1836, it was 6,927; in 1840, 9,124; in 1850, 21,019; and by 1860, just before the Civil War, Detroit boasted the very respectable population of 45,619.

This growth was aided by the new transportation and the Erie Canal. The immigrants, mostly farmers, had produce to sell from their new farms, and the canal opened up a market for Michigan crops in the East. Commenting on the economic benefits of the canal just prior to its opening, the *New York Spectator* declared:

> A barrel of potashes, flour or any produce can be transportated from Detroit to Buffalo with as little expense through Lake Erie, as a like quantity can be transported by land in a western part of this state to the canal from places which lie twenty-five or thirty miles from the canal route.[23]

When completed, the canal reduced the cost of the shipment of produce from Buffalo to New York from $100 to $8 a ton.[24] As a result, the eastern cities, particularly New York, became good customers for Michigan corn, wheat, flour, and pork. Most of this produce of course left for the East from the warehouses and wharfs of Detroit's busy waterfront.

Banks for the Mercantile Center

During this period of growth, with the city's economic base and commercial interests expanding, the territorial government chartered four new banks. Along with the now prosperous Bank of Michigan, it was expected that these institutions would establish in Detroit a sound banking system.

The first of these banks was the Merchants' and Mechanics' Bank of Michigan, incorporated by the legislative council on April 2, 1827. Under the terms of its charter, the bank was authorized to do a combined banking and insurance business. In addition, the bank was required to subscribe to $4,000 of the stock of a new steam powered flour mill to be built "at or near Detroit." [25]

The backers of the new bank probably viewed the insurance business as an unimportant sideline, but the charter required that while the bank must keep its banking and insurance functions separate, it could not begin operations until $60,000 in specie had been paid-in to run the insurance business. The minimum to be paid-in for the banking function was only $20,000, which could easily have been secured from New York capitalists. The requirement of the extra $60,000 may have been the factor which caused the failure of the scheme. Whatever the reason, the new charter was not utilized and no attempt was ever made to organize a bank under its articles.[26]

The next bank to be incorporated was the Farmers and Mechanics' Bank of Michigan, chartered November 5, 1829, with an authorized capitalization of $100,000. John R. Williams, who had earlier resigned as president of the Bank of Michigan, was one of the first directors. The bank began business in June 1830, in rented quarters; then in 1832 it built its own building on the south side of Jefferson between Griswold and Shelby. From the beginning, the bank was well managed and, in 1834, it was authorized to open a branch at St. Joseph in Berrien County and to increase its capital to $400,000. At this time the bank was sold to eastern capitalists and during the next three years continued to be an extremely profitable operation. In 1837, for example, the bank declared a dividend for the previous year of 30 percent on each share of stock.[27]

The corporation that was eventually to be Detroit's fifth bank was chartered on March 7, 1834, as the Michigan Insurance Company. Although incorporated as an insurance company, it never transacted any insurance business and in fact was not organized for business of any kind until January 15, 1838. On that date stock for the Michigan Insurance Company Bank was placed up for subscription. Under its new name the company opened for business on January 24, with a paid-in capital of $20,000 and located at the northeast corner of Jefferson Avenue and Shelby Street. There was some doubt as to whether the company could legally carry on a banking business under the terms of its original charter, but it was allowed to open by authority of a clause in the state banking law.[28]

The last of the Detroit banks chartered by the territorial legislative council was the Michigan State Bank. The act was passed on March 26, 1835, and authorized a capital of $100,000. The bank began business on the north side of Jefferson between Bates and Woodward, then in 1837 moved its offices across Jefferson to the bulding which had been occupied by the Bank of Michigan. With the city's commercial life booming, and only two other banks in operation at that time, the future of the Michigan State Bank, at the outset at least, seemed very bright indeed.[29]

Thus within a matter of two decades Detroit had been transformed from an impoverished wilderness outpost to a thriving mercantile center. Now that the city was growing, as were so many of the other towns and villages throughout the territory, the citizens of Michigan began to think in terms of statehood.

"AN ACT TO ORGANIZE AND REGULATE . . ."

The New England settlers who poured into the Michigan Territory quickly found that they had little liking for the autocratic rule of the Governor and Judges, a form of government in whose affairs they had no voice. Governor Cass was aware of this discontent and made plans to do something about it. The first change came in 1819 when, largely through Cass's efforts, the Michigan Territory was granted the right to elect a delegate to Congress. The first man sent to represent the territory was William Woodbridge, a close friend of Cass. Woodbridge sat in Congress with a voice and no vote. He was succeeded by Solomon Sibley, another Cass associate. The territory's third representative, elected in 1825, was Father Gabriel Richard, the first Roman Catholic priest ever to sit in the halls of Congress.

The next step in governmental advancement came in 1824 when the rule of the Governor and Judges ended and a representative system was instituted through an elected legislative council. The council was comprised of nine members chosen by the president from a list of eighteen who had been elected by the voters of the territory. In the same year Detroit reorganized its municipal government and, for the first time, elected a mayor, a clerk, and five aldermen. The first man to be elected mayor was John R. Williams who at the time was serving as president of the Bank of Michigan.

In order that the legislative council would have a place to meet, a capitol was built. Under the Woodward Plan of 1807, such a building was supposed to have stood in Grand Circus Park, which was still too far out in the country in 1824. Another site was selected, the small triangular plot of ground fronting on State Street and the head of Griswold. It is today known as Capitol Park. Finally completed in 1828 at a cost of $21,000, the capitol was two stories in height and topped by a graceful tower 140 feet high, to the top of which citizens and visitors climbed for a breath-taking view of the town, river and countryside. The building was of classic design with lofty pillars across the front. It could have been a large Congregational church in some out-of-the-way New Hampshire valley.

The building continued to serve as the capitol until 1847 when Lansing became the capital city. After Detroit ceased to be the center of government, the Old Capitol, as it eventually came to be known, was used for a variety of purposes. It was first used as a union school and quarters for what was to become the Detroit Public Library. It later served as the city's high school until it was destroyed by fire in 1893.

When Lewis Cass resigned as governor to go to Washington in 1831, he was succeeded by George B. Porter. A year before Cass departed, President Jackson appointed Virginia aristocrat John T. Mason to be secretary of the territory. When he came to Detroit he was accompanied by his son, Stevens T. Mason, an engaging young man who attracted the favorable attention of Cass. When John Mason resigned after only a few months service, he prevailed upon Jackson, with the endorsement of Cass, to name his nineteen-year-old son Stevens as his successor. For the next several years, the young man was the outstanding figure in Detroit and Michigan.

When Governor Porter assumed his new duties, he did not work very hard at the job and was frequently absent from Michigan for long periods. That meant that Stevens T. Mason had to fill in as governor. Then in July 1834, Porter died and Mason became acting governor on a full-time basis. Mason did such a creditable job that, in 1835, when Michigan declared herself a state, he was elected the first governor even though he was only 24 years old. In addition to electing a governor in 1835, the citizens of the territory also adopted a constitution. Because of a boundary dispute with Ohio, however, it was not until January 26, 1837, that Michigan was officially admitted to the Union as the 26th state.

At the time Michigan became a state, public land sales were at their peak. During 1836 the sale of land by the United States at its offices in Detroit, Monroe, Kalamazoo, Flint, and Ionia had been greater than those in any other state. More than four million acres, one fourth of all the land sold in that year by all United States land offices, were sold in Michigan.[30] One of the major factors in this land boom was the availability of easy credit.

Until 1833 the Bank of the United States had dominated the banks of the nation; conservatively managed by Nicholas Biddle, its president, its notes circulated as money and drove from circulation the notes of shaky state banks. In 1832, President Jackson launched his "war on the Bank," vetoing an act passed by Congress to renew the charter of the bank, which was due to expire in 1836. Jackson's triumphant reelection in 1832 indicated that he had popular support. Prospective settlers and speculators who found it hard to borrow money clamored for easier credit, and they were confident that if the Bank of the United States, dominated by the rich and well-born of the East, could be destroyed, money would become more abundant and would be easier to borrow. In this they were right. The amount of paper money per capita circulating in 1830 was only $6.69; by 1835 it had risen to $9.86, and two years later it went up to $13.87.[31]

In 1833 Jackson halted the deposit of government funds in the Bank of the United States before its charter expired, and directed that the monies be deposited in seven state banks, one each in Philadelphia and Baltimore, two in Boston, and three in New York. Six of these banks were closely associated with Jackson's advisors and were popularly referred to as the "pet banks." By June 1836 a total of 33 state banks were being used as depositories. This increased to 84 banks by August 1837. In Detroit, the Farmers and Mechanics' Bank and the Bank of Michigan received deposits totaling $2,267,174. These were the only banks in Michigan to be designated depositories for government funds.[32]

The distribution of these funds had the effect of encouraging the establishment of state banks throughout the country. Between 1829 and 1837, their number increased from 329 to 788, their note circulation rose from $48,000,000 to $149,000,000, and their loans went up from $137,000,000 to $525,000,000.[33] The result was inflationary. Prices rose, debtors paid off their loans with cheap money and borrowed more for speculative purposes.

During this time, government income from the sales of public land and revenues from the high tariff were increasing at such a rate that in 1835 the national debt was paid in full, and a surplus began to accumulate in the United States Treasury. Embarrassed by this unusual circumstance, Congress directed that all money over $5,000,000 in the Treasury on January 1, 1837, should be apportioned among the states according to their representation in the electoral college and distributed in quarterly payments as an indefinite loan. When the law was passed in June 1836, the surplus was about $50,000,000.[34]

Even though Michigan was still three weeks from official admission to the Union, she was included in the surplus distribution of January 1837. With her three electoral votes, one for each of the two senators and one for the single congressman, Michigan's share of the surplus amounted to $381,535.31 and the first installment of

$95,383.83 was deposited in the Michigan State Bank. Two more installments were paid before the law was repealed in 1837 at the request of President Martin Van Buren.[35]

Although the sums distributed to the states were technically loans, most of the states treated them as gifts and made no effort to repay them. Some states used the money for canals and other internal improvements; a number invested in bank or railroad stock and used the interest in support of public schools. In Michigan's case the money was earmarked for canal and railroad construction. Of the $286,751.49 actually received by Michigan, only $26,751.49 was ever spent on internal improvements. The remaining $260,000 was siphoned off into the general fund to defray the current expenses of the state. This evidently was not an unusual occurrence, for in the judgment of many contemporary observers, the distribution of the surplus, in the majority of cases, had only encouraged waste and extravagance.[36]

As Michigan neared statehood, optimism was in the air. The population was growing; money was abundant and cheap; and land sales were booming. Promoters and businessmen entertained extravagant visions of immediate wealth through land speculation, and canal and railroad construction. Michigan had just attained statehood, and government funds were pouring into the state's banks.

At the beginning of 1837, there were sixteen chartered banks in operation in Michigan; three were located in Detroit and thirteen in the interior. The total capitalization of these sixteen banks was $7,100,000, although their actual paid-in capital was only $1,500,000.[37] In addition to the Bank of Michigan, whose charter had been granted by the Governor and Judges, the Territorial Council had incorporated nine banks and the state legislature in 1835 and 1836 chartered nine more. Of this total of nineteen banking corporations, two never opened for business and one other was located in Green Bay country, which was set off as the Territory of Wisconsin in 1836. Of the sixteen banks in operation, the Bank of Michigan, the Farmers and Mechanics' Bank of Michigan, and the Bank of the River Raisin each had been authorized to open a branch. In addition to these banks, several other banking associations had been established by railroad companies and insurance corporations through amendment to their charters.[38]

This would seem to have been a sufficient number of banks to meet the needs of the people of Detroit and Michigan. But there was a demand for still more banks and easier credit. As a consequence of

Jackson's bitter condemnation of the Bank of the United States, it had become the fashion to regard banks as being monopolies of the monied interests and to view with suspicion the charters granted by state legislatures. It was widely believed that such charters granted special privileges to the few. The democratic westerner believed that banking, like the manufacture of cloth, ought to be open to anyone who wanted to go into business.

Thus when the January session of the legislature opened, the tables of the committees on banks in both houses were loaded with petitions, and the pressure for the granting of bank charters was very heavy. Because there were so many petitions it was decided to pass a general banking law in place of individual charters. Accordingly, a bill was introduced and after many amendments, was finally passed by both houses of the legislature, and became law on March 15, 1837. Entitled "An act to organize and regulate banking associations," it was more familiarly known as the General Banking Law of 1837.[39]

The new banking act empowered any twelve landowners to form a banking association by applying to a county treasurer and clerk. Capital stock to the amount of not less than $50,000 or more than $300,000 was to be subscribed and 30 percent was required to be paid-in in specie before the bank could open for business. The amount of bills each bank could issue and circulate, and the amount of loans and discounts, could not exceed two-and-a-half times the total paid-in capital. The directors of the new banks were required to furnish securities for the payment of all debts contracted and the redemption of all notes issued. These securities, which could consist of bonds or mortgages, had to be approved by the state auditor general. Also, the directors were required to "make oath faithfully to perform their official duties, and to keep and report a true statement of the affairs and condition of the association."

In addition to these provisions, an act to appoint a bank commissioner and adopt a safety fund system had been approved by the legislature in 1836. The bank commissioner (later increased to three commissioners) was to visit all the banks in the state once every three months, inspect their books, and check to see that they held the correct amount of specie in their vaults. The safety fund system was modeled after the type then in operation in New York. It required each bank to deposit with the state treasurer, at the beginning of each year, a sum equal to one-half of one percent on the paid-in capital stock. This fund was to be used to pay creditors should any of the banks fail. In New York the system proved to be inadequate and was abandoned.[40] A similar future was in store for the safety fund in Michigan.

The General Banking Law of 1837, with all its amendments, was considered a model. However, while it was carefully written and included a number of safeguards, the law was, within a few short months, to spell disaster for banking in Detroit and Michigan. Perhaps the law would have worked if times had been normal, but they were not. President Jackson's war on the Bank of the United States had resulted in relaxing restraints on state banks. In addition to the withdrawal of government funds from the Bank of the United States and the distribution of the surplus, Jackson had issued his famous Specie Circular. Dated July 11, 1836, the circular was issued in an attempt to decrease land speculation and specified that all payments for public lands had to be made in specie after August 15, 1836. Men who had expected to make payments for their real estate purchases in bank notes had to find specie with which to pay or default and thus lose their lands.

The issuance of the Specie Circular touched off a wild scramble for specie. As the amount of available coin steadily decreased, people began to hoard gold and silver money. The dearth of specie that resulted and the consequent contraction of bank notes in circulation (because of diminished specie reserves in bank vaults) forced banks to reduce their loans.

Nevertheless, economic activity remained high during the remainder of 1836. Then, in the fall of the year, the specie shortage in America began to affect the economy of Great Britain. Americans had been importing large quantities of goods from Britain through such means as sales of farm produce and shares in business ventures to meet the specie shortage. To stop the outward flow of metal, the Bank of England raised its rates and refused to pay American suppliers of commodities in specie. This policy created a crisis in New York banks, for their supplies of gold were thus diminished at the same time the banks of the West were draining them of specie. The situation became so critical that on May 10, 1837, the New York banks suspended specie payments.[41]

The news of the suspension by the eastern banks reached Detroit on May 17 and quickly spread. Late in the day a citizens meeting was held at city hall and a resolution was passed calling on local banks to also suspend specie payments. As a result, the next day the following notice appeared in a local paper:[42]

TO THE PUBLIC

BANK NOTICE—At a meeting of the Board of Directors of all the banks

53

in the City this afternoon, it was *RESOLVED,* that in consequence of intelligence of a general suspension of specie payments in the Eastern States, it has been deemed a course of proper precaution on the part of the banks of Detroit and their branches to adopt a like measure until further notice; and in the meantime the business of the banks will in other respects be conducted as usual.

Detroit, May 17, 1837

The situation bordered on the chaotic, and on June 12 Governor Mason called the legislature into a special session to take action in the emergency. At this special session, a law was passed which relieved all Michigan banks of the requirement that they pay out coin for their notes.[43] Here was an extraordinary opportunity to make money. New banks were quickly organized, apparently with the principal purpose of issuing notes which were not redeemable in cash. During the next 18 months, 55 banks were organized and 49 of these are believed to have started operation.[44] These were the infamous wildcat banks of Michigan.

It would have been quite impossible for such a large number of banks to have been established if the law concerning paid-in capital had been strictly enforced. But all sorts of dodges as well as wholesale fraud were resorted to by the organizers of these banks in order to evade the law. Specie was sent ahead from one bank to another in advance of the bank inspectors. Gold and silver never circulated so freely or traveled so rapidly. Sometimes the specie was transported during the night. On at least one occasion, specie was handed through the back door as the bank commissioner was walking in the front.

Some banks, however, were caught by the bank commissioners without even borrowed specie on hand. The Bank of Sandstone, for instance, never had any specie, and although its liabilities exceeded $38,000, it had no assets of any kind at the time it was examined. The Exchange Bank of Shiawassee threw open its safe to disclose only seven copper coins and a very small number of notes, while it had bills in circulation in the amount of $22,261. The Jackson County Bank placed before the bank inspectors several large strongboxes that appeared to be filled with coin. Upon opening the boxes, the commissioners found, below a layer of silver dollars, that the boxes were filled with nails and pieces of glass. When the commissioners arrived at the Lenawee County Bank to examine their books, they found the required amount of specie on hand. Believing that all was not as it appeared to be, the commissioners returned unexpectedly a few days later and found the total amount of specie in the bank's vault to be $34.20. This was for a bank with a circulation of bills amounting to more than $20,000. Some of the banks tried to get by with specie certificates, certifying that the specie had been received to be held on deposit. Others tried to use stock notes instead of actually paying in specie. In spite of their lack of hard cash, the banks issued handsome notes that pledged the bank to pay to the bearer on demand so many dollars in specie. And they issued them in enormous quantities.[45]

Many of these wildcat banks were located in inaccessible and out of the way places. Two of the banks were opened in purely farming communities, towns with only one or two merchants each. Many were located in towns like Singapore (Allegan County) and Goodrich (Lapeer County), towns which do not exist today. Seven of these wildcat banks were established in Washtenaw County alone—a county which at the time had a population of about 20,000.

For a brief time the demand for borrowed money was so great that almost none of the notes were presented for redemption in specie. On one occasion, a Detroiter made his way to the Bank of Brest in Monroe County, planning to exchange $1,200 in notes for specie. The president of the institution received him with cordiality, wined him and dined him, and told him he could not redeem the notes just then, but was expecting a shipment of gold and silver within a few days.

Another story was told of a stranger who had lost his way in the woods of Shiawassee County. Toward nightfall, looking for a place to spend the night, he followed what he thought was a logging trail through the woods when suddenly he came to a clearing that contained a large frame structure across the front of which was a conspicuous sign proclaiming it to be the Bank of Shiawassee. "It was one of the wild-cats quartered in the native haunts of that animal, the depths of the forest." [46]

No one knows for certain why the banks were called "wildcats." One contemporary reported that the notes of the different banks organized under the General Banking Law were called "wild cat," "tom cat," "red dog," and other names according to the fancied solvency of the particular institution.[47] One authority says that the name was first used by Oliver Newberry, one of Detroit's leading merchants of the period. A customer brought in a parcel of bills to pay up an account and Newberry refused to accept them saying he would have nothing to do with "that wild cat stuff." [48] Another report

55

says the term came from Missouri. The governor of that territory approved an act, "To encourage the killing of wolves, panthers, and wildcats." The bounties were paid with legal tender certificates called "wildcat certificates." [49] Whether any of these were the origin of the term no one is able to say. Very likely the name "wildcat" was applied to a bank on some occasion in jest, and it seemed so peculiarly appropriate that it stuck.

THE PANIC OF 1837

The depression that began in the East with the New York banks suspending specie payment in 1837 did not at first affect Michigan. When it did reach the state in 1839, however, it descended with a fury. Two of the factors that contributed to the hard times in Michigan were the wildcat banks and the state's internal improvement program.

The people of Michigan were especially conscious of the benefits they had derived from the Erie Canal, which had been built by the state of New York, and they believed that their own state should undertake similar projects. As a result, the constitution of 1835 had made it the duty of the legislature to appropriate funds for the improvement of roads, canals, and navigable waters.

In March 1837, along with the General Banking Law, the legislature undertook to sponsor a staggering program of railroad and canal construction. In fact, several bills had to be enacted to cover the various phases of the program. Three railroads and two canals were planned to span the lower peninsula from East to West. One railroad, the Southern, was to be built from Monroe to New Buffalo on Lake Michigan; another, the Central, from Detroit to the mouth of the St. Joseph River; and the third, the Northern, from Port Huron to Grand Rapids. Steamships on the Grand River would complete the connection of this line with Lake Michigan.

A canal was to be dug from Mount Clemens on the Clinton River to the mouth of the Kalamazoo, and another to link the Saginaw with the Maple, a tributary of the Grand. The Saginaw-Grand River Canal was to begin at the forks of the Bad River, 15 miles above Saginaw, and terminate at the bend of the Maple, 32 miles from its confluence with the Grand River. In addition to these, a canal was to be constructed around the falls of the St. Mary's River between Lake Superior and Lake Huron.

To finance this program of internal improvements, the legislature authorized Governor Mason to negotiate a loan of five million dollars. This was the amount the governor had suggested in his message to the legislature. In June 1838, after several trips East, the governor made an agreement with the Morris Canal and Banking Company of New York to act as agent for the sale of bonds to raise the five million.

By the end of 1838, some construction had begun. One hundred and ten miles had been cleared for the line of the Northern Railroad, the Southern had reached Adrian, and the Central ran its first train from Detroit to Ann Arbor on October 17. Both the Clinton and Kalamazoo and the Saginaw canals were under construction, and the Grand and Kalamazoo rivers had been made navigable, the first as far as the rapids, and the second to Allegan.

The only project that did not get off to a good start was the canal around the rapids of the St. Mary's River. A contract for construction had been made in September 1838. In May 1839, the contractor appeared at the Sault with a gang of workmen and began to dig. He was warned by the commandant of the military post at the site not to interfere with the millrace of a sawmill used by the fort. Disregarding the warning, the contractor continued his operations in such a way as to endanger the flow of water to the mill. When he refused to desist, an officer appeared with a detachment of regulars and forcibly removed the workmen from the scene.

In August, Michigan and the War Department reached an agreement on the route of the canal, but the contractor refused to resume work, and the project was abandoned. It is believed that the contractor, not liking the job and fearing that the state would not be able to pay for the work, intentionally caused the interference of the military officers. [It was not until 1853 that a second attempt at building a canal at the Sault was undertaken. This time the project was a success with the first ships passing through the locks in June 1855.]

Even though all the projects were underway, progress was very slow primarily due to the lack of funds. It was quickly discovered that five million dollars, a colossal sum in those days, was just not enough. Then, in early 1840, the whole program collapsed. On April 1, the Morris Canal and Banking Company defaulted on the payment of the quarterly installment of the bonds and within a few months both this company and the Bank of the United States of Pennsylvania, which had joined as a purchaser of the bonds, failed. When the state demanded that the bonds on which the holders had not advanced any money be surrendered, it was discovered that the two banks had deposited the bonds with bankers in England as security for loans of their own.

There ensued a series of negotiations and dealings extending over a long period of years that were so complicated as to defy description. In the end, the state redeemed some of the bonds at about 30 cents on the dollar, while interest and principal on others were paid in full. Unfortunately, as a result of this financial disaster, Michigan's credit standing was ruined and the ambitious program of internal improvements came to an end. The railroads were eventually sold to private corporations, but the canals were abandoned.[50]

While the state was struggling with its internal improvement program, its banking structure collapsed completely as a result of the fraudulent practices and excessive issue of depreciated paper money by wildcat banks. The public reaction is graphically recorded in the diary of Silas Beebe, a farmer moving to Michigan from Utica, New York, who had stopped over in Detroit on his way to the interior. His entry for March 15, 1858, reads:

> Nothing is talked of but the "wild cat" banks, some of which are showing the stuff they are made of, and proving themselves rotten to the core. There is scarcely a single one of the whole number (about 60) whose bills will be received at the stores for goods, while many a farmer had sold his produce, and some even their farms for this worthless trash. Most of the laborers and mechanics hold all their receipts and earnings for the last six months in these worthless rags which they cannot use. We hear almost daily of the arrest of Presidents, Directors, and Cashiers for fraud, and injunctions placed upon the banks.[51]

In an attempt to bring some order to this situation, the state bank commissioners tried to force the weaker banks to call in their notes and to reduce their indebtedness. In this they had little success. The legislature tried to strengthen the General Banking Law with a series of amendments. This was not successful either. Then in 1838, the legislature suspended the General Banking Law for one year, and the following year decreed that no more banks could be formed under its provisions. Financial disaster could not be averted, however, and bank failures became a daily occurrence. By the end of 1839, over 40 banks were in the hands of receivers, and something in excess of $1,500,000 in worthless bank notes was left in the hands of individuals throughout the state.[52]

In April 1839, the legislature established a State Bank of Michigan with nine branches, modeled after the very successful State Bank of Indiana, but the backers were unable to raise the necessary capital and the bank went out of existence without ever having opened its doors for business.[53] By 1840 there remained in operation only five of the older chartered banks and four which were organized under the General Banking Law. The final blow came when a case brought before the state supreme court in 1844 resulted in a decision that the General Banking Law of 1837 had never been constitutional.

Thus by 1839 Michigan was plummeted into a depression that was to last until the mid 1840s. Money which had once been so plentiful was no longer available. Land sales dropped off drastically as did the price of farm products. Flour, for example, which had been selling in Detroit for $16.00 a barrel fell to $8.00 in 1839 and $2.25 in 1842. By 1841 it would have been difficult to find an acre of land in the state whose title had not been encumbered for back taxes, mortgaged for individual debt, or pledged to redeem the bills of wildcat banks.[54]

The difficulties of carrying on business activities during this period are epitomized in a letter written in December 1838, by James W. King of Clinton, Michigan, to the New York firm of Phelps Dodge from which he had purchased $500.00 worth of tin:

> Your letter came to hand Requesting an answer Respecting your Clame In Regard to it I ecknolage you had ought to had your pay Long time ago—But oing to the wild Cat Curincy and some of the Chartered Banks it bin impossible to do eny thing with money wee Sold our Goods to Smith & Landon They wur to pay the Demand on account of they Being ingaged in the Wild Cat Banks they had to Leave the country. I had to take the goods to secure myself & Sold them out on a Credit inpreference to take the kind of money that was in Circulation —until some two months pas I have stopd the lending Business and am making my Colections this winter if you want it before I Can Colect it I will Sattisfy the Demand By good notes against good farmers & Back them myself if it wood make them enny Better—or if you will be patient Little Longer I will Pay you as soon as I Can Colect it money is scarce hear Mr. Shelly has not paid me for the tin I hold his note now—But that is nothing to do with you & If you must forbar with me a Little Longer and it Shall Come together with the inress.[55]

Of the forty-nine banks that had gone into operation under the General Banking Law, only one had been established in Detroit. This was the Detroit City Bank. It was organized in December 1837, with an authorized capitalization of $200,000, of which $60,000 was paid-in. With offices on Jefferson Avenue the bank did an active business from the first day it began operations. In a short time, however, the directors found themselves overextended and in February 1839, they were forced to close the bank.[56] Unfortunately this was not the only Detroit banking institution to go out of business in 1839. Within a matter of months, the Michigan State Bank, and the Farmers and Mechanics' Bank of Michigan were also in the hands of receivers.

The Michigan State Bank suspended payments in late February 1839, and the Farmers and Mechanics' Bank suspended payments the following October. As was the case with the Detroit City Bank, the failure of these two was due primarily to overextension. With the depression intensifying and creditors demanding payments, it was discovered that these banks had been doing a larger business than their capital warranted and that much of the discount paper they held was uncollectable.

The failure of the Michigan State Bank was a particularly critical financial blow to Michigan. Not only was the Michigan State Bank the depository of the state treasury, it was also the local bank handling the five million dollar internal improvement loan. When it closed, the bank held the entire state treasury in its vault.[57]

Detroit's other chartered bank, the powerful Bank of Michigan, was also facing very difficult times. In 1838 the bank had moved into a new building at the southwest corner of Griswold and Jefferson. This structure was the first in Detroit to be built of dressed stone. In June the bank declared a dividend of 12 percent for the first 6 months of the year; and, then, during the winter of 1836–37, the bank found itself overextended and heavy withdrawals began to seriously reduce its specie reserves. Fortunately the bank was able to survive this crisis through the careful management of its affairs by the president and cashier. The next crisis came in May 1837, when the Bank of Michigan joined the other banks of the city and suspended specie payments. The suspension continued for a year until the eastern banks resumed specie payments; and, on May 16, 1838, the Bank of Michigan along with the Farmers and Mechanics' Bank again began to redeem its notes in coin.

When the Michigan State Bank failed early in 1839, the Bank of Michigan was designated as the state depository. Any benefits the bank might have gained through this transaction were only temporary. In 1840 the Morris Canal and Banking Company failed and was shortly followed by the Bank of the United States of Pennsylvania. As agents for the sale of bonds to raise the five million dollars for internal improvements, the two banks owed the state about three million dollars at the time they suspended. Payments on these bonds were due in $250,000 installments every three months; and the Bank of Michigan had been advancing money to the state in anticipation of these installments. Thus, the failure of the two eastern banks effectively ruined the Bank of Michigan.

Earlier, the bank had received a loan of $300,000 in cash from its eastern owners. Even this could not save the bank for, unfortunately, most of its loans had been secured by real estate. When these loans became due and payments could not be made, the bank was forced to accept land in lieu of cash. The situation continued to deteriorate and the bank's notes gradually fell to 35 cents on the dollar. Finally, in August 1841, the Bank of Michigan closed its doors and began to wind up its affairs.* [58]

When the Bank of Michigan went out of business, the Michigan Insurance Company remained as Detroit's only banking house. Even though it had begun banking operations in 1838, the company was conservatively managed and as a result was able to survive the depression. In July 1842, the Bank of St. Clair moved its offices to Detroit. Originally chartered in March 1836, the bank's new quarters were located on Jefferson Avenue. This institution soon followed the pattern of the other chartered banks in the city and went out of business in 1845. After the Bank of St. Clair closed, only three of the old charter banks remained in operation in the state; of the 55 wildcat banks, not one had survived. [59]

By the mid 1840s, the depression began to subside. There was no repetition of the wild speculation of the early 1830s, but Michigan citizens began to take a somewhat more optimistic outlook on their future. A few men in Saginaw were proving that Michigan pine had an eastern market. A copper rush and the discovery of iron in the Upper Peninsula also helped to give the state the lift it needed to emerge from the doldrums of the late thirties and early forties.

Banking in Detroit was also taking on a somewhat more promising outlook. It is true that the experiences of the years following 1837 had created a deep antipathy among Detroiters toward banks and bankers, an attitude that was to continue for many years. In fact, during the 1840s, practically the only money in circulation consisted

---

* Although the Bank of Michigan was controlled by eastern financiers, many local investors suffered when the bank failed. One Detroiter who suffered heavily was Lewis Cass. The Governor lost $32,000 in the crash. [60]

of coinage of the United States mint: gold coins plus a limited number of silver dollars, half-dollars, dimes, and half-dimes. After a series of litigations in 1845, the Michigan State Bank was able to reopen. When it had suspended, the bank's affairs had been placed in the hands of an assignee who operated the receivership very astutely. Within three years, the assignee had paid all the bank's obligations and had managed to salvage 20 percent of the original capital. The bank's stock was then sold at 15 percent of its face value to a group of Detroit's leading businessmen; and Charles C. Trowbridge was elected the bank's new president. By the time the bank began business in its old quarters on the south side of Jefferson Avenue, the new directors had been able to accumulate a paid-in capital of $70,000.[61]

In the same year that the Michigan State Bank reopened, the Farmers and Mechanics' Bank began proceedings to resume its business. By 1849, the directors had collected enough specie to offset the bank's indebtedness and, in that year, the institution was granted a new 20-year charter.

The Michigan Insurance Company, while doing a moderately successful business, was still running into an occasional problem due to the fact that it had been chartered as an insurance company. This situation was finally rectified in 1849 when a new charter was obtained, which included in its articles all banking privileges. It continued to do well and soon became Detroit's and Michigan's leading banking institution.[62]

Thus by 1849 banking in Detroit was once again in a sound position. And, with the Michigan State Bank, the Farmers and Mechanics' Bank, and the Michigan Insurance Company Bank all reorganized and operating successfully, Detroit's banking needs appeared to be sufficiently supplied, at least for the business and commercial interests of the city.

Detroit Savings Fund Institute

DETROIT IN 1849

Detroit had recovered from the depression of the late 1830s and early 1840s and, by 1849, was once again a growing commercial center. The city's population numbered 19,000 inhabitants, and the first indications of industrial growth were evident. A man by the name of John Brennan had started a boiler shop in 1847; the Michigan Iron Foundry was established in 1848; and the boot and shoe business and the manufacture of tobacco products were also underway. There was a group of sawmills along the riverfront below Belle Isle and another group of them along the river near Springwells. There were also several shipyards in operation. In addition to these, there were many light industries—the shops and factories turning out products for household or farm use. These manufacturing operations, however, were as yet on a relatively small scale and Detroit was still largely a town of wholesale and retail establishments.* [1]

Detroit's wholesale and retail trade was extensive in 1849 and the

* The federal census of 1850 reported a little more than eleven million dollars worth of manufactured products for the state of Michigan with slightly less than two million dollars of this total for the city of Detroit. [2]

merchants offered a wide variety of goods for sale; groceries, wines, liquors, tea, drugs, patent medicines, books, stationery, office supplies, lumber, building supplies, farming equipment, dry goods, ready-made clothing, hats, gloves, fur robes, soap, sperm and wax candles, rifles, shotguns, and hunting supplies. Rowe and Company, located on Jefferson, dealt in "fresh and pickled oysters, lobsters and clams, also fruits, sardines, sauces and pickles." Down the street from Rowe and Company was Silberman and Hersch, suppliers of cigars, tobacco, and snuff. R. W. King and Company, also on Jefferson Avenue, sold china, glassware, and crockery while the Scotch Store, on the corner of Jefferson and Woodward, was one of the popular dry goods stores of the day.

Even though the city's economic interests were expanding, the busiest place in town was still the waterfront. Detroit did a fairly large freight handling and forwarding business, and the city's docks and warehouses were piled high with merchandise waiting for shipment to the East or the upper lakes. During the shipping season, steamers, propellers, barques, scows, sloops, and schooners could be seen loading and off-loading cargo and passengers at the city's wharves. The entire tonnage of shipping on the upper lakes in 1849 amounted to 160,000 tons and was valued at over eight million dollars.

By far the most exciting boats to see and to travel on in 1849 were the fast, new lake steamers. The Michigan Central Railroad built and operated three of these luxurious steamboats: the *Atlantic*, the *Mayflower*, and the *Ocean*. This fleet carried passengers and freight between Buffalo, Cleveland, Detroit, Milwaukee, and Chicago. The *Mayflower* was built in Detroit and completed her trial runs in May 1849. One of the most noted lake steamers of her day, she had 85 staterooms and could carry 300 cabin passengers and a still greater number of deck or steerage passengers. On board one of these luxury steamers, a man and his family could travel from Buffalo to Detroit in the amazing time of only 16 hours.

For those travelers who preferred to come by rail, there were two railroads serving Detroit in 1849. The Detroit and Pontiac Railroad had begun operations in May 1838. Their line ran out Dequindre on the same right-of-way the Grand Trunk uses today. There was a spur line from Dequindre, down the middle of Gratiot Avenue, to the depot which in 1849 was located at the corner of Gratiot and Farmer. Because of citizens' protests (the east side residents opposed having the rails on Gratiot, with trains running past their homes, spewing sparks, and scaring their horses and cows), the route was changed in 1852. The trains then ran down Dequindre to Atwater and then east to Brush Street, where a new depot was built. It still stands today as the Brush Street Station.

Detroit's other railroad was the Michigan Central. First chartered as the Detroit & St. Joseph Railroad in 1832, the company also began operation in 1838. Incorporated as the Michigan Central Railroad Company in 1846, the concern was sold to eastern businessmen for two million dollars. The Michigan Central line came from Kalamazoo (it reached Chicago in 1852) and down Michigan Avenue to Griswold Street, then to the new depot at the foot of Third Street near the riverfront. The fine new Michigan Central Depot had been built in 1848 and, the following year, the rail yards were expanded and a new domed engine house or roundhouse was built just west of the depot. Along with its supporting shops, factories, and repair buildings, the Michigan Central became one of Detroit's transportation centers. In 1849 the railroad carried 152,672 passengers and 81,066 tons of freight. Its operating expenses were $301,649 and its net earnings were $390,323.

On arriving in Detroit, a traveler had the choice of a number of excellent hotels. There was, of course, Andrew's Railroad Hotel facing Campus Martius, next to the Detroit and Pontiac Railroad Depot. There was the National Hotel on Woodward at Fort Street, where a weary traveler could obtain a room for 75 cents a night; or the famous Michigan Exchange at Jefferson and Shelby, where a very good evening meal could be had for 25 cents. For those who arrived by train at the Michigan Central Depot, there was Johnson's Hotel up Third Street at the corner of Jefferson.

In May 1848 a fire swept through the lower part of the city. While it had been contained to a district bounded by Randolph Street and Woodward Avenue, and from Jefferson Avenue down to the river, almost every building in the area had been destroyed. The damage was estimated at $300,000. New buildings were springing up in this area in 1849 and one of them was a new hotel, the Biddle House. Built on the southeast corner of Jefferson Avenue and Randolph Street, it was to become one of Detroit's leading hotels for the next half century. Presidents, generals, statesmen, and foreign dignitaries were all, at one time or another, guests at the Biddle House.

Fire was constantly a menace in Detroit, and the firemen of this time played an important part in the life of the city. The fire companies were independent volunteer organizations that worked in intense rivalry. No public parade or local pageant was considered complete without a turnout of the fire companies. The competition in brilliancy of uniform and decoration of apparatus was very keen and contests of speed and efficiency were frequent. There were four engine companies and two independent hose companies in 1844; then, in 1849, two more companies, the Union, No. 7, and the Mechanics, No. 8, were organized.

Since water mains did not have sufficient pressure for fighting fires at this time, the most common fire apparatus was the hand-powered pump engine. The first steam fire engine seen in Detroit was one which passed through the city on its way to Chicago in 1859. In 1860 the city purchased a steamer from the Amoskeag Company of New Hampshire at a cost of $3,150, and the last hand engine was finally retired from service in 1865.

In 1849 the telegraph was still a novelty in Detroit. The first telegraph line in Michigan ran from Detroit to Ypsilanti and went into operation on November 29, 1847. The first telegraph office was located in a rear room on the second story of a building at the northeast corner of Jefferson and Cass. In early 1848 the line was opened to Buffalo, and by 1849 it was completed from Detroit to Chicago.

Detroiters of 1849 had a wide choice of churches to attend on Sunday mornings. By far the most numerous parishes were those of the Roman Catholic faith—the two largest Catholic churches were Ste. Anne's and SS. Peter and Paul. Ste. Anne's had been constructed after the fire of 1805. SS. Peter and Paul was a new church in 1849, the building having been completed in 1848. This church still stands today on the north side of Jefferson at St. Antoine.

The Episcopalians also had a choice of churches. There was old St. Paul's on the east side of Woodward near Larned, next to the First Presbyterian Church; and there was the new Mariners' Church built in 1849 on the west side of Woodward at Woodbridge. Congregationalists, Lutherans, and Methodists also had their churches. The Baptists had their First Church on Fort at Griswold. The Second Baptist Church, which had been organized in 1836, was Detroit's first black church. Located on the southside of Lafayette near Beaubien, the Bethel A.M.E. Church was Detroit's second black church. Organized in 1841, the church was incorporated on July 30, 1849. [In 1973 construction was begun on a new church at Warren and the Chrysler Freeway on the city's near east side.]

The bell in the tower of the First Presbyterian Church on Woodward at Larned was rung at 6 o'clock in the morning, at noon, and at 6 o'clock in the evening. It also sounded the curfew over the city at 9 o'clock. There were too many saloons and taverns in town that existed solely for the purpose of selling strong ale and whiskey at 3 cents a glass, and the curfew was sounded to warn disorderly persons off the public streets.

While the commercial life of the city was located on Atwater, Woodbridge, and Jefferson, the residential sections of Detroit in 1849 were situated along Fort, West Lafayette, and East Jefferson. There were many fine homes in Detroit at this time. The town's leading citizen, Lewis Cass, recently returned from Paris, built a splendid new home in 1842 on the northwest corner of Cass and Fort streets. Mrs. Solomon Sibley's home was built in 1848 on the south side of Jefferson Avenue. It still stands today, next door to Christ Episcopal Church.

The parlors and drawing rooms of the homes were lighted by tallow and stearin candles, and lamps adapted for the use of lard and sperm oil. Soon after 1849 came the introduction of camphene, a burning fluid which was a highly inflammable mixture of alcohol, turpentine, and camphor gum. Many fires and explosions resulted from its use, and it was soon discontinued in favor of refined petroleum oil, or kerosene. The first use of gas in Detroit was by H. R. Johnson, who installed a small gas-producing plant for lighting his hotel located on Third Street near the Michigan Central Depot. In 1851 the first public gas plant was installed in Detroit.

Having been the capital of the territory, and until recently the capital of the state, Detroit was the location of many governmental offices. There was of course the Old Capitol Building at the head of Griswold, and the Wayne County building at the southeast corner of Congress and Griswold. The County Building, a plain two-story brick structure, was built in 1844.

The City Hall was an unattractive three-story brick building which stood in the middle of what is now Cadillac Square, then known as Michigan Grand Avenue. Built in 1835 it faced toward Woodward Avenue. Butchers' stalls and fish stalls occupied the ground floor. On the second floor were the city offices, and on the third floor was a council room and public hall where religious services, theatrical productions, concerts, and other social functions were frequently held.

The federal government had taken over the Bank of Michigan Building on the southwest corner of Jefferson Avenue and Griswold Street. There the United States Court, marshall, and other officials were housed. The local U.S. Land Office occupied the basement with an entrance on Griswold. The Customs House was on Griswold between Jefferson and Woodbridge. Offices of the local Indian commissioner, surveyor, and commissary were scattered about in other buildings.

Jefferson Avenue in 1849 was paved from curb to curb between Third and Brush streets. In wet weather, the unpaved streets were impassable for heavily loaded wagons. The new pavement was of cobblestones, laid on ten inches of sand to deaden the noise and facilitate drainage. Construction costs of the new pavement were: 15 cents a yard for excavation, 50 cents a square yard for paving and 21 cents per lineal foot for curbing. In this same year, the first crosswalks were laid of alternate strips of cobblestones and flat stones, and alleys were paved between Woodward Avenue and Griswold Street and State Street and Grand River Avenue.

While Detroit was a growing, bustling town in 1849, it also had its disasters and setbacks. In the summer of that year, the dreaded cholera struck, and before it had run its course, 336 citizens died. The first cases were reported in late May. Announcements began to appear in the *Detroit Free Press* and the *Detroit Daily Advertiser* giving instructions as issued by the Board of Health. Citizens were warned to clean up their yards, the streets, and alleys. This was of little help, and the newspapers soon began listing the deaths of friends, neighbors, and loved ones. To try to combat the spread of the cholera, some of the townspeople burned large kettles of pitch at night in front of their homes and at intervals along the streets. But the cholera continued to spread and it was not until September that the epidemic came to an end.

Detroit had its share of happy times, too. Crane and Company's Oriental Circus came to town on June 7, 1849. There was a grand parade headed by a large chariot drawn by ten Syrian camels. The handbills and posters advertised, "band music, clowns, trained ponies, exciting horse races, etc., etc." All this and more for an admission price of only 25 cents.

Michigan's first state fair was held in the closing days of September 1849. The fair grounds were located on the west side of Woodward between Columbia and Vernor. Farmers and city folk alike came from all over the state to view prize-winning farm animals and equipment, domestic handicraft such as needle work, and a multitude of fruits, flowers, vegetables and field crops.

Detroit in 1849 was indeed a thriving commercial center, and this growth was supported by the sound banking operations of the city's three banks: the Michigan State Bank, the Farmers and Mechanics' Bank, and the Michigan Insurance Company Bank. Since 1845, these three banks had all been reorganized; and, in 1849, both the Michigan Insurance Company Bank and the Farmers and Mechanics' Bank had been granted revised charters. In addition to these revised charters, the state legislature also issued charters to two new banking institutions in 1849. One of the charters was for the Peninsular Bank. This bank was incorporated on March 28, with an authorized capital of $100,000. The directors first met on April 5, 1849; and on October 22, the bank opened in a building just west of the Farmers and Mechanics' Bank on the south side of Jefferson Avenue between Shelby and Griswold.

However, the Peninsular Bank was a bank of issue, a commercial institution similar to the three banks already doing business at this time—serving the interests of local merchants and businessmen. What Detroit needed was a bank for the workingman, an institution where tradesmen, mechanics, and laborers would be encouraged to invest their small savings at interest; a bank where their money would be protected and yet have an opportunity to grow. The other charter issued by the state legislature in 1849 was for just such a bank. It was called the Detroit Savings Fund Institute.

"A BANK FOR THE INDUSTRIOUS AND PRUDENT"

On March 5, 1849, Governor Epaphroditus Ransom signed an authorizing act incorporating the Detroit Savings Fund Institute. The signing of this charter meant not only a new bank for Detroit, it also represented a new idea in banking. The Detroit Savings Fund Institute differed from the other banks then established in Detroit and Michigan in that it was not a commercial banking house concerned solely with commerce and trade. It was founded as a

69

savings bank. As envisioned by the trustees, the purpose of the Detroit Savings Fund Institute was described:

> The design of the Institution is to afford to those who are desirous of saving money, but who have not acquired sufficient to purchase a share in the banks, railroads, or a sum in public stocks, the means of employing their money to advantage, without running the risk of losing it, as they are too frequently exposed to do, by lending it to individuals, who either fail or defraud them. It is intended to encourage the industrious and prudent, and to induce those who have not hitherto been such, to lessen their unnecessary expense, and to save and lay by something for a period of life when they will be less able to earn a support.[3]

The idea of the savings bank was first developed in Europe at the time of the industrial revolution and the formation of a permanent wage-earning class. These savings institutions grew out of benevolent organizations formed to promote thrift among the working class and thus improve their welfare. The first such bank was founded in Hamburg, Germany in 1778. Other savings banks were established throughout Western Europe following the French Revolution and its accompanying social upheaval.

In England the church sponsored the establishment of savings institutions. In Great Britain the first savings bank, self-sustaining and catering to a wide public, was founded by the Reverend Henry Duncan at Ruthwell Parish in Dumfriesshire, Scotland in 1810. Within the next few years the idea of the savings bank was rapidly taken up in England and soon spread to the United States.

With the European savings societies as a model, the first savings bank in the United States, the Philadelphia Savings Fund Society, began business in November 1816 although the first savings bank to be chartered was the Provident Institution for Savings in Boston, which opened for business on December 2, 1816. In the following years savings banks were established in most of the important towns in the New England and North Atlantic states. These institutions were founded by public-spirited citizens who organized themselves into self-perpetuating boards of trustees and served without pay in the management of the community savings bank. The formation of savings banks in the United States coincided with the beginnings of industrial development when people were moving away from the farms to employment in small business and industries of the cities and towns. When the New England settlers began their migration into Michigan they brought with them, along with their household and personal belongings, the idea of the savings institution.

70

The single most important factor in the success of a savings bank at this time was the public confidence in the officers and directors. Fortunately, the man who was instrumental in the formation of the Detroit Savings Fund Institute had this public trust. His name was Elon Farnsworth—one of Detroit's most respected citizens. Farnsworth was born in Vermont in 1799, and there he received his early formal education. At the age of 25, he packed his bags and, like so many of his Yankee neighbors, set out for Michigan. In his coat pocket Farnsworth carried this letter of introduction written by DeWitt Clinton, governor of New York, addressed to Lewis Cass:[4]

> Albany, September 17, 1824
>
> Sir,
> I have the pleasure of introducing to you Mr. Elon Farnsworth, a respectable young gentleman of Vermont, whom you will find worthy of your favorable notice, and who visits your Country with a view to settlement in it.
>
> I am yours respectfully
> DeWitt Clinton
>
> To Gov. Cass

Cass was impressed by young Farnsworth and introduced him to his friend Solomon Sibley, who took him into his law office, where Farnsworth began to study law. Farnsworth held his first public office in 1834–35 as a member of the sixth and last Legislative Council of the Territory of Michigan. He served as representative from Wayne County. In 1836, when the state government was organized, a court of chancery was created and Farnsworth was appointed its first judge or chancellor. This court was established to hear equity cases as opposed to common-law jurisdictions, which were separate and vested in another court. Farnsworth served as chancellor of the state until 1842 at which time he resigned because of poor health.

During his term as chancellor, Farnsworth served as a regent of the University of Michigan. In 1846 he was reappointed regent and continued to hold the position until he resigned in 1858.

From 1843 to 1845, Farnsworth served as state attorney general. In the meantime, he had been nominated for governor in 1839 by the Democratic party. Unfortunately the Democrats were blamed for the depression that had resulted from the panic of 1837, and Farnsworth was defeated by the Whig candidate, William Woodbridge, 19,070 to 17,782.

An indication of Farnsworth's feeling of obligation to public service is evidenced by his acceptance of reappointment as chancellor in 1846. Following the passage of an act to eliminate the court of chancery, the incumbent, Randolph Manning, resigned. Governor Felch was left with no one to fill out the unexpired term. A public office with less than a year to run had little appeal, and yet it was essential that its affairs be put in order before the supreme court assumed the duties of the position. Governor Felch appealed to Farnsworth, who at first refused to consider a reappointment but finally relented and accepted. He was formally reappointed June 1, 1846, and continued until March 1, 1847, when the court was abolished. Farnsworth proved to be such an outstanding jurist and respected member of the bar that even after the court was abolished, he continued for the remainder of his life to be addressed as Chancellor Farnsworth.[5]

When the Michigan Central Railroad was reorganized in 1846, Farnsworth was elected to the Board of Directors. As the only member of the board living in Detroit (the other six members were from Boston, Albany, and New York City), he was designated resident director. This was a position he held for nearly 20 years.

Elon Farnsworth had realized the need for a savings bank in Detroit and the need for a group of respected citizens to serve as its directors. Thus, he enlisted the aid of ten prominent Detroiters to assist him in establishing the Savings Fund Institute. There was David Smart, a merchant, and a forwarding and commission agent. Smart, a Scot, was also president of the Fire Department Society and a member of Engine Company No. 3. John Palmer was a dry goods merchant. His store, located on Jefferson Avenue, was one of the best-known establishments in town. Later, Palmer was one of the first directors of the Detroit Board of Trade. Zina Pitcher was one of Detroit's most prominent physicians. He had a lifelong interest in education and in 1843 was president of the Detroit Board of Education and later served as a regent of the University of Michigan. Dr. Pitcher also served two terms, in 1841 and again in 1843, as Detroit's mayor. Charles Moran was a large land owner and over the years had held a number of public positions. Moran was a Frenchman whose ancestors were contemporary with Cadillac. Shubael Conant, one of Detroit's oldest residents, was a fur dealer and merchant. Conant had also long been an active member of the Detroit Anti-Slavery Society. Then there were Benjamin B. Kercheval, Levi Cook, James A. Hicks, George M. Rich, and Gurdon Williams, all merchants and businessmen of good character, integrity, and financial responsibility.

A preliminary draft for a bill to incorporate the bank was drawn up and presented to George R. Griswold, the state senator from Detroit. On January 24, 1849, Senator Griswold reported the bill to the senate. Early in February it was read a second time, and on February 17 the bill was read for a third time. Finally on March 5, 1849, the charter was approved by both houses of the legislature and sent to the governor for his signature.[6]

The charter provided that the Savings Fund Institute was "to receive on deposit all such sums of money as should from time to time be offered by tradesmen, mechanics, laborers, servants, minors, and others for investment." The deposits were to be repaid to them at such time and with such interest and under such regulations as the board of trustees should from time to time prescribe. It was a pure and simple trust; there was no corporate capital.[7]

The charter also provided among other injunctions, that the bank should

not issue any bill or note to circulate as money. Any trustee, officer or agent of said company who shall use any of the funds except as in this act provided, or issue or cause to be issued any bill or note designated or intended to be circulated as money, shall be deemed guilty of a misdemeanor, and on conviction thereof shall be punished by imprisonment in the State Prison not more than ten years, and by fine not exceeding ten thousand dollars or both, in the discretion of the court.[8]

It is true that these injunctions were strict—the lessons from the General Banking Law of 1837 had been painfully learned.

Other restrictions imposed on the bank related to how the board of trustees might invest deposits made with them, stating in Section 5 for example that they might "invest . . . in any public stock of the United States, or of the State of Michigan, or upon bond secured by mortgage upon unencumbered real estate worth at least double the amount loaned. . . ." The bank itself, however, was limited in what real estate it could hold and convey. It was restricted to

1st, such as shall be necessary and convenient for an office as place for the transaction of business. 2nd— Such as shall be mortgaged or otherwise conveyed to it as security for money loaned. 3rd— Such as shall be conveyed to it in payment of indebtedness.* [9]

Shortly after the charter was issued, the trustees gathered at Farnsworth's law office to hold their first official meeting as directors

* A copy of "An Act to Incorporate the Detroit Savings Fund Institute" will be found in Appendix A.

of the bank. Farnsworth was appointed chairman of the meeting, and the first order of business was the reading of Gurdon Williams' letter of resignation. The resignation was accepted, and by a unanimous vote, Henry N. Walker was chosen to fill the vacancy.[10] This proved to be a very wise choice, for Walker, a long-time personal friend of Farnsworth, became one of the principal officers of the bank and was instrumental in its early success.

Henry Nelson Walker was born on November 30, 1811, in Chautauqua County, New York; and, upon coming to Detroit in 1834, he entered the law office of Elon Farnsworth and Asher B. Bates as a law student. In 1835 he was admitted to the bar; and when Farnsworth became chancellor in 1836, the firm was continued as Bates and Walker. In 1837, undoubtedly with Farnsworth's backing, Walker was admitted to practice in the state court of chancery; and in 1845 he succeeded Farnsworth as state attorney general, serving from 1845 to 1848. In 1846 he was admitted to the bar of the United States Supreme Court on the motion of Daniel Webster.

It was during this period that Walker entered the railroad business and within a short time became an expert in railroad affairs and one of Michigan's most successful railroad lawyers. He took an active part, as attorney general, in the sale of the Michigan Central Railroad in 1846; and in 1848, he became president of the Oakland and Ottawa Railroad. When this railroad consolidated with the Detroit and Pontiac Railroad to become the Detroit and Milwaukee Railroad, he continued to serve as president of the reorganized corporation until 1858.[11]

When the Michigan Insurance Company Bank was rechartered in 1849, Walker became its vice president. When he was elected a trustee of the Savings Fund Institute, he continued as a director of the Insurance Company Bank.* As a result, and not a surprising one at that, the Michigan Insurance Company Bank became a major Savings Institute depositor. During the early years of the bank's existence, the Insurance Company Bank was its only corporate depositor. The importance of the Michigan Insurance Company Bank's account can be measured by the fact that individuals deposited $2313.24 during 1849; the Insurance Bank deposited $973.76.[12]

* Serving as a director of two banks at the same time was not an unheard of practice in 1849. Benjamin B. Kercheval was a trustee of the Savings Institute and also a director of the Peninsular Bank. Charles Howard, who was mayor of Detroit in 1849, did Walker and Kercheval one better. Howard was simultaneously president of both the Peninsular Bank and the Farmers and Mechanics' Bank.[13]

In addition to Walker's election, the trustees had a number of other items to consider. The most important of these was the appointment of a committee to draft a set of rules and regulations to govern the operations of the bank. Farnsworth, Walker, and Shubael Conant were selected as the committee members.

On May 9, 1849, the trustees met again at Farnsworth's office and the committee presented their draft of the by-laws. After some discussion these regulations were unanimously adopted.* [14]

The by-laws stated that sums as small as one dollar would be accepted on deposit. Interest, at the rate of "four per centum per annum," would be paid only on accounts of five dollars and above. Section 16 of the by-laws established the hours of business which were to be "Mondays, Wednesdays, and Fridays, except holidays, from the hours of ten A.M., to one o'clock, P.M. . . ."

Two of the major sections of the by-laws concerned the appointment and duties of the finance committee. The trustees were to annually appoint "from their own number, two persons, who with the President and Vice President shall constitute a finance committee. . . ." It was to be the finance committee's duty to see that all moneys deposited in the bank were properly invested in such public stocks as were authorized by the charter. When the bank was opened for business, the running of its affairs came under the complete control and direction of the finance committee. [15]

With the by-laws approved, the trustees elected officers and finance committee members. By a unanimous vote Elon Farnsworth was elected president and Henry Walker vice president. Shubael Conant and Zina Pitcher were elected to serve with Farnsworth and Walker as members of the finance committee. Once the finance committee was formed they were to prepare the by-laws for publication, to rent an office, "and to do all other acts and things necessary to open the Institute for business." [16]

The final order of business for the day was the acceptance of Charles Moran's resignation and the election of Samuel Lewis to fill the vacancy. Lewis, who was a member of the firm of Dudgeon, Lewis & Graves, forwarding and commission merchants, had been one of the first men in the city to invest in steamboat construction.

As one of their first tasks, the finance committee members turned their attention to the problem of locating and renting office space for the bank. The story of the bank's first quarters goes back to 1818 and

* A complete set of the first "By-Laws and Regulations" will be found in Appendix B.

the arrival in Detroit of the paddlesteamer *Walk-in-the-Water.* Two of the passengers on that historic voyage were Mrs. Julia Anderson and her sister, Charlotte Taylor. Mrs. Anderson was the new bride of Colonel John Anderson of the U.S. Army who was escorting the ladies to Detroit where he was stationed. The Anderson home was on the northwest corner of Woodward and Woodbridge, at that time part of the city's residential district. Charlotte Taylor, who possessed a considerable fortune, purchased the property from the Andersons in 1822, and all three continued to live in the home until Colonel Anderson's death in 1834. A year or two later, Mrs. Anderson and Miss Taylor moved to a house on Rowland Street, where Miss Taylor died in February 1840, and Mrs. Anderson in October 1842.

By the terms of Miss Taylor's will, her fortune was left to her sister with the express provision that it be used at the latter's death for the founding of a church for mariners. This church was to minister to the religious needs of Great Lakes' sailors and was to be patterned after the seamen's bethels established in a number of Atlantic seaports.[17]

When Mrs. Anderson died, her will stated specifically that such a church was to be built. The church was to be named "Mariners' Church of Detroit"; it was to be built of stone; it was to be situated on the Anderson property at Woodward Avenue and Woodbridge, facing Woodward; and it was to be endowed. Following the settlement of the will, the Michigan Legislature enacted a bill to incorporate the church as an Episcopal church with a board of nine trustees. The board was composed of Henry P. Baldwin, president; James V. Campbell, secretary; Charles C. Trowbridge, treasurer; and board members Alexander H. Adams, Henry Chipman, Alexander D. Fraser, James A. Hicks, Mason Palmer, and Elon Farnsworth.[18]

Unfortunately, Mrs. Anderson's fortune was not as great as she had believed and the trustees were faced with a number of problems in building the church. Mrs. Anderson's estate was comprised of the Woodward Avenue lot fronting 50 feet on Woodward and 100 feet on Woodbridge; a second adjacent lot fronting 100 feet on Woodbridge and 40 feet on Griswold; and $13,600 in cash. It was soon discovered that the cost of constructing a stone building was far greater than Mrs. Anderson's estate would allow, which would mean that nothing would be left for the endowment. Then, also, the stipulation that the church had to front on Woodward (which was in the heart of the city's business district), prevented the trustees from using this lot for business purposes while building the church on the rear lot facing Woodbridge or Griswold.[19]

76

Unwilling to leave the new church without an assured income or to encumber it with a debt, the trustees hit upon the plan of devoting the ground floor of the structure to business uses and the upper story to the church; the church to be reached by a broad stairway leading up from Woodbridge at the rear of the building. In addition to this, it was decided to erect on the lot at the rear of the church two substantial brick stores fronting on Woodbridge. The cost of the construction of the church and the two stores on the Woodbridge-Griswold lot came to $17,590.94, practically $4,000 in excess of Mrs. Anderson's bequest; but the money borrowed was made a lien upon the Woodbridge-Griswold property alone, leaving the church entirely free from debt. The rental income from the two buildings on Woodbridge, which was estimated at $600 annually, was to be assigned to the liquidation of the debt. The income from the businesses in the church building itself, estimated at $900 annually, was to be used for the endowment specified in Mrs. Anderson's will.[20]

In April 1849, the existing structures on the two lots were removed and the construction of the stores and the church was begun. By August, the two brick stores were completed; and, in December, the church was consecrated.* [21]

The first occupants of the ground floor of the church were the U.S. Post Office and Gleason F. Lewis, an exchange broker. The Post Office remained a tenant of the church until 1860, when a new government office building was constructed at the northwest corner of Griswold and Larned.

With the Woodward shops rented, the church trustees were faced with finding tenants for the building on the Woodbridge-Griswold property. With Elon Farnsworth and James A. Hicks on the board, the trustees did not have to look far. The building on the corner of Woodbridge and Griswold was rented as quarters for the Detroit Savings Fund Institute while the other structure was leased to

* By 1875 the church's congregation, which in the mid-1850s had been a prosperous one, dwindled to just a few families. The advent of the lake steamer drove the sailing ship from the lakes, and the few mariners who had attended the church soon disappeared. As the years passed, the church deteriorated into a run-down building. In the 1950s, however, when the city developed its civic center, Mariners' Church was renovated and moved to the southwest corner of Randolph Street and Woodward Avenue. There, this venerable church stands today, one of Detroit's historic landmarks. The church was only moved about three city blocks but because of the size and age of the building it was moved, literally, at a snail's pace. The move was begun on December 17, 1954, and completed on April 12, 1955.[22]

Farnsworth for use as his law office.*

With office space rented, officers elected, and by-laws published, the Detroit Savings Fund Institute was finally ready to open. On Wednesday evening, August 15, 1849, the following notice appeared in the *Detroit Free Press*:

> The Detroit Savings Fund Institute—We are glad to learn that the institution chartered last winter under the above title, is now organized, and ready to transact business.
>
> The days for receipt of Deposits, are for the present, Mondays, Wednesdays, and Fridays, from ten to one o'clock. From the character of the trustees and officers of this institution, we have no doubt it will prove one of great usefulness to that class for whose benefit it is particularly designed. The office is at the corner of Griswold and Woodbridge streets, near the Customs House.

On Friday, August 17, the bank opened promptly at 10 A.M. The first day's business brought in six depositors and $41.00. One of these first depositors was Elon Farnsworth's daughter, Caroline. Her account was opened for one dollar.

In its early years the bank had no regular cashier. William A. Butler, who officially held the office of secretary, also filled in as the cashier. Although his duties at the Savings Fund Institute would not have been arduous, since the bank was open only three days a week from 10 A.M. until 1 P.M. and the number of persons availing themselves of his services was small, he soon found that his own banking and exchange business prevented his devoting sufficient time to the activities of the new venture. He was succeeded by William Walker, who filled the position until 1855 when a full-time cashier was appointed.[23]

An indication of the bank's limited facilities can be gained from studying its expenses during its first two years of operation. For example, rent of $75 was paid quarterly to the trustees of Mariners' Church; other expenditures were for wood (in the amount of $1.50) and for its cutting-cost: 75 cents. The wood was burned in a stove which had been purchased for $8, with stove pipe an additional 38 cents; shovel and tongs were purchased for 75 cents. The cost of

---

* There are many references stating that the Savings Fund Institute was located next to the Post Office on the ground floor of the church. The confusion comes in part from the fact that in many cases the two rentals are listed as Post Office and Bank, or Banking Office. Gleason Lewis, an exchange broker, was the Post Office's neighbor. In the mid-nineteenth century exchange brokers were known as private bankers and their offices were often referred to as banking houses, banking offices, or simply banks.[24]

advertising for the first year amounted to $10 and printing costs were $9.25. In addition, there were expenses for pamphlets, paper, a blank account book, ink, and sundries. Total expenses for the year came to $355.36.[25]

During the first months of operation, the bank had relatively few customers. This fact was emphasized by an editorial comment in the *Detroit Daily Advertiser* for August 31, 1849, which stated:

> It may be important to many of our readers to know that there is in operation in our city an institution where minors, servants, laborers, and others, can deposit their savings and receive interest for their money. The Trustees . . . are among our best citizens.

This was followed by an article in the *Detroit Free Press* of October 24th that urged:

> . . . As but comparatively few of those classes to whom it [the bank] is intended more especially to benefit, are aware of the facilities it affords to them and the profits to them by their deposits, it will doubtless, require two or three years time for this bank to grow . . . , but the officers are confident that it will continue to increase in importance and usefulness, and fully meet the expectations of the trustees and the public.
>
> Many apprentices, young men, and females, who are getting small salaries, and who are in the habit of putting the small amounts saved, in the hands of some friend or allowing them to remain idle in their trunks, will do well to embrace the opportunity presented by the Savings Bank of increasing their capital.

At this time over 30 individuals had opened accounts and the sums deposited amounted to several hundred dollars. By the end of 1849, the number of depositors had reached 56 and deposits totaled $3,287.[26]

The *Free Press*'s prediction that it would take two to three years for the bank to grow was a pessimistic one, for on January 10, 1850, that same paper reported that business was "rapidly increasing" and that over $700 had been deposited since the first of the year. In fact, business became so good that the bank soon outgrew its offices on Woodbridge and moved to new quarters on Woodward Avenue, four doors north of Mariners' Church. And, by July 1851, the number of depositors had grown to 320, with total deposits amounting to about $25,000.[27]

At this time, loans made by the bank usually realized a return of ten percent, although some references to a higher rate are evident, the latter probably due to a basic minimum fee. Deposits continued to grow and, on October 22, 1851, an important investment was made: a new safe was purchased for $125.

Certainly the officers and trustees were astute businessmen, for the Institute continued to expand and prosper. Its growth was such that in 1855 the bank again had to move to larger quarters, and it was at this time that the bank acquired its first regular cashier.

The Detroit Savings Fund Institute's first full-time cashier was Alexander H. Adams. Adams was born in Cincinnati, Ohio, February 2, 1813, and came to Detroit in 1836. Prior to his coming to Detroit, Adams was employed by the Cincinnati branch of the Second United States Bank. Soon after his arrival here, he was appointed to the state Board of Commissioners for Internal Improvements, a position he held for five years. Shortly after this, he went to work for the Michigan Central Railroad, where he became a close acquaintance of Elon Farnsworth. And, along with Farnsworth, Adams was on the first board of trustees for Mariners' Church.[28]

When the Michigan State Bank was reorganized in 1845, Adams was appointed bookkeeper and cashier pro-tem. In 1847 he was elected to the position of cashier with a salary of $900. Since the charter of the Michigan State Bank expired in 1855, the officers began making preparation to liquidate the bank in the fall of 1854. Adams tendered his resignation on September 25, 1854, to take effect the following January. The directors of the bank accepted his resignation stating:

> Resolved that the board cannot do justice to their own feelings in their severing a connection which has existed for many years, without testifying in the most unqualified manner, their respect for Alexander Adams as a man and an officer, and their entire appreciation of his past valuable services to this bank.[29]

In January, Adams left the employ of the Michigan State Bank; and on April 30, 1855, he was appointed to the position of cashier with the Detroit Savings Fund Institute.[30] This was the beginning of a long and successful partnership for both Adams and the bank.

In addition to Adams' appointment, the trustees, at their April 30th meeting, elected Edward Lyon and Henry P. Baldwin to fill the vacancies created by the deaths of trustees James A. Hicks and Benjamin B. Kercheval. Edward Lyon was the owner of one of Detroit's leading hotels, the Michigan Exchange. Henry P. Baldwin, one of Detroit's most respected citizens, was a very successful manufacturer and wholesaler of boots and shoes. He was president of the first board of trustees for Mariners' Church and numerous civic and social organizations. From 1845 to 1855, he was a director of the Michigan State Bank; from 1869 to 1873, he served as governor of Michigan.

The new office that the bank moved into was the Old Michigan State Bank Building on the south side of Jefferson Avenue between Woodward and Bates. This change of quarters was a decided improvement for the bank. For the first time, the Detroit Savings Fund Institute was in a building that had been designed for banking purposes. Following its move to new quarters in 1855, the bank's growth continued; by the end of 1856, deposits totaled $144,521.[31] Thus by 1857 the Detroit Savings Fund Institute was a sound and prosperous banking enterprise. Since its founding in 1849, the bank had continued to expand; in 1857 it was to face its first financial crisis.

PANIC OF 1857

The panic of 1857 was a typical bust following a typical American boom. The decade following the Mexican War saw speculation run riot in railroad construction, growth of manufacturing, development of the wheat belt, and growth of poorly regulated state banking. Land speculation and the opening of the California gold fields had also contributed to this nation-wide spirit of expansion.

The lack of effective organization of the nation's banking system combined with a number of factors in the securities market to make the panic of 1857 a very serious one, particularly in the rising industrial areas of the East and the agricultural sections of the Middle West. There had been a short period of financial difficulty in 1851, and in 1853 a somewhat more serious one—both aggravated by the federal government's poorly directed treasury policy. American railroads which had been selling their securities abroad found the market reduced by the outbreak of the Crimean War. Several states felt obliged to come to the aid of half-finished railroads, and this action weakened the state bonds which were held as collateral for bank notes. As a result, some banks in Ohio, Indiana, and Illinois were forced to suspend specie payments in May 1854.

The situation was not improved by the news that fraudulent stock had been issued by the New York, New Haven & Hartford Railroad, and that 3,000 shares of the New York and Harlem Railroad had been forged; there were also rumors of irregularities in Illinois Central issues. Even the railroads which were untouched by these activities were in a precarious condition. With a capital of $491,000,000, the nation's railroads had run up a debt of $417,000,000; against an income of $48,000,000 in 1856–57, they had interest charges of $25,000,000. All these factors combined to create a highly inflammable situation in the money market.[32]

The immediate spark to the panic of 1857 was the failure of the Ohio Life Insurance and Trust Company, which had its head office in Cincinnati, with an agent in New York. It had never done much insurance business in spite of its name, but received a few deposits, made loans, and acted as transfer agent for the state of Ohio. The company had a reputation for conservative banking; and at the head office in Cincinnati no note could be discounted without the approval of the directors. Its agent in New York had unlimited powers, and his speculations in railroad securities resulted in losses greater than the company's capital and surplus. It became known that the New York office had been obliged to close its doors on August 24, 1857. Most of the New York banks were holders of its drafts, and they were immediately called on by their nervous correspondents throughout the country to remit their balances. As a result, New York bank deposits fell from $64,000,000 to $43,000,000 during the next two months.[33]

Stock prices fell rapidly; and exchange brokers found it almost impossible to borrow on their collateral, which consisted primarily of railroad securities. The New York banks had little to lend on call as their balances were reduced. Money rates soared to a peak of five percent per month. Finally on October 12, all the banks in New York City, except The Chemical Bank, were forced to stop redemption of their notes.

The New York banks were able to resume specie payments in mid-December—by that time the damage had been done. The panic had quickly spread and with the approach of winter, unemployment grew, breadlines formed, and ominous signs of social unrest appeared. The depression continued for several months; and while there was some improvement in the East in the spring of 1858, the hard times continued in many Midwestern states until well into 1859 and even 1860.

Michigan was one of the states hardest hit and one of the slowest to recover. Conditions in Michigan were aggravated by a poor wheat crop and a depressed lumber business. In 1857, 132 businesses with liabilities of $2,518,000 failed in the state. In 1858, an additional 147 companies, with liabilities of $2,779,404, also went out of business.[34]

In Detroit great numbers of working men were released from their jobs; and, as in many eastern cities, breadlines became common sights. Detroiters were also faced with the unhappy reality of children begging, door to door, for food and clothing. Another segment of Detroit's laboring class that suffered were the newly formed trade unions. During the 1850s the printers, the carpenters, the stonecutters, and the iron molders had organized. The depression, however, practically wiped out these unions and they were forced to begin their organizing all over again.

Detroit's banks were also hard hit by the panic. As was previously noted, the Michigan State Bank wound up its affairs when its charter expired in 1855. So well was this bank managed that in 1857, when its books were finally closed, a dividend of 20 percent was paid on its capital stock. The Detroit Savings Fund Institute had agreed to receive and hold any of the bank's circulating notes, and when these bills were redeemed in 1858, a final dividend of three percent was paid to the stockholders. The depression had no effect on the closing of the Michigan State Bank or on the payment of its dividends;[35] one of Detroit's other banks was not so fortunate.

The Peninsular Bank had done a very profitable business ever since its opening in 1849, paying semi-annual dividends of five percent. In August 1853, the directors voted to increase the capital stock by $100,000, and in 1856 it was again increased by $150,000. Later in that same year, an extra dividend of 25 percent from surplus profits was divided among the stockholders. However, the bank was overextended and, within a few months, the tide set in the other direction and losses began to multiply. Finally, because of pressures from bankers in the East, the Peninsular Bank suspended specie payments on October 1, 1857.

The business of the bank was placed in the hands of an executive committee and, in February 1858, specie payments were resumed. In 1861 the bank's stock was reduced from $350,000 to $106,000; after the passage of the National Banking Act in 1863, no banking business of any amount was done. The Peninsular Bank never really recovered from the panic of 1857 and finally closed its doors in 1870, four years before its charter was to expire.[36]

The Farmers and Mechanics' Bank, which in February 1857 had moved its offices to a building on the southwest corner of Jefferson and Woodward, was also forced into suspension in October. Unlike the Peninsular Bank, however, the Farmers and Mechanics' Bank was able to resume specie payments and through careful management was able to continue a successful banking operation.

In 1855 Detroit's largest bank, the Michigan Insurance Company Bank, moved into the old Bank of Michigan Building on the southwest corner of Jefferson and Griswold. When the panic hit in 1857, the Michigan Insurance Company Bank immediately came to the aid of the Peninsular Bank and the Farmers and Mechanics' Bank. Unfortunately, the Insurance Bank did not have the resources to save the Peninsular and the Farmers and Mechanics' from suspension.

By inducing its own customers to accept drafts instead of specie, and because of the confidence that the public had in the bank's officers, the Insurance Bank was able to continue business all through the panic without suspension. Very soon, depositors came in with specie in such quantities that it was shipped to New York and sold. When its charter expired in 1860, the bank was reorganized with a capitalization of $200,000, and it was to continue a successful business for another ten years.

The Savings Fund Institute also suffered during the panic. As the other Detroit banks were facing the problem of suspension, the Institute was faced with the loss of deposits. The bank's deposits, which had reached a height of $144,521, soon dropped to $71,051. In order to save the bank, President Farnsworth devoted his entire attention to its operation—this to the exclusion of his duties as a director of the Michigan Central Railroad and his personal law practice. Because of its conservative management, the bank was able to retain the confidence of its depositors and, fortunately, at no time during this period was the Institute forced to close its doors. There is little doubt that, but for Farnsworth's diligence, the Detroit Savings Fund Institute would have failed during the panic of 1857.[37] As the city emerged from the depression, so did the Savings Fund Institute; and by the end of 1859 deposits had climbed to a new high of $176,048.

During the 1850s President Farnsworth and Vice-President Walker were both very busy men. In June 1853, when construction of the canal around the St. Mary's River was begun, the cost was estimated at about $50,000. Congress had passed an act granting 750,000 acres of public land to the state; this land was to be sold and the revenue used to finance the construction of the canal. However, the costs of construction far surpassed the original estimates. As the canal neared completion, costs mounted to almost one million dollars. In an effort to raise more revenue, the St. Mary's Falls Ship Canal Company commissioned Elon Farnsworth to go to Europe to sell bonds and the public lands. Unfortunately, Europe was in the throes of the Crimean War, and investors were little interested in the project. Farnsworth, however, was able to sell some of the land and bonds; and the canal was completed in late May of 1855.[38]

Farnsworth was also instrumental, along with James F. Joy and Henry Walker, in having the Great Western Railroad built from Buffalo across the lower Ontario peninsula to Windsor. Up to this time there was no rail connection from Detroit to the East; all freight and passengers had to travel by water. The steamers built by the Michigan Central Railroad had proved to be very successful; but with the winter shutdown of lake navigation, the fleet was useless. At the urging of the Michigan Central and other members of Detroit's business community, Henry Walker wrote a series of articles for the local papers discussing the importance of the extension of the Great Western to Detroit. Farnsworth, Joy, and Walker traveled to Toronto and Buffalo and raised $180,000 in subscriptions for the project.[39] Construction was immediately begun, and in January 1854 the road was opened. Thus, freight could be shipped from Detroit year round, and for the first time, a traveler from Chicago using the Michigan Central could make connections on the Great Western to the Niagara River, where he could board the New York Central for Albany and New York.

In addition to his banking and railroading interests, Henry Walker was active in a number of other business ventures. In the early 1850s, he made a number of investments in vast tracts of pine lands in northern Michigan and in several saw mills at the mouth of the Saginaw River. Along with his outstate property, Walker also invested in land in the vicinity of Hamtramck. Land was one type of investment affected by the panic of 1857, and Walker lost a considerable sum of money during the depression. The setback was only temporary for, in 1861, Walker purchased the *Detroit Free Press* and for several years was its sole owner and editor. Walker continued to take an active part in the paper's operation until 1875, when he sold his interest. In addition to these activities, he also served as Detroit city historiographer from 1843 to 1845, and as the city's postmaster during 1859 and 1860.[40]

With the Detroit Savings Fund Institute growing during the late 1850s, the trustees saw the need of changing the by-laws. At their January 18, 1857 meeting, the trustees voted to amend the by-laws to reflect this expansion. As a result, interest on all deposits above five dollars was increased from four percent to five percent annually. With deposits growing, the responsibilities of the finance committee were also growing, and the trustees voted to increase the committee's size to five members. At this time it was also decided to increase the hours that the Institute would be open for business. The new hours were now 9 A.M. to 1 P.M. and 3 P.M. to 4 P.M. Monday through Friday and 6 P.M. to 8 P.M. Saturdays. The new hours presented no real problem for Alexander Adams, the cashier, because he now had an assistant; William Lyster had just recently been hired as bookkeeper. In recognition of their faithful service and the extended hours, Adams's salary was raised to $1800 annually and Lyster's to $700.[41]

In late 1856, David Smart had died, and the trustees elected Henry Ledyard to fill the vacancy. Ledyard, who had served in a number of civic positions such as alderman and school inspector, was one of the directors of the Michigan State Bank when it was reorganized in 1845. Ledyard also served two terms as Detroit's mayor.

As deposits began to increase following the panic of 1857, the trustees determined that larger quarters were needed. In November 1859, trustee Samuel Lewis submitted a proposal to lease to the Institute banking offices in his new building. Then in the process of construction, the building was located on the east side of Griswold between Larned and Congress. Shubael Conant, John Palmer, and Edward Lyon were appointed a committee to examine the building to determine if indeed it would be suitable for banking purposes and to report their findings to the other trustees.[42]

The committee, assisted by the architect and the contractor, inspected the building thoroughly. One area they examined very closely was the building's vault. The vault was constructed of brick reinforced by iron bars, with walls ten inches thick, and a floor and ceiling each one-and-a-half feet thick. The iron bars reinforcing the walls, ceiling, and floor were placed five inches apart and were one inch wide and ⅜ of an inch thick. There was one problem—the vault was built over the cellar. And, while the committee felt the vault would be safe from fire, they did not feel it would be as safe from burglars as was the vault in the present offices on Jefferson Avenue. The walls of this vault were constructed of stone and cement; the floor was solid masonry and built on the foundation of the building.[43]

The problem was resolved when Mr. Lewis agreed to rent both the first floor and basement to the Institute at $900 per year and to furnish the office space to the satisfaction of the trustees. The lease was to be renewable for a period of ten years.[44]

86

The construction and furnishing of Lewis's building was soon completed and, on May 1, 1860, the Detroit Savings Fund Institute moved into its new offices.[45] With this move the bank was once again a close neighbor of the Post Office. Earlier in the year, the Post Office had moved from the ground floor of Mariners' Church to quarters in the new federal building on the northwest corner of Griswold and Larned.

Following the move into its new offices, the Detroit Savings Fund Institute continued to prosper, and by the beginning of 1861, deposits had grown to $285,508 and depositors to 1,186.[46] The year of 1861 was to be a period of continued growth for the Institute; the year of 1861 was also to bring the storm of civil war.

CIVIL WAR

Great wars inevitably bring about drastic permanent changes in the economic and social life of a country. Once committed to arms, belligerents seldom regain their prewar status. The demands of the Civil War were directly responsible for the culmination of the American industrial revolution, causing the greatest forward surge in technical achievement that the world had seen up to that time and laying the groundwork for the rise of big business in the postwar decades.

The more immediate effect of the war was to precipitate a severe though short-lived panic in the North. The apprehension of many eastern merchants had been well founded. When the war began, southern interests owed the banks and business establishments of the North close to $300,000,000—practically all of which was a total loss.

In spite of this staggering write-off, the following spring saw a revival of prosperity resulting from the insatiable needs of a rapidly expanding army. Manufacturing, protected by an increasing tariff, responded to the crisis by turning out products on a hitherto unprecedented scale. The Homestead Act of 1862 (which granted 160 acres of land free in return for five years' occupancy and a fee of $10 for registration, or for $1.25 an acre and 14 months' residence on it), brought a new flood of immigration to the United States with a consequent increase in vitally needed agricultural production.

The battlefields of the Civil War were far away and did not touch Detroit directly; the city's role was that of home front. Detroit sent a total of about 6,000 soldiers to the battlefields during the four years of the Civil War. When President Lincoln announced a state of war on April 17, 1861, and called for volunteers, a wave of patriotic fervor swept the city. A citizens' mass meeting was held on April 18 across the street from the Detroit Savings Fund Institute, in front of the Post Office.

First to answer Lincoln's call was the First Michigan Infantry composed of militia companies drawn from Detroit and other Michigan towns. Orders for the formation of the First Michigan were issued April 24 and, on May 2nd, the regiment was mustered into service. The Detroit unit, Company A, consisted of the Detroit Light Guard [an organization which has provided the nucleus of the local militia and national guard down to the present time]. Trained at Fort Wayne, which was located south of Detroit on the river, the regiment was presented its colors in a ceremony in Campus Martius for which nearly all Detroit turned out. The First Michigan was the first western regiment to arrive at Washington. It was badly mauled at Bull Run, after which, being a three-month regiment, it was disbanded.

As a device to encourage enlistments, local officials decided in July 1862 to pay a bounty of $50 for each single man, and $100 for each married man who volunteered. The city council initially pledged $40,000 for the payment of the bounties, and a committee was appointed to oversee their distribution. The chairman of the committee was Elon Farnsworth, who held this position for the remainder of the war; and during that time his committee paid out a total of $203,000 in bounties.[47]

Another distinguished Civil War regiment was the Twenty-fourth Infantry composed almost entirely of Detroit and Wayne County volunteers. It trained at the old fair grounds, then at Woodward and Canfield avenues, and arrived at the front in time to take part in the battle of Antietam, after which it was incorporated into the famous Iron Brigade. It opened the battle of Gettysburg on July 1, 1863, and was almost completely destroyed while holding up the Confederate advance until the mass of the Army of the Potomac could get into position. Its casualty rate was the highest of any Union regiment in the battle.

The recruiting of the Twenty-fourth was tarnished by a deplorable race riot in March 1863. The regiment had no part in the affair, which was largely a protest against conscription, and disenchantment with emancipation and war policies generally. Violence against the city's blacks reached the riot stage during the morning of March 6, when a mob of hoodlums swept through the lower east side along Brush and Beaubien streets between Monroe and Congress. It was in that area that most of the blacks lived. City officials were slow to respond to the crisis, and by late afternoon the disturbance reached fever pitch. Many blacks were beaten and some were killed; many more were forced to flee their homes. Some crossed the river to Canada for refuge. A large part of the district was burned, and damage from fire, looting, and vandalism was extensive. Order was not restored until nightfall when federal troops were brought in from Fort Wayne and Ypsilanti.

The riot was only an incident and did not reflect the feelings of most Detroiters. In fact, a strong anti-slavery and abolition sentiment had developed early in the city and after the mid 1830s Detroit became an important last station on the Underground Railroad. Thousands of slaves—no one knows the exact number—escaping from the South were passed along established routes which took them through Ohio, Indiana or Illinois into Michigan and to Detroit. En route they were hidden at night or by day, as circumstances demanded, in the cellars or barns of sympathetic farmers and townspeople who guided them from one station to another. In Detroit they were usually hidden in the livery barn of Seymour Finney's Temperance House. The hotel was at the southeast corner of Woodward and Gratiot. The stable was a block away at the northeast corner of State and Griswold across the street from the old capitol. [A bronze plaque on the wall of the Detroit Bank & Trust Company branch office now marks the location.*] After hiding in the barn until the way was clear, the fugitives were escorted across the river to Canadian sanctuary. [Large numbers of blacks in Windsor and southwestern Ontario today trace their ancestry back to passengers on the Underground Railroad.]

Throughout the war, Detroit supplied munitions and food for the Union armies; the city was a principal distribution point for supplies from Michigan towns and farms. Financing the war presented a more

* The tablet is on the Griswold Street side of the building and reads:
This tablet marks the site of Detroit's "Underground Railway Station." A large brick building known as "the Finney House Barn," was located here, and used as a depot for helping slaves gain freedom into Canada from 1833 until the Civil War. Detroit was one of the important "stations" on the route to Canada and the anti-slavery society organized in 1837, aided the liberation of thousands of slaves.

89

difficult problem for the government than supplying its material needs. The national fiscal machinery was totally inadequate to meet the demands of a major conflict. Salmon P. Chase, secretary of the treasury, was a lawyer suddenly called upon to be a financier and he found the transition a difficult one.

In August 1861, Secretary Chase went to New York and met with the banks of New York, Philadelphia, and Boston. A loan was arranged in the amount of $150,000,000 secured by bonds which the banks might resell to the public. To the surprise of the banks, which had thought that the loan would be made in the form of book credits, the secretary demanded specie because of his interpretation of existing law. This required far more gold than the banks possessed, with the result that the loan had to be made in three installments. Even then, it dangerously depleted the banks' gold reserves.

Secretary Chase had reasoned that the gold would be paid out by the U.S. Treasury in discharge of its obligations and would then flow back to the banks. Much of it did not, and the shortage of specie grew increasingly acute as hoarding became more prevalent. Specie payment was suspended by the banks in December 1861, and the government followed suit immediately.

It soon became obvious that the notes of the state banks could not meet the demand for a circulating medium. Early in 1862, Congress authorized its first government note issue in an amount which, with subsequent increases, eventually reached $450,000,000. These were the famous greenbacks, so called because the backs of the notes were printed in green ink. Following the principle of Gresham's Law that cheap money drives out the stronger currency, hard money almost disappeared from circulation. The greenbacks depreciated and prices soared during the next three years. Wages also rose, but not to the same degree, involving much hardship on the lower-income group.

Although Secretary Chase had consented with reluctance to the issuance of greenbacks, he did not consider them a substitute for a national currency, the issuance of which he believed to be of major importance. To this end, as well as to create a new market for government bonds to finance the war, the National Banking Act was passed in early 1863.

The object of the act was to bring the banks under federal control. Existing banks might take out federal charters at which time they would deposit with the Treasury government bonds equal to one-third of their capital, against which they might issue notes up to

90 percent of the market value of the bonds. Thus, once and for all, with the passage of this act, a uniform paper currency was provided which made possible the elimination of the motley array of state bank paper which had so long plagued the economy. In 1862, for example, nearly 1,600 state banks were circulating paper money at various discounts.

These state bank notes were eliminated gradually by taxation, not by the act. A two percent tax had been levied on state bank notes by the internal revenue legislation of 1862. In 1866, in order to give the national banks a monopoly of note issue and increase the market for government bonds, the tax was increased to ten percent. At such a rate there was no more profit in the issue of state bank notes. Only notes of the national banks therefore remained in circulation, and it was no longer necessary for merchants to consult the Bank Note Detector to learn the value of the money their customers were offering. In spite of its inflexibility, the national bank note gave the country for the first time a note issue which was uniform in value and this, it should be observed, in spite of the fact that it was not legal tender.

In 1864 the National Banking Act was revised. The revision allowed reserve requirements to be adjusted more closely to the ratios of cash which the banks had been accustomed to keeping before the war. In addition, the revised act improved the banking structure by raising standards and gradually forcing state banks to improve their operations.

Following the revision of the act, the number of national banks increased rapidly. Many new banks were organized, and an even larger number of state banks changed to national charters. By the end of 1865, there were 1601 in all, with 171,000,000 notes outstanding, backed by government bonds. Conversely, with the inauguration of the national banking system, the number of state banks declined. In 1863 there had been 1466 incorporated banks in the northern states, with 239,000,000 notes outstanding. By 1865 the number was down to 349. However, the trend was eventually reversed as notes became less important than deposits. Several decades later the number of state banks became equal to that of the national banks.[48]

In Detroit several national banks were established following the passage of the National Banking Act of 1863. The First National Bank was organized almost entirely through the efforts of Philo Parsons, one of Detroit's most prominent businessmen. The first stockholders meeting was held on September 2, 1863, and a month later the bank opened for business in its offices on Griswold Street. In December 1864, the bank's charter was purchased by the officers of the State Bank of Michigan. A new board of directors took over the bank's operation and increased its capital to $200,000. The State Bank of Michigan had been organized in February 1859, with a capital of $50,000. It was the only bank to be established in Detroit between 1849 and the passage of the National Banking Act. When the bank's officers purchased the charter of the First National Bank, the operations of the State Bank were discontinued.

The Second National Bank was opened for business on November 4, 1863, in a building on the southwest corner of Jefferson and Woodward avenues. The bank began with a capital of $500,000, and its first president was Henry P. Baldwin, then a trustee of the Detroit Savings Fund Institute. In 1865 the bank's capital was increased to one million dollars, making it one of the largest banks in the West. The American Exchange National Bank was organized in 1865 with a capital of $250,000. This bank was the successor of the banking business of A. H. Dey and was located on Griswold Street.

On June 25, 1865, the Michigan Insurance Company was reorganized as the National Insurance Bank. Four years later, the bank's charter expired. The directors decided not to renew the charter; and this bank, which had served Detroit and Detroiters so well for so many years, was not reopened.

During the Civil War years, the Detroit Savings Fund Institute continued to prosper. By the end of 1862, deposits had grown to $464,467.57 and depositors to 1,958; two years later the figures were $591,206.57 and 2,315, respectively.[49] As deposits increased, the finance committee diversified the bank's investments. By the end of the war, the bank held over $100,000 in bonds of the United States, the State of Michigan, the State of Missouri, Wayne County, the City of Detroit, the Detroit and Milwaukee Railroad, and the New York Central Park Company.[50]

The Civil War years also witnessed an expansion of the bank's staff. In July 1861, Charles H. Safford was appointed teller at a salary of $600 per year. Two years later the three employees received pay raises which increased their annual salaries to: Alexander H. Adams, cashier, $2000; J. W. Pitcher, bookkeeper, $900; and Safford, teller, $700. In January 1865, an assistant teller, Charles G. Zeigler, was added to the staff, giving the Institute a total of four employees: a cashier, a bookkeeper, a teller, and an assistant teller.[51]

The Civil War finally ended on Palm Sunday, April 9, 1865, when

Lee's armies surrendered at Appomattox. The United States, matured by common suffering, surveyed the wreckage and faced the future uncertainly, little knowing that it stood on the threshold of an industrial and business expansion which, in little more than a half a century, would make it the richest and strongest nation in the world. Detroit was to play a vital role in this industrial and financial growth.

4

Detroit Savings Bank

MINING, RAILROADS, AND CONSUMER GOODS

The growth of manufacturing that followed the Civil War had its beginnings in Detroit and Michigan in the early 1840s. Initial sources of this expansion came from copper, iron, and lumber.

The existence of copper in the Upper Peninsula of Michigan was known from the earliest times. While the French had learned of it from the Indians, the exploration of the upper Great Lakes by Cass, Houghton, and others was due in part to the desire to locate these copper deposits. It was not until 1841 that extraction and refining of copper ore began on a commercial basis. Necessitated to a large extent by steamship and logging engine manufacture, copper and brass became important factors in Detroit's economy in the 1850s; and the mining of copper quickly developed into a major industry, supported by large injections of local and eastern capital.

Substantial deposits of iron ore were discovered in 1844, about the time the copper industry began to boom. Within a decade, Michigan became the leading producer of iron ore, and a new industrial era dawned for Detroit. Located on a water route accessible to the ingredients—ore and limestone—for making pig iron and steel, Detroit took on a new importance as a center of heavy industry.

94

This importance was enhanced when the St. Mary's River ship canal was opened in 1855. It made the transportation of raw materials to Detroit mills and foundries easier, faster, and more economical. Industrial development was greatly accelerated as a result of the Soo Canal. By the time of the Civil War, it appeared as though Detroit would be the great iron and steel producing center of the United States, a position eventually preempted by Pittsburgh and the Chicago area.

Detroit has always had its sawmills, but it was never a lumber town in the sense that Saginaw, Bay City, Muskegon, and other Michigan cities were. There was little actual lumbering around Detroit. Even before the Civil War, cordwood had to be imported from other areas of Michigan and from Canada. Nevertheless, much Detroit capital went into lumbering; and several Detroiters amassed great fortunes from the industry in the latter part of the nineteenth century.

The availability of good hardwood in Michigan led to flourishing woodworking businesses at Detroit in which wood and skilled woodworkers were required. Wagon and carriage building was one, and of course shipbuilding was another. Furniture was also made, and like carriage building, the industry was not extensive in Detroit. Even if comparatively small, the carriage and wagon business employed a number of highly skilled workmen, whose craftsmanship proved essential when the making of automobile bodies, frames, and wheels began.

Shortly after the Civil War broke out, the copper, iron, and lumbering industries were beset by a number of problems. During the first year of the war, the price of copper dropped to 17 cents a pound; at that time 20 cents a pound was considered a fair price. The domestic market was disorganized, and Confederate privateers threatened to cut off the foreign market for copper. But recovery came fast. As government orders for brass buttons, copper canteens, bronze cannon, and naval equipment began to accumulate, prices rose. They were up to 46.3 cents a pound by 1860 and to 36 cents in 1865. Oddly enough, production did not keep pace with higher prices. In fact, production fell by a million-and-a-half pounds in 1862, another half-million in 1863, and still another half-million in 1864. The reason seems to have been that the scarce labor supply was being diverted to the development of new mines that had not yet gone into full production. Despite the fall-off in production, 70

Elon Farnsworth, president of the Detroit Savings Fund Institute, 1849–77. Courtesy of the Burton Historical Collection, Detroit Public Library.

Detroit in 1855. At this time, the Detroit Savings Fund Institute was located in the old Michigan State Bank Building on the south side of Jefferson Avenue between Woodward and Bates. Courtesy of the Burton Historical Collection, Detroit Public Library.

A citizen's mass meeting was held at the outbreak of the Civil War on April 18, 1861 in front of the new Post Office across the street from the Detroit Savings Fund Institute. Courtesy of the Burton Historical Collection, Detroit Public Library.

The livery barn of Seymour Finney's Temperance House. Used as a station on the Underground Railroad prior to the Civil War, the barn was located at Griswold and State streets on the site later occupied by the Detroit Savings Bank main office. Courtesy of the Burton Historical Collection, Detroit Public Library.

The Detroit Savings Bank Building at Griswold and Larned in 1881. Erected in 1878 by Sidney D. Miller and known as the Bank Chambers, this was the home of the Detroit Savings Bank until 1906. Courtesy of the Burton Historical Collection, Detroit Public Library.

Bank staff on the steps of the Bank Chambers, Larned and Griswold, 1881. Courtesy of Detroit Bank and Trust.

Alexander H. Adams, president of the Detroit Savings Bank, 1878–83. Courtesy of the Burton Historical Collection, Detroit Public Library.

Detroit in 1887, the year the Michigan Bankers Association was founded. Courtesy of the Burton Historical Collection, Detroit Public Library.

Main banking room, Bank Chambers, 1890. Courtesy of Detroit Bank and Trust.

Henry Ford and his quadricycle at his Bagley Avenue garage. Courtesy of the Automotive History Collection, Detroit Public Library.

Sidney D. Miller, president of the Detroit Savings Bank, 1883–1904. Reprinted from George I. Reed, *Bench and Bar of Michigan* (Chicago, 1897), p. 246.

King's and Detroit's first automobile. Charles B. King is at the tiller of his car in 1896. Courtesy of the Burton Historical Collection, Detroit Public Library.

DeWitt C. Delamater, president of the Detroit Savings Bank, 1904–19; chairman of the board, 1919–25. Courtesy of the Burton Historical Collection, Detroit Public Library.

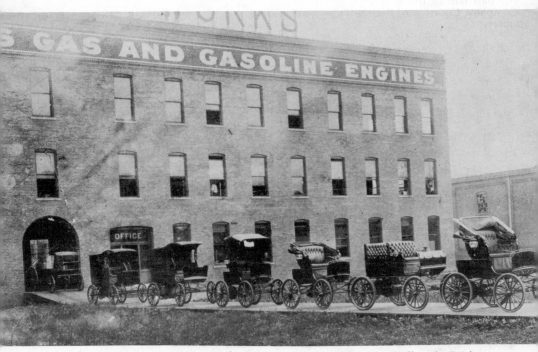

The Olds Motor Works on East Jefferson near the Belle Isle Bridge. Opened in 1899, the factory burned to the ground in March 1901. Courtesy of the Automotive History Collection, Detroit Public Library.

Detroit Savings Bank, branch no. 1, Gratiot–St. Antoine. Designed by Detroit architect Albert Kahn, this building was opened in 1909. Courtesy of Detroit Bank and Trust.

Penobscot Building, main office of the Detroit Savings Bank from 1906–21. The bank occupied the entire west half of the ground floor. The east half of the ground floor was occupied by the Detroit Trust Company. Courtesy of the Burton Historical Collection, Detroit Public Library.

Second Liberty Loan Drive held in Cadillac Square, October 1918.
Courtesy of the Burton Historical Collection, Detroit Public Library.

George S. Baker, president
of the Detroit Savings
Bank, 1919–27. Courtesy of
Detroit Bank and Trust.

Detroit Savings Bank Building (formerly the Chamber of Commerce Building), Griswold at State. This was the main office of the Detroit Savings Bank and later The Detroit Bank from 1921–63. Courtesy of Detroit Bank and Trust.

The Detroit Trust Company Building at West Fort and Shelby was built in 1915. The addition was erected in 1926. Courtesy of Detroit Bank and Trust.

percent of the nation's copper came from Michigan mines during the Civil War.[1]

Like the copper-mining industry, the iron-ore industry had a lean year in 1861. Production at all the mines declined drastically. This may have been partly due to a labor shortage, but it is also attributed to the fact that Detroit and Cleveland (the main markets for Michigan ore) had a large surplus on hand at the beginning of the year, and buyers ceased purchasing additional supplies due to the uncertainties at the beginning of the war. Revival of iron production was even more rapid than that of copper. In 1862 the leading mines produced more ore than in any previous year. Production increased thereafter, stimulated by wartime demand.[2]

At the beginning of the war, the lumber industry was hit even harder than copper and iron mining. Not only was the market glutted at the outbreak of hostilities but also the war emergency made it difficult for the lumbermen to secure capital with which to conduct their business. Labor shortage was acute, and higher wages had to be paid to workmen. Although the price of lumber went up, almost doubling by 1865, the lumber business did not fully recover until after the war.[3]

Another industry that developed just prior to the Civil War was the production of salt. Douglass Houghton had found salt springs in the Saginaw region; little was done to develop this resource until 1859. In that year the state legislature considered a bill to pay a bounty of ten cents a barrel for the production of salt. The proposal was subjected to ridicule, apparently because the lawmakers did not believe salt could be produced in Michigan. An anonymous legislator, probably in jest, suggested an amendment to make the bounty ten cents a bushel, and the bill was passed and signed by the governor in that form. A group of investors promptly formed the East Saginaw Salt Company and immediately began operations. A well was bored, and the necessary facilities for evaporating the brine were erected. In 1860 the company turned out 10,772 barrels of five bushels each, and tripled their production the following year. Other companies were organized, and when the increasing output threatened to empty the state treasury, the legislature repealed the bounty law.[4]

During this period the production of salt was closely linked with lumbering. Seasoned lumber was used for the construction of salt vats and salt works while slab wood and other scrap from the sawmills were used as fuel to evaporate the water from the brine. By 1880 Michigan was supplying half the salt to the nation, and the output in 1890 was more than 3,800,000 barrels.[5]

In the 1880s, salt-making moved southward from the Saginaw Valley along the Detroit and St. Clair rivers. For many years it had been known that a deep vein of rock salt underlay the soil in the vicinity of Detroit. The first use of the resource was made when a well was sunk near Wyandotte to provide salt for making the soda ash used in the manufacture of glass. At first, water was forced through the rock formations, and a strong brine was brought to the surface. This was the start of the alkali industry in Detroit. It was not until 1910 that a deep shaft was sunk and the mining of rock salt was begun.[6]

Heavy Industry

Detroit's first real heavy industry was the manufacture of railroad cars, wheels, and other equipment. It had its beginnings about 1840. At that time there were no rail connections beyond the state's borders, and most of what Michigan needed in the form of rolling stock and equipment it had to produce itself. Along with rail equipment shops, a number of foundries and machine and boiler works sprang up, furnishing boilers and engines for the new mining industries, sawmills, and ships.

A physician, Dr. George B. Russel, provided the first major impetus to railroad equipment manufacturing in 1853, when he organized a company which became the Detroit Car & Manufacturing Company. Starting with a small plant on Gratiot, operations soon expanded to larger shops at the foot of Beaubien and then on Monroe Street. Competitors entered the field, such as the Michigan Car Company in 1865 and the Peninsular Car Works in 1885. In 1892 several of these concerns merged, including the Russel interests and Michigan Car, and in 1899 they were taken over by the American Car & Foundry Company.

In 1871 George Pullman bought a plant in the area bounded by Monroe, St. Aubin, Macomb, and the railroad; and for eight years Detroit was the main center for the manufacturing of the Pullman sleeping car. In 1879 chief operations were moved to Chicago, but cars continued to be built in Detroit until 1893. In 1868 Detroiter William Davis invented the refrigerator car and interested local meat packer George H. Hammond, who provided him with capital. An enterprising man, Hammond also founded the Hammond-Standish Company, which became the largest meat packer in Michigan. The first shipment by refrigerator car was made from Detroit to Boston in 1869, and Detroit gained a new industry. These railway industries naturally encouraged other inventions, and many new railroading ideas and mechanical improvements came out of the Detroit shops. Not the least of these was the railroad track cleaner and snow plow, the invention of Augustus Day.

Railroad equipment and other metal products which rolled out of Detroit factories in increasing quantities required a basic metals industry, which Detroit was quick to provide. Behind this local enterprise was the figure of a most remarkable man, Eber Brock Ward. Ward's family settled in Michigan soon after the War of 1812, and through shrewdness and hard work, young Ward prospered and became one of the developers of Michigan industry. His interests were broad. They included the ownership of timber and ore lands, newspapers, railroads, steamship and insurance companies, glass manufacturing, and banking. He was one of the promoters of the Soo Canal and one of the first to take advantage of it.

With a group of local financiers, Ward organized the Eureka Iron and Steel Works in 1853 on a 2,200-acre site in Wyandotte—where a big furnace and a tremendous plant were erected. It was an ideal location: northern ore and limestone could be brought in cheaply by water; extensive beech forests were nearby to supply the charcoal with which most steel was then made; and it was close to a growing market which eventually became nationwide. It was in the Eureka furnace in 1864 that the first commercial steel was produced in the United States by the Bessemer process.

The Eureka Works prospered, and Ward prospered with it. He was probably Detroit's wealthiest man and its first millionaire. After his death in 1875, the company began to falter. First, the use of charcoal gave way to coke, which was more efficient and readily available to the steel plants located near the Pennsylvanian and Illinois coal fields. Second, a depression discouraged company officials and stockholders from modernizing the plant. Ultimately the business closed, and, in the 1890s, the Eureka Works were razed except for part of the furnace and the office building. They remained for many years as a reminder of how close the Detroit area came to being the steel producing center of the United States.

Another industry that had an early start in Detroit was the

manufacturing of stoves, which began locally in the 1830s. At that time most stoves were made at either Albany or Troy, New York. When a cast iron part of a stove broke, a new part had to be ordered from the East. Because it took so long to get a replacement part, the Hydraulic Iron Works in Detroit began making parts for the local market and was successful enough to branch out into the production of complete stoves. In 1861 Jeremiah Dwyer, who had worked in an Albany stove works and as an apprentice with Hydraulic, opened his own stove company in Detroit. He did well, and three years later, two Detroit industrialists put up the necessary capital for expansion. Dwyer's small operation became the Detroit Stove Works, and in 1871 the Michigan Stove Company. Other companies, notably the Peninsular Stove Company, also entered the field in the 1870s and 80s, and for more than 50 years the manufacturing of stoves and kitchen ranges was Detroit's leading industry.

Tobacco, Drugs, and Shoes

The production of tobacco products, particularly chewing tobacco, was another one of Detroit's early leading industries. There were several firms although two men in particular dominated the industry: one was John J. Bagley, the other was Daniel Scotten. Both served apprenticeships in the first tobacco business established in Detroit in 1840 by George Miller, who had a store and factory on the west side of Woodward just below Jefferson. Dan Scotten and his brother Oren went into business for themselves in 1856, their most famous product being Hiawatha, a chewing tobacco. Bagley started three years earlier, and made and sold a brand of chewing tobacco called Mayflower. Both Bagley and Scotten were astute businessmen. Scotten proved his shrewdness just before the outbreak of the Civil War. With all the capital and credit he could lay his hands on, he bought southern tobacco until his warehouse bulged. In addition to chewing tobacco, Detroit firms were also major producers of pipe tobacco and cigars.

The Civil War greatly stimulated manufacturing in Detroit and Michigan. Between 1860 and 1870, the number of manufacturing establishments increased in the state by 174 percent, and the amount of capital invested by 201 percent.[7] In Detroit, the Michigan Car Company, the Detroit Bridge and Iron Works, the Detroit Safe Company, and the E. T. Barnum Wire and Iron Works were among the plants started during the war. In 1864–65 the Detroit Board of Trade built a large new structure on the southeast corner of

Woodbridge and Shelby streets. In spite of the 1855 prohibition law, a law passed by the legislature in 1863 permitted the manufacturing of beer, and this legislation resulted in the launching of a number of new breweries.

Other important industries established about the time of the Civil War included paints, varnish, drugs, chemicals, and shoes. Why Detroit became a center for paint manufacturing is difficult to explain. Possibly shipbuilding, furniture making, and woodworking had something to do with it; certainly the Civil War era of Midwest expansion and settlement caused thousands of new city homes, farmhouses, and barns to be built, and they had to be painted. Perhaps, though, the best explanation is that men with the knowledge of paint-making settled in Detroit and went into business. The two Berry brothers were the first. They opened a small shop in 1858 and mixed their first supply of paint in a 30-gallon tub. Other well-known paint concerns established in the 1860s and 1870s were Boydell Brothers, Detroit White Lead Works, and Acme Lead and Color Works.

Of great importance to Detroit's economic development was the drug and pharmaceutical industry which gained a firm foothold. The production of drugs grew from the activities of a number of local druggists who manufactured their own pills, tonics, and ointments. There was a great demand for these products; physicians were neither numerous nor proficient, particularly in the rural communities, and people had to doctor themselves and their livestock.

As an industry, it started in 1845 when Jacob Farrand began to make pills in his combination drug and grocery store on Woodward near Jefferson. Eventually his business expanded, and, as Farrand, Williams & Company, became one of the Midwest's leading wholesale drug firms. In 1865 Frederick Stearns opened a drugstore on Jefferson near Brush Street and before long was doing a substantial business in the manufacturing of not only regular pharmaceuticals, but also so-called patent medicines, toothpaste, perfume, and other toilet articles. After outgrowing several plants, Stearns built a large factory and laboratory on East Jefferson at Bellevue.

Detroit's major pharmaceutical concern is Parke, Davis & Company, which dates back to 1867. It was founded by Dr. Samuel Duffield, a member of a distinguished local family. Dr. Duffield began making pharmaceuticals over a drugstore at Cass and Henry, and the building soon was completely taken over as a factory. Duffield was joined by two partners, Harvey C. Parke and George S. Davis. Then he withdrew from the management, and the firm became Parke, Davis & Company. In 1873 a new location was selected on the river near the foot of Joseph Campau. [The company's greatly expanded plant still occupies the site. With branches all over the world, Parke, Davis & Company, now a wholly-owned subsidiary of Warner-Lambert, is one of the leaders in the drug field, and one of Detroit's best known as well as one of its oldest businesses.]

Some druggists went in different directions. Theodore Eaton, for instance, entered the wholesale drug business in 1855 and then branched out into the field of chemicals. James Vernor, on the other hand, liked to mix soft drinks in his drugstore and concocted a ginger ale. As a result the ginger ale business soon overshadowed the drugstore, and for over a century Vernor's Ginger Ale has been a household item enjoyed by generations of children and adults.

For a while toward the end of the last century, Detroit gave promise of becoming a major shoe manufacturing center. The most important company in the field was built largely by the drive and genius of one man—Hazen S. Pingree. There were, however, two important shoe companies in Detroit prior to Pingree's entering the business. The earliest was the pre-Civil War firm of Henry P. Baldwin who was a very successful businessman and for several years served as a trustee of the Detroit Savings Fund Institute. Primarily a wholesale and retail business, Baldwin's firm did some custom shoemaking. The other firm was the company of Richard H. Fyfe. An employee of Baldwin, Fyfe branched out for himself and opened a store on Woodward Avenue. For many years the R. H. Fyfe Company was one of Detroit's most familiar business names.

Following service in the Civil War, Hazen S. Pingree moved to Detroit and found employment as a cobbler with Fyfe and Baldwin. Pingree opened his own factory in partnership with Charles A. Smith in 1866. Before long their plant at Woodbridge and Griswold employed more than 700 people. The shoe industry continued to prosper in Detroit until Pingree's death. When he died, the local industry pretty much died with him.

No account of Detroit's business activity would be complete without reference to the seed industry, which was established largely by Dexter M. Ferry. His packets of seeds, grown on his own seed farms in or on the outskirts of Detroit, made farms and gardens bloom all across the country. Ferry came to Detroit from Rochester, New York, in 1852 and found work as a clerk in a book and stationery store. In 1867 he entered the seed business, taking over the small

101

concern of Miles T. Gardner, who operated a farm and nursery on Michigan Avenue near Eloise. Ferry established his own farm of 300 acres at Grand River and what is now West Grand Boulevard. He also built a large warehouse and office building on downtown Brush Street between Lafayette and Monroe. This building was completely destroyed in 1886 by one of the city's most spectacular fires. It was rebuilt, however, and the structure still stands, and is used for storage and office purposes. In later years, D. M. Ferry & Company acquired a new and larger farm near Rochester, Michigan, and as a result of a merger, the firm became Ferry, Morse Seed Company.

By 1880 Detroit's industrial production was valued at $30,181,416 with a capital investment in manufacturing of $15,594,479. At this time there were 919 manufacturing establishments employing 16,110 workers and paying $6,306,460 in wages. Some of the products that were manufactured are listed below.

Products Being Manufactured in 1880 [8]

Type of Product	Value of Production
iron and steel	$ 2,498,634
foundry and machine shop products	1,808,355
meat packing	1,721,231
railroad cars	1,448,756
chewing tobacco and snuff	1,212,146
cigars and cigarettes	1,196,870
cigar boxes	103,000
seeds	1,194,066
breweries	1,143,601
boots and shoes	1,108,225
shipbuilding	738,975
paints and varnish	452,000
drugs and patent medicines	295,400
safes and vaults	165,400
cooperage*	266,400
blacksmithing*	109,350
saddlery and harnesses*	120,700
hoop skirts*	208,500

* These industries have long since vanished from an important position in Detroit's economy.

This development of industry in Detroit also resulted in a growth in population. In 1860 the city's population stood at 45,619; by 1870 it had grown to 79,577; and by 1880 to 116,000.

As manufacturing and industry grew in Detroit, so did the city's banks and banking system. This growth, during the years following the Civil War, was also influenced by a number of changes in Michigan's banking laws. And one Detroit bank that grew and prospered during this period was the Detroit Savings Fund Institute.

TRADESMEN, MECHANICS, AND LABORERS

In 1849 the voters of Michigan, by the lopsided margin of 33,193 to 4,095, approved a proposal for the general revision of the state's constitution. Behind this overwhelming desire for a new constitution was the ferment of Jacksonian democracy. Michigan's first constitution had been framed before the implications of Jackson's ideas for state government were generally understood. These included the choice of public officials by election rather than by appointment and limitation upon the authority of the legislature. A convention met in Lansing on June 3, 1850. In November, the voters, by a huge majority, approved the constitution which had been drawn up by the convention.

More than twice as long as the first constitution, the state's second constitution was much more detailed. The greater length was the result of incorporating in the document many restrictions on the powers of the legislature. For example, the lawmakers were prohibited from passing special acts of incorporation. Henceforth, all corporations had to be formed under general law, thus assuring that no group would get special favors. Also, the legislature was forbidden to engage the state in building or financing internal improvements (a reflection of the antagonisms created by the five million dollar loan to finance the Internal Improvement Program of 1837). Borrowing in the name of the state was limited to a total of $50,000. In addition, the new constitution specified that officers and stockholders of any banking association issuing notes or paper credits to circulate as money "shall be individually liable for all debts contracted during their term, equally and ratably to the extent of their respective shares"; that the legislature was prohibited from authorizing or sanctioning the suspension of specie payments; and that no general banking law could be enacted until it had been approved by a majority vote of the people at a general election.[9]

By the repeal of the General Banking Act of 1837 the incorporation of banks was limited to special charters; under the constitution

103

of 1850 no special charters could be granted. As a result, during a period of nearly 20 years only 2 banks were formed in Michigan: the Detroit Savings Fund Institute, and the Peninsular Bank, both chartered in 1849 at Detroit.

As Michigan's population grew, and as industry and manufacturing became major factors in the state's economy, it became evident that a new banking law was needed. Thus, early in the legislative session of 1857, a bill was introduced "To authorize the business of banking." The bill passed both houses of the legislature on February 15, and at the general election in November 1858, it was approved by the people of the state and became law.[10]

Virtually all that was lacking in the law of 1837 was embodied in the new banking law of 1857. Heavy fines and prison terms could be levied against dishonest bank officers and directors, and stockholders were individually liable for all debts contracted by their bank in proportion to the number of shares they held. The law also stipulated that each bank was to keep a register listing the names and addresses of all shareholders and the date of purchase or transfer of their stock. This register was "to be open for public inspection during business hours, subject to a penalty of $100 for every day's neglect, and a refusal by any officer to exhibit such book shall subject such officer to a penalty of $50 and costs, for the benefit of the township library."[11] Either the bankers of the day adhered strictly to the law or this clause was never enforced, for there is no record of any library ever having been built with funds collected from bank fines.

While the new law closed most of the loopholes found in the General Banking Act of 1837, it lacked one essential element—it did not provide for a state banking commissioner or examiner. Although power was given to the state treasurer, attorney general, or any committee appointed by the legislature to investigate the condition of a bank, no regular examination was required.

The passage of the General Banking Act of 1857 had, at first, little effect on the formation of new banks in Detroit and Michigan. In fact, during the 12 years following its adoption, only 15 state banks were organized under the new law.[12]

By the end of 1870 there were six banks in operation in Detroit. There was the First National Bank, which in March 1869 had moved to the old Bank of Michigan Building on Jefferson and Griswold; the Second National Bank at the southwest corner of Griswold and Congress; and the American Exchange National Bank on Griswold

Street. The Merchants and Manufacturer's Bank, which had been organized on May 13, 1869, opened for business on June 1 of that year with a capital of $100,000. Its first offices were in the Bank Block on Griswold. The Mechanics' Bank, with offices in the Butler Block on Griswold opposite the post office, had been organized in September 1870. This bank was the successor to the private banking firm of William B. Butler and Company, which had been in business since 1847. Detroit's sixth bank, the Detroit Savings Fund Institute, was also on Griswold next door to the Mechanics' Bank. By 1870 Griswold Street had become the center of Detroit's financial district, a position which it still holds to this day.

Following the Civil War, the Detroit Savings Fund Institute continued to prosper, and by 1870 deposits had grown to over one million dollars. When the Finance Committee met to examine the bank's books on April 20, 1870, the following statement was issued:

	Amount
Cash on hand	$ 201,121
Mortgages	366,083
Bills receivable	323,104
Cash on deposit in New York banks	119,521
Funds invested in bonds	249,285
Surplus	207,656
Total Resources	$1,259,615.[13]

In 1870 the trustees passed a resolution that was to mean a significant change in the bank's operation. At their meeting of February 21, the trustees agreed to pay President Farnsworth a salary. Up to this time Farnsworth, like the other trustees, had received no remuneration for his services. But the office of president had, by this date, taken on greater responsibilities. During the panic of 1857 Farnsworth had ceased to serve as the Institute's lawyer, and Sidney D. Miller, a prominent young attorney, was retained. In 1866, because of pressing bank business, Farnsworth had resigned as a director of the Michigan Central Railroad. The trustees resolved that, "the salary of the President be fixed at three hundred dollars per year from the time he took charge of the Institute—for services as President and also in full for professional services rendered by him." [14]

In addition to failing to provide for a state banking commissioner, the General Banking Law of 1857 also failed to provide any machinery for the formation and regulation of savings banks. In 1871 this defect was corrected with the passage of an amendment to the state banking law. Passed by the legislature on March 31, 1871, the amendment was designed to encourage the formation of state banks.* Its principal feature was that it allowed a state bank to maintain both a savings and a commercial department. Simply stated, the amendment allowed any group of five or more individuals to organize banks, associations, or corporations which were to be known as savings banks. In cities with a population of 20,000 or less, the new banks were required to have a capital of not less than $25,000. In cities with populations greater than 20,000, the minimum capital was set at $50,000. Savings banks organized under this amendment were allowed to receive on deposit "all such sums of money as shall from time to time be offered by tradesmen, mechanics, laborers, servants, minors, and others, for the purpose of safe-keeping." It was required that two-thirds of the savings deposits had to be invested in United States bonds, or the bonds of the State of Michigan or its municipalities. Finally, any bank or association existing under Michigan law was allowed to reorganize under the provisions of this act.[15]

The first bank to be reorganized under the new law was the Detroit Savings Fund Institute. In mid-June 1871, the trustees met in a special session and passed a resolution to reorganize the Institute, stating

> that such reorganization be effected by filing Articles of Association as required . . . under which the name of said reorganized Corporation shall be the "Detroit Savings Bank" and it shall be based upon a capital stock of Two Hundred Thousand Dollars, with provisions allowing the increase thereof to an amount not exceeding one million dollars.[16]

On July 18 the trustees met again, and in order that the final reorganization be approved by a full board, two new trustees had to be appointed to fill vacancies caused by the death of John Palmer and the resignation of George M. Rich. The two men elected were cashier Alexander Adams, and the Institute's lawyer, Sidney D. Miller. Following their election the board unanimously confirmed the resolution introduced at the meeting in June. With this vote the Detroit Savings Fund Institute officially became the Detroit Savings Bank. On July 21 the Articles of Association were filed with the Michigan Secretary of State, and on the following day the directors met to execute the transfer.† [17]

---

* While the amendment was passed March 31, 1871, it was not to take effect until July 16—90 days after the final adjournment of the legislature.
† The complete Articles of Association will be found in Appendix C.

Capital stock of the Detroit Savings Bank was divided into two thousand shares of $100 each. Each of the eleven trustees of the Detroit Savings Fund Institute subscribed to 150 shares, with the remaining 350 shares being held in trust by Henry Walker. The re-organized bank was to be managed by a Board of Directors of nine stockholders. Elon Farnsworth, Henry N. Walker, Henry P. Bridge, Alexander Lewis, Samuel Lewis, Edward Lyon, Willard Parker, Zina Pitcher, and Edmund Trowbridge comprised the first board. Elon Farnsworth was elected president, Henry Walker vice-president, and Alexander Adams cashier. Of the original eleven trustees who founded the Detroit Savings Fund Institute, only Chancellor Farnsworth and Dr. Pitcher remained.

Following the election of officers, the board's first order of business was the adoption of a set of by-laws. The new by-laws spelled out the duties of the various officers, and described the bank's seal, the procedure for transferring real estate, the methods for increasing and transferring the bank's stock, the duties of the finance committee, the paying of expenses, and the recording of the minutes of the board meetings. A variety of other items dealing with the bank's organization and operation were also included.[18]

By the end of its first year of operation as the Detroit Savings Bank, assets had grown to $1,965,380. This was made up of: loans, $1,204,000; cash on hand, $312,795; and bonds, $440,320. The bonds that the bank had invested in were varied. There were of course federal, Michigan, Wayne County, and City of Detroit bonds in addition to bonds of the State of Missouri, the New York Central Park Authority, the Detroit Car Works, the Detroit City Railroad Company, the Detroit and Milwaukee Railroad, and the Detroit and Hamtramck Iron Company. Primarily, the loans were for mortgages, but several had been made to local industries. Typical of these were loans to the Hargreaves Manufacturing Company and to Eber Brock Ward for expansion of the Wyandotte Rolling Mill. Located at Howard and 18th streets, the Hargreaves Company manufactured mouldings, frames, and mirrors. The Wyandotte Rolling Mill was a part of Ward's vast Eureka Iron and Steel Works.[19]

Savings deposits had at this date risen to $1,652,490, and the bank's hours had been increased so that depositors could now transact their business daily from 9 A.M. to 1 P.M. and 2 P.M. to 4 P.M.[20] In 1872, daily meant Monday through Saturday. In November 1874, the hours were extended again, the bank remaining open from 6 P.M. to 8 P.M. on Monday and Saturday evenings.

The year 1872 also marked the first of a number of changes that were to take place on the Board of Directors. On April 5, 1872, Dr. Zina Pitcher died. As one of the last of the original trustees of the Detroit Savings Fund Institute, his fellow directors were greatly saddened at his passing.

During the five years following Dr. Pitcher's death, several more vacancies occurred on the board. These were filled by George Hendrie, George Jerome, Frederick B. Sibley, and Thomas Ferguson. Hendrie, a native of Scotland, was owner of Hendrie and Company, cartage and trucking agents. Later, he became director of the Detroit City Railroad Company, then the city's major streetcar line. George Jerome, one of Detroit's most prominent lawyers, was general counsel for the Detroit and Milwaukee Railroad and had also been active in state politics. Frederick Sibley, son of early Detroit Judge Solomon Sibley, owned and operated a large limestone quarry near Trenton, Michigan. The offices and dock of F. B. Sibley & Company were on east Atwater Street. Ferguson was a partner of Merrell & Ferguson, general agents, Mutual Life Insurance Company of New York. On September 2, 1875, Henry P. Bridge resigned as director and Alexander H. Adams, the bank's cashier, was elected in his place.

The Detroit Savings Bank was not the only bank to prosper in the year following the passage of the amendment to the General Banking Law. By 1873 Detroit's banking community had grown to ten members. In addition to the Detroit Savings Bank and the other five institutions already mentioned, there was the City Bank, which had been organized in the spring of 1872. Incorporated with a capital of $50,000, the bank was the successor of the private banking concern of Kanady & Taylor. The German American Bank was organized in August 1871, with a capitalization of $100,000. Located on West Larned, the German American Bank was the successor to the banking house of Edward Kanter, who had begun his banking business in August 1868. The People's Savings Bank, located on Jefferson Avenue, was organized on January 1, 1871, with a capitalization of $60,000, and the following April it moved its offices to the southeast corner of Griswold and Congress. On July 1, 1874 the capital stock was increased to $125,000, and on January 1, 1878, to $250,000.

The Wayne County Savings Bank was organized October 22, 1871. Originally located on the northwest corner of Griswold and Congress streets, the bank moved in December 1876, to Congress Street, immediately in back of its old offices. This new building was erected by the bank at a cost of $110,000 including the lot. In September 1875, the bank's original capital of $30,000 was increased to $150,000. In addition to its banking operations, the Wayne County Savings Bank was the first in the city to offer its customers the use of safety deposit boxes. In 1872 the bank's officers formed the Safe Deposit Company. Housed in the same building as the bank, the boxes could be rented for $5.00 to $75.00 per year. [On March 29, 1871, a law had been adopted providing for the organization of trust, deposit, and security companies.[21]] Along with the People's Savings Bank and the Detroit Savings Bank, the Wayne County Savings Bank was to become one of Detroit's major banking institutions.[22]

As was true in Detroit, the late 1860s and early 1870s was a period marked by prosperity throughout the United States, particularly in the areas of industrial expansion and railroad construction. By the spring of 1873, it had become evident that almost every type of industry had been stimulated beyond its needs in anticipation of still greater profits. The building of new railroads, which between 1869 and 1873 had increased the total capital invested in railroads from two to nearly four billion dollars, had overreached itself.

Finally in the fall of 1873 a full scale panic occurred. The panic was not precipitated by the banks but rather by the failure of a number of important eastern investment firms. The New York Stock Exchange closed for two days, and bankruptcy overtook a host of companies and individuals. This was the tenth year of the existence of the national banking system, and there were 1,980 banks in operation. Deposits in these banks fell more than $100,000,000 in a little over six months.[23]

The depression following the panic proved to be one of the worst in American history. For the two years 1876–77 business failures numbered more than 18,000. A majority of American railroads went into bankruptcy; more than two-thirds of the iron mills and furnaces lay idle; and by the beginning of 1875, over 500,000 men were out of work. In the absence of organized public relief, destitution and hunger far outstripped the efforts of charity to keep up. Wage reductions caused a series of serious labor strikes; beggary, prostitution, and crime increased; and political and economic radicalism gained ground.

The depression also hit Detroit very hard. Many workers were on the streets, particularly those formerly employed in the city's factories and railroad shops. And, as could be expected with unemployment high, deposits in Detroit banks fell. Deposits in the Detroit Savings Bank, which had risen to $1,744,960 by the end of 1872, fell to

$1,351,492 by 1876.[24] Similar decreases were felt by banks throughout the state. Fortunately, Michigan's banking structure was strong enough to survive the panic and ensuing depression in good order. In Detroit only the newly formed City Bank was forced to close its doors.

In addition to a drop in deposits, the Detroit Savings Bank was faced with other losses during the depression; and to hold the line on expenses, salaries were cut. No new employees were hired, and the existing staff had to double up on their duties. Frequently, payments on personal loans were delinquent. Many of these caused serious difficulties for the bank because mortgages had served as collateral. The bank also had trouble collecting on many of its industrial loans. Typical of these were loans that had been made to the Detroit Car Works, and the Detroit and Hamtramck Iron Company.[25]

At the height of the depression the bank suffered another loss. A loss of a far different nature, this was a personal loss that could not be measured in loans and mortgages and deposits. On March 24, 1877, President Elon Farnsworth died. He had been ill for several months and was recuperating at his home on East Jefferson between Rivard and Riopelle when he was stricken. Farnsworth was survived by his wife, Hannah Blake Farnsworth. The Farnsworths had married in 1830 and had lived at their home on East Jefferson since 1835. His old friend Henry Walker prepared this resolution which was read into the minutes of the Board of Directors:

> The Hon. Elon Farnsworth after a continuous service of twenty-eight years as president of this Institution, having departed this life on the Twenty-Fourth instant, his associates place upon record their testimony to the ability, faithfulness, and integrity with which he filled his office and discharged his trust.
>
> To this official recognition most justly due they heartily add their tribute of the loss of a personal friend, whose qualities need no higher eulogium than the silent grief of all with whom he has acted here during this long period of his life.[26]

His passing was felt by many segments of the community, and special resolutions in his honor were passed by several of the city's civic and professional organizations. Former Governor Adelphus Felch wrote this about President Farnsworth:

> The characteristics governing him as chancellor were carried into the administration of the bank during its formative years. As a banker he was clear-headed, prudent, of sound judgment, inflexible in the

discharge of his duties, straightforward and above reproach. He left a record most clean as a man of spotless honor and complete integrity.[27]

Shortly after Farnsworth's death, James McMillan was elected to the Board of Directors. McMillan was one of Detroit's most successful businessmen. When the Michigan Car Company was founded, he was appointed manager. Later, with John Newberry, he formed the firm of Newberry and McMillan, which became one of the city's largest companies, with controlling interests in railroads and railroad equipment companies, shipbuilding, and steamship lines. McMillan was later to serve with distinction as United States senator from Michigan.

Though Farnsworth's vacancy on the board was filled, a new president was not immediately elected. In the interim Vice-President Walker assumed the management of the bank's affairs. Finally on January 17, 1878, the board elected Alexander Adams to succeed the late President Farnsworth. Because of Adams's proven ability as cashier, he continued to hold that office for another four years while serving as president. The directors had complete confidence in his ability and good judgment, and as both president and cashier, Adams soon became the practical manager of the bank with unlimited power and discretion.[28]

Shortly after Adams became president, the depression began to ease, and within months it gave way to good times. Depositors once again began to return to the bank. Business increased at such a rate, in fact, that the directors were soon faced with the problem of finding larger office space.

As early as July 1875, the directors had considered moving into new quarters; after lengthy discussion, the idea was abandoned. Then early in 1878, with the depression on the decline, the idea was once again brought up. President Adams read to the directors a letter he received several days earlier from Sidney D. Miller.[29] Miller had purchased the property at the northeast corner of Griswold and Larned and was planning to erect a new office building there. Miller's letter inquired if the bank would be interested in renting part of the main floor for its offices.

A committee of President Adams and Directors Lyon and Ferguson was appointed to meet with Miller to discuss his proposal. On March 2 the committee reported to the board that they were very pleased with Miller's presentation and that the new building would have a number of advantages. First, and possibly most important, the new building would be erected in the heart of Detroit's financial district, at the intersection of two of the city's busiest streets. Secondly, the main banking room would be considerably larger, allowing for better accommodations for customers. In addition, there would be more working space for the employees, an office for the cashier, and a more spacious board room for the directors. Also the new building would contain a larger and better constructed vault, there would be plenty of natural light and ventilation, all rooms would be heated by steam (at no cost to the bank), and finally—of all things—electricity would be available.

After the board had heard and discussed the committee's report, Director Lewis submitted a proposition to continue the bank's lease in its present quarters, which he owned. Miller was asking for a rental fee of $3000 annually; Lewis was willing to settle for $1500 "and to pay for all gas consumed by the Bank during the day time." After considerable debate Lewis withdrew his motion, and the directors voted to adopt the committee's report and accept Sidney Miller's proposal.[30]

With the Detroit Savings Bank agreeing to terms, Miller was able to proceed with the planning of his new building. The architectural firm of Lloyd and Pearce was retained; drawings and specifications were prepared; and by the end of May, construction had begun.* The cost of construction was originally estimated at $30,000, with a completion date of late September. Owing to a number of delays, the final cost was somewhat higher, and the building was not ready for occupancy until early December. Finally, just before Christmas, the bank moved into its new quarters.[31]

The best description of the building appeared in the *Detroit Free Press*—written just before the bank moved in:

> The handsome, red-stained brick block, recently completed by Sidney D. Miller, at the northeast corner of Larned and Griswold streets, had not been christened yet, and on the Wall street of Detroit it is referred to as "the new Savings Bank block." Mr. Miller and his associates, however, hope soon to give it a name. The former strongly objects to having his own name attached to the block, and "Bank Chambers" has been suggested with some prospect of its being accepted. A reporter of *The Free Press* yesterday strolled through the elegant building, which for the time being is known as "80 Griswold street." It may be described as a four-story, red brick with basement,

---

* Gordon W. Lloyd and John Pearce were local architects. Their office was on W. Fort Street between Griswold and Shelby.

and brown stone front for the lower story. Its exterior architectural adornments are plain and neat. The chief features of the building in its entirety are its properties of light and ventilation, its ease of access, excellent interior arrangement and its handsome finish. It has a frontage of 50 feet on Griswold street and 80 on Larned street, with an alley in the rear. The entire ground floor is occupied by the Detroit Savings Bank and the offices of George Hendrie and the Detroit City Railway. Under the latter offices is a fine, light basement office as yet unrented. Commencing from the basement two tiers of vaults run through the entire building to the roof, thus giving every office a large, roomy vault. The Detroit Savings Bank's offices are elegantly finished in black walnut. The main office is 40 x 50 feet in size, and is lighted by windows facing both Larned and Griswold streets. The directors' room in the rear is finished with marble mantel and a grate, and there are two sets of lavatories and closets containing water and all the conveniences. There is also a large cloak-room. The vault has a passage way all round it.

The City Railway offices are approached from the hallway on Griswold street, or from Larned street at the corner of the alley. The main office of the railway company is large and roomy, being 30 x 50 feet. These offices are four feet above the banking floor.

At the head of the broad, easy stairway on the second floor is the office of C. C. Trowbridge, late receiver of the Detroit & Milwaukee Railway. To the right is the elegant suite of offices in which Sidney D. Miller and his associates, John H. Bissell and Fred T. Sibley, are cosily ensconced. The suite comprises three large rooms facing Larned street, appropriately furnished, and carpeted with a pretty figure of body brussels.

The entire corner of the second floor is occupied by the Mutual Life Insurance Company of New York, Merrell & Ferguson, General Agents. These gentlemen are agents for seven States, and their home offices are here. The main public office is fifteen by twenty feet in size; Mr. Ferguson has a private office, and there are also a large store-room and a handsome vault, with closets and wash rooms. Messrs. Merrell & Ferguson are just moving into their new quarters.

The second and third floors are finished in ash and butternut, with natural oil finish. The third floor has several offices, that of Douglas & Bowen fronting on Larned street.

The fourth floor is finished in pine. The offices fronting on Griswold street are occupied by Mason & Rice, architects. Judge Campbell has also an office on this floor, and parties are negotiating for the other offices. The building is heated by steam, but each office has a grate for use when desirable.

The windows in the rear of the building are protected by heavy iron shutters. The elevator is a hydraulic one, a cistern containing 1,200 gallons of water, being located in the cellar, and a tank in the top of the building contains 1,000 gallons.[32]

Now that the bank had moved into this fine new building, it appeared to most Detroiters that the Detroit Savings Bank was planning to continue serving the citizens of this city for many years to come.

PANIC, DEPRESSION, AND RECOVERY

The Detroit Savings Bank had now been in existence for over 30 years, and during all this time the directors had held the complete confidence of the people of Detroit. This confidence had enabled the bank to survive two serious financial panics and to develop into one of the city's soundest financial institutions. In 1881 a situation developed which threatened to destroy this public trust. On June 27, 1881, Henry M. Walker, who had served as the bank's vice-president since 1849, was asked to resign from the board of directors. Over the years Walker had made and lost several fortunes. During the panic of 1857 he lost a considerable portion of his real estate and lumbering holdings. Through careful management he was able to recover these losses. He then invested heavily in railroading and copper mining in the Upper Peninsula. Unfortunately Walker was again completely wiped out, this time by the depression that followed the panic of 1873. After losing all of his Upper Peninsula investments, he was forced to sell his remaining real estate as well as his interest in the *Detroit Free Press*. By 1881 he was deeply in debt. Because of his long and valuable service to the bank, Walker was retained as one of the bank's legal counsels and continued to serve in this capacity until his death in 1886.[33] The reputation of the directors and officers was critical to the bank's existence. Any loss in confidence in these men could have spelled disaster for the bank.

In June 1881, the legislature passed a law which required every bank to hold an annual stockholders meeting the first Monday in May, at which directors were to be elected.[34] On May 1, 1882, the stockholders of the Detroit Savings Bank met and elected the following nine directors: Alexander H. Adams, Thomas Ferguson, George Hendrie, George Jerome, Edward Lyon, James McMillan, Frederick B. Sibley, William K. Muir, and Sidney D. Miller. Muir, who had served as superintendent of the Detroit & Milwaukee Railroad and later as president of the Eureka Iron and Steel Works, had first been elected to the board in 1879 following the resignation of Samuel Lewis. Miller was elected to fill the vacancy created by the resignation of Henry Walker.[35]

The following day the new board met and elected Alexander Adams president, and Thomas Ferguson vice-president and secretary. Because of the growth of the bank, Adams was no longer able to serve as both president and cashier. In his place the board promoted Eustace C. Bowman to the position of cashier. Bowman, who had previously been a clerk at the First National Bank of Detroit, began working at the Detroit Savings Bank in April 1881, as assistant cashier and collections and discount clerk. Bowman had proven his ability in banking affairs; and his election to cashier marked the beginning of many years of distinguished service to the Detroit Savings Bank and to the city's financial community.

By the end of 1882 there were 12 chartered banks in Detroit. These institutions had an aggregate capital of $3,700,000; loans and discounts of $16,793,000; and deposits totaling $20,239,000.[36] While these statistics may not seem impressive by today's standards, they did indicate a prosperous and active banking community. Since the panic of 1873, the volume of banking business had been steadily increasing and, to handle the volume of transactions, the city's bankers decided to form a clearing house.

There had been talk for several years about establishing a clearing house but nothing had been done. Then, in 1882, Frederick W. Hayes, cashier of the Merchants and Manufacturers' National Bank, was sent to New York to study the workings of that city's clearing house.* When Hayes returned to Detroit, an agreement was signed to set up an experimental clearing house for two weeks. Beginning on February 6, 1883, the bank clerks and messengers gathered each noon at the Merchants and Manufacturers' Bank to clear the transactions of the preceding 24 hours. The bankers who had participated in the trial, including Alexander Adams, were so well satisfied with its operation that they called a meeting to draft a constitution, by-laws, and rules for a permanent organization. The meeting was held on March 6, and Henry P. Baldwin, president of the Detroit National Bank, was elected president of the Detroit Clearing House Association and Frederick Hayes was elected manager.[37] Total clearings for the first year amounted to $131,410,450, with the largest day's clearing reaching $794,941.[38] In 1887 the Detroit Clearing House Association

* The New York Clearing House is the oldest clearing house in the United States. Founded in 1853, its primary purpose was for the exchanging of checks and paying resulting balances among member banks. The London Clearing House, perhaps the oldest official organization of its kind, began operation as early as 1773.[39]

moved into the Newberry and McMillan Building, located on the southeast corner of Griswold and Larned across the street from the Detroit Savings Bank.

On November 27, 1883, President Adams chaired a routine board meeting. The only business transacted that day was the reading and approval of the finance committee's report on loans and bills discounted. Six days later this simple two line statement was recorded in the minutes of the board of directors: "Alexander H. Adams, President, died on Saturday evening, Dec. 1, 1883, at 10 o'clock." [40]

Mr. Adams had served the bank for over 28 years as cashier, director, and finally president. Although 71 years old, he had been in excellent health and was working at the bank on the day he died. His sudden death came as a shock to his many friends.[41] As a tribute, the directors of the Detroit Savings Bank prepared a memorial resolution, which was entered into the official minutes of the bank. The resolution read in part:

> Throughout his connections with the Institution he has been recognized by the Board and by other Banks as well as by the Community at large as the responsible manager . . . (and) active head of the Institution. As such, he was . . . trusted by his associates and by all who have conducted business with the Bank and through all the varied fortunes of the Bank in prosperity and in vicissitudes he has stood at his post of duty and faithfully discharged the Trusts reposed in him.[42]

At the annual stockholders meeting in May 1884, Sidney D. Miller was elected president succeeding Alexander H. Adams. The selection of Miller was an excellent choice. Not a banker by profession, he had long been active in the city's business community as one of Detroit's most prominent attorneys. At various times he had served as an officer or director of the Eureka Iron and Steel Works, the Detroit City Railroad Company, and the Detroit & Milwaukee Railroad. Miller was also active in many civic affairs. From 1870 to 1891, he served as a member of the police commission and for many years was a vestryman at Christ Episcopal Church. He also served two terms on the Board of Education, Committee on Library, and as such was one of the real founders of the Detroit Public Library.

As soon as he assumed office, Miller made a complete examination of the bank's books. Upon finishing the study, he addressed a letter to the board setting forth his findings and his recommendations for the future operations of the bank. The letter in part stated:

> 1st. Four fifths of our Liabilities are to those who commit their money to our care (1) for safe keeping and (2) for Investment for

Accumulation and therefore are trust funds and should be so employed.

It seems a reasonable interpretation of the terms of this trust derived from the provisions of the statute and our agreement with Depositors as well as the experience of the past, to say that one fifth of these Deposits should be as carefully invested as we would individually endeavor to invest trust funds left in our keeping.

2nd. The remaining one fifth of our Liabilities being the average current Reserve Funds of our current Depositors, may be employed by us in legitimate commercial paper readily available to meet the demand Liability assumed by us to those depositors.[43]

Miller further stated that while it was impractical to attempt to establish definite rules which would always be applicable to the operation of the bank, he did believe that investments should be made along the following lines: first, he recommended that a larger amount be invested in United States bonds and the interest deposits in national banks reduced; second, that the amount invested in bills discounted should be reduced and that commercial and accommodation discounts on time paper should be kept within the amount of the average commercial deposits; and finally, that a further study be made to determine to what extent, and in what types of securities, demand loans should be permitted.

That Miller's recommendations were sound is borne out by the fact that by 1888, the bank's total resources had grown from $2,500,000 to better than $3,850,000—this in a period of only six years. During this time bond investments had more than doubled, increasing from $414,500 to $912,000. Mortgage investments had shown an even larger gain, increasing from $360,400 to $1,148,000. Bills discounted had been reduced by over $300,000, from $1,380,000 to $1,063,000, while cash reserves (primarily funds on deposit in other banks) had been slightly reduced from $660,000 to $644,000. Meanwhile savings deposits had grown from $2,300,000 to $3,015,000, and commercial deposits from $340,000 to more than $385,000.* [44]

In his report of 1888 Miller pointed out that since 1878, the bank's deposits had grown from less than $1,600,000 to more than $3,000,000, and yet this increase had been "gradual and not spasmodic at any time." Also, that while business had doubled, expenses had remained about the same. Miller concluded his report saying:

It is proper to refer to the fact of the constant gradual growth of the Bank and to anticipate a reasonable degree of prosperity in the future if we continue the conservative policy heretofore acted upon.[45]

* The first commercial accounts had been opened in 1875.[46]

This growth of the Detroit Savings Bank was occurring at a time when banking was expanding in Detroit as well as throughout the state of Michigan. The increase in the number of banks during the 1880s resulted from the return of prosperity following the depression of the mid-70s and the growth of the state. In Detroit the number of banks had grown to 21 by the end of 1888—of these 13 were state chartered banks and 8 were national banks. Throughout Michigan, state banks, which had numbered only 7 in 1871 when the state banking law was amended, had increased to 80 by 1889. National banks had increased from 43 in 1871 to 110 at the beginning of 1889. In addition to these, the number of private banks had also grown. It is estimated that in 1887 there were a total of about 375 banks of all kinds in Michigan.[47]

In that year (1887) the Michigan Bankers Association was formed. The first annual meeting was held in Detroit on October 26, 1887, and a constitution was drawn up. A desire to bring about a thorough revision of the state's banking laws may have been the impetus for the organization of the association.* At any rate, its first project was to draw up a bill for the revision of the state laws. As was required by the state constitution, the bill had to be submitted to the voters for approval. This was done in 1888, and it received the approval of the electors and went into effect January 7, 1889. The new law clarified and markedly liberalized state banking regulations. One noteworthy feature of the act was the establishment of the office of state banking commissioner. The commissioner was given the authority to examine state banks, require periodic reports of their condition, and to enforce the provisions of the law.[48]

The new law resulted in the reversal of the dominance of national banks in Michigan, which had existed ever since the Civil War. Twenty-seven new state banks were established during the first two years under the new law. In Detroit two new state banks were organized. The Detroit River Savings Bank opened on Woodward Avenue near Jefferson in April, and in October the City Savings Bank began business on Griswold north of Fort Street. Also in the new law were provisions for the organization of building and loan associations, and by 1891 no less than 78 of these institutions were established in Michigan. Seven of these building and loan associations opened for business in Detroit.[49]

* As early as February, 1887, President Miller and a number of other Detroit bankers had met with state Senator Monroe to discuss changes in the banking law.[50]

The prosperity of the 1880s came to an end in 1893 when another world-wide financial panic occurred. When the Philadelphia and Reading Railroad went bankrupt in February 1893, the panic which developed ushered in a depression that was to be one of the most severe in the nation's history. The effect of the Reading bankruptcy was somewhat offset by President Grover Cleveland's inauguration and a belief among members of the business community that the president would "maintain our national credit and avert financial disaster." Failures among smaller financial and industrial firms developed, however, and grew in number. Then, on May 5, the supposedly solid National Cordage Company failed and touched off a stock market collapse and the panic. By the end of 1893, some 500 banks and 16,000 business firms had been financially ruined. The winter of 1893–94, and the summer following, witnessed widespread unemployment, strikes met by violence, and a march upon Washington by "Coxey's Army."* Wheat and cotton prices collapsed and economic activity declined about 25 percent. The depression did not lift substantially until the poor European crops of 1897 stimulated American exports and the importation of gold.[51]

While the banking system of Detroit and Michigan felt the impact of the panic of 1893, the number of bank failures was not large. This was due in large measure to wise and timely action by the banks of Detroit. It was recognized by the Detroit bankers that the large and sound banks would suffer from the failure of the weaker banks of the city, and for that reason it was determined that all should stand or fall together. Adopting a plan which had been utilized in New York, the Detroit Clearing House Association set up a loan committee, authorized to accept from the member banks bills receivable and securities on which loan certificates could be issued, bearing seven percent interest. These certificates could be used in settling balances at the clearing house. Certificates to the total amount of about half a million dollars were issued. The use of these certificates benefited not only Detroit depositors, but also those outstate, for it enabled the Detroit banks, with which outstate banks deposited a large part of their reserves, to meet the call from the latter for funds. Confidence in the ability of the banks to pay off their depositors was strongly bolstered by this action, and as a result not one bank in the city

* Led by Populist Jacob S. Coxey of Ohio, a group of 400–500 jobless men marched on Washington, April 30, 1894, to deliver to Congress their demands for relief. When he tried to speak on the steps of the Capitol, Coxey was arrested for trespassing on the Capitol grounds, and his "army" disbanded.

failed. In the entire state only fifteen banks were forced into liquidation, and of these, nine were private banks, and only one was a large concern.[52]

Forced to curtail their loans, the banks found it necessary to call in loans when they became due. Many local industries, unable to borrow funds for carrying on their business, were compelled to close down. Consequently, thousands of men were unemployed, and much hardship resulted. In the winter of 1893–94, more than 25,000 men in Detroit lost their jobs. The City Poor Commission was overwhelmed with applications for relief, and large numbers of men were employed in public works. In an effort to relieve some of the hardship, Detroit Mayor Hazen S. Pingree had the City Hall lawn, public parks, and other vacant land plowed up and turned into vegetable gardens on which Detroit's poor families could grow their own food. They were known as Ping's Potato Patches, and while it may be doubted that they actually saved anyone from starvation, they were very popular.

In 1892 deposits at the Detroit Savings Bank had risen to a record high of $5,140,000; but by the end of 1893, they fell to $4,375,000.[53] In the summer of 1893 withdrawals from savings deposits were extremely heavy, and President Miller predicted that during the month of July alone, the cash resources of the bank would be reduced by more than $100,000. To meet the anticipated cash crisis, the board authorized Miller to travel to New York and Boston to arrange for credit with eastern banks in any amount up to $200,000. The securities he was to use as collateral were City of Detroit bonds, of which the bank held $291,000, worth more than $300,000.

Miller immediately left for the East and was able to make an arrangement with the American Exchange National Bank of New York for an "open credit of $100,000." In mid-August, Miller again went to New York to make certain the bank would be able to draw upon its special deposits in several New York banks as the need required. Miller received assurances from the New York bankers that they would be able to meet their obligations, and he deposited with the American Exchange National Bank checks drawn on the Farmers Loan & Trust Company, the National Citizens Bank, and the Washington Trust Company totaling $50,000. The American National was to hold these checks for the Detroit Savings Bank and if it became necessary, purchase currency with the checks and forward the cash to Detroit.[54] To further bolster the bank's reserves, President Miller negotiated with a Canadian insurance company in Toronto for the sale of Detroit City Water Bonds for $57,200 in American gold.[55]

As the depression wore on, deposits at the Detroit Savings Bank continued to fall, reaching a low of $4,325,000 by the end of 1894. During the following year, Detroit's economy began an upswing and deposits at the bank, both savings and commercial, began to grow. By the end of 1896 they reached $4,855,000, and by 1898, $5,609,000.[56] One other indication that the depression had finally run its course came in early 1898 when the Michigan Peninsular Car Company received a contract for the construction of 1,000 railroad cars for the Michigan Central Railroad. Good times had once again returned to Detroit.

From May 1884, when Miller was elected president, to 1892, there were no changes on the board. While this was a period of stability, there was one problem—attendance. In fact, at the time Miller was elected president, there had been a problem of getting a quorum for many of the board meetings. In the fall of 1885, the directors passed a resolution stating that "from and including this date (October 6) each Director who shall attend promptly the weekly board meetings on Mondays at 11:00 A.M. shall receive $5.00 for such attendance." Vice-President Ferguson wanted stronger language and proposed that the phrase "who is present in the Board Room ready for business not later than ten minutes past 11 o'clock" be added. Discussion of the resolution was taken up at the end of the meeting and was passed, but evidently the habitual latecomers were present because Ferguson's amendment was voted down.[57] Thereafter, attendance at the board meetings improved, and there was no further mention of tardiness.

At the end of 50 years of service, deposits at the Detroit Savings Bank had risen to over six million dollars. In that same year (1899) the state legislature enacted a law requiring that "the capital of banks having deposits exceeding five millions of dollars shall be increased to a sum of not less than four hundred thousand dollars." Since the capital stock of the Detroit Savings Bank was still $200,000, and deposits had long since passed the five-million-dollar mark, the president was directed to call a special meeting of the stockholders to approve a stock increase to $400,000. The meeting was held on Thursday, January 18, 1900, and the stockholders voted to offer the additional stock at $100 per share. Detroiters evidently considered the new stock to be a sound investment, for by the end of March all of the outstanding shares were purchased.[58]

In June 1901, President Miller reported to the board on the results of a detailed study of the bank's condition that he had undertaken. His report showed that the bank's resources were at an all time high of $7,623,350, which included a surplus in excess of $100,000. The report further stated that "real estate mortgages are the principal item of our resources (and) the main reliance of this bank during its existence." At this time the bank held 1,524 separate mortgages totaling $2,884,000; $1,662,000 in United States, municipal, and private bonds; and had $1,200,000 in cash on hand and on deposit in other banks. Miller concluded his report by stating that in his opinion the Detroit Savings Bank was in an "excellent condition." [59]

President Miller was not the only one to believe that the Detroit Savings Bank was in an excellent condition. While Miller had been making his study, the state banking department was making one of its own. Upon completion of the state's examination, Commissioner George L. Maltz sent the following letter to President Miller:

> The Detroit Savings Bank has received the formal official certificate of this Department that it is in satisfactory condition for the continuance of business.
>
> It is just and proper to add, in this separate statement, a few words of commendation occasioned by the careful special examination, required by the statute and recently concluded by the Deputy Commissioner and a force of Examiners, extending over a period of many days, whose detailed reports have been submitted to and thoroughly considered by me.
>
> It is seldom that an old bank engaged in business practically for half a century, with so large and mixed departments, involving dealings now with more than ten thousand customers and with so great a variety of assets, can completely place itself in the hands of skilled experts and come forth from the ordeal so free of criticism.
>
> I judge from the report to me, as well as from my personal investigation, that the credit is due not merely to the Board and its officers, but to those who have charge of the daily detailed work, which has been found, in each department to be thoroughly accurate and exceptionally correct; and it is due to the men who so readily and intelligently responded to every inquiry by the examiners, that I ask you to make acknowledgment to them for their faithful services to the Bank, and indirectly to the State.[60]

There was a change on the board of directors following the death of James McMillan on August 19, 1902. McMillan's vacancy was filled by his son, Philip H. McMillan, who was elected to the board on September 30, 1902. Philip McMillan took over management of his father's varied financial holdings at the time of the latter's death. This included the controlling interests in both the Detroit & Cleveland Navigation Company and the Detroit Shipbuilding Company. He later served as secretary-treasurer of the Packard Motor Car Company, secretary-treasurer of the *Detroit Free Press,* as well as director of a number of other firms.

In early 1904, Sidney D. Miller's health began to fail, and in February the 73-year-old bank president traveled to Florida in the hopes that the warmer climate would serve as the needed tonic. Unfortunately, his condition worsened, and on April 2, 1904, Miller died at the Hotel Ponce de Leon in St. Augustine. In tribute to his nearly half century of service to the bank, the directors adopted a resolution which was "ordered spread upon the record" and which read in part:

> The hand that molded, guided and governed the affairs of this Bank with entire faithfulness and signal ability so many years is now stilled by death, but its impress upon the character and reputation of the institution will endure through the future. Just as he in his career as a banker was wise, prudent, honest, conservative, liberal and just, so has he stamped his character upon this institution, until in this community it has become the synonym of safety, security, stability, fidelity and conservatism.[61]

At the time of his death, Sidney Miller was considered one of Detroit's leading financial men. The local newspapers carried lengthy articles on his many contributions to the city. The *Detroit Free Press* of April 4, stated:

> (Detroit) will miss him. . . . His was the success that is unselfish. He found time to give his personal efforts to the community. He became a working part of that society, assisting in the administration of its laws, the construction of its government, the support of its churches and charities. He was a man of the people, conscious of his moral and ethical obligations to his brother citizen and these he discharged to the letter.

Miller's death came at the end of an era in Detroit. The city, its people, its industry, and its banks were about to enter a period of growth, expansion, and prosperity never before known. Coming to an end was the city's reliance on the horse and wagon. Detroit was about to enter the age of the motorcar.

123

The Age of the Motorcar

Today Detroit is known as the Motor Capital; yet the industry's beginnings were anything but spectacular. A local railroad mechanic, Charles B. King, assembled his auto in John Lauer's machine shop on the east side of St. Antoine Street just below Jefferson Avenue. His automobile was the first to appear on the streets of Detroit. On the night of March 6, 1896, the machine was ready for its trial run. Wrapped up in a short coat for protection against the cold, King climbed into the vehicle and grasped the steering tiller. One of his assistants spun the crank, the engine sputtered, King threw in the clutch, and Detroit's first automobile moved uncertainly up St. Antoine toward Jefferson.

At Jefferson, King turned west and drove to Woodward where he turned north and chugged up to Cadillac Square. Then the motor died, and there is no account of how King got his machine back to Lauer's. Epochal as that short trip was, it stirred only casual public interest. On the following day, the *Free Press* carried only a brief account, buried on its back page: "The first horseless carriage seen in this city was out on the streets last night. . . . The apparatus seemed to work all right, and it went at the rate of five or six miles an hour at an even rate of speed." The longest account of King's feat was a quarter column on an inside page of the *Journal*. The *Tribune* gave it only three lines.

King, however, was not the only Detroiter tinkering with a horseless carriage in 1896. On the north side of Bagley Avenue between Grand River and Clifford lived the night-shift engineer of the Edison Illuminating Company [the present day Detroit Edison Company]. His name was Henry Ford. There was a small brick shed at the rear of his Bagley Avenue house, and in his spare time Ford worked out there, putting together a machine much like King's in appearance. He finally got it assembled on June 4, but to get it on the street, Ford had to knock out part of the shed's wall. Ford cranked up his quadricycle, as he called it, and no one was more surprised than he when it started.[1]

At the time, neither Ford nor King had any idea they were launching a great industry. King became more interested in art and music and, after his first machine, did not contribute much to the automobile industry in Detroit. Ford was merely playing with a mechanical toy. If he had any ideas of developing or improving his machine, it was to increase its speed and stamina and perhaps race it against a horse or another automobile. It would be almost five years before he awoke to its commercial possibilities.

It was Ransom E. Olds of Lansing who first started manufacturing automobiles in Detroit. He began his experiments in Lansing prior to 1895, working with a friend, Fred Clark. Olds's father made stationary engines and Clark's father made carriages. The two young men joined forces and built a car which they called the Oldsmobile. They organized the Olds Motor Works in Lansing in 1897 and then had a difference of opinion. Olds bought out Clark, sought financial backing and found it in Detroit. His benefactor was Samuel L. Smith, who had made a fortune in copper and lumber. He gambled $199,600 on the venture, with these provisions: that the manufacturing be done in Detroit; that he control 95 percent of the stock; and that his two sons, recently graduated from college, be given jobs in the company.[2] As a result, the Olds Motor Works opened for business in 1899 in a small factory on East Jefferson near the Belle Isle Bridge, where the Uniroyal tire plant now stands. The first Oldsmobiles were good machines. They ran well on paved streets and the company sold all it could make, which was not many. The Olds cost $2,382 which only the wealthy could afford.[3]

Then Olds had a lucky break, which he probably did not

appreciate at the time. On March 9, 1901, fire completely destroyed his plant. All the plans and machinery for producing the Oldsmobile were lost. The only thing saved was a small experimental model with a curved dash. Shortly thereafter the company's operations were moved back to Lansing and of necessity were concentrated on making this smaller car. Although the ties with Detroit were not broken, Olds was no longer able to machine parts in his own factory. The manufacture of his cars became essentially an assembly process. Work was farmed out to a dozen or more suppliers, most of them Detroit shops. The Leland-Faulconer machine shop on Trombley at Dequindre, headed by Henry M. Leland, built the motors; John and Horace Dodge, who had recently been making bicycles in Windsor, supplied transmissions; the Briscoe Manufacturing Company produced radiators; and a young fellow named Fisher, one of seven brothers from Norwalk, Ohio, was hired to help make bodies. Consequently, the Olds was produced more economically. The price of the curved-dash smaller car was drastically reduced to $625. Within a year the company was turning out the first popular low-priced car and making about 25 percent of all autos built in the United States.[4]

Meanwhile, Henry Ford continued to improve his model, obtained financial backing, and organized the Detroit Automobile Company in 1898. This venture was not a success. Ford left the firm and in 1901 formed the Henry Ford Automobile Company in a shop on Park Place. His second venture was no more successful than the first; but he kept working, making improvements and winning recognition for himself and his car by racing. He hired Barney Oldfield to drive for him, and in 1901 Oldfield set a record of 60 miles an hour on the Grosse Pointe track. Ford personally drove a race on the ice of Lake St. Clair in 1904 which set a new world speed record of 93 miles per hour.

With the publicity he received, Ford was ready for a fresh start. He found new financial backing, and, on June 16, 1903, the Ford Motor Company was incorporated and commenced operations in a factory on Mack Avenue at Bellevue. Among those who furnished the money (actually only $28,000 in working capital was paid in) were Alexander Y. Malcomson, a coal dealer; John S. Gray, a banker; and Horace H. Rackham, an attorney. John and Horace Dodge, who contracted to make parts for Ford in their shop on Beaubien at Fort and later in larger quarters on Monroe at Hastings, were given shares in payment. Malcomson's bookkeeper, James S. Couzens, put in $2,500 and joined the Ford Motor Company as its business manager. In 1919 Ford bought him out for $29,308,857, a substantial part of which Couzens returned to the community as a philanthropist.[5]

The new Ford idea was to build a car that would provide basic transportation not only for city dwellers, but for farmers and small town residents as well. The latter needed a machine that would get them up hills and through spring quagmires. Ford envisioned a mass-produced, low-priced auto so simple in construction that the farmer's hired hand could repair it. The concept paid off handsomely right from the start. In the first year of operation, 1,708 cars were sold. As it quickly became evident that the one-story Mack Avenue plant would not suffice, Ford moved in 1906 to larger quarters on Piquette Avenue at Beaubien. There in 1908 he began production of that automotive wonder of all time—the Model T. Ford was soon unable to meet demand, and within two years the company was six months behind on deliveries. So another move was made. Famed Detroit architect Albert Kahn was called upon to design a radically new plant, the site for which was far out Woodward in Highland Park. Kahn pioneered in industrial architecture for Ford, utilizing reinforced concrete and glass as structural elements, and providing facilities which brought the work to the man instead of sending the man to the work. Ground was broken in 1909, and by January 1, 1910, the Highland Park factory was in partial operation.[6]

In 1913 something new was developed at the Highland Park plant. The first automatic assembly line was put in operation. Standardization of parts had already been perfected by Ford at the plant. Now these parts were made to flow in a continuous stream to the moving line, reaching it just as they were needed by a worker who performed only a single operation. At the end of the line the body was skidded down an incline just in time to land on the assembled chassis. It was bolted into place and driven away under its own power. By this system, production was made more economical, more efficient, and given an almost unlimited quantity potential.[7]

While the assembly line was an important milepost, Ford's next inovation staggered the competition. On January 12, 1914, Ford announced that henceforth each production worker in his plant would be paid $5.00 for an eight-hour shift. To workers for whom $2.75 a day or less was standard pay for unskilled or semi-skilled labor, this sounded like a new gold strike. Men left their farms in Michigan and other states and headed for Detroit. Job-seekers even came from as far away as Europe. Other employers screamed "foul" and "socialism" as their employees quit and lined up at the Ford hiring gates. So dense was the throng of job applicants that it was necessary on one occasion to use fire hoses to disperse them.[8]

There were, however, strings attached to the five dollars-a-day. In order to earn that rate a man had to be on the payroll for six months and even after that had to be "worthy" of it. That certainly did not discourage the job-hunters who poured into Detroit.

The Detroit Automobile Company meanwhile got along very well without Ford. After his departure, Henry M. Leland was called in to take charge, and soon thereafter his Leland & Faulconer Manufacturing Company was merged with the auto concern. In 1903, the same year Ford launched his new enterprise, Leland and his associates put their first car on the market under the name of Cadillac. Not long afterwards, the name of the company was changed to the Cadillac Motor Car Company, operations being conducted in a plant at Cass and Amsterdam.

Others were watching Olds, Ford, and Leland with interest, and more than one part-time mechanic was at work in his own barn or in rented quarters in a shop somewhere in Detroit. A case in point was David D. Buick, a capable engineer in the plumbing supply business. He was successful in inventing a method of applying porcelain to bathtubs, toilets, and wash basins. He became interested in automobiles, and in 1903 built a car which he named for himself. Unfortunately, he used up his resources in doing so and was forced to sell out. The company was purchased by Flint wagon-maker William C. Durant. Operations were moved to Flint, and after two or three years of extremely hard going, Buick Motors experienced a turn in its fortunes and began to prosper. Durant had a keen head for figures, foresight, with a streak of the gambler in him. He realized that there were too many individual companies entering the field, that competition would stifle many of them, and that the industry's salvation and progress depended upon the centralization of resources, production, and marketing. A combine which would offer the individual a range of cars to choose from according to his needs and his pocketbook was Durant's great idea.

With this as his plan, he formed the General Motors Company in 1908 with Buick as the cornerstone (General Motors Corporation was formed in 1919). He offered to buy out Henry Ford and almost succeeded—at the last minute the deal fell through. Two years later Cadillac was acquired, then Oakland (manufactured in Pontiac and the parent of the Pontiac car). Olds became part of the new company, and then General Motors bought Chevrolet, at that time produced in Detroit, and moved it to Flint. With Chevrolet, Durant now had a low-priced car, one that would compete with the Ford Model T. Other companies, particularly firms making parts and accessories, were added from time to time. With its head office in Detroit and its manufacturing activities widely scattered, General Motors was on its way to becoming the giant of all American industrial enterprises.[9]

The year 1903 saw yet another famous Detroit car launched. That was the Packard, originally built at Warren, Ohio. On a trip to New York, Henry B. Joy and his brother-in-law, Truman H. Newberry, both wealthy Detroiters, saw the Packard for the first time and were impressed by the ease with which it could be started. Shortly thereafter, they acquired the company, moved it to Detroit, and began production in a plant designed by Albert Kahn on East Grand Boulevard near Mt. Elliott.[10] In its new plant, the Packard Company flourished, building a quality passenger car and a durable truck.

There were other companies that followed Packard. In 1904 Jonathan Maxwell, who had been Olds's factory manager, persuaded Benjamin Briscoe to back him in building a new car. Briscoe had a plant which turned out stampings for several of the early motor companies. He found the money, and soon the famed Maxwell was on the streets, rolling out of a factory at East Jefferson near Connors. From time to time during the next dozen years Maxwell either bought or merged with such pioneer companies as Chalmers, Metzger, Brush (the favorite light runabout of doctors), Columbia, and Flanders. The Maxwell was the genesis of the third of the Big Three. After World War I, the company ran into trouble and one-time railroad master mechanic Walter P. Chrysler was called in to put the company on its feet.

Chrysler had previously worked for Buick, where he had been plant superintendent. He surrounded himself with some superb talent in the persons of K. T. Keller and James M. Zeder. In 1925 he reorganized the company and the Chrysler Corporation was born.[11]

The years before 1910 saw many others enter the field: Hupp and Paige in 1908, and Hudson in 1909.* Hudson was organized by Roy D.

---

* Of the 202 different makes of automobiles being produced in 1910, only 4 remain today: Buick, Cadillac, Ford and Oldsmobile.[12]

Chapin, a former Olds employee, with the financial backing of department store owner J. L. Hudson. Still others such as Krit, Saxon, Liberty, and Rickenbacker appeared on the scene. In 1914 the Dodge brothers left Ford and established the Dodge Brothers Company, producing the Dodge car in a new plant in Hamtramck. They prospered with a fine line of well-built, moderately-priced cars and sturdy trucks. With the death of both brothers in 1920, the company faltered, and Walter Chrysler, seeking to emulate General Motors, bought the Dodge company in 1928 for one of the largest cash deals in history.

Why Detroit?

What was peculiar about Detroit that it so quickly became the heart and nerve center of the automobile industry? The horseless carriage was not invented in Detroit; it appeared on the streets of other cities months and even years before Charles King took his first ride. Companies were already manufacturing autos in other cities and states before Detroit entered the field. The answer lies in Detroit's background, its economic climate, and its tradition.

More than most other cities, Detroit possessed the ingredients for building the automobile. First of all, it had been for several years the center of the marine gasoline-engine industry, building the power units for the launches and motor boats on the Great Lakes. The shops were here, the know-how was here, the supply of skilled labor was here. In 1901 the price of gasoline tumbled when the first Texas oil gusher, Spindletop, came in. The cost of fuel fell from about a dollar to a few cents a gallon, cinching the future of the gas combustion engine over the short-ranged electric and the sometimes dangerous steamer. Second, Detroit was the center of the malleable iron manufacturing industry; it had plants which could turn out castings; and it had others which were turning out springs, copper and brass parts and fittings, and paints and varnishes. While there were no large companies engaged in manufacturing wagons and carriages, there were several small ones; so finding body makers, wheelwrights, and blacksmiths was no problem. The era of northern lumbering was passing, and there was a huge supply of labor with basic or developable mechanical aptitudes. Finally, Detroit had capital and plenty of it. In the second half of the nineteenth century, fortunes had been made in lumber, mining, and shipping. Thus risk capital was available to finance ventures which gave promise of being economically sound. That was why Detroit became preeminent in the industry: capital, skilled labor, and material were all at hand without the necessity of going afield for essentials.[13]

Along with automobile manufacturing, the first decade of the century witnessed the mushrooming of the great parts and accessories companies. Although many started as small shops, they grew and prospered along parallel lines by obtaining contracts from the motor manufacturers. Among some of the more important, especially from the standpoint of Detroit's economy, were Murray Manufacturing Company, McCord Manufacturing Company, Briggs Manufacturing Company, and Kelsey Wheel Company [present-day Kelsey-Hayes Corporation].

Even local people sometimes thought of Detroit as a one-industry town. That was a gross misconception. True, the stove and railroad industries were on the decline, but there still were pharmaceuticals, marine equipment, and shipbuilding. Attracted by a skilled labor supply, other new industries came to Detroit. In 1904, for example, the Arithmometer Company of St. Louis, which made adding machines, moved to Detroit and occupied a building at Second and Amsterdam. The following year it was incorporated as the Burroughs Adding Machine Company, later changed to the Burroughs Corporation. [Its headquarters continue to be at the site of the original plant, although its operations are now virtually worldwide.] Salt mining and chemicals also accounted for much of the new employment.

To coordinate and stimulate the city's growing business activity, the Detroit Board of Commerce was organized in 1903. One of the Board's founding members was Detroit Savings Bank President Sidney D. Miller.[14]

BRANCHING OUT

Primarily because of industrial expansion, Detroit experienced a rapid growth, almost tripling in population between 1880 and 1900. During approximately the same period, the area of the city nearly doubled, due to annexations. When the Bank Chambers was built in 1878, there were fifteen square miles within the city's boundaries. By 1900, the area was slightly more than 28 square miles. The new areas added were largely residential, accommodating the greater number of people who were establishing homes in Detroit.

This expansion meant that an increasingly larger proportion of the public lived farther than ever before from the Detroit Savings Bank.

Whereas in 1880, the Bank Chambers was either within walking distance or a short streetcar ride for most customers, the situation in 1900 was considerably different. By that time, it took more than an easy stroll to reach the corner of Larned and Griswold. It was beyond walking distance for most people. Public transportation also became a problem. From the outlying districts, it became necessary to transfer from one line to another, often at added expense and inconvenience. The board of directors was aware of this situation, and realized that a bank located in the heart of the downtown business district could not adequately serve the outlying areas.

As early as July 1887, the directors discussed a plan to alleviate this problem. It was suggested by the cashier, Eustace C. Bowman, that the bank establish a number of offices at outlying points in the city, where deposits could be received at certain regular hours. Although the idea was debated at some length, there is no record of any action being taken or any further discussion being held.[15]

In June 1890, the board again attempted to meet this problem and approved a plan whereby customers could make savings deposits with certain selected agents throughout the city. In most every case, these agents were local neighborhood merchants. A customer would make a deposit in the sum of 5, 10, 25, or 50 cents with the agent and would receive in return a "deposit token" to be pasted on a card. Each card held 20 tokens and when full, was accepted by the bank on deposit as $1, $2, $5, or $10. The card was sent to the bank by the merchant, or the customer could take his card to the bank himself.[16]

Agents were located throughout the city. Deposits could be made at Henry Cleland's drugstore on Montcalm at Clifford; at Callian's Book and Stationery Shop on Jefferson Avenue; at Judge's Cigar Store on Grand River; at George W. Dufrene's grocery on Rivard and Congress streets; at Hodge's Notions on West Fort; at William Smith's barbershop on Crogham [present day Monroe]; and at John Alexander's dry goods store on Chene near Larned. In all there were 73 designated agents. In addition to the local merchants, deposits could be made at Cadieux's General Store in Grosse Pointe; at Michael Greiner's general store at Connor's Creek out Gratiot; at John Scott's general store and postoffice in Delray; and at Laing and Fleming's drugstore in Windsor.[17] The plan met with some acceptance but was not the success the bank had hoped for, and within a few years the arrangement was discontinued.

Nothing more was done to solve this problem of reaching customers in the outlying districts of the city until 1903. At a board meeting in March of that year, the directors decided, after lengthy discussion, that a committee should be formed to consider the advisability of establishing permanent branch offices.[18] While the city's first branch bank had been opened in May 1889 by the Home Savings Bank, the concept of branch banking was still relatively new in Detroit.[19] Of the 20 banks doing business in the city in 1903, only six had branch offices.*

After several months of study, the committee's recommendation was to open a branch office, and on November 19, 1903, a special board meeting was held to discuss the details. This meeting's outcome was the appointment of another committee consisting of Directors Anderson, Delamater, McMillan, Miller, and Muir who were to prepare a list of suitable locations. The committee's suggestion for a site was the corner of Gratiot and St. Antoine avenues, on the city's east side, on property already owned by the bank.[20]

It was not until June 1904, however, that the final decision as to the location of the branch was made. At a special meeting on June 24, the board instructed the president to rent office space in a vacant store on Gratiot just west of St. Antoine.[21] For some unexplained reason, it was decided at that time not to build the branch on the bank property at the corner.

A lease was signed and, within a short time, the remodeling of the interior of the store was begun. In late September the work was finally completed; and, on October 3, 1904, the Detroit Savings Bank opened its first branch office. The manager of the branch was Joseph A. Petz; Edward J. Dee was the assistant. The first day's business was brisk, with $4300 deposited in savings accounts and $1600 in commercial accounts. By January 1905, deposits totaled nearly $100,000.[22]

When the branch was opened, Gratiot and St. Antoine was a locality where many prominent Detroiters maintained their businesses. Gratiot Avenue was a cedar block road from Woodward to Randolph Street. From Randolph past St. Antoine to McDougall, Gratiot was paved with stone, while beyond McDougall to past the city limits it was again paved with cedar blocks.[23]

The branch continued to do such a good business that in 1909 a new building, designed by Albert Kahn, was constructed at the corner of Gratiot and St. Antoine. This was to serve as the home of

* These 6 banks had a combined total of only 9 branches. By 1929, the city's 16 banks had a total of 307 branches.[24]

branch number one for the next 51 years. From the date the branch opened until the early 1930s, the bulk of the business transacted was of a savings nature.[25]

The Detroit Savings Bank opened its second branch on July 15, 1905, in a rented store at the corner of Dix [later Vernor] and Junction on the city's west side, in a predominately Irish and German neighborhood. On the first day of business, thirty accounts were opened, totaling $2000. The branch's first manager was Edward J. Dee, who continued as manager until 1913 when he was promoted as first superintendent of branches. When branch number two was opened, Dee had a staff of one, Edward Kast, who served as teller, bookkeeper, and messenger all rolled into one.[26]

The bank did not establish its third branch until 1909, when three new offices were opened. Branch number three opened its doors for business on April 22, 1909, in space rented on the ground floor of a store on the west side of Woodward between Milwaukee and Grand Boulevard. Business was immediately successful and by 1914 had increased to such an extent that the board of directors decided to move the branch into larger, permanent quarters. In April 1914, property on the southeast corner of Milwaukee and Woodward was purchased for $60,000. It was not until July of the following year that Albert Kahn's plans were approved and construction of a building started. Once begun, construction was soon completed, and the new building opened in 1916.[27]

When this branch originally opened for business in 1909, such factories as the Cadillac Motor Car Company, Everette-Metzger-Flanders Company, Ford Motor Company, Fisher Body Corporation, and the Regal Motor Car Company were located nearby. By the 1920s most of these companies had departed from the area. New customers came from the two giant office buildings in the New Center area, the General Motors Building which opened in 1921, and the Fisher Building which opened in 1929.

Branch number four, situated at the intersection of Grand River and Warren avenues, was opened for business on June 3, 1909. The residents of this neighborhood were mainly factory workers employed in the plants in the area. Although several large factories were nearby, savings deposits were about double the commercial deposits well into the 1930s. Competition for customers in this area was keen. When the new building was opened in 1927, for example, there were branches of five other banks along the adjacent eight block stretch of Grand River.[28]

On September 30, 1909, the Jefferson-Hilger Branch opened as the fifth unit of the Detroit Savings Bank branch system. This was in the district previously known as Fairview Village, a predominantly residential area. The branch was one block beyond the end of the Detroit United Railway lines, but the interurban passed its door on its way to Mt. Clemens.

During the next seven years, the bank opened eight new offices, bringing to 13 the total number of branches. With the coming of World War I, the opening of new branch offices came to an end, at least temporarily. With the signing of the armistice, however, plans for the construction of more branches were made. Detroit had experienced a phenomenal growth in population during the 20-year period from 1900 to 1920. In 1900 the city's population was 285,704; by 1910 it had increased to 465,766; and by 1920 it had almost doubled to 993,678. By this time the competition for bank customers had become very keen and the city's 18 banks were operating 170 branches.[29] In the six years from 1920 to 1925, the Detroit Savings Bank opened 12 new buildings, almost doubling its number of branch offices.

The three branches opened in 1925 were all located in thinly populated areas that were soon to become growing residential neighborhoods. The opening of these branches, numbers 23, 24, and 25, also marked, for all intents, the end of branch office expansion by the Detroit Savings Bank for the next 20 years. During this 20-year period, only 6 branches were opened. It was not until the end of World War II that another major branch office building program was to take place. The growth of the Detroit Savings Banks during the first quarter of the twentieth century brought on both an expansion of branch offices and a resultant growth in staff.

In 1878 when the Bank Chambers was opened, the staff consisted of ten employees from president/cashier to messenger. In 1882 President Adams felt he could no longer adequately perform the duties of both president and cashier; hence, assistant cashier Eustace C. Bowman was promoted to cashier. The bank's staff then numbered twelve. Besides the president and the cashier, there were two tellers, two assistant tellers, two bookkeepers, one clerk, one assistant clerk, one janitor-watchman, and a messenger. Salaries for these employees went from $2,100 for the cashier and $1,800 for the tellers to $400 for the assistant clerk and $264 for the messenger.[30] These were all annual salaries.

In 1882, carpenters in Detroit and neighboring communities were paid from $2 to $3 a day; bricklayers, $2.50 to $3; woodcutters, $22 to $26 a month with board; farm hands, $16 to $25 a month with board; and female domestics, $1.50 to $3.50 a week with board. Prices were generally low, although they varied considerably, being higher usually in the outlying towns and villages than in Detroit. A brief list of prices follows:

roast beef	10 to 16 cents a pound
corned beef	5 to 10 cents a pound
fresh pork	10 to 15 cents a pound
ham	10 to 18 cents a pound
chickens	8 to 18 cents a pound
butter	20 to 35 cents a pound
coffee	14 to 30 cents a pound
sugar	10 to 12½ cents a pound
potatoes	40 cents to $1 a bushel
milk	4 to 8 cents a quart
eggs	12 to 30 cents a dozen[31]

During the next 20 years, the bank's staff grew slowly reaching only 17 by the turn of the century and the opening of the first branch office. Then a regular boom took place, and by 1916 when the 13th branch opened, the bank's staff numbered over 90. As more branches were opened following World War I, the growth in staff continued, reaching a high of 331 in 1929.[32]

During this period of the early development of the branch system, the directors of the Detroit Savings Bank were confronted with a number of other very important tasks. The first of these was to select a new president to replace Sidney D. Miller.

WORLD WAR I

When Sidney D. Miller died on April 2, 1904, the directors of the Detroit Savings Bank immediately began their search for his successor. They did not have to look far. On April 19, 1904, they selected Director DeWitt C. Delamater. Born in Buellville, New York, in 1844, young Delamater was ten years old when his family moved to Jackson, Michigan. He began his business life in that city and later moved to Detroit. In 1890 he helped organize the wholesale hardware firm of Freeman-Delamater & Company and served as its secretary and treasurer. In 1900 he became the company's president and chief executive officer. In 1910 the firm name was changed to Delamater Hardware Company; and Delamater was its president until 1917, when the business was sold.

In 1897, when Delamater was elected a director of the bank, he was also serving as secretary and director of the Buhl Stamping Company. In 1901 he served on the executive council of Detroit's Bi-Centenary Committee and was president of the Merchants and Manufacturers' Exchange. At the time of his election as president of the bank, DeWitt C. Delamater was considered to be one of the city's leading businessmen. The next 20 years were to prove that the bank's board of directors had made a wise selection.

Following President Delamater's election, Frederick B. Sibley resigned as vice-president (though he continued to serve as director until his death in 1907), and Director Charles A. Dean was elected in his place. To fill the vacancy on the board created by President Miller's death, the directors elected his son Sidney T. Miller. A senior partner in the law firm of Miller, Canfield, Paddock and Stone, Miller was one of Detroit's most distinguished lawyers. In addition to his position at the Detroit Savings Bank, Miller was director of the Wyandotte Savings Bank, the Detroit Trust Company, and the U.S. Radiator Corporation. For several years he also served as a Detroit Library Commissioner. During World War I, he was Michigan Director of the American Red Cross.

At the time Delamater became president, the bank was in excellent condition, and deposits were at an all-time high of $7,480,926.[33] In fact the bank was growing at such a rate that the board determined new banking offices were needed. On February 3, 1905, a special meeting of the board was held to discuss the possibility of moving from the Bank Chambers to the Penobscot Building, which was then being constructed on Fort Street between Griswold and Shelby.*[34] A week later the board met again, and the president and secretary were authorized to accept the offer of the owners of the building and to complete all arrangements necessary for the move. It had been agreed to lease the office space for the period of at least ten years, with rent for the first five years at $7,500, and for the second five years at $10,000 per annum.[35]

Construction of the building was delayed several times because

* The "old" Penobscot Building, as it is sometimes called today, still stands next door to the "new" 47-floor Penobscot Building which was built in 1928 at the corner of Griswold and Fort streets.[36]

of labor strikes by the construction crews.[37] The building was finally completed, and on February 27, 1906, the board held its first meeting in the new banking office.[38] The following article appeared in a local newspaper about a month after the bank moved:

> In February last, the bank was moved to its handsome new quarters in the Penobscot building, just completed, on Fort st. west. Here it has a home of which it may well be proud, as may likewise the Detroit public. It is said that the Penobscot is classed as the finest office building in the State of Michigan, and its 14 floors contain the headquarters of many of the most important financial and professional institutions in the city.
>
> The Detroit Savings Bank occupies the entire west half of the ground floor, the arrangement and equipment throughout being especially designed and made. The office, spacious and elegant, is finely finished in marble and mahogany, with metal grille work and every possible convenience of arrangement and furnishing. The large staff of specially trained attaches and department officers are stationed in spacious offices and from the president's office in the front to the directors' room in the rear, the whole appearance is rich, dignified and in faultless taste. Every facility for the carrying on of the business of banking after modern methods is found here, and every possible convenience for customers and visitors.*
>
> The safety and protection of the property of the bank and its contents are guarded with jealous care. Bolts and bars, iron and steel, locks and improved machinery making the strongboxes and safe deposit vaults proof against interference. One of the important new features of the big vault where the cash of the bank is deposited, is the heavy electric part of an electrical system so elaborate and yet so sensitive and complete in its nature and detailed construction that the slight moving of a curtain during the night—even the insertion of so much as a pin point into the curtain's body—will turn in an immediate signal to the offices of the Still Alarm close at hand, whence will come immediate and well-equipped response.
>
> This, while the newest feature of the protective system of the bank, having but a few counterparts as yet in the world, is but a single one of the almost innumerable precautions taken to insure the safety of the patrons of the bank from loss. Among all the important institutions of its class there is none that commands—and deserves—a higher degree of public confidence and good will than the Detroit Savings Bank.[39]

Following the move into the Penobscot Building, the Detroit Savings Bank continued its period of growth. This was aided by the

---

* One unique convenience was for the lady customers. When the new offices were opened, a separate department with a private entrance for women was established and a woman teller was hired to conduct this phase of the business. This innovation did not prove successful, however, and the department was abandoned. The bank's only other female employee at this time was the president's secretary.[40]

industrial expansion then occurring in Detroit. The companies were turning to the city's banks for loans in order to expand their facilities and increase their production and services. The minutes of the board of directors of the Detroit Savings Bank show frequent entries for loans to a variety of companies. Loans were made to the Michigan Copper and Brass Company; the Packard Motor Car Company; the Bagley Land Company; the *Detroit Free Press*; the Gale Manufacturing Company; and the Detroit Range Boiler Company.[41]

While these transactions were all with commercial customers, the bank was still primarily a savings institution. At the end of 1906, deposits stood at $8,346,145, consisting of $7,642,556 in savings and $703,589 in commercial deposits.[42] Deposits continued to grow after 1906, and in 1911 they passed the $10,000,000 level.*

After DeWitt Delamater's election as president, there were a number of changes on the board of directors. In February 1905, Strathearn Hendrie was elected director to fill the vacancy created when the board was expanded to ten members at the annual meeting of that year. Strathearn Hendrie, the son of director George Hendrie, followed his father in the interurban business. In 1906 Arthur M. Parker, a prominent businessman and secretary and treasurer of the Detroit Range Boiler Company was elected to the board. That same year John M. Dwyer was elected to fill the vacancy created when the board was expanded to 11 members. Dwyer was a senior partner of Dwyer & Vhay, a wholesale grocery firm. He was also vice-president of the Peninsular Savings Bank. In 1909 when William K. Anderson died, his vacancy was filled by Paul F. Bagley. In the 1890s Bagley entered his father's tobacco business. He later served as president of the Bagley Land Company, and as a director of the Union Trust Company.

Further changes occurred on the board in 1913, when three directors were elected: David S. Carter, Jerome H. Remick, and Robert Henkel. Carter was a director of Larned-Carter, an overall uniform-manufacturing company. He also served as a director of the Detroit & Cleveland Navigation Company, and the Grosse Pointe

---

* The $10,000,000 mark was an important moment in the bank's history. Kenneth Paton was an assistant bookkeeper in 1911, and many years later when he was vice-president and cashier, he told the following story. "The morning the bank passed the $10,000,000 milestone Mr. John Barron, then general bookkeeper, told me to ask Mr. Cyrus Boss, cashier of the bank, to come to the general bookkeeping department immediately. Mr. Boss came at once, and I can still picture these two fine men congratulating each other, shaking hands, and laughing gleefully. The entire office force joined in the celebration a moment later."[43]

Bank. Remick was owner of the J. H. Remick Music Company, one of the largest music publishing houses in the world. He was also president and general manager of the Detroit Creamery Company; director of the *Detroit Free Press*; director of Parke, Davis & Company; and a director of the Paige Motor Car Company. Robert Henkel was president of the Commercial Milling Company and secretary-treasurer of the Detroit Barrel Company.*

In addition to the election of three directors, the year 1913 brought an increase in the bank's capitalization. At a special meeting on October 2, 1913, the stockholders approved a capital stock increase of $350,000, raising the bank's capitalization from $400,000 to $750,000.[44] The increase was made to allow the bank to handle its rapidly expanding business. The following editorial appeared in "The Mercantile and Financial Times" shortly after the stockholders meeting:

> The Detroit Savings Bank has had its hands full and the additional working capital will materially assist the bank in reaching out after a desirable class of business, such as is waiting it and the other local banking institutions on account of the unexampled prosperity which this city and state are now enjoying.
>
> It has been stated that the bank's business was never in a sounder nor more prosperous condition than at the present time.
>
> The Detroit Savings Bank has facilities of the most complete character. For effecting collections in this territory, handling the accounts and other business of out-of-town clients it affords a superior service and to local business houses and individuals it must strongly appeal on account of its long experience in the banking world here.
>
> And if we again lay stress upon the liberality, yet progressiveness, of its management we add a very good reason why patronage is being and ought to be, extended the institution in steadily increasing volume.[45]

The year 1913 ended on a firm note with the bank's capital at $750,000 and deposits at a high of $12,030,525.[46] President Delamater's ten years as the bank's chief executive officer had been highly successful ones. The decade had been a period of continued growth. The only set-back had come with a brief but severe panic in 1907.

* Henkel's milling company built and operated a large flour mill at the foot of Randolph Street. Later sold to the Robin Hood Flour Company, the mill was torn down in 1973 to make way for the new Renaissance Center. The Detroit Bank and Trust Company was one of the major financial institutions that invested in the partnership which put together the down-payment money for the center's first construction phase.[47]

The Panic of 1907 and the Federal Reserve System

The panic began in New York City. Over-speculation was once again the primary cause, but behind that lay the competitive struggle between the new trust companies, acting as commercial banks with inadequate reserve requirements, and the more conservative and better regulated commercial banks. The panic was precipitated by the Knickerbocker Trust Company, which closed its doors on October 22, and by the failure on the following day of the Westinghouse Electric and Manufacturing Company. Prices collapsed on the New York Stock Exchange. To head off the panic, the U.S. Treasury Department and J. P. Morgan & Company each loaned $25,000,000 to the New York banks, and the acute stage of the crisis passed in December.

While bank suspensions and failures occurred throughout the country, the panic served one good purpose in that it emphasized the inelasticity of the national banking system and the need of its correction. During the following year, a National Monetary Commission was appointed to make a study of the banking situation and report to Congress. As a result of this report the Federal Reserve Act was passed on December 22, 1913, creating the Federal Reserve System.

The new Federal Reserve System provided for a regional system of twelve Federal Reserve banks, each to act as a central bank for its district. The operations of these regional banks were to be supervised and coordinated by a Federal Reserve Board located in Washington.

All national banks were required to join the system, and state banks and trust companies could join upon fulfilling certain requirements. Stock in the Federal Reserve banks was to be subscribed for by member banks in the amount of six percent of their capital and surplus.

The Federal Reserve banks were empowered to hold deposits for member banks and to clear and collect checks for them; to discount certain types of paper for member banks; to fix a rate of discount on such paper; to sell and buy coin; to issue Federal Reserve notes; and to act as fiscal agent for the federal government. Thus, through a bit of lucky timing, the country's financial machinery was put into shape just in time to meet the demands that would be placed upon it by World War I.

Like most state banks, the Detroit Savings Bank did not join the Federal Reserve System until after the United States had entered the First World War. At their meeting of October 16, 1917, the directors voted to apply for membership and a week later they made written application to purchase stock in the Federal Reserve Bank of Chicago.[48]

Shortly after World War I began in Europe, a conference of clearing house associations from the Federal Reserve cities was held in Washington. The conference recommended that a gold fund be established to check the outflow of gold from the United States and to relieve the international exchange system. A committee report requested that the national and state banks in the reserve cities contribute $100,000,000 to the fund. In response to this request, the board of directors of the Detroit Savings Bank authorized a subscription in the amount of $55,000 to the fund in gold and gold certificates.[49]

The Great War

When World War I broke out in Europe, President Wilson called for strict neutrality on the part of the United States. As the fighting continued and increased in fury, and as American lives were lost through submarine attacks on merchant ships, a feeling of moral indignation was aroused in the public's mind. Finally on April 6, 1917, President Wilson called upon Congress to declare war on Germany.

With the entry of the United States into the war, it became apparent that large sums of money, in excess of tax receipts, would be needed to conduct the war. To obtain the necessary funds, the Treasury resorted to borrowing through a series of bond issues. The first four issues were known as "Liberty Loans," while the fifth and last was called the "Victory Loan."

The issues were bought between May 14, 1917, and April 21, 1919, in the total amount of $21,478,250. Liberty Loans were long-term bonds bearing from 3½ percent to 4½ percent interest. The Victory Loan consisted of two series of three- to four-year notes bearing interest from 3¾ percent to 4¾ percent.

Heavy demands were made on local banks to finance the many war industries which mushroomed in Detroit, but the banks' major role in the war was to assist in the sale of Liberty Bonds. Just as soon as the Treasury Department announced plans for the first Liberty Loan drive, the Detroit Savings Bank, in cooperation with the other banks of the city, set out to raise the $20,000,000 in bonds which the Treasury had assigned as Detroit's quota.

The disposal of the bonds was accomplished by direct sales to the public. A Liberty Loan Committee was organized and "4-minute speakers" gave high-powered sales talks in theaters, hotels, and restaurants. Ministers made pleas from their pulpits for the purchase of bonds, and mass meetings were held in the downtown area. To those who could not afford to purchase the bonds outright, the banks assisted by lending money, at a rate no higher than the interest on the bonds, the smallest denomination available being $50. In this way it was possible to secure the funds wanted and to obtain oversubscriptions on each issue.

The first drive was typical of the other four. Early in June 1917, Detroit businessmen assembled in the Board of Commerce auditorium and underwrote $5,700,000 for their employees. Henry Ford was the first and largest subscriber, taking $1,250,000 for his employees. Later that month Ford personally subscribed for $5,000,000 in Liberty Bonds. The Detroit Savings Bank was also one of the larger subscribers taking $750,000 in bonds.[50]

While the bank was actively supporting the Liberty Loans it was also faced with a serious manpower problem. In June 1917, the State Banking Commissioner notified the bank that during a recent examination, the state examiners had discovered major errors in the accounting at several branch banks. The report stated in part that, "in the opinion of the examiner some of the employees do not appear to be equal to the task of performing the work." The directors replied that the bank was having trouble "procuring sufficient help to do the work required." [51]

To solve this dilemma, the bank began hiring women. At the beginning of the war, the bank had only five women on the staff out of a total of more than 90 employees. Three of the women served as secretaries, one was the telephone operator, and the fifth managed the Women's Department. When an acute shortage of male help developed after the first wartime draft, the bank for the first time began to employ women as bookkeepers and clerks.[52]

Evidently, this solved the problem, for in his next report the Banking Commissioner found no major errors in the bookkeeping and concluded his letter with this statement: "From the examiner's report, it is very evident that your bank continues to have the careful and conscientious attention of officers and directors." [53] It was also at this time that the bank qualified as a depository for U.S. Postal Savings and for federal and state public money.

Detroit's automobile industry also went to war in 1917. Nearly every conceivable type of military equipment was turned out by the automotive and allied industries. Guns, ammunition, even the tin hats of the doughboys were produced in large quantities. The first major automobile order from the government came six weeks after the declaration of war. It was for 3,000 Ford ambulances.

One notable Detroit product was the famous Liberty engine for Allied aircraft. Designed by Packard's chief engineer Colonel Jesse G. Vincent, it was built by Packard, Ford, Cadillac, and a new concern, the Lincoln Motor Company, organized in 1917 by Henry M. Leland and his son Wilfred. Lincoln was the principal builder of Liberty engines. A plant was constructed at Warren and Livernois, and the area around it was made hideous day and night by the deafening roar of hundreds of engines being block tested in open fields surrounding the factory.

The Ford Rouge plant, under construction when the war broke out, was used for the production of Eagle boats, small but fast vessels designed for patrol and anti-submarine warfare. Out at the Highland Park plant, Ford was turning out Whippet tanks.

In the late summer of 1918, the German armies began to collapse, and on November 11 an armistice was signed. A few days before the 11th, a premature announcement of peace resulted in general rejoicing followed by disappointment. But the word that flashed on November 11 was official and authentic, and Detroiters laid down their tools, quit their offices, homes, and classrooms, and poured into the downtown streets to celebrate.

The war years brought considerable growth to the Detroit Savings Bank, as is evidenced by the following statistics:

	Resources	Savings Deposits	Commercial Deposits
1914	$14,056,619	$10,606,614	$1,476,216
1918	$20,798,766	$15,344,162	$3,013,992
1919	$27,672,952	$18,756,604	$4,921,394[54]

The Great War was finally over, the celebrating had ended, and Detroit was ready to return to normal. Yet the decade of the 1920s turned out to be anything but normal.

THE TWENTIES

The year 1919 marked the end of 15 years as president of the Detroit Savings Bank for DeWitt C. Delamater. They had been years of growth and prosperity for the bank. At 75 years of age, Delamater decided the responsibilities had become too heavy and on October 31, he resigned as president and was elected the bank's first chairman of the board.[55] In December, cashier George S. Baker was elected a director of the bank and, following the annual stockholders meeting of January 13, 1920, he was elected to succeed DeWitt Delamater as president and chief executive officer.

George S. Baker was born in Boston, Massachusetts, in 1873 and came to Detroit with his family in 1889. In 1890 he was employed by the Citizens' Savings Bank as a messenger and eventually worked his way up to auditor. During this period he attended the Detroit College of Law, and although he received his degree and was admitted to the state bar, he never was a practicing attorney. In 1906 he left the Citizens' Savings Bank to accept the position of treasurer of the University of Michigan. Then, in 1911, he left Ann Arbor and returned to Detroit as an assistant cashier of the Detroit Savings Bank. Following the death of Cyrus Boss in 1912, Baker was promoted to cashier, and in 1918 he was appointed vice-president and cashier.

At their meeting of January 13, 1920, the stockholders also voted to increase the size of the board to 16 members (although only 15 positions were filled at the time) and elected three new directors: James T. McMillan, Ralph N. Stoepel and David M. Whitney.[56] McMillan, the grandson of former director James McMillan, was general superintendent (and later president) of the Detroit & Cleveland Navigation Company. He was also a director of the Packard Motor Car Company, and the Detroit Trust Company.

The industrial expansion of the war years was followed by a short but severe business depression. After reaching a peak in May 1920, commodity prices began to decline rapidly, and this gave rise to an unprecedented cancellation of orders for goods. Money became extremely tight, although the stringency did not become acute until autumn. A noticeable exodus of gold from the country caused a marked advance in money rates; and by the end of the year, industrial stocks on the New York Stock Exchange declined by 30 percent. The depression continued throughout 1921 and was characterized by industrial inactivity, business failures caused by the fall of commodity prices, and a major decline in foreign trade.

The Detroit Savings Bank was directly affected by the depression of 1920–21. In June 1920, the bank's resources were at an all-time high of $30,919,724, with investments in real estate mortgages and bonds at $17,041,628, and loans and discounts at $6,414,693. Savings deposits had reached a high of $19,932,438 while commercial deposits stood at $4,666,733.[57] By February 1921, assets had fallen to $28,657,185 and by March 1922, reached a low of $28,096,530. Thereafter the economy began to improve; and by the fall of 1922 the bank's resources had reached $30,507,412, with mortgages and bonds at $21,690,262, and loans and discounts at $4,061,723. Savings deposits stood at $19,698,087, with commercial deposits at $4,061,359.[58]

The depression of 1920–21 was followed by a period of prosperity such as the country never before had experienced. One of the major factors in this prosperity was the growth of the automotive industry. In 1917 United States production of cars and trucks was 1,873,949 units. In 1918 war work lowered the output although 1919 saw cars rolling out of plants at a rate equal to 1917.* With some declines, but mostly showing steady increases, domestic production rose year by year until 1929, when the 5,000,000-unit mark was broken for the first time. Not until 1948 was that figure reached again.[59]

Several factors contributed to this growth throughout the decade of the 1920s. It was a growth which led to the day when the production of motor vehicles and all the ramifications of a mighty enterprise made the automotive industry America's number one manufacturing activity, both from the standpoint of the value of the product and the number of people employed. This reflected an ever-expanding market, both domestic and foreign, mainly domestic. Millions of soldiers learned to rely on the automobile during the war and became accustomed to using it. A car was one of the first things a veteran wanted when he returned to civilian life. The invention and perfection of the self-starter by Charles F. Kettering made the auto more accessible to women by eliminating the crank and the broken wrists and sprained shoulders which usually went with it. Cadillac was the first to adopt the starter as standard equipment in 1912; by 1914 it was standard or optional on most models; and by 1920 it was standard equipment on virtually all cars. The ladies began to give up their glassed-in electrics—"show cases on wheels"—for the gasoline-powered automobile.

Other innovations also contributed to the industry's growth. Little gadgets such as the automatic windshield wiper became a common piece of equipment on all cars. The Dodge brothers pioneered in all-steel bodies for their cars and in a better enameling process.

* While many of Detroit's auto plants were converted to the production of war materials, the conversion was never a complete one. Production of cars for the domestic civilian market was not halted (as in World War II), although it was slowed down.[60]

Larger balloon type tires made for better riding. Perhaps the most radical change in the 1920s was the introduction of closed cars, in which Hudson was prominent. While closed cars had been manufactured earlier, the price was too high to attract many buyers. In 1922 Hudson came out with a closed car selling for only six percent more than the open model. Just as in the case of other improvements, all automobile makers were forced to recognize the change and adopt it. By 1925 more than half of the American cars sold were of the closed type.

Out of the upsurge in sales and production emerged General Motors, Chrysler, and Ford as the Big Three. The day of the small independent was coming to a close. Some of the latter, like Auburn, Cord, Essex, Franklin, and Paige-Detroit never recovered from the depression of the 1930s, while others like Packard and Studebaker went out of business after World War II. It was not all smooth competitive driving even for the giants, as Henry Ford found out. His Model T, the famed Tin Lizzie, ruled the low-priced field until 1925 when good roads, a supply of cheap used cars, and the classier Chevrolet gave Ford trouble. By 1926 Ford sales were running a poor second to Chevrolet, and the next year the Model T was discontinued after fifteen million had been produced. The Model A appeared in the fall of 1927 and Ford was back in competition, although the Ford Motor Company never again had the field to itself as it did in the heyday of the Model T. After 1927, Ford reluctantly conformed to the practice established in the business, that of bringing out a new model every year.

Like the automobile industry, the Detroit Savings Bank experienced a period of great prosperity during the decade of the 1920s. One major move was an increase in the bank's capitalization. At a special meeting held February 26, 1920, the stockholders approved a stock increase of $750,000, bringing the bank's total capitalization to $1,500,000. At this time plans were also discussed for methods of financing a new main office building.[61]

As early as January 1912, the board of directors had been considering moving out of the Penobscot Building and into larger quarters.[62] Committees were formed to study various sites which were finally narrowed down to two: the Detroit Opera House Building on Campus Martius, and the 12-story Chamber of Commerce Building on the corner of State and Griswold streets. At a special meeting of the board in September 1915, it was decided that the bank should own or control its own main office building. With this plan in mind, a committee consisting of Directors Charles A. Dean, Philip H. McMillan and Sidney T. Miller was appointed to negotiate with the owners of the two buildings.[63] The Clark family, owners of the Opera House Building, were only willing to lease office space. However, the owners of the Chamber of Commerce Building, a group of Boston financiers, indicated that they were willing to sell their property.[64]

The committee traveled to Boston to ascertain what kind of an arrangement might be made for the acquisition of the Chamber of Commerce Building. After several proposals and counter-proposals, a plan was finally settled upon, and on November 3, 1915, the board decided to purchase the building. The following day a cash price of $850,000 was agreed to.* [65]

Albert Kahn was commissioned by the bank, and at a special board meeting on July 17, 1918, he submitted plans for extensive improvements and alterations of the building.[66] For the next several months Kahn met regularly with the board to discuss the changes in detail. Kahn recommended that the first four stories of the exterior of the building be faced with a red granite, replacing the red stone facing then being used. The pressed brick and terra cotta facings on the upper stories were to remain the same as when the building was constructed in 1894.[67] Extensive alterations for the interior of the building were also recommended. These consisted of modernizing the first floor and converting the second floor into a mezzanine, building safe deposit vaults, and reinforcing the building throughout with steel girders.†

Alterations were completed in the spring of 1921, and arrangements were made with the newly organized Commercial State Savings Bank to sublet the offices in the Penobscot Building. In May, the Detroit Savings Bank moved into its new quarters and on May 31, 1921, the directors held their first board meeting in the new offices.[68]

When the bank moved into the Detroit Savings Bank Building, as the Chamber of Commerce Building was now to be known, it occupied the basement and first three floors of the building, renting out the offices on the upper nine floors. One important addition to the bank's operation made at this time was the formation of the

---

* On April 3, 1920, the Detroit Savings Bank Building Company was organized. The company was established primarily to own and manage the new main office for the bank.[69]

† For a short time a branch office was opened in the Chamber of Commerce Building but when alterations were begun in May 1920, this temporary branch was closed.[70]

Detroit Savings Safe Deposit Company.[71] It was incorporated as a company, separate from the bank, to own and operate the safe deposit vault in the new banking house. The safe deposit boxes were installed in a modern steel and concrete vault, the entrance to which was guarded by a ten-ton steel door. These new quarters with up-to-date equipment and accommodations were a far cry from the facilities in either of the bank's two previous locations.

Back in 1889 a nest of 106 boxes had been installed in the Bank Chambers exclusively for the convenience of the bank's clients. The original 106 boxes were housed in a movable iron safe, and no more than one customer at a time was allowed access to the vault. When the bank moved into the Penobscot Building in 1906, the original 106 boxes were transferred to the office and an additional 440 boxes were installed. When the Safe Deposit Company was incorporated, the facilities were expanded in the new building to include 2,475 boxes of various sizes.* [Today, the Detroit Savings Safe Deposit Company has 63,703 boxes in the main office and in 56 of the bank's branches.]

With the return to prosperity following the depression of 1920–21, the Detroit Savings Bank grew at a rapid pace. In the fall of 1922, the bank's assets were listed at $30,507,412; by the fall of 1929, this figure had climbed to $55,578,932. During these seven years, mortgages and bonds grew from $21,690,262 to $29,888,173, while loans and discounts were increased from $4,061,723 to $17,731,676.[72] Typical of the loans made at this time were to: the Detroit Creamery Company; the Peninsular Stove Company; the City of Detroit; and the Cities Service Company. Not all of the bank's customers were major companies or big government. The minutes of the board of directors record frequent loans to small independent firms like the Beilfield Tire Company, and the Gladwin Farm and Cattle Company.[73]

In August 1925, the directors were saddened to learn of the death of the Chairman of the Board, DeWitt C. Delamater. To fill his vacancy on the board, the directors elected Sidney T. Miller, Jr., the son of director Sidney T. Miller. After returning from military service in Europe in World War I, young Miller began his law practice and soon became one of Detroit's best known corporation lawyers. In addition to being a director of the Detroit Savings Bank, Miller was a director of the Detroit Trust Company, and the Wyandotte Savings

* In order to serve its customers more conveniently, a branch of the Detroit Savings Safe Deposit Company was opened at the new Grand River-Joy Road office in November 1929. A second branch was opened in the remodeled Woodward-Milwaukee office in March 1934.[74]

Bank. In April 1925, the board had been brought up to its full complement of 16 directors by the election of James H. Doherty. Doherty had joined the bank in 1888 as a general assistant at the age of 18. At the time of his election to the board, he was vice-president and cashier, having been appointed to that position when George Baker was elected president.

On September 13, 1927, the board of directors was shocked with the news of the sudden death of President George Baker at the age of 54. He was stricken while on vacation in Atlantic City. As the bank's chief executive for nearly eight years, Baker had earned the respect of all his fellow officers and employees. At the time of his death, George S. Baker was considered one of Detroit's leading bankers.[75]

To succeed President Baker, the board of directors immediately set out to locate a banker of the highest caliber available. On November 1, 1927, Director John M. Dwyer was elected chairman of the board of directors; and as chairman, his first duty was to announce the selection of Walter L. Dunham as the bank's new president.[76] Dunham had come to Detroit from New Orleans in 1910 as a cashier for the Ford Motor Company and, in the intervening years, held a series of responsible banking positions. In 1912 he became a vice-president of the Highland Park State Bank (Henry Ford's bank) and in 1920 accepted a similar position with Detroit's Dime Savings Bank. In 1923 he became vice-president of the First National Bank-Detroit holding that position until his election as president and director of the Detroit Savings Bank on November 1, 1927. At the time of his move to the Detroit Savings Bank, Dunham was a director of the Detroit Trust Company, the Industrial Morris Plan Bank, the McCord Radiator Company, and was first vice-president of the Michigan Bankers' Association.

Reporting on his election as president, the *Detroit Free Press* of November 2, 1927 said this of Walter Dunham:

> Few bankers have a wider acquaintance through Michigan and in the principal cities of the United States, and Mr. Dwyer feels that (Dunham's) introduction to the Detroit Savings Bank as president will enlarge the circle of that bank's influence.

At the annual shareholders meeting in January 1928, the board of directors was enlarged by the election of Edward D. Stair, who was one of Detroit's most prominent citizens. Since 1906 he had been owner and publisher of the *Detroit Free Press*. At the time of his election as a director of the bank he held similar positions with the

Paige Motor Car Company, the Detroit Creamery Company, the Detroit Trust Company, and the Detroit Fire and Marine Insurance Company.

As the bank began the year 1929, it showed an increased volume of business that not only reflected the prosperity of Detroit, but was also an index of the bank's activity. Resources stood at $51,284,337 with savings deposits at $32,016,645 and commercial deposits at $12,932,454. In the last year alone the number of depositors had grown from 99,991 to 107,429. At the annual meeting of January 8, 1929, President Dunham told the stockholders, "The situation with respect to 1929 your officers believe to be most encouraging." [77]

The first months of 1929 did nothing except confirm President Dunham's statement. Business was booming, employment in Detroit was high, and the automobile industry hit a new peak in production. Then on October 24, 1929, the New York Stock Exchange collapsed. The market continued its plunge until November 13 and ushered in the worst financial panic the United States had ever experienced.

6

Governor Comstock's Proclamation

MERGERS AND CONSOLIDATIONS

The causes of the depression which followed the October crash did not originate in Detroit. They were worldwide—a result of the war with its ensuing inflation as well as the European financial and political collapses. The stock market break was a signal for the general economic collapse which followed almost immediately. Thousands lost their money in the market; everything tightened up and the boom of the twenties deflated. When the great reservoir of easy money and credit dried up almost overnight, the public stopped buying.

Detroit, due to its industrial nature and heavy reliance on the automobile industry, was one of the first cities to feel the effects. Michigan, as well as Detroit, had prospered throughout the decade of the 1920s. Hordes of workers from all over the United States migrated to Michigan to work in the automobile factories. Detroit became largely a one-industry area; almost everyone was dependent directly or indirectly upon the automobile industry. According to the 1927 *United States Census of Manufacturers,* over 56 percent of the total production of Detroit in that year represented motor vehicles, bodies, and parts.[1] *The United States Census of Population* for 1930 shows that between the years 1919 and 1929 the value of manufacturing in Detroit increased by 64.2 percent, largely because of the phenomenal growth of the automobile industry.[2]

In 1929, there were 5,337,087 vehicles produced. In 1930, production was down to 3,362,820; and, in 1932, it touched bottom with an output of only 1,331,860.[3] That meant extensive layoffs in the factories. Suddenly thousands of Detroit workers were out of jobs. Lacking resources, they could not pay their bills, they could no longer obtain credit at the corner grocery store, and the merchants themselves began to feel the pinch.*

It was not only the factory workers who were distressed. Middle- and upper-income families saw their savings wiped out and their jobs vanish. Most businesses, to stay alive, drastically cut salaries and wages. Speculators who had borrowed money were called upon to raise collateral; businessmen who had borrowed on increased inventory were called upon to reduce their indebtedness. Detroit went from silk-shirt affluence to hunger in a matter of a few short months.

The most dramatic incident of the depression occurred early in 1933 when the banks of Michigan were closed by the decree of Governor William A. Comstock. The causes of the bank holiday were many, but one important factor was the particular way banking had developed in Detroit following the First World War.

Between the years of 1914 and 1929 the number of financial institutions in the city of Detroit more than doubled. In 1914 there were 10 state banks, 3 trust companies, and 3 national banks. By 1929 there were 15 state banks, 4 industrial banks, 12 trust companies, and 2 national banks in operation. In 1914 the following state banks and trust companies were doing business: Detroit Savings Bank, American State Bank of Detroit, Central Savings Bank, Dime Savings Bank, Federal State Bank, German American Bank, Peninsular State Bank, People's State Bank, United Savings Bank of Detroit, Wayne County & Home Savings Bank, Detroit Trust Company, Security Trust Company, and the Union Trust Company. Their total resources were $172,600,748, while their total deposits amounted to $139,548,771.[4]

Detroit's three national banks in 1914 included: First National Bank, National Bank of Commerce of Detroit, and the Old Detroit National Bank. Their total resources were $69,054,828 with deposits at

---

* Federal Reserve statistics show that employment in the automobile industry was reduced by more than 45 percent in the year following the stock market crash of October 1929.[5]

$55,217,113. Thus the city's total banking assets in 1914 were $241,655,576 with deposits totaling $194,765,884.

Detroit's largest state bank in 1913 was the Wayne County Savings Bank, which had been founded in 1871. In 1913 this bank merged with the Home Savings Bank to become the Wayne County & Home Savings Bank. The Home Savings Bank had first opened for business on January 2, 1889, in the McGraw Building on Griswold Street. Following the consolidation, the Wayne County & Home Savings Bank moved into its newly constructed office building at the corner of Michigan Avenue and Griswold. In October 1914, the Wayne County & Home Savings Bank acquired the Michigan Savings Bank, which had first opened its doors in April 1872. With the acquisition of the Michigan Savings Bank, the resources of the Wayne County & Home Savings Bank totaled $37,406,369.

The year following the merger of Detroit's two largest state banks saw the merger of the city's two largest national banks. The First National Bank had been chartered on October 5, 1863. In 1908 it had acquired the Commercial National Bank. The Second National Bank was chartered October 7, 1863, just two days after the First National. When the Second National's charter expired in 1883, it was reorganized as the Detroit National Bank, and in 1903 it became the Old Detroit National. In 1912 the American Exchange National Bank was absorbed by the Old Detroit. Then in 1914 the First National and the Old Detroit National merged and became the First and Old Detroit National Bank. The resources of the new bank were $55,501,701. With this merger, the First and Old Detroit became one of the strongest national banks outside of New York and Chicago. In 1919 the bank bought Detroit's famous Pontchartrain Hotel at the southeast corner of Woodward Avenue and Cadillac Square and, in February 1922, completed on that site the tallest bank building in Michigan—the 24-story First National Bank Building. When the First and Old Detroit moved into its new offices, the name of the bank was officially changed to the First National Bank-Detroit. In 1928 the bank again expanded as the result of a merger, absorbing the Central Savings Bank.

In the spring of 1914 when the First National and the Old Detroit National consolidated, the announcement was made that a number of well-known businessmen were organizing a new national bank to be known as the Merchant's National Bank. Capitalized at one million dollars, the new bank moved into the offices recently vacated by the Old Detroit National Bank in the Buhl block at the corner of Griswold and Congress streets. On the first day of business, the bank met with instant success receiving over one million dollars in deposits.

In 1916 three new state banks and one new trust company were organized. First, the Guaranty Trust Company of Detroit was chartered and commenced business on May 22, 1916, with a capitalization of $300,000. Second, on March 1, 1916, the Highland Park State Bank of Detroit was organized with a capital of $500,000. Third, in June 1918, the Highland Park State Bank changed its name to Bank of Detroit. Then, on April 24, 1916, the Michigan State Bank of Detroit opened its doors in offices at the corner of Junction and Norton on the city's near west side. At the end of April 1916, the Commonwealth Savings Bank commenced business with an initial paid-in capital of $258,600 in offices in the Hammond Building at Fort and Griswold streets. In 1919 a consolidation was effected with the Federal State Bank, forming the Commonwealth Federal State Bank. The Federal State Bank had originally been the Metropolitan State Bank; the name change occurred in January 1914.

Two new trust companies were formed in Detroit in 1917, and one state bank changed its name. The new institutions were the Bankers Trust Company, and the American Loan & Trust Company. Both of these companies were capitalized at $300,000. The Bankers Trust opened for business in offices on West Congress between Griswold and Shelby, while the American Loan & Trust had quarters on the southwest corner of Griswold and Larned. In 1924 the corporate name of the American Loan & Trust Company was changed to the American Trust Company. Following the declaration of war by the United States in April 1917, the German American Bank changed its name to the First State Bank of Detroit.

Also, the year 1917 witnessed the passage of an important banking act by the state legislature. Provisions of Act 296, of the Public Acts of 1917, allowed the formation of a new type of financial institution in Michigan—the industrial bank.[6] Act 296 detailed the procedures for the incorporation, powers, supervision, and control of these new banks. The industrial bank was to derive its funds through a form of savings known as investment shares, and to invest these funds by specializing in the financing of businesses through the assignment of pledged accounts. The first bank to be formed under this act was the Industrial Morris Plan Bank of Detroit. Organized with a capital of

155

$500,000, the bank commenced business on August 16, 1917, in offices in the Farwell Building on Griswold between State and Grand River.

In 1918 a branch of the Federal Reserve Bank of Chicago was opened in Detroit. The branch began operations on March 18, in offices in the Congress Building at the corner of Congress and Griswold streets. The opening of this branch was in line with Federal Reserve policy to bring Reserve facilities nearer to certain of the larger cities separated by long distances from the 12 District Banks. This step was made possible by an amendment to the Federal Reserve Act in 1917. All branches were assigned a specific capital and a definite territory in which they were to render the same services as the District Bank itself. They were to hold the legal reserve balances of their members; lend them reserve money; perform collection services; store, receive, and pay out currency; make available wire transfer facilities; and provide safekeeping service for United States securities. The territory served by the Detroit Branch included the 19 counties in the immediate metropolitan area.*

The growth of banking that Detroit was witnessing was also being experienced throughout the rest of the state. By 1920 there were 113 national banks in Michigan, only a slight gain over 1910, but the number of state banks showed a major increase. There were 544 state banks in 1920 as compared with 397 in 1910. Of this number, 157 had become members of the Federal Reserve system. These were the larger state banks, representing almost 72 percent of the state's banking resources. Also, in 1920, there were 11 trust companies and 2 industrial banks. The number of depositors was much larger for state banks than for national banks. While the former had 553,770 commercial accounts and 1,579,439 savings accounts, the latter had a total of just over 500,000 depositors. Bank accounts had also increased. Whereas the average savings account in state banks in 1910 had been $273, it was $332 in 1920. Commercial deposits showed a more marked gain. In 1910, the average was $447 for state banks and $423 in national banks, while in 1920 the average for state banks was $671, and for national banks it was $1,214.[7]

Following the opening of the Federal Reserve Branch, no further banking institutions were established in Detroit until 1921; in that

* After January 1, 1954, the territory of the Detroit Branch was expanded to include the entire Lower Peninsula of Michigan. From the beginning, the Upper Peninsula was in the territory of the Federal Reserve Bank of Minneapolis.[8]

year, two new state banks opened their doors. The Continental Bank of Detroit commenced business in January 1921. Organized in the fall of the previous year, it began operations with a paid-in capital of $700,000. On May 25, 1925, the affairs of the Continental Bank were taken over by the Central Savings Bank of Detroit. The second bank to open in 1921 was the Commercial State Savings Bank, which commenced business in August with an authorized paid-in capital stock of $1,000,000. On June 27, 1927, the Commonwealth Federal Savings Bank of Detroit absorbed the Commercial State Savings Bank under the name of Commonwealth Commercial State Bank.

From 1923 to 1925, four new trust companies were chartered in the city. The Fidelity Trust Company opened its doors on September 10, 1923, with capital stock amounting to $500,000. The Standard Trust Company, which had been organized in March 1924, commenced business on January 26, 1925. In May 1925, the United States Trust Company began business and, like the Standard Trust Company, had an authorized capitalization of $300,000. Although the Guardian Trust Company was organized in December 1924, with a capitalization of one million dollars, the company did not actually begin business until July of the following year.

Additional bank openings and consolidations occurred in 1927. The Guardian Detroit Bank was organized in April as an affiliate company of the Guardian Trust Company with a capitalization of five million dollars and a surplus in excess of three million dollars. In June of 1927, the Guaranty State Bank was organized by interests connected with the Guaranty Trust Company. Capitalization was at two million dollars with a surplus of just over one million dollars. This bank opened for business in offices in the Guaranty Trust Building on Woodward Avenue at Congress.

On March 21, 1927, the Griswold National Bank of Detroit and the First State Bank of Detroit consolidated under the title of Griswold-First State Bank. The Griswold National Bank had originally been chartered on November 11, 1925. At the time of its consolidation, the new bank's resources stood at better than $50,000,000. Offices of the Griswold-First State were located in the Union Trust Building [the present day Guardian Building].

During this period three new industrial banks were opened in the city. On the last day of 1926, the Michigan Industrial Bank commenced operations. Organized in September 1926 with a capitalization of $200,000, it opened for business in offices at 161 West

157

Congress between Griswold and Shelby streets. The city's third and fourth industrial banks were opened in 1928, the City Industrial Bank in January, and the Metropolitan Industrial Bank in September. The City Industrial Bank opened its doors at 1248 Washington Boulevard with a capital stock of $125,000. The Metropolitan Industrial Bank was located at 134 Lafayette Boulevard and began its operations with a capitalization of $100,000. Also in 1928, the Detroit Trust Company and the Security Trust Company began plans for a merger under the name of the Detroit and Security Trust Company. Not until August of the following year, however, was the consolidation completed. In October 1930, the Detroit and Security Trust Company changed its name to Detroit Trust Company.

In addition to these developments, the year 1928 marked the largest bank merger in the history of the state up to that time. On February 15, 1928, the People's State Bank of Detroit and the Wayne County & Home Savings Bank consolidated to become the People's Wayne County Bank. This new bank had resources of $313,117,236, with savings deposits of $163,011,870, and commercial deposits of $86,315,500. Branches of the two banks were, of course, also merged giving the People's Wayne County Bank a branch system of 92 offices resulting in its being Detroit's largest banking institution. In comparison, the city's second largest state bank was the Dime Savings Bank with 24 branches and resources of $69,797,697. The third largest state bank was the Peninsular State Bank with 30 branches and resources of $55,096,682. The Detroit Savings Bank ranked sixth with 26 branch offices and resources totaling $50,306,311. The city's largest national bank, the First National, had resources totaling $182,886,437.

In 1929 there were three important banking mergers in the city. On February 28, the Griswold-First State Bank consolidated with the National Bank of Commerce of Detroit under the latter's name. On May 27, the Merchant's National Bank was merged with the Dime Savings Bank. Then, on the following day, the Dime Savings Bank changed its name and became the Bank of Michigan. On December 27, the Central Trust Company joined with the Equitable Trust Company and formed the Equitable and Central Trust Company. The Equitable Trust Company had been established on November 16, 1926. The Central Trust Company had been organized in December 1928, and commenced business on January 23, 1929 with a capitalization of one million dollars. Shortly after the Central Trust Company opened, it absorbed the American Trust Company. On January 20,

1932, the Equitable and Central Trust Company was renamed the Equitable Trust Company.

It was also in 1929 that the state legislature enacted a completely new banking law, superseding the General Banking Law of 1888 and all the amendments to that law.[9] One important provision of the new law prescribed the method by which banks might merge or consolidate. It provided for the establishment of trust departments by banks and enlarged the limit of investment in commercial paper on personal securities. This law set the stage for the formation of two giant holding companies by Detroit bankers: the Guardian Detroit Union Group, Incorporated, and the Detroit Bankers Company. Through an exchange of stock, the Guardian Group acquired control of nine large banks and trust companies in the Detroit area and those of an equal number of leading banks outstate. It owned about 40 percent of the stock of 6 other banks and secured a direct or indirect control over 5 other financial institutions. The Bankers Group secured control of 11 banks by stock exchange and obtained a minority interest in a number of others.

Both the Guardian Group and the Bankers Group were founded on the assumption that banking resources and profits would continue to increase. The stock market crash was considered to be an unfortunate but temporary setback. The downward trends of the major economic indexes in early 1930 did not materially alter the convictions of the directors of these two groups. They were certain that "prosperity was just around the corner" and that the Detroit banks could withstand any temporary pressures.[10] In this assessment, they were to be proven very wrong.

"SHOUT IT FROM THE HOUSETOPS"

Group banking, as a form of multiple banking, had come to be used more extensively than ever before during the 1929 to 1932 period. Bankers throughout the country rushed to take advantage of the new system. In Michigan, the Guardian Detroit Union Group, Incorporated, and the Detroit Bankers Company, the two competing groups which almost completely dominated the banking structure of metropolitan Detroit, were incorporated within less than 30 days of each other.

The Guardian Detroit Union Group, was formed through the

159

merger of two earlier group systems. The first of these, the pioneer group banking operation in Michigan, was established May 17, 1928, through the Union Commerce Investment Company, later known as the Union Commerce Corporation. The Union Commerce Investment Company was incorporated under the laws of the state of Delaware on May 17, 1928, as a holding company, and acquired the stock of the Union Trust Company which had as subsidiaries the Union Title and Guaranty Company and the Union Building Company, firms organized to enable the Union Trust Company to acquire real estate and build its own office building. Also the Union Commerce Investment Company acquired the stock of the Union Company, a company organized to take over the business and profits obtained by the Union Trust Company in the form of commissions for loans brought about as agents for insurance companies. The Union Commerce Investment Company also acquired a controlling or a strong minority interest in the Michigan Industrial Bank of Detroit and 15 other financial institutions in the city and in outstate Michigan.

At the time of incorporation in 1928, the capitalization of the Union Commerce Investment Company was five million dollars. This had to be increased several times to take care of new acquisitions, and then prior to the merger with the Guardian Detroit Group, Incorporated, the name of the company was changed to the Union Commerce Corporation.

The Guardian Detroit Group, Incorporated, was formed as a holding company on May 9, 1929. The major part of the stock was issued immediately to acquire the stock of the Guardian Detroit Bank. By acquiring the Guardian Detroit Bank, the Guardian Detroit Group immediately gained control over three financial institutions since the Guardian Detroit Bank had two affiliates—the Guardian Detroit Company and the Guardian Detroit Trust Company.

The Guardian Detroit Bank had been organized in April 1927, to meet a banking need which had arisen as a result of the tremendous growth in the automobile industry and the following rapid rise in population in Detroit and the Detroit area. Organized specifically to take over ownership of the Guardian Detroit Bank and its affiliates and to operate as a group, the Guardian Detroit Group then set out to acquire new banks, both in and out of Detroit, in order to expand its operations. In the five months after its birth in May 1929, the Guardian Detroit Group acquired the Bank of Detroit and six other financial institutions in Highland Park, Dearborn, Jackson, and Port Huron.

Capitalization of the Guardian Detroit Group was originally $7,500,000; but from time to time this was increased, finally reaching $50,000,000. It was at this time that the name was changed to Guardian Detroit Union Group, Incorporated, in preparation for the merger with the Union Commerce Corporation. These two major banking groups merged on December 16, 1929 through an exchange of shares of stocks of the two corporations, and the resulting group became known as the Guardian Detroit Union Group, Incorporated. This group then either controlled or had a strong minority interest in 32 separate financial institutions, most of which were either in the city of Detroit or in the metropolitan area.[11]

The Detroit Bankers Company was incorporated under the laws of Michigan on January 8, 1930, as a holding company. Though this date was some three months after the stock market crash, negotiations had been under way for some time. Final plans were completed on October 9, 1929, when the articles of association were signed by the 12 incorporators. The guiding light in the early days of the corporation was Julius H. Haass, who became the first president of the group. Public knowledge about the group first came on October 5, 1929, when the stockholders of five of Detroit's largest banks were notified that during the previous month, the boards of directors of these banks had passed resolutions recommending that the stockholders exchange their shares for shares of the projected Detroit Bankers Company.

John Ballantyne, who became president of the Detroit Bankers Company upon the death of Julius Haass, stated that the company was primarily organized to obtain control of the five banking institutions with their many branches in the city of Detroit. These banks were the People's Wayne County Bank, the First National Bank-Detroit, the Detroit Trust Company, the Bank of Michigan, and the Peninsular State Bank.

In a letter to the stockholders of each of the banks to be brought into the Detroit Bankers Company, the drafters attempted to persuade them to become a part of the Detroit Bankers Company. The stockholders of the five banks were told that dividends in the amount of 17 percent annually would be paid on the common stock of the new company each quarter. They were also told that the Detroit Bankers Company would have, at the time of the exchange of stock, combined capital, surplus, and undivided profits of about $90,000,000, and $725,000,000 in resources, representing 60 percent of the total banking resources in Detroit, with 192 branches and serving approximately 900,000 depositors and clients. The plan of the group company was to carry on the business of the individual institutions as they were.

The authorized capital of the Detroit Bankers Company was just in excess of $50,000,000. Shortly after the final act of incorporation in early January 1930, the Detroit Bankers Company, through the exchange of stock proposed the previous October, acquired almost all the common stock of the five above mentioned banking institutions. Then, after the company began its operation, additional unit banks and non-banking companies were acquired.[12]

Several factors were important in prompting the consolidation movement in Detroit. Banking institutions then in existence were unable to furnish adequate services to the unique industrial development in the city. The automobile had produced a few giants of industry, and, in turn, giant banking institutions were required to handle their active commercial accounts and loan requirements. Secondly, there were some banking institutions which wished to extend their operations throughout the city. They could do this by consolidating with other banks already maintaining branches. This cause was probably dominant in three of the more important consolidations of the period: the absorption on January 10, 1928 by the First National Bank of the Central Savings Bank which operated 29 branches and was engaged mainly in a savings business; the absorption on February 28, 1929, by the National Bank of Commerce of the Griswold-First State Bank which operated 17 branches and also had a large savings department; and the merger on June 30, 1930, of the Bank of Detroit with the Guardian Detroit Bank. The latter was almost completely a commercial bank and had no branches, while the Bank of Detroit operated 19 branches and had developed a large savings business. Thirdly, once the consolidation and group movement was underway, there was a certain pressure to keep pace with the competing group.[13] This is apparent from the fact that the Guardian Group and the Bankers Group started operations within a few weeks of each other and within a year had developed to the point where the two groups controlled more than 87 percent of the total banking resources of Detroit. To be added to these more specific causes of the movement toward the group system were the desire to lessen competition, and the desire for greater profits and power.

It was also anticipated that the formation of the Guardian Detroit Union Group and the Detroit Bankers Company would stabilize the city's banking situation.[14] Unfortunately this did not occur. As the depression deepened, the condition of the banks in Detroit and in the rest of the state became very serious. In Michigan from December 1929 to December 1932, as a result of failures and mergers, the number of banks was reduced by about 25 percent, and deposits declined 32 percent.[15] During this period nearly two hundred banks failed.* Not only were unprecedented numbers of people in Detroit and Michigan out of work, but the meager savings that some had managed to hold onto were jeopardized by this wave of bank failures.

The withdrawal of funds by depositors to meet current needs or because of doubts regarding the soundness of financial institutions caused many of the banks that remained opened to be hard-pressed. These banks had their funds invested in mortgages on buildings—investments that may have seemed perfectly safe a few years before. During the depression, the value of real estate plunged to such a low point that the mortgages in many instances far exceeded the amount for which the property could be sold. To tide them over, the banks secured loans from the newly formed Reconstruction Finance Corporation. Unfortunately, in July of 1932, Congress provided that all such loans be made public. The result was that when a bank borrowed from the RFC, depositors became wary and withdrew their money even faster, placing their cash in safety deposit boxes or in the United States Postal Savings system.

In Detroit the bank failures began with the closing of the Standard Trust Company in January 1930. This was followed by the failure of the Michigan State Bank of Detroit on April 27, 1931; the Metropolitan Trust Company (which had first opened in Highland Park in 1925 and moved to Detroit in 1929) on June 18, 1931; the Guaranty Trust Company of Detroit on July 1, 1931; the Fidelity Bank and Trust Company on October 7, 1931; and the Northwestern State Bank (which had opened in 1915) on August 3, 1932. When the Northwestern State Bank closed, it was taken over by the state banking commission and was only able to make an immediate distribution of 40 percent of its deposits.

* Throughout the United States, over 5,700 banks had failed between 1921 and 1929. During 1930–32, an additional 5,100 became insolvent.[16]

163

On March 31, 1931, a major setback occurred when Detroit's third largest state bank, the American State Bank of Detroit, with 27 branches and resources of more than $54,000,000, closed its doors. When the books showed only seven million dollars cash on hand and in other banks to meet immediate liabilities exceeding $26,000,000, the bank had little choice but to liquidate. Fortunately for the bank's customers, deposits were guaranteed by Detroit Clearing House Association members and the bank was then absorbed by the People's Wayne County Bank. The Detroit Savings Bank, as a member of the Detroit Clearing House Association, participated by subscribing to 3.4 percent of the guaranty.[17]

The facts concerning the general state of banking in the city and the condition of the local banks undoubtedly were grim enough to impair the confidence of Detroit depositors. But far more than the bare statistics were reported as the Detroit newspapers gave considerable space to the city's banking problems.

In addition to the newspaper coverage, Detroiters were exposed to the zealous criticism of Father Charles E. Coughlin. In 1932 this Roman Catholic priest was receiving considerable local and national publicity from his extremely violent denunciations of the banking system. His speeches, many delivered over the radio, were highly emotional and often contained comments adverse to both the monetary system and Detroit bankers. Excerpts from his pronouncements indicate the tone of Father Coughlin's comments:

> Now for the creation of the Federal Reserve Bank [sic]—now for the second attempt to establish the bankers' bank—the masterpiece of international bankers—the high treason of high finance . . .
> Moreover, the Federal Reserve Bank can conscript 3% of time deposits and from 7 to 10 and 13% of demand deposits of all national banks. In other words part of your life's earnings, of your deposits, of your savings go to this profit making, private corporation.[18]

One effect of his references to Detroit bankers as "criminal banksters" and his condemnation of their practices was a discernible increase over the usual rate of deposit withdrawals on days immediately following his speeches. The First National Bank estimated that it lost over one million dollars of deposits per week as the result of Father Coughlin's speeches.[19] Thus Detroiters were confronted, in many instances, with seriously adverse opinions, and half-truths when being informed about the condition of the city's banks.

Finally, in early 1933, the banking situation in Detroit reached crisis proportions. Apparently by coincidence, the two national banks of the two group systems, the Guardian Union National Bank of Commerce and the First National Bank-Detroit, were examined by federal bank examiners on January 27 and 28, 1933. At the conclusion, in letters to the directors, each of the banks was declared to be solvent.[20]

During the first days of February, however, officials of the RFC were informed that Detroit was in precarious circumstances because of serious trouble at the Union Guardian Trust Company. The urgent demand was for ready cash. Since there was some rumor that the company could not realize on its assets, the officials of the Union Guardian Trust Company knew that it must be prepared to pay off all deposits at 100 cents on the dollar. Because the Union Guardian Trust Company had deposits of approximately $20,000,000 and held not more than $6,000,000 in liquid assets, it was absolutely necessary that outside help be obtained. The Guardian Group decided to ask for a loan large enough to sustain the Union Guardian Trust Company in its present difficulty and to put the whole group on a reasonably sound basis. Therefore, a $50,000,000 RFC loan was requested. This amount, added to a loan made in 1932, would have totaled $65,000,000 loaned to the entire Guardian Group.

When the RFC examiners were unable to find enough collateral to justify the new loan, the RFC promised to provide a part of the amount ($37,000,000) if the large depositors would guarantee the remainder. Edsel Ford was a director of both the Union Guardian Trust Company and of the Guardian Group, and the Ford Motor Company had large deposits in the Guardian banks and in the First National Bank. Officers of General Motors and Chrysler, also large depositors, agreed to contribute to a local fund if Henry Ford would do the same. Always leary of banks, the motor tycoon not only refused, but at one point even threatened to withdraw all of his deposits.[21]

By Thursday, February 9, the situation had become so crucial that President Hoover called Senators Couzens and Vandenberg of Michigan, Secretary of the Treasury Mills, and Charles Miller, president of the RFC, to the White House for a conference. James Couzens was the senior senator from Michigan and a member of the Senate Committee on Banking and Currency. Unfortunately he came to the meeting without a clear understanding of what it was about. He mistakenly gained the impression that the RFC was ready to grant an excessive loan to the Detroit banks based on insufficient security, whereas the intention of the officers and President Hoover was just the opposite. Still confused, Couzens left the meeting, declaring that if such a monstrous thing was done, he would "shout it from the housetops." That statement, in the opinion of Couzen's defenders, gave rise to the legend, long persistent, that it was he who wrecked the Michigan banks by blocking RFC relief.[22]

It has been pointed out several times by authoritive sources that James Couzens and Henry Ford had been antagonistic toward each other for several years. Senator Couzens, who had made a fortune with the Ford Motor Company, had sold his holdings after several disagreements with Mr. Ford. At the time of the banking crisis both men were in positions to determine the destiny of banking in Detroit—Couzens because of his influential position in the Senate, Ford because of his large deposits in the city's two major banks. A substantial withdrawal by Ford from either bank could have forced a closure. Whether the personal animosity between Henry Ford and James Couzens was a significant factor in the Detroit banking crisis has been debated for many years. Whether or not either was truly at fault, the newspapers carried stories of their feud which only helped to undermine the confidence among depositors of the city's banking system.

On Friday, February 10, Secretary of Commerce Roy D. Chapin and Assistant Secretary of the Treasury Arthur Ballantine came to Detroit to attempt to keep the Union Guardian Trust Company and others of the Guardian Group open until Saturday noon. Sunday was Lincoln's Birthday, and thus Monday, the 13th of February, was a regular banking holiday. There would then be two and one-half days of closed bank time in which to find a solution to the problems of the Detroit banks.

From Friday until Sunday, Chapin and Ballantine exerted every influence to raise new capital in Detroit to save the situation. They had little success because of the sentiment aroused by rumors about the Union Guardian Trust Company and by the daily statements of Senator Couzens that the banks of Detroit were hopelessly insolvent. By Sunday the situation had become so bad that bankers, industrialists, and community leaders gathered to discuss the crises. This was not just a meeting of Detroit bankers but of financial men from all over the country. For in addition to representatives from all the Detroit Clearing House Association member banks (which included Walter L. Dunham, president of the Detroit Savings Bank; Robert O. Lord, president of the Guardian National Bank of Commerce; Ernest Kanzler, chairman of the board of the same bank; Clifford Longley, president of the Union Guardian Trust Company), also in attendance were Roy D. Chapin, secretary of commerce; Arthur A. Ballantine, assistant secretary of the treasury; John K. McKee, representing the RFC; B. K. Patterson, vice-president of the Guardian Detroit Union Group, Incorporated; Alfred P. Leyburn, chief examiner of the Seventh Federal Reserve District; and Malcolm C. Taylor, deputy commissioner of banking for the state of Michigan.[23]

The meetings continued until late Monday evening. No solution for the problem of meeting the immediate needs of the Union Guardian Trust Company could be found, and it was decided that the Union Guardian could not open for business on Tuesday morning. Fearing that as soon as word of its failure was spread about there would be runs on other banks which would also have to close, drastic measures were advocated. Governor William A. Comstock was called to the meeting from Lansing and asked to issue a bank holiday proclamation, closing all banks in the state effective February 14. He agreed and the proclamation was written out at the Detroit Club during the night of the 13th.[24] Shortly after midnight, Comstock and his press secretary walked around the corner to the offices of the *Detroit Free Press* and dictated the following public announcement:

Whereas in view of the acute financial emergency now existing in the city of Detroit and throughout the state of Michigan, I deem it necessary in the public interest and for the preservation of the public peace, health and safety, and for the equal safeguarding without preference of the rights of all depositors in the banks and trust companies of this state and at the request of the Michigan Bankers Association and the Detroit Clearing House and after consultation with the banking authorities, both national and state, representatives of the United States Treasury Department, the Banking Department of the State of Michigan, the Federal Reserve Bank, the Reconstruction Finance Corporation, and with the United States Department of Commerce, I hereby proclaim the days from Tuesday, February 14, 1933, to Tuesday, February 21, 1933, both dates inclusive, to be public holidays during which time all banks, trust companies, and other financial institutions conducting a banking or trust business within the state of Michigan shall not be opened for the transaction of banking or trust business, the same to be recognized, classed and treated, and have the same effect in the respect to such banks, trust companies, and other financial institutions as other legal holidays under the laws of the state, provided that it shall not affect the making or execution of agreements or instruments in writing or interfere with judicial proceedings.

Dated this Fourteenth day of February, 1933, 1:32 A.M.

William A. Comstock
Signed
Governor of the State of Michigan[25]

A NATIONAL HOLIDAY

Detroit was in a state of shock and disbelief on the morning of Tuesday, February 14, 1933. People who did business by check found they had no funds available. Employers were unable to meet their payrolls and merchants could not pay their bills. Business at every level was suddenly paralyzed. The only cash was what people had in their pockets or cash registers, or in safety deposit boxes where, admittedly, a lot was being hoarded. The bad news, however, was taken quietly. Many people had the idea that the Federal Reserve System made it impossible for banks to go broke, and there was widespread confidence that in due course all the banks would reopen. Unfortunately the following weeks were to prove this belief to be anything but true.

On Wednesday morning, the *Detroit Free Press* published a second statement by Governor Comstock, which allowed depositors in Michigan banks to withdraw up to five percent of their balances beginning the following day. The paper reported that more than $26,000,000 would be available for depositors from Detroit banks. Withdrawals were to be made by counter receipts, and all payments were to be in cash. That night $40,000,000 in currency was shipped into Detroit from New York and Chicago.[26]

There was no great rush to withdraw funds on Thursday morning. In fact only $4,610,000 of the available $26,117,000 was taken out. This amounted to only 17½ percent of the usable amount, less than would be expected during a routine day's business.[27] The city's banks reported the following withdrawals:

	Available	Withdrawal
1. First National	$18,000,000	$2,995,000
2. Guardian National	5,200,000	1,200,000
3. Detroit Savings	1,500,000	219,000
4. Commonwealth-Commercial	600,000	100,000
5. United Savings	567,000	63,000
6. Industrial Morris Plan	250,000	33,000

Safety deposit vaults were opened as usual on Thursday and remained open during regular banking hours. The Detroit Stock Exchange was ordered to remain closed, and all brokerage houses were prohibited from trading in the stocks of any banks. Life insurance companies announced that checks drawn on Detroit banks would be accepted as conditional payment of premiums due.

Withdrawals under the five percent limitation continued for the remainder of the week but at a slow pace. At the Detroit Savings Bank, for example, only $55,500 was withdrawn on Friday and the following day customers were no more numerous than on a typical Saturday.[28]

While these adjustments were taking place during the week, officials were considering the merits of various reopening proposals. President Hoover proposed a clearing house scrip plan under which the Detroit Clearing House Association would issue scrip to be available on a *pro rata* basis to meet depositors' claims. Detroit bankers were skeptical of using scrip. They had misgivings that the bank assets supporting the issue would be insufficient to justify a *pro rata* distribution large enough to accommodate Detroit's needs.

The scrip plan was also opposed by the Federal Reserve Board. They favored a plan (formulated by James Broderick, New York commissioner of banking) under which the banks would act, in effect, as their own receivers. The banks would reopen with a *pro rata* credit to each deposit account equal to its share of good assets. The major disadvantage of the Broderick Plan was that a partial payment of depositors' claims would constitute an act of technical insolvency. For banks to reopen under this arrangement, special enabling legislation would be required on both state and national levels. President Hoover was advised that national legislation could not be passed without the risk of a general panic.[29]

In light of this warning and the hesitancy to issue scrip, conferences to discuss the problems of reopening were continued. Over the next several days many suggestions for reopening were made, but no direct action was taken and confusion increased. Many outstate banks in the Lower Peninsula refused to allow the five percent withdrawals, claiming that to reopen under those conditions would mean failure. Under the governor's statement, the outstate banks would have been able to draw only five percent of their reserves and other balances deposited in Detroit banks. They contended that to meet the demands for five percent of their own deposit liabilities would be impossible unless they could draw more freely on their own reserves. On the other hand, banks in the Upper Peninsula of Michigan had entirely ignored the bank holiday

169

proclamation. Basing their position on the fact that they were in the Ninth (Minneapolis) District of the Federal Reserve System, they maintained normal banking operations.[30]

On Monday, February 20, Senator Couzens introduced a resolution on the floor of the Senate to enable the controller of the currency to place all national banks under the same restrictions as their respective states might prescribe for local financial institutions.[31] In Michigan, Governor Comstock obtained retroactive legislative approval of his holiday proclamation and began preparing legislation which, assuming passage of the Couzens resolution, would permit the reopening of Michigan banks.

The next day Governor Comstock extended the holiday, although the restrictions were less severe. To Detroit bankers, the provisions of the new declaration seemed vague and ambiguous, and they were uncertain as to how the restrictions should be interpreted and applied. As a result, the Detroit Clearing House Association announced that its member banks would continue the five percent limit rather than risk possible legal repercussions from the new directives.[32]

On Wednesday, Washington's Birthday, a new RFC proposal was made. It involved a loan of $100,000,000 to the First National Bank and $35,000,000 to the Guardian National Bank to permit those institutions to organize new banks. However, following an RFC examination of the collateral offered to cover the loans, it was discovered that the collateral would support only a $78,000,000 loan—$54,000,000 to the First National Bank and $24,000,000 to the Guardian National Bank.[33]

Following the RFC examination, Henry and Edsel Ford announced that they were prepared to match the $8,250,000 necessary to open the two new banks. Reaction in Detroit was jubilant. Newspaper headlines read "Bank with Hank," and editorials described the offer as "public spirited and generous." The names of the two new banks were to be the People's National Bank (the old First National), and the Manufacturers National Bank (the old Guardian National).[34]

Since the issuance of Comstock's proclamation, the directors and senior officers of the Detroit Savings Bank had been meeting daily in an effort to develop a plan that would allow their bank to reopen on a full-time basis. During the week of February 20, Director Sidney T. Miller, Jr., made several trips to Lansing in an attempt to convince state officials that the Detroit Savings Bank was sound, and that it should be allowed to reopen. In this attempt, Miller was successful and the state banking commissioner gave the Detroit Savings Bank permission to reopen effective Monday, February 27. As can be imagined the bank was extremely busy as a torrent of business poured in—the lobby of the main office was jammed to capacity with customers. Amazingly enough, the majority of these customers were depositing money rather than withdrawing from their accounts. In addition there were many who waited patiently in line for hours to open new accounts. A mountain of cash and checks was stuffed in boxes, bags, trays, drawers, even waste paper baskets, or just piled on the floor, overflowing the tellers' cages. In an effort to keep up with the paper work, the staff worked late into the night tabulating all the business transacted during the day.[35]

Questioned as to his reaction to the day President Dunham told a newspaper reporter:

> I'm delighted at the way in which things worked out and our board of directors expressed the same feeling after their meeting this noon.
> I find many of our customers needed the banking facilities we are now offering them and that we have solved many of their problems by our action. We believe we will be able to be of even greater service as the days go on.[36]

The following day business was even heavier as "money came in by the bucketful," and on each day for the remainder of the week, depsoits exceeded withdrawals in savings accounts by tens-of-thou-sands-of-dollars.[37] The faith that Sidney T. Miller, Jr., and the other directors had in the Detroit Savings Bank was well-founded. During the week of February 27, 1933, the Detroit Savings Bank was the only financial institution in the city able to provide full banking services to the citizens of Detroit.

Even though the Detroit Savings Bank was able to reopen, the city's banking situation took a turn for the worse as events made it clear that the Ford plan to open the two new banks would not be carried out. This became apparent on the evening of Tuesday, February 28, when the directors of the First National met and came to the general conclusion that it would be inadvisable to go ahead with the plan. Their reasoning was based on several factors. First, the Michigan Clearing House Association, representing outstate banks, expressed the fear that reserve deposits would not be given prefer-ence. Second, the directors indicated that they were reacting to the protests of depositors, and other customers who were against the

171

plan. Thirdly, the directors concluded that Ford would completely dominate the new banks and that it was very likely that many bankers would lose their positions. Lastly, a major problem arose when word was received that a $20,000,000 loan to the First National Bank would not be renewed. This loan, extended by the Central Hanover Bank in New York, had been secured by assets which were now impounded as a result of the Michigan holiday proclamation. Every proposal for the resumption of banking in Detroit had automatically included the renewal of this loan as part of the bank's resources.[38]

In the two weeks following the governor's proclamation, no workable solution had been developed and Detroit's situation remained serious. The RFC and other governmental agencies could do no more under existing law. The one private plan for reopening had failed.

On February 28, Governor Comstock extended the banking holiday again, this time for four days until March 4.[39] Following the original proclamation there had been hope in neighboring states that the problems of the Michigan banking system could be solved. When the holiday passed and the banks still did not open, other states were forced to proclaim state-wide holidays to protect their depositors and the whole financial system.

Saturday, March 4, found most of the banks throughout the country closed by gubernatorial proclamation or by their own choice. March 4 also marked the inauguration of Franklin D. Roosevelt, and during the evening of the following day the new president issued an order declaring a national bank holiday.[40]

Roosevelt's proclamation was originally to be in effect for four days. Then on March 9, the holiday was extended indefinitely.[41] That same day, Congress enacted an emergency banking law, under which the president announced, two days later, the reopening of banks in the 12 Federal Reserve cities beginning Monday, March 13. On Tuesday the banks in the more than 250 cities with clearing house associations were to be allowed to reopen, and on the following day all other banks which were members of the Federal Reserve system were to be allowed to open. Only those banks which the federal examiners found 100 percent solvent, however, were to be allowed to reopen under this timetable. The banks were to open under a license system, and without this federal license no bank could reopen for business. For those banks which were not found to be sound, a system of conservators was set up to take charge in the interest of their depositors.[42]

Federal legislation left to the states the matter of setting up conditions under which state banks, not members of the Federal Reserve System, might reopen. In Lansing, the new banking legislation resulted in a legislative snarl between the house and the senate. Finally on March 21, the new state banking bill became law with the signature of Governor Comstock.[43] It was amended three times in the next four months. The law permitted the banking commissioner to take over banks and manage them as conservator and either to continue them in limited operation or close them under receiverships. Solvent banks were to be permitted to resume full operation.

On Tuesday, March 14, the Detroit Savings Bank, the United Savings Bank, the Industrial Morris Plan Bank, and the Leonard Thrift Bank reopened. The Commonwealth-Commercial State Bank also opened but on a limited basis; the bank continued to limit savings withdrawals to five percent. Not until Thursday, March 16, did the Commonwealth-Commercial State Bank resume full operations. Thus, because the United Savings Bank had no commercial department, and the Industrial Morris Plan Bank and the Leonard Thrift Bank were both industrial banks, the Detroit Savings Bank was the only full service commercial bank in operation in Detroit for the first two days following the reopening of the city's banks.[44]

While the city's five independent banks were allowed to reopen, Detroit's two national banks could not be certified as sound and were ordered closed. Conservators were appointed on March 13, and the First National Bank-Detroit and the Guardian National Bank of Commerce, with 800,000 depositors, were compelled to liquidate.* The two large holding companies, of which these two banks were parts, were also liquidated. Fortunately, the assets of member institutions had not been merged, so a few of the sound organizations in the groups, such as the Detroit Trust Company, were able to survive.

On March 31, 1933, Circuit Judge Adolph F. Marschner appointed former Michigan governor Alex J. Groesbeck receiver for the Guardian Detroit Union Group, and named former Judge William Connolly as receiver for the Detroit Bankers Company. In each case, Judge Marschner selected a man who had the complete confidence of the

---

* Paul C. Keyes was appointed conservator for the First National while B. C. Schram was appointed conservator for the Guardian National.[45]

community. He referred to Groesbeck at the time as "one of the few men in Michigan able and responsible enough for such a position of trust." [46] The fact that these men took control went far in allaying public fear as well as helping to restore confidence in a situation from which confidence had all but vanished.

Following the appointments of Groesbeck and Connolly, machinery was set in motion to collect liability assessments from the stockholders of the two holding companies. A pay-off plan for depositors in both the Guardian National and the First National was inaugurated which involved the purchase of claims of small depositors by the large depositors.* About 116,000 depositors in the Guardian National, with individual balances of $1,000 or less, were paid off in full; a total of 600,000 depositors of the First National, with accounts of $300 or less also were paid in full. [47]

Not until 1949 could the banking commissioner announce that the process of liquidation of state banks and trust companies, closed during the depression, was complete. A total of 436 state banks and trust companies, having deposits of $481,229,914 were closed by Governor Comstock's proclamation of February 14, 1933. Of these, 207—slightly less than one-half—were permitted to reopen following the holiday. Of the remainder, 170 were authorized to reorganize and 59 were placed in receivership. In the institutions which were reorganized, the total payments to depositors totaled 93.8 percent of the amount on deposit at the time of reorganization. Depositors of the 59 institutions which were placed in receivership ultimately regained 85.4 percent of the $56,000,000 on deposit at the time the banks were closed. Of the total amount on deposit in all the state banking institutions at the time of the bank holiday, 96.11 percent was eventually returned to depositors. [48]

To replace the First National Bank-Detroit and the Guardian National Bank of Commerce, two new national banks were organized. The National Bank of Detroit was chartered March 21, 1933, and opened for business on March 24. The Manufacturers National Bank of Detroit was chartered July 28, 1933, and commenced operations on August 15. The RFC invested $12,500,000 in preferred stock for the National Bank of Detroit, while the General Motors Corporation underwrote a matching $12,500,000 of common stock. [49] The more

* This plan was developed and implemented by Jesse H. Jones, an RFC director, and Edward D. Stair, chairman of the Bankers Group and a former director of the Detroit Savings Bank. [50]

liquid assets of the two defunct banks and the RFC loans to the conservators of these latter institutions on their remaining assets, were placed on deposit with the National Bank of Detroit, making possible a 30 percent distribution to depositors.*

General Motors entered the banking field reluctantly, fearing that its actions might be misinterpreted by the public. Accordingly, the company offered to sell any or all of its 500,000 shares of bank stock at the original subscription price of $25.00 per share. Only 50,000 shares were purchased—20,000 by the Chrysler Corporation—by the time the initial offering was completed.[51]

Detroit was able to organize its other new national bank as a result of the efforts of Henry and Edsel Ford. The Manufacturers National Bank acquired the deposits and liabilities and received cash and qualifying assets of the Highland Park State Bank, the Dearborn State Bank, and the Guardian Bank of Dearborn on August 13, 1933. Later the bank absorbed the People's Wayne County Bank of Highland Park, and the People's Wayne County Bank of Dearborn. Organized entirely without governmental assistance, the Fords subscribed the original capital of three million dollars for the new bank.[52]

In an attempt to make another bank holiday all but impossible, the Federal Deposit Insurance Corporation was established by Congress on June 16, 1933. The system became effective January 1, 1934, and guaranteed the safety of deposits in Federal Reserve banks up to $2500. Although the provisions were to be in force for only one year, they were extended twice, and the amount of coverage was raised to $5,000. The Banking Act of 1935 altered the original plan but left coverage at $5,000 until it was raised again by the Federal Deposit Insurance Act of September 21, 1950. On that date, the coverage for each individual account was increased to $10,000, which was extended on September 1, 1967 to $15,000, and then again on April 30, 1970 to $20,000.

The FDIC is an independent agency of the federal government and is administered by a three-man board of directors appointed by the president and approved by the Senate. The comptroller of the currency, by virtue of his office, is automatically one of the directors. Operating funds are not appropriated; they come from assessments levied upon insured banks, based upon their deposit structures and from investments. All national banks must be members of the FDIC.

* The RFC lent $214,000,000 and $16,000,000, respectively, to the conservators of the First National Bank and the Guardian National Bank.[53]

175

State banks have the option of membership. While the coverage is available to commercial banks, mutual savings banks, and industrial banks, it is not available to savings and loan associations or credit unions.

Even though the city's banks were open once again, there were still some troubled times ahead for the citizens of Detroit. Because of the depression, the city was faced with a massive loss of funds. At that time, the principal source of municipal revenue was the general property tax. Lacking money, people were unable to pay their taxes, and city revenues dried up. The situation continued to worsen until April 1933, when the city found its treasury empty. In order to meet its payroll the city issued eight million dollars in scrip to pay off municipal employees.[54] Public employees were relatively fortunate. Most of them kept their jobs, and few knew the necessity of applying for public relief as did many of their fellow-Detroiters.

As spring turned into summer, Detroit's banking and money situation began to ease. With the opening of the Manufacturers National Bank in August, the city's banking community numbered ten members: the Detroit Savings Bank, Commonwealth-Commercial State Bank, United Savings Bank, Industrial Morris Plan Bank, Merchants Bank of Detroit (name changed from Leonard Thrift Bank, July 24, 1933), Bankers Trust Company, Detroit Trust Company, Equitable Trust Company, National Bank of Detroit, and Manufacturers National Bank.[55]

Following the bank holiday, the Detroit Savings Bank experienced a tremendous growth of resources. In the fall of 1932, the bank's assets were reported at $42,597,358; by October, 1933, this figure had reached $61,278,725. Loans and discounts had increased slightly during this period, while mortgage investments had dropped slightly. The bank's major gain was in holdings of bonds and securities. This type of investment almost doubled, going from $11,868,608 to $20,968,077 in this one year. Savings deposits had also increased slightly rising from $24,362,617 to $26,299,161, but commercial deposits took an amazing jump, increasing from $6,579,072 in the fall of 1932 to $21,362,937 a year later.* [56]

On several occasions prior to the bank holiday, the Detroit Savings Bank had been criticized as being old fashioned, conserva-

* Though times were improving, the bank still carried many loans which were later to be charged off as: "bad debt; bankruptcy—no assets; elderly man—no worthwhile assets; estate hopelessly insolvent." [57]

tive, and lacking in ambition. The bank's board of directors and officers, however, had held firmly to their judgment as to the direction the bank should take. Following the crisis of February and March, the citizens of Detroit flocked to the bank by the thousands. Many of its former critics became depositors, and by the fall of 1933, the Detroit Savings Bank had grown to such a degree that it was now Michigan's leading state bank.[58]

The years 1930 to 1933 had brought many changes to the Detroit Savings Bank. Not the least of these were a number of changes on the bank's board of directors. The most important of these board changes occurred on October 31, 1933, when President Walter L. Dunham submitted his resignation to the board of directors at their regular Tuesday morning meeting. Dunham explained to the board that he felt he must retire because of his poor health. Actually, he had wanted to resign in late 1932, but because of the banking crisis had continued at his post and for the past month had been acting board chairman during the illness of John M. Dwyer. By the fall of 1933 Dunham felt the bank, having over 110,000 depositors, was in an excellent condition.[59]

Dunham's resignation came as a surprise to Detroit's financial and business community.[60] He had been president of the Michigan Bankers Association for the year 1928–29, and since the bank holiday, had served as president of the Detroit Clearing House Association.

President Dunham's resignation was accepted by the board with regret at their meeting of November 7, 1933. Although he wanted to resign immediately, Dunham agreed to continue as president until a successor was found. Also at the November 7 meeting, Vice-President Wilson Fleming was appointed to the newly created position of executive vice-president.

In recognition of Dunham's six years of service as president, the directors recorded a letter of appreciation in their minutes, which read in part:

> (We) wish to express our deep appreciation of the conscientious devotion you have given the affairs of the Bank at all times since your advent here, and most particularly your fine courageous work during the troublesome days last Winter and Spring which played such a large part in helping this Bank to render satisfactory service when it was temporarily called upon to do all of the banking business of the City of Detroit.[61]

On December 5, 1933, the board of directors elected young Joseph M. Dodge, a vice-president at the National Bank of Detroit, to succeed Dunham as the bank's seventh president. Since the Detroit

Savings Bank had just weathered the worst financial storm in the country's history, Dodge was accepting this position of leadership at a very critical time. The next several years were to be difficult ones, but during the period of Joseph M. Dodge's presidency, the Detroit Savings Bank was to emerge as one of the nation's leading financial institutions.

Mr. Dodge at the Helm

THE RECOVERY ROAD

Joseph Morrell Dodge was a local boy—born in Detroit in 1890. Following his graduation from Old Central High School, in 1908, he began his business career as a clerk for the Standard Accident Insurance Company. A few months later, he accepted a position with the Central Savings Bank, where he rose from bank messenger to general bookkeeper. In 1911 he left the Central Savings Bank to join the accounting firm of R. T. Hollis & Company, where he taught himself accounting.

In early 1912, Joseph Dodge got his first big break when he went to work for the Michigan State Banking Department as an assistant bank examiner. The next five years were productive ones for young Dodge, and by 1916 he had risen to the dual position of examiner-at-large for the state banking department and secretary of the Michigan Securities Commission. While a state examiner, he exposed a famous case of double-dealing by a bank in Jackson; and as a securities examiner, he uncovered a series of fraudulent stock manipulations by the Charlevoix Rock Product Company.[1] At an early age, Joseph Dodge established himself among banking circles as a good man to send for when a tough job had to be done.

Dodge left the state banking department in December 1916 to accept a position as operations officer with the Highland Park State

179

Bank of Detroit [later the Bank of Detroit]. In his letter of resignation to the state banking commissioner, Dodge wrote that he felt this new job would be a challenging one and that the Highland Park State Bank was an "active, vigorous, forward looking bank with great promise." [2]

Whether or not Dodge found his new job to be as rewarding as he had expected is not clear for in 1918 he left the bank to go to work for the T. C. Doyle Agency.* Thomas Doyle owned Detroit's largest Dodge automobile dealership with a central new car agency and several used car lots.† Joseph Dodge began with the agency as its comptroller. During the next several years, he played an active part in the growth of the Doyle Agency and by 1929 had attained the position of vice-president and general manager. It was during this period that Dodge and Doyle became very close friends.

With the stock market crash of October 1929, the bottom fell out of the new car market. Dodge made a series of recommendations to Doyle on ways to cut costs and lower expenses in an attempt to save the business. Dodge's recommendations even included a 50 percent cut in his own salary. He worked hard and long to keep the company's head above water, but it was a losing battle. Finally, in December 1931, Dodge could no longer justify even his own reduced salary and over Doyle's repeated protests, he resigned. In his letter of resignation to Doyle he wrote, "Fourteen years to spend on a business and have to start over again is not such a pleasant outlook." [3]

The early months of 1932 were difficult ones indeed. In early August, Dodge wrote to Thomas Doyle that he had obtained a position with the First National Bank-Detroit.[4] Months of long hard work had paid off for Dodge, and his new position was as vice-president and assistant to the chairman of the board. In addition to his duties as a vice-president of the bank, he also served as secretary to the governing committee of the board of directors of the Detroit Bankers Company.

While March 1933 brought the closing of the First National Bank by the federal government, it did not bring to a close Joseph Dodge's

---

* Thomas C. Doyle was the son of State Banking Commissioner Edward H. Doyle. Dodge went to work at the agency on the recommendation of his former boss.[5]
† Joseph M. Dodge was not related to the Detroit Dodge family of automobile fame and fortune.

banking career. Later in the month, when the National Bank of Detroit was organized, Dodge was retained as a vice-president by the new bank's board of directors. In his new position, Dodge was given the task of selecting $131,000,000 of assets which were to be purchased by the National Bank of Detroit from the now closed First National and Guardian National banks. The proceeds from these purchases were used to make the first payments to the depositors of the closed banks. He also supervised the recording and handling of all the bank's purchased assets and successfully closed the contracts with the receivers.[6]

It was at this point of his career that Joseph M. Dodge resigned as a vice-president of the National Bank of Detroit to accept the invitation of the Detroit Savings Bank to become its new president. The directors of the Detroit Savings Bank were looking for a man who would be able to take a firm hold of any situation, a strong leader, a man of ideas. The directors found such a man in Joseph M. Dodge.

Dodge had not been personally hurt with the closing of the banks in March 1933, but he was so deeply moved by the disaster that he then and there acquired a philosophy by which he was to guide the Detroit Savings Bank:

American banks have a primary obligation, which is the safety of the depositors' money—it is not to be freely distributed among borrowers who have more optimism than assets; banks have an obligation to the nation to maintain the strictest kind of conservatism—there can be no speculative boom unless it is financed . . . by bank loans.[7]

President Dodge set to work on his new job at once. The first order of business was a special shareholders' meeting held December 21, 1933, at which a stock increase was approved. Because funds available for investment from the private sector had virtually disappeared, the bank's capital stock was increased in the amount of $4,000,000 by issuing 200,000 shares of cumulative preferred stock at $20 a share to the Reconstruction Finance Corporation.[8] This $4,000,000 in preferred stock was to be in addition to the $1,500,000 of common stock already on the bank's books.

During the early months of 1934 President Dodge reported to the board of directors on several new programs that the bank was undertaking. The Detroit Savings Bank had previously been designated a special depository of public monies under an act of Congress of 1917. The amount of public monies to be deposited was now to be increased from $2,000,000 to $5,000,000. At the same time, an increase in postal savings, from $2,000,000 to $5,000,000, was also authorized. Dodge also informed the board on the progress of the expansion of safety deposit facilities at the main office, on the growth of deposits at branch offices, and on the increase of safety deposit box rentals.[9]

In the spring of 1934 a rather serious problem arose. Many of the bank's staff were having to work long overtime hours, particularly in the branches. This condition was brought on by the extensive increase in business. A survey was taken at this time, and it was discovered that the three major reasons customers were opening new accounts at the bank were: (1) convenience of location, (2) reputation of the bank, (3) recommendation of friends.[10] As a result of this business increase, it was decided to hire more staff. In February 1933, the bank's staff numbered 225; by the end of 1934 the staff had increased to over 500, and a Personnel Department was established.[11]

When the State Banking Department appeared for the bank's regular examination in July 1934, the examiners reported that the bank was still carrying several undesirable lines of credit and listed a large number of loans as either slow, doubtful, or loss. In total, however, the bank examiners were very pleased with what they found at the Detroit Savings Bank and complimented the board of directors on "the excellent improvement in all departments since the advent of President Dodge." [12] This opinion was supported by a very favorable mention of the Detroit Savings Bank in the *American Banker* of August 2, 1934. On that date the bank was listed as 63rd out of the 100 largest banks in the United States. This was a jump from 82nd as of December 1933, and from 123rd as of December 1932.[13]

At the end of Dodge's first year as president, the bank's resources had increased from $60,323,800 to $92,107,145. During this period, commercial deposits had grown from $22,822,359 to $32,592,320, while savings deposits had jumped from $26,129,355 to $45,079,038. In December, the bank received a letter from Eugene Stevens, chairman of the Federal Reserve Bank of Chicago, who commented most favorably on this growth and on the administration of the bank.[14] Joseph Dodge's first year with the Detroit Savings Bank had been a highly successful one.

When the board's examining committee made its semi-annual report in January 1935, a major change was recommended. During the past year, the growth of the bank had been so extensive that the old method of making a physical check of all assets as well as the verification of all liabilities by the examining committee itself was impossible. The committee deemed it advisable "to rely on certified reports from each department, embodying all necessary details. The thorough reorganization which this bank has experienced under the direction of our President Dodge has made this possible." [15]

An article in the *Detroit Free Press* of January 20, 1935 indicated that better times were ahead for Detroit and its citizens. The announcement in the paper that day stated that the Detroit Savings Bank was prepared, during the year 1935, to loan up to five million dollars on first mortgages for new residence construction in metropolitan Detroit. Also, that the bank was prepared to rewrite and extend terms of mortgages currently held. All of these loans were to be made under the regulations and provisions of Title 2 of the National Housing Act. This new service represented the first major attempt at mortgage financing undertaken by any Detroit financial institution since 1929. All that was needed was state approval. [16]

Approval came on February 20, 1935, when a bill to release $40,000,000 from Michigan banks for home construction was signed by Governor Frank D. Fitzgerald. Qualified Michigan banks were authorized to make loans under Title 2 of the National Housing Act up to 80 percent of the appraised valuation of mortgaged property and for a 20-year duration. The Detroit Savings Bank made the first loan in the state under this act the day following its passage. This loan was in the amount of $2500 on a new two-story brick home being constructed in the northwest section of the city. [17]

Other requests for mortgages followed quickly and, in early August, the bank closed its 100th FHA loan bringing to a total of $410,450 money invested in new and refinanced home mortgages. [18] Bearing an interest rate of five percent per annum, the payments on these new loans were to be made monthly and for periods not to exceed 20 years.

Not only did these loans help to get Detroit's economy moving, they were also a very desirable bank investment. Their government insurance feature eliminated the possibility of the bank having to absorb the property in case foreclosure proceedings were necessary for the collection of the loan. The bank continued to be a major participant in FHA mortgages and by 1939 was among the 50 largest mortgage lenders, including finance companies, in the United States.[19]

During the remainder of the year 1935, the bank continued to experience the same growth under Dodge's leadership as had occurred in 1934. By the close of the year, the bank's resources had passed the $100,000,000 mark, reaching $115,470,421 with savings deposits of $56,919,714 and commercial deposits of $45,702,256. During the two-year period of mid-1933 to mid-1935, total branch deposits alone had climbed from $14,986,900 to $49,841,000.[20]

The Detroit Bank

At the annual meeting of January 14, 1936, the stockholders unanimously voted, upon the recommendation of President Dodge and the board of directors, to change the bank's name from the Detroit Savings Bank to The Detroit Bank.[21] With the memory of bank mergers, consolidations, and closings still fresh in the public's mind, this change was not lightly undertaken. The name change had the serious consideration of the bank's officers for the better part of a year. The advisability of the change was carefully reviewed with the Michigan State Banking Department, the Federal Reserve Bank, and the Reconstruction Finance Corporation. Also, during this period, the name change was discussed quite freely among the staff, with customers, stockholders, friends, and other bankers in order to determine the reaction to the idea and to remove as much of the element of surprise as possible when the change actually became effective.

At the time of the bank holiday in February 1933, many corporation and business accounts were transferred to the Detroit Savings Bank. Many of these corporations used their checking privilege for the payment of accounts outside the state of Michigan and the city of Detroit. In doing so they were frequently asked how they happened to or why they decided to do business with a savings bank, as in most states, particularly in the East, a bank using the word "savings" in its name was by law exclusively a savings bank without checking accounts, and in some states was always a mutual savings bank.[22]

This point had been emphasized by President Dodge in July when he reported to the board of directors on a letter he had received from the Proctor & Gamble Company of Cincinnati. The company had an account with the Detroit Savings Bank in excess of $100,000 and were planning to transfer this money to another Detroit bank stating:

For quite a long time we have had in mind transferring our commercial deposit account from your bank to one of the commercial banks in Detroit. As you undoubtedly know, our account was established with the Detroit Savings Bank on a more or less temporary basis during the time of the banking panic. It was our intention to move it to a commercial bank as soon as banking conditions assumed normal proportions, and we now have decided to make the transfer on August 1. We very much appreciate the service your bank has rendered our Detroit District Office for the past several years, and we want you to know that the move we are making is not because of any dissatisfaction, but rather in keeping with our policy of carrying deposit accounts in commercial banks.[23]

Dodge emphasized to the board that the bank's current name was a handicap to further commercial growth, and cited several other instances of the attitudes of bankers, corporations, and individuals in this regard. He expressed the belief that a change of corporate name might prove beneficial and first offered as a suggestion the name "Detroit State Bank." The directors recognized the importance of Dodge's suggestions, but after lengthy discussion decided to postpone any change until the annual meeting in January.[24]

The name Detroit Savings Bank had been suitable as long as the institution was doing business almost exclusively in Detroit and with the largest part of its deposits being savings deposits, and with commercial accounts almost entirely restricted to a service of convenience for savings customers. The circumstances following the bank holiday changed the position and community usefulness of the bank, giving it a much wider field of activity. In 1935 fewer than 60 banks in the United States had deposits in excess of $100,000,000; the Detroit Savings Bank was one of them. By this time, the bank's position had become national with respect to the connections of its clients and customers, particularly corporations, and as a depository for other banks. The name change was a very simple and reasonable move. It was a move toward eliminating a condition which President Dodge felt was a handicap to the bank's future progress.[25]

In April 1936, the board was shocked to learn of the death of Sidney T. Miller, Jr. A director since 1925, young Miller had served as chairman of the board's executive committee since December 1933. Miller was held in the highest regard and his opinion frequently sought. His passing was a severe loss to the bank. In an attempt to express their feelings, his fellow directors prepared a memorial resolution which read in part:

The initiative, courage, and leadership he displayed during the dark

185

days of the banking crisis won the unstinted admiration of his associates.[26]

By mid-1936 the bank's financial situation had grown to a point that in August a check for $200,000 was forwarded to the Reconstruction Finance Corporation to retire a corresponding amount of the bank's preferred stock. This first payment, made out of earnings, reduced the outstanding amount of preferred stock from $4,000,000 to $3,800,000. By retiring this preferred stock, the bank was able to save $7000 a year in preferred stock dividends and to increase the equity of the common stockholders by $200,000.[27]

As the bank's services, operations, and staff were expanded, it became evident that additional main office space was needed.* To handle this increased activity, a two-year main office modernization program had been started in early 1934. This expansion program was developed by President Dodge. His plan called for the gradual taking-over of more space in the main building, regrouping the departments on the various floors, and rearranging the departments internally.[28]

By the fall of 1936, the first stage of the modernization program was complete. The bank now occupied the first six floors and basement of the building. Its basement was occupied by enlarged safety deposit vaults and facilities, along with locker and stock rooms. The lobby and mezzanine floors were devoted to expanded tellers' cages and quarters for the commercial and savings contract officers. The completely rebuilt third floor centralized the entire commercial loan division, plus the discount, collateral, and credit department. Originally located on the first floor, the executive offices were now housed in fine new quarters also on the third floor. The fourth floor housed all the commercial bookkeeping operations with the accounting and auditing departments. Along with the newly installed switchboard on the fifth floor were the miscellaneous operating departments, such as personnel, monthly payment loan, and bond investment. The sixth floor was shared by the realty management and mortgage department. Later the ninth and tenth floors were modernized for private office rental purposes, while the seventh, eighth, eleventh, and twelfth floors were left for future bank expansion.[29]

In order to allow state banking institutions to take full advantage

* The staff had grown from 500 in December 1934 to 600 by August 1937. And by January 1938, the bank was 42nd on the list of the nation's 100 largest banks.[30]

of the new federal banking legislation, the Michigan State Legislature passed in 1937 a new definitive banking law titled "The Michigan Financial Institutions Act." [31] It completely revised the laws relating to state banks, industrial banks, trust companies, small loan companies, and safe and collateral deposit companies. It authorized state banks to cooperate with and secure the benefits made available by federal agencies such as the Federal Deposit Insurance Corporation and the Federal Housing Administration. One provision, which later attracted much notice because of allegations that it was passed as a result of bribery, established regulations for branch banking.

The act set forth minimum capital stock requirements of $25,000 in villages having a population of 2,500 or less; $100,000 in towns with a population of more than 6,000 and less than 30,000; $150,000 in communities of 30,000 to 100,000; $200,000 in cities of 100,000 to 300,000; and $500,000 in cities of over 300,000 population. A surplus of at least 25 percent of capital was required, and shareholders' liability was limited to the amount of stock held. Ordinary real estate loans could not be made in an amount exceeding 50 percent of appraised value, except under provisions of the National Housing Act, in which as high as 80 percent of the appraised value might be loaned. It also prohibited any bank from being affiliated with issuing, floating, underwriting, selling, or distributing stocks, bonds, and other securities. A major provision of the new act which directly affected The Detroit Bank, terminated the requirements for segregating commercial, savings, and industrial loan business and assets on the part of any state bank.[32]

The growth that The Detroit Bank was experiencing in the mid-thirties was also being witnessed by other segments of Detroit's economic community. Gradually, a better financial base was beginning to be built in the city, and purchasing power was being restored. People's confidence was returning and with it the first signs of prosperity. Just as Detroit was one of the first cities to feel the depression, so it was one of the first to find the recovery road. A car-hungry nation began to buy automobiles, and in 1936 the auto industry produced nearly 4,500,000 cars and trucks.[33] Many observers claim Detroit's major industry led the nation out of the depression and set it on the road to normalcy.

Full recovery, however, did not come smoothly or all at once. When it appeared in 1937 that all was well again, there was a recession. Reflecting this downturn in the city's economy, President Dodge reported to the board of directors in January 1938, on his

187

plans for the coming year. Dodge stated that it would not be the intention of management to press for increased earnings during 1938. It was his recommendation that "under the present disturbed conditions, particular emphasis be placed upon the protection of principal investments, avoidance of unnecessary risks in loans and investments, and substantial liquidity." [34] The major programs of the bank were to be the preferred stock retirement and dividend, the common stock dividend, and the continued improvement in internal operating efficiency and equipment. With these safely covered, there was to be no deliberate attempt to equal or exceed any past period earnings.

Dodge's recommendations were sound ones. The recession of the late thirties had little real effect on the bank and during this time the bank's resources continued to expand. By the end of 1938, assets reached $145,968,927; and by the end of 1939, assets reached $165,537,555.[35] This growth was reflected in increases in the bank's capital stock of $300,000 in January 1939, and $360,000 a year later. Primarily, the need for capital stock increases was due to the growth of deposits. The issuing of new stock had been delayed until earnings were free to maintain dividends. It was determined that small issues, made periodically, were preferable to large increases. Large increases would have to be underwritten and might have changed the complexion of the ownership of the bank.[36]

At this date, there were several changes on the bank's board of directors. The year 1938 marked the passing of directors Roehm and Doherty. James Doherty had begun his career with the bank in 1888, rising to assistant cashier in 1911, vice-president in 1918, and director in 1925. During his nearly 50 years of service he had worked in every department in the bank.

To fill one of the vacancies on the board, Ferris D. Stone was elected director on April 19, 1938. Stone was a senior partner in the law firm of Miller, Canfield, Paddock and Stone. In addition to his duties at the bank, Stone served as president of the Detroit Bar Association and as a trustee of Harper Hospital and Hillsdale College. The second vacancy was not filled.

There were no further changes on the board until 1940. On May 19 of that year Sidney T. Miller, the senior director of the bank, passed away. He had become a director in 1904 following the death of his father Sidney D. Miller, who at that time was the bank's president. With the death of Sidney T. Miller, a continuous period of

85 years of distinguished service to the bank by the Miller family ended.[37]

The year 1940 also marked the end of ten long years of depression. In the political and social sector, it was a period occupied with experiments to accomplish relief, recovery, and reform. In the field of banking, the net effect of the depression was the drastic reduction of the number of financial institutions doing business. This was particularly true in Detroit and Michigan.

At the close of the year 1930, there were 14 state banks and 2 national banks doing business in Detroit, and 566 state banks and 124 national banks in operation outstate. Ten years later, the numbers had been reduced to 7 and 2, and 349 and 74, respectively. The number of trust companies was reduced during the same period from 9 to 4 in the city, and from 12 to 7 outstate. Because of changes in the state banking laws and the differences in the method of reporting, it is difficult to compare the changes in the amounts deposited in state banks. However, in national banks throughout the state, demand deposits in 1930 numbered 176,111 while in 1940 the number was down to 157,266. Time deposits in national banks in 1930 numbered 535,053 as compared with 640,000 in 1940.[38]

By the end of the decade of the thirties, a measure of prosperity had returned although full recovery was not to come from social legislation and financial pump-priming. Full recovery was to come with the onslaught of the blitzkrieg and the marching feet of invading armies.

A NEW BATTLE FRONT

It was a Sunday afternoon like most early winter Sunday afternoons in Detroit. Not much was going on. Those who had gone to church were back home. Many had had their dinners and were catching naps. The day was cloudy, the temperature was a raw 36 degrees, with a trace of rain. It was a good day to be indoors. A philharmonic program was being broadcast by one of the radio networks and the local audience was large. Yet it was not a typical Sunday afternoon in Detroit or anywhere else. It was December 7, 1941, a remarkably fateful day. It was, as President Roosevelt said, "a day that will live in infamy."

Suddenly about 3 P.M., there was a break in the radio program and an excited voice announced: "We interrupt this program to bring you a special news bulletin. The White House has announced that the Japanese have attacked Pearl Harbor. Please stay tuned to this station for further details." With no more warning than that, the United States was at war.

The shock was great; the immediate reaction on the part of the average citizen was anger. Yet the shock wore off quickly because America's ultimate participation in the war had generally been taken for granted. It was just a question of when. Unlike World War I, World War II did not catch the country totally unprepared for involvement. December 7, 1941, found the country well on the way toward mobilization.

Nazi Germany had invaded Poland on September 1, 1939, and the European phase of the war was underway. In less than six months, the United States started on its program of preparedness. Large amounts of war materials were produced not only for United States forces but also for those of Great Britain and France. After the fall of France in the summer of 1940, President Roosevelt gambled on sending war materials to Britain; had the gamble failed, that material might have fallen to Hitler. Under the Lend-Lease Act, the president was empowered to send materials of war to any nation the defense of which he considered vital to the defense of the United States. It was during this period that the United States was called the "Arsenal of Democracy," and this designation came to be applied particularly to Detroit.

Long before Pearl Harbor, plants in Detroit and Michigan, particularly the automotive plants, were heavily committed to the production of war materials. On September 16, 1940, the "Conscription of Industry Act" was passed. This empowered the president, through the heads of the War or Navy Departments, to place orders with corporations, firms, or manufacturing concerns for such products or materials as were required. By January 1941, 24 corporations in Detroit and Michigan had each been awarded contracts for $1,000,000 or more.[39]

To finance this production, the government turned to the nation's banks. On October 9, 1940, the "Assignment of Claims Act" became law, setting up a basis by which banks could participate in the lending of funds. This act enabled the banks to do three things: (1) lend for the creation of new plants and facilities; (2) lend for the production of supplies; (3) lend for the construction of arsenals, bases, and other projects.[40]

To coordinate the production of war materials, the United States National Defense Council was created in 1940. William S. Knudsen, president of General Motors, was made its chairman; and in 1941 he resigned from his civilian job to become director of the Office of Production Management. It was apparent by 1941 what American and Allied war needs would be, and it was equally apparent to men like Knudsen that the automobile industry and its associate companies were best equipped to fill those needs. The problem was how to do it most quickly and efficiently. Parts for tanks, planes, and guns were vastly different from parts for Fords, Chevrolets, and Packards, and yet the basic principles of engineering and production were much the same. It became necessary to find out which companies could most easily manufacture the new products of war—products with which they were then unfamiliar.

The solution was found by Knudsen and the noted flier James Doolittle, who had both been assigned the job of coordinating facilities for the production of aircraft. Working with the newly created Automotive Council for War Production, they accumulated all the various parts that would be required. These were spread out in a sort of museum display in the former Graham-Paige plant on West Warren at Wyoming. Parts manufacturers, tool makers, and other suppliers were then invited to inspect the display. Representatives of more than 1,500 companies walked up and down the aisles looking at the samples. As each representative found something his plant was equipped to turn out, he was given a contract or subcontract.[41]

More was needed than willingness and know-how. The machine that could stamp out an automobile fender could not forge a sheet of armor plate for a tank. Gradually, the old machines and tools were moved out of the auto plants and stored for the duration in warehouses or under tarpaulins in open fields. The tool makers went to work, and soon new machinery designed for war production was moved in. More plants were required also, involving capital expenditures the manufacturers were not always in a position to make. That obstacle was overcome by the government's construction of huge new arsenals and factories. These were then turned over to the auto companies to operate. Chrysler ran the great tank arsenal in Warren, Hudson Motor Car Company took over the management of the Navy gun arsenal in Center Line, and General Motors operated a tank arsenal near Flint. The Ford Motor Company assumed the responsibility for building B-24 Liberator bombers at the Willow Run plant, which was constructed at a cost of better than $100,000,000.[42]

191

In August 1941, the production of automobiles for the civilian market began to be curtailed; on February 9, 1942, it came to a complete halt, not to be resumed until late 1945 and early 1946.[43] All the industry's efforts were now concentrated on the output of war material.

The miracle of conversion to war production by the automotive industry was perhaps best described by Lt. General Brehon B. Somervell, commanding general of the Army's Services of Supply when he said:

> The road ahead is dim with the dust of battles still unfought. How long that road is, no one can know. But it is shorter than it would have been had not our enemies misjudged us and themselves. For, when Hitler put his war on wheels, he ran it straight down our alley. When he hitched his chariot to an internal combustion engine, he opened up a new battle front—a front we know well. It's called Detroit.[44]

A few figures will show the extent of the production of war materials in the Detroit metropolitan area. The Chrysler tank arsenal turned out more than 25,000 tanks—General Grants, General Shermans, and General Pershings. The rate of output sometimes reached 1,000 tanks a month. In addition, Chrysler plants turned out Bofors anti-aircraft guns, light ammunition, pontoons, aircraft engines, aircraft fuselage sections and parts, and a variety of other items.

Out at Willow Run, the first B-24 bomber came off the lines September 10, 1942. There were 8,685 of the huge aircraft built there, more aircraft than were produced at any other plant in the nation. Other Ford plants were producing aircraft engines, amphibians, tank destroyers, and gun directors.

General Motors manufactured more than 2,300 separate items ranging from tiny ball bearings to 30-ton tanks. The corporation also produced airplanes, airplane engines and parts, guns, shells, and marine diesel engines. Aviation items, however, accounted for more than 40 percent of the dollar volume of the war deliveries from General Motors.

The plants of the other automotive companies were equally productive. Packard built thousands of Rolls-Royce aircraft engines, and marine engines for PT boats; Studebaker produced Wright Cyclone aircraft engines, and heavy duty cargo trucks; Nash turned out two-stage, supercharged, 2,000-horsepower Pratt and Whitney airplane engines; and Hudson built engines for landing craft, aircraft engine parts, suspension units for M-5 tanks, and other armament products. In addition, all these companies turned out military vehicles of all types in an unending stream. At the Ford Rouge plant a new kind of light vehicle was developed and tested. It was named the Jeep. Ford built them and so did the Willys plant in Toledo. Both Ford and Willys were also making jet propelled buzz bombs toward the end of the war.

From September 1, 1939, to V-J Day in 1945, the automobile industry delivered to the government almost $50,000,000,000 worth of war materials. Over 39 percent was comprised of military vehicles and parts. Another 13 percent went for tank production. Marine equipment, guns, artillery, and ammunition were among the other major items. Almost 4,000,000 engines of various types were made. Tank production, armored cars, and other combat vehicles totaled about 200,000.[45]

As was the case in 1917, the federal government turned to issuing bonds of small denominations to finance the production of war materials. These new bonds were called Savings or Defense Bonds and were issued in three series; E, F, and G. They were first placed on sale on May 1, 1941, at post offices, banks and other financial institutions throughout the country. The Detroit Bank actively promoted the sale of Savings Bonds among its employees and by mid-June 1941, 98 percent of the bank's staff was participating in the program. Also, the bank actively promoted the sale of Defense Bonds to the citizens of Detroit. By the fall of 1941, the bank ranked third in the sale of bonds in the 7th Federal Reserve District, trailing only the National Bank of Detroit and the First National Bank of Chicago.[46]

The attack on Pearl Harbor caused a tremendous increase in the sale of Savings Bonds at the bank's main office and 29 branches. A total of 16,064 bonds with a maturity value of $2,960,150 were sold during December 1941. As a comparison, the bank had sold 5,068 bonds with a maturity value of $786,575 during the preceding month of November.[47]

With the official entry of the United States into the war, bond drives were established by the U.S. Treasury Department. In all, there were eight public offerings of these securities. Offered in November 1942, the First War Loan placed no sales quotas on banks and was not organized for a public selling campaign. The Second War Loan, which ran from April 12 to May 1, 1943, saw the start of an organized selling effort through the nation's banks. The sales team for The Detroit Bank consisted of 13 officers, all the branch managers, and 11 securities salesmen from the Banking Division of the War Finance

Committee for Michigan. The selling pattern set in the Second War Loan was generally followed in the succeeding drives.

On December 31, 1945, the last of the public drives for subscriptions to government securities for financing World War II came to a close. The Victory Loan Drive (as the Eighth War Loan Drive was officially called) was oversubscribed by The Detroit Bank as were the quotas for all the previous drives. In all, The Detroit Bank sold $356,066,664 worth of Savings Bonds during the seven organized loan campaigns.[48]

Soon after the declaration of war, price controls and rationing went into effect. Detroiters were virtually frozen into their jobs and could not quit or transfer without the consent of the War Labor Board. Wages were also frozen, but to offset that, ceilings and controls were placed on rents and the prices of food, clothing, and other essential items. To assure enough material for the armed forces and our hard-pressed Allies, rationing of gasoline and tires was ordered, thus materially limiting automobile travel. Once busy highways were almost deserted except for huge trucks, buses, and cars on essential missions. To get back and forth to work, Detroiters were encouraged to organize car pools. Most people were able to keep their cars running, however, and replacement parts continued to be manufactured. Citizens hoarded their gasoline coupons to enable them to go on short trips. Somehow Michigan's army of deer hunters always managed to make the northward trek in November. Later in 1942, shortages of many commodities resulted in the rationing of meat, canned goods, shoes, clothes, and unhappily, liquor and cigarettes. During this rationing period, The Detroit Bank serviced over 4,500 ration banking accounts covering sugar, processed foods, meats, shoes, gasoline, and fuel oil.[49]

The Detroit Bank also actively participated in the war effort by extending loans and lines of credit to industries engaged in the production of war materials. Typical of these corporations were Packard Motor Car Company, Nash-Kelvinator Corporation, Gray Marine Motors Company, and General Motors Corporation, to name only a few.

Direct financing of the war through large-scale purchases of government securities was also undertaken by The Detroit Bank. Holdings of these securities at the close of 1943, for example, represented 67 percent of the bank's total deposits.[50] These large government deposits were allowed following a change in the state banking law. Public Act No. 82, signed in April of 1943, permitted state banks in Michigan to accept without limit:

> . . . War loan deposits or other similar deposits of the United States of America when such deposits are established coincidentally with the purchase of obligations of the United States of America by or through any institution subject to the provisions of this Act.[51]

Prior to this time state banks in Michigan had been subject to a limitation of ten percent of their total deposits and were required to receive prior approval from the State Banking Department before accepting a federal deposit.

The Detroit Bank served the nation in ways other than the lending of money and the selling of defense bonds. In October 1942, President Joseph Dodge was asked to undertake the chairmanship of the Price Adjustment Board of the Army Air Forces for the Central Procurement District. With headquarters in Detroit and offices in Chicago, Cleveland, and Cincinnati, Dodge helped organize the 13-state midwest operation. His responsibility as chairman was to renegotiate government wartime contracts held by midwestern firms in order to help cut the level of federal spending. Dodge's handling of this post received national attention. Government officials, industrialists, bankers, and contractors reported on his fair tactics and able handling of renegotiation matters. Dodge's outstanding work, aided by his fine reputation as a banker, culminated in his selection, by Secretary of War Henry L. Stimson, to fill a similar post at the national level.[52]

In September 1943, Joseph Dodge was appointed Chairman of the War Department Price Adjustment Board. Simultaneously with this appointment, Dodge became director of a new headquarters staff division of the Army Service Forces, known as the Renegotiation Division. Following his appointment, Dodge immediately left for Washington, although he continued to hold the position of president and chief executive officer of The Detroit Bank. Because it would be necessary for Dodge to spend an enormous amount of time in Washington, he recommended the appointments of vice-presidents Raymond T. Perring and Charles H. Hewitt as administrative assistants to the president. Under this delegation of authority, Hewitt served as administrative assistant with respect to bank operations, while Perring assumed direct responsibility for the quality and distribution of the bank's assets. Dodge accepted his new position in Washington with the understanding that he would be able to return to Detroit at regular intervals to attend board meetings and continue general supervision over the operations of the bank.[53]

Following Dodge's arrival in Washington, the War Department Price Adjustment Board was reorganized. Then, in February 1944, the board was phased out and the War Contracts Price Adjustment Board was created. This board's responsibility was to adjust prices for the War, Navy, and Treasury departments, the Maritime Commission, the War Shipping Administration, and the Reconstruction Finance Corporation; and Joseph Dodge was asked to serve as the board's chairman.

Dodge's first job was to prepare a two-inch-thick instruction manual to explain the operation of the new board and the regulations for renegotiation procedures. Once the work of the board was underway, contractors came to know Joseph Dodge as a man with a stern eye for any large profits made out of the war. By the late summer of 1944, Dodge had the board running smoothly. Thus he felt he could resign his post in good faith and return to Detroit and the bank.*

During the war years, there were a number of changes at The Detroit Bank. In February 1943, the Detroit Savings Bank Building Company wound up its affairs and was dissolved. Since the directors felt that there was no longer any advantage in keeping the corporate entity alive, The Detroit Bank exercised its option to purchase the main office building, and the Building Company ceased to exist. To operate and manage the main office a Building Department was established within the bank, and all the Building Company employees were transferred to the department.[54]

Another departmental change occurred in August 1944, when the bank bought and remodeled a spacious three-story building on Times Square for storage and purchasing facilities. During the latter part of February 1945, the Purchasing and Archives departments moved to this new location. This building was within five minutes' walking distance of the main office. Moving these departments to new quarters freed valuable floor space for the expansion of customer service facilities at the main banking building.[55]

There were also a number of changes on the bank's board of directors during the years 1941–45. Following the death of Sidney T.

---

* Secretary Stimson's successor, Robert Patterson, observed that the War Contracts Price Adjustment Board, which renegotiated some $190 billion of contracts between 1942 and 1945 and recovered some $11 billion, had done its work with "not one breath of scandal." [56]

Miller, Sr., in the spring of 1940, the membership of the board remained at ten until the close of 1943.

At the annual stockholders' meeting of January 11, 1944, H. Lynn Pierson was elected to the board to fill the vacancy caused by the death of Director Hubbard. It was decided at this time not to fill Director Viger's vacancy. H. Lynn Pierson was president and director of the Detroit Harvester Company, and had held this office since the formation of the company in 1922. Pierson was also a director of the Provident Loan and Savings Society of Detroit; the Eaton Manufacturing Company; the Standard Accident Insurance Company; the Detroit Branch of the Federal Reserve Bank of Chicago; and a member of the advisory committee for the Reconstruction Finance Corporation. At this time Pierson was also the current president and director of the Detroit Board of Commerce.

On June 18, 1945, Director Ferris D. Stone died. To fill this vacancy, the board elected prominent Detroit attorney Cleveland Thurber, who had been a member of the law firm of Miller, Canfield, Paddock and Stone since 1922. Thurber was also a director of Parke, Davis & Company; the Detroit Trust Company; and the Whitney Realty Company, Ltd.

As could be expected, the war years witnessed a major growth in the resources of The Detroit Bank. Under the leadership of President Joseph M. Dodge, the bank's total resources more than doubled during this period. At the close of business in December 1940, the resources of The Detroit Bank stood at $222,731,681; by December 31, 1945, they had reached $527,414,606. The major gain came in the form of United States Treasury Bills and Certificates, and from other United States securities. At the end of 1940 this figure stood at almost $51,000,000; by 1945 it had climbed to over $386,500,000. Total deposits during this period jumped from $211,522,716 to $509,695,998.[57]

This growth of The Detroit Bank was reflected in increases in the bank's common stock and decreases in its preferred stock. In 1940 the bank's capital investment was $3,530,000 of preferred stock and $2,160,000 of common stock. By January 1946, these figures stood at $3,370,000 and $3,000,000 respectively.[58]

On June 6, 1944, the great Allied armada landed on the beaches of Normandy. Gradually the enemy was pushed back and the end drew near. On May 8, 1945, Nazi Germany, or what was left of it, surrendered. The war effort did not slacken, however. There was still a job remaining, and on August 6, the United States administered the coup-de-grace to Japanese war hopes, when the first atomic bomb was exploded over Hiroshima.

With the dreadful destruction caused by the A-bomb, the Japanese realized that their cause was lost. On August 14 the shattered and defeated Japanese Empire surrendered. When the news reached Detroit, it was carnival time again. As they did at the end of World War I, Detroiters celebrated, only in greater numbers. It was estimated that half a million people poured into the downtown streets to stage a giant victory celebration.

The Detroit Bank had experienced a tremendous growth during the war years. It was now to enter an equally great period of expansion, a decade that was to be marked by a high level of business activity and general prosperity.

TO BERLIN, TOKYO, AND WASHINGTON

The smoke of battle had barely cleared when the United States began its aid programs to nations which only weeks before had been the enemy. In this rebuilding of Germany and Japan, The Detroit Bank was to play an active role through its President Joseph M. Dodge. On August 15, 1945, the War Department announced the appointment of Joseph Dodge as Financial Advisor to the American Commander in Germany. He was handpicked for this job by General Lucius Clay.

To put it bluntly, Germany's financial structure was a mess, and it was Joseph Dodge's conviction that if Europe was to survive, Germany had to be resuscitated. Basically, Dodge's job was to plan Germany's financial rehabilitation; it was a job which would have floored any ordinary man. His first task was to lay out a plan for reforming the old centralized German banking system. Dodge based his plan on the American Federal Reserve System of setting up land (state) banks limited to branches in separate states.

The second problem was the horrendous glut of Germany's currency, which was throwing the country into a barter economy and paralyzing its industry. Dodge's recommendations were drastic: to reduce the currency 90 percent by requiring Germans to turn in ten old Reichsmarks for one new Deutschmark. This reduction was followed by the imposition of mortgages and capital levies on real estate, plants, and inventories. The income from this was used to compensate those hurt the worst by the conversion and those who had been hurt worst by the war. It was an effort to spread the burden of defeat.

The Dodge plan was tough, but it worked. It revived the German economy. The Germans themselves acknowledged their debt to Detroiter Joseph Dodge. Jacques Rueff, revered as an authority among European economists, called the German monetary reform brought about by the Dodge Plan "the greatest success ever achieved in the field of monetary policy . . . no one can doubt that the decisive upward swing in the German economy was initiated with the currency reforms . . . it meant for the corpse of Germany the signal to 'rise and walk'. . . ." [59]

Joseph Dodge's success was also acknowledged by the United States Government. Following his return home in June 1946, Dodge was awarded the Medal for Merit—this nation's highest civilian war award. The citation accompanying the medal, signed by President Truman, stated that the medal was awarded "for exceptionally meritorious conduct in the performance of outstanding services to the United Nations," and for displaying "extraordinary financial acumen combined with executive ability of the highest order." [60]

During his assignment in Germany, Dodge had taken a trip through the Russian zone to Leipzig and Dresden. He had also visited Czechoslovakia and Austria. In both countries he met with the financial ministers and officials of the national banks, with the purpose of investigating the monetary and financial situation of these countries resulting from the war.

No sooner had Dodge settled back in Detroit when he was asked to return to Europe. At the request of President Truman and Secretary of State George C. Marshall, Dodge was appointed head of the American delegation on the Four-Power Commission which was formed to break the deadlock over the Austrian Peace Treaty. For five weeks Dodge sat across the table from his Russian counterpart, hammering out a solution. At these meetings he verbally dueled with the Russians (who called him a tool of Wall Street), but he finally succeeded in helping to develop a proposal that established the basic formula of the final settlement. At the conclusion of the meetings, Dodge spent two months as adviser on Austrian affairs to Secretary of State Marshall at the foreign ministers' meeting in London. [61]

Following his return to the United States, Joseph Dodge was elected president of the American Bankers Association for 1947–48. As president of the ABA, Dodge spent the better part of a year touring the nation to fight inflation—offering an anti-inflation program based on voluntary credit restraint. He traveled 15,000 miles urging member bankers to emphasize loans that increased production and distribution, while discouraging those that increased purchasing power. Dodge's program, backed by President Truman and other government officials and later adopted by the Federal Reserve Board, was to keep prices down by easing demands for goods and lowering the supply of money.[62]

During 1944 and 1945 Dodge had served as president of the Michigan Bankers Association. In 1951–52 he was to hold the same office for the Association of Reserve City Bankers.* Thus Joseph Dodge became one of only six bankers in the United States to serve as president of his state banking association, the American Bankers Association, and the Association of Reserve City Bankers. In 1936, 1940, and again in 1951, Joseph Dodge also served as president of the Detroit Clearing House Association.

In late 1948, Washington belatedly turned a worried eye upon Japan, then in the midst of a peculiarly Oriental inflation. The Japanese budget had not been balanced since 1930. All fiscal controls had collapsed with the surrender of the Japanese government. In the three years following the end of the war, prices had rocketed to 200 times the prewar level. In an attempt to solve this dilemma, President Truman once again called on Joseph M. Dodge.

On January 20, 1949, the White House announced the appointment of Dodge as Financial Advisor to General Douglas MacArthur, with the rank of U.S. Minister. Acting under the U.S. Government's Nine Point Stabilization Directive of December 1948, Dodge and his staff of fiscal and economic experts were instructed to balance Japan's budget and to help rebuild her shattered economy.

Following his appointment, Dodge left immediately for Japan. Upon his arrival in Tokyo, he began a long series of meetings, listening patiently through interpreters to the Japanese. Item by item, he went over their budget, wrestling with Asiatic obscurities and philosophies. No "miscellaneous" got by his scrutiny. One such "miscellaneous," after much probing, turned out to be payment for 20 geisha girls.[63]

Japanese fiscal officials required some convincing of the rightness

* The Association of Reserve City Bankers includes as members the principal officers of the nation's larger banks. Limited to 450, membership is composed exclusively of bank officers active in the administration of banks in designated reserve or central reserve cities, transacting a correspondent bank business.[64]

of Dodge's stringent measures, which included eliminating internal government subsidies, setting a single rate of exchange for the yen, cutting domestic consumption, and providing for budget surpluses and tax reductions. Dodge did not try to ram his cure down their throats. But having absolute authority, he was in a position to persuade them, and some were ready in the end to admit he was right. When Dodge left Tokyo in May 1949, Japan had its first balanced budget in 19 years. One member of the mission summed up Dodge's results this way: "By early '50 the yen meant something, and thieves now stole money instead of clothes." [65]

Not everyone had plaudits for Dodge's efforts. A number of Japanese newspapers attacked his plan as deflationary and ruinous. The decisions Dodge had to make were difficult ones. Often they caused temporary hardships and were unpopular with those directly affected who could not see the ultimate goal.

One young man who was particularly hard hit later wrote to Dodge how he had hated the anti-inflationary measures which, by taking the props out from under worthless stocks, had plunged his family into extreme poverty, making it necessary for him to end his education abruptly and go to work. He had come to realize, however, that in spite of his own hardships, Dodge's plan had been the best one for his country, and he wanted Dodge to know of his change of heart.[66]

Through all of these negotiations, Joseph Dodge kept the good will and respect of both sides. He presented the aspect of a man out to do a job, hard-driving, efficient, unbiased, and supremely capable; a hard man to quarrel with because he was able to present his case with such exactitude.

After he returned to Detroit, Dodge was called back to Tokyo on two different occasions to help iron out budgetary problems; first by General MacArthur in the fall of 1950, and then by General Matthew Ridgeway a year later. Each trip Dodge made was followed by a debt and tax reduction for the Japanese.

In recognition of his outstanding achievements while in Japan, Joseph Dodge was presented with the Decoration for Exceptional Civilian Service from the United States Army. The presentation was made by Secretary of the Army Frank Pace, Jr., at a special ceremony in the Pentagon on September 8, 1950. A citation was included with the Decoration and read in part:

The magnitude of his financial knowledge and the unlimited scope of his initiative made possible a program in Japan of economic stabilization unparalleled in modern history. . . .[67]

Among the congratulatory messages received by Dodge at the time of this presentation was a cablegram from Shigeru Yoshida, Japanese Prime Minister, which read:

Congratulations on the Army's Exceptional Civilian Award you have received. I rejoice at the official recognition accorded to your historic contribution to Japan's economic stabilization—a contribution whose significance and value will grow greater with the years.[68]

With the end of the war, Detroit's industry returned to the production of peacetime goods, particularly automobiles. There were still over 25,000,000 cars on the road in 1945, only 4,000,000 less than in 1941. But a great many of them were decrepit and ready for the junkpile. During the war, workers had earned high wages, and because of rationing, they were unable to spend their earnings except for essentials. Accordingly, when the war ended, there was a pent-up demand for cars that took years to fill.

Advance planning helped to speed the reconversion of war plants to the civilian production of automobiles. War production was cut back after the surrender of Germany in the spring of 1945, and substantial progress was made toward reconversion during the summer. One company turned out several hundred cars before Japan surrendered. When the Japanese capitulated in August, war contracts were cancelled and reconversion began in earnest. By the end of 1945, 75,000 cars had been built, enough to supply about two to each of the 33,000 dealers in the nation.[69]

Like the automotive companies, Detroit's other industries resumed peacetime production at the end of the war. To finance this reconversion, they turned to the city's banks. Loans and lines of credit extended by The Detroit Bank which was being transformed from a primarily savings bank to a full-range commercial bank. Lines of credit were extended to a larger number of national corporations including automotive companies.[70]

A sampling of the loans made at this time by The Detroit Bank illustrate the types of industries the bank was now accommodating. In the spring of 1947, the bank made a loan of $1,000,000 to a major railroad. This was part of a $19,000,000 loan being handled by the Bank of America in San Francisco. The purpose of the loan was to finance the purchase of new diesel locomotives by the railroad.

Loans to local companies were represented by a participation of $1,250,000 of a $5,000,000 loan to Parke, Davis & Company. In December 1946, the bank loaned a larger sum to a major automobile manufacturer. This was part of a larger $10,000,000 loan to the company which was participated in by a number of major banks. Not all the loans were made to corporations, however. In the fall of 1947, for example, a $750,000 loan was negotiated with the University of Detroit.[71]

The year 1949 marked the end of the first hundred years of the life of The Detroit Bank. In honor of the anniversary, a special medallion was struck and given to bank customers; a special historical issue of the *Teller*, the bank's employee magazine, was published; and Blue Cloud, a Sioux Indian Chief, met and talked with visitors at a number of open houses held at the main office and many of the branches.

The bank had come a long way from its very small beginnings behind Mariners' Church. Illustrating this growth was the expansion of the bank since the end of the war. In December 1945, the bank's resources were $527,414,605; by the end of 1949, they had reached $576,912,235, an increase of almost $50,000,000. Major gains were made in real estate loans which increased from $10,572,998 to $64,759,835 during this time, and loans and discounts which grew from $29,475,900 to $56,964,596. On the other side of the ledger, demand deposits (commercial deposits) grew from $261,830,842 to $277,758,089, while savings deposits increased from $247,865,157 to $273,922,050. The total number of depositors' accounts grew from 325,000 to 350,000 in this four-year period.[72]

The years immediately following the war also brought changes to the bank's board of directors. On September 6, 1946, James T. McMillan died and his vacancy was filled by the election of his son, James McMillan. Young McMillan began his business career with the Detroit & Cleveland Navigation Company as a freight clerk in 1934, rising to general manager in 1942 and finally to president and director. At the time of his election to the bank's board, McMillan was also a director of the Detroit Trust Company, the Packard Motor Car Company, and the Ferry Morse Seed Company. From 1938 to 1943 McMillan had served as a director of the Detroit Board of Commerce. The election of young McMillan marked the fourth generation of his family to serve on the bank's board of directors.

Further additions were made to the board on October 23, 1951 when Walker L. Cisler was elected director. In November 1945, Cisler returned from military duty and assumed his responsibilities as chief engineer of power plants for the Detroit Edison Company. Considered an authority in his field, Cisler later became president, then chairman of the board of Detroit Edison, and one of Detroit's most influential leaders. Six weeks following Cisler's election, Director Claude M. Harmon died. This vacancy was not immediately filled, leaving the board's membership at an even dozen.

The year 1951 also marked an important change in the bank's management structure. At the annual meeting of January 9, vice-presidents Raymond T. Perring and Charles H. Hewitt were each promoted to positions of executive vice-president. Perring headed the bank's investment department while Hewitt was responsible for bank operations.[73]

In the fall of 1952, President Joseph Dodge was again called to government service, this time as director of the bureau of the budget for President-elect Dwight D. Eisenhower. Dodge's appointment was the first major one Eisenhower settled on. While he was still campaigning, Eisenhower came to the conclusion that the office of budget director was among the several most important he had to fill. General Lucius Clay suggested Dodge, whom Eisenhower remembered well from his service in Germany.

In addition to the position of budget director, President-elect Eisenhower also asked Joseph Dodge to serve as his advance representative in Washington. In that connection, Dodge worked closely with the man he eventually succeeded as budget director, Frederick J. Lawton, gathering information for Eisenhower on the budget he was to inherit from outgoing President Truman. Under President Eisenhower the Bureau of the Budget had an important place as a coordinating agency during a period of reversion to peacetime and an attempt to reform international trade relations. As budget director, Dodge became one of Eisenhower's most valued advisers. This is underscored by the fact that Dodge reported directly to the president and was asked to sit with all meetings of the Cabinet and the National Security Council.[74]

Joseph Dodge accepted this position in Washington only because he knew that he would be able to leave the operation of The Detroit Bank in very capable hands; these hands belonged to Executive Vice-President Raymond T. Perring. At their regular meeting of December 30, 1952, the bank's board of directors elected Joseph Dodge as chairman of the board and elected Perring as president. The directors amended the bank's by-laws to provide that the chairman would be the chief executive officer and would have general management and direction of its business. It also provided that the president would have the powers and duties of the chairman in the latter's absence or disability.[75]

Raymond T. Perring was elected the eighth president of The Detroit Bank at the age of 47. He was born in Detroit and attended Wayne State University and the University of Michigan, where he received his master's degree from the School of Business Administration in 1927. After his graduation, Perring was employed as an accountant in the Trust Department of the Union Trust Company. Six months later, on January 23, 1928, he joined the staff of the Detroit Savings Bank and helped to organize the bank's Credit Department. In 1931, he was made manager of that department and secretary of the Executive Committee. Two years later Perring was appointed assistant vice-president, and in 1939 was named head of the Bond Investment Department. During that year he also served as president of the Michigan Chapter of the Robert Morris Associates, an organization of bank credit managers. In 1941 Perring was appointed vice-president and ten years later was made executive vice-president and chairman of the Officers Loan Committee.

After President Eisenhower's inauguration, Joseph Dodge assumed his new duties as Director of the Bureau of the Budget. To prepare for induction in that office, he resigned January 15, 1953, as chairman of the board and director of The Detroit Bank. Following Dodge's resignation, the directors appointed Director Cleveland Thurber as acting chairman of the board. As acting chairman, Thurber, who was also the bank's legal counsel, presided at the meetings of the board of directors and the Executive Committee. During this period Thurber acted primarily as consultant and adviser on matters of policy rather than in an executive or operating capacity.[76]

To fill the vacancy on the board created by Dodge's resignation, the board of directors elected Executive Vice-President Charles H. Hewitt at their regular meeting of January 20, 1953. Hewitt began his banking career with the State Savings Bank of Ann Arbor. He left Ann Arbor in 1929 to accept a position with the State Banking Commission as an examiner. In April 1932, Hewitt became an examiner for the Detroit Loan Agency of the Reconstruction Finance Corporation rising to the position of manager by 1937. After a brief second sojourn with the State Banking Department, this time as deputy banking commissioner, Hewitt joined The Detroit Bank as a vice-president on January 3, 1938. On January 9, 1951, he was appointed executive vice-president.

In early 1954 Joseph Dodge resigned his position as budget director to return to Detroit and the bank. (He resumed his duties as the bank's chief executive officer on April 16, following his re-election as director and chairman of the board on April 6.) Joseph Dodge's resignation as budget director was accepted by President Eisenhower with regret and only if he could call Dodge back to Washington in case of an emergency. On March 4, 1954, President Eisenhower wrote to Joseph Dodge to express his thanks for a job well done stating:

> Your services during these past 14 months in office have been invaluable to the country. Your competence and knowledge in an exceedingly difficult field have immeasurably helped solve the gigantic fiscal and management problems that have faced this administration.[77]

President Eisenhower held Joseph Dodge to his promise that he would return to Washington if the president needed him. In August 1954, Dodge went back to Washington as a consultant to the President's Advisory Committee on Government Organization. This was followed by a request to serve as coordinator of the foreign economic activities of the United States in December 1954; as a member of the President's Special Committee to Study the United States Military Assistance Program in 1958–59; and as a consultant to the National Security Council in 1959. In September 1955, Dodge had been appointed, by the secretary of the treasury, to serve as a member of the United States delegation to the Annual Meeting of the International Monetary Fund and the International Bank for Reconstruction and Development held in Istanbul, Turkey.

Throughout the ten years following the end of the Second World War, Detroit's population expanded into the east and northwest sections of the city. To keep up with this shift of population, The Detroit Bank opened nine new branch offices during this period. In addition, the bank moved a number of established branches to more advantageous locations, and remodeled and modernized several others.

Extensive remodeling and modernization were also carried out in the main office building. In 1948 substantial changes were made on the main floor, mezzanine and lower lobby as well as on a number of the upper floors. In 1951 the third floor, which housed the administrative offices and the commercial loan department, was extensively modernized and rearranged. By this date the bank occupied all the floors of the main office building. In 1956, 10,000 additional square feet of floor space were provided for main office operations by leasing the entire eighth floor of the adjoining Griswold Building.[78]

In 1953 The Detroit Bank established its first downtown branch and its first suburban branch. On May 4, Branch 36 opened in the David Whitney Building, one of the city's leading office buildings, located at Woodward Avenue and Grand Circus Park. This facility enabled the bank to give improved service in the downtown area and relieve the pressure on the main office. On August 31, Branch 37 opened in temporary quarters on the property of Northland Center, the gigantic retail shopping development under construction in suburban Southfield. At the time of its opening, Northland, with 80 retail shops and the J. L. Hudson Department Store, was the world's largest regional shopping center. In March 1954, Northland Center was completed and the bank's branch was moved into permanent quarters.[79]

During this period, the growth of the branch system was accompanied by a growth in the bank's personnel. At the beginning of the Second World War, the bank's staff numbered 644. Ten years later (1951), the staff had nearly doubled, growing to a total of 1,103, including 45 officers. By the end of 1955 the staff numbered 1,233. Of this total, 677 were in the main office and 556 were in the branches.[80]

Throughout the decade following the end of World War II, the resources of The Detroit Bank grew substantially from $527,414,606 in 1945 to $839,318,740 by the end of 1955.[81] This growth was accompanied by an increase in capital stock. In 1946 the bank's capitalization stood at $6,370,000, comprised of $3,370,000 of preferred and $3,000,000 of common stock. Following this date the bank's common stock was periodically increased, reaching $6,500,000 in 1952. On April 29 of that year a special stockholders' meeting was held at which approval was given to increase the bank's common stock by an additional $1,000,000. This increased the capital stock of The Detroit Bank to $7,500,000 of 375,000 shares of common stock. The purpose of this sale was to retire the remaining $2,000,000 of outstanding preferred stock. This was completed by May 1952. Additional sales of common stock were later held, increasing the bank's capital funds to $8,250,000 by December 1955.[82]

By the end of 1955, The Detroit Bank had grown to be one of the leading financial institutions in the United States. The ten years following the war had been a decade of growth and expansion. The decade ahead, however, was to witness an even greater growth. It was to begin with 1956, a pivotal year in the history of The Detroit Bank.

A New Direction

A BILLION DOLLAR BANK

While The Detroit Bank had witnessed many changes during the 20-year period that followed Michigan's banking holiday, significant changes were also occurring to the other members of Detroit's banking community. By the end of 1933, there were 11 financial institutions conducting business in the city. [At the beginning of 1956 this number had been reduced to 8.] There were three state banks, two industrial banks, four trust companies, and two national banks operating in Detroit as of December 1933. The state banks included the Detroit Savings Bank, the Commonwealth-Commercial State Bank, and the United Savings Bank; the industrial banks were the Industrial Morris Plan Bank and the Merchants Bank; the Bankers Trust, the Detroit Trust, the Equitable Trust, and the Union Guardian Trust were the four trust companies; while the National Bank of Detroit and the Manufacturers National were the city's two national banks.[1]

The first change following the bank holiday came in 1936. On August 3 of that year the Michigan Industrial Bank was allowed to reopen by the state banking department. Since the holiday, this bank had been in receivership and under the control of the state banking commissioner.

Following the holiday, the first new state bank to be established in Detroit was the Wabeek State Bank of Detroit. Organized July 1,

1938, it had an initial capitalization of $800,000. The bank was formed by the stockholders of the Wabeek State Bank, Birmingham, which had been organized in 1933 by Senator James Couzens. These two banks were consolidated a month after the formation of the second bank under the name Wabeek State Bank of Detroit, and the Fisher Building was designated as its main office. As of September 1, 1938, the Birmingham bank's offices in Ferndale and Birmingham were opened as branches of the new bank. The principal officers of the bank at the time of the consolidation were Frank Couzens, chairman of the board, and George B. Judson, president.

The same year that the Wabeek State Bank opened in Detroit, the Commonwealth-Commercial State Bank made the first of two name changes when it became the Commonwealth Bank. [The second change occurred on February 2, 1953, when it took on its present name of Bank of the Commonwealth.]

There were no further changes in Detroit's banking community until 1941. At the close of business on December 31, 1940, the Industrial Morris Plan Bank went into voluntary liquidation and sold substantially all of its assets to a newly organized national bank institution known as the Industrial National Bank. On January 2, 1941, the bank opened its doors for business as a national bank.

A series of consolidations by the city's four trust companies were the next changes to come about. On February 17, 1943, the Union Guardian Trust Company and the Detroit Trust Company consolidated under the latter's name. This was followed in November 1948, by a merger of the city's other two trust companies, the Equitable Trust and the Bankers Trust. These two joined under the name of Bankers-Equitable Trust Company. Then on October 26, 1951, the Detroit Trust and the Bankers-Equitable Trust consolidated under the name of the Detroit Trust Company. With this merger, Detroit Trust became the only independent trust company in the city.

In 1949 a new financial institution was opened in Detroit under the name of the City Bank. Organized as a state bank on January 31, the new bank commenced business on March 1. With a capital stock of one million dollars, City Bank's main office was located in the Penobscot Building at Griswold and Fort from where it still operates today.

On June 30, 1952, the United Savings Bank went into voluntary liquidation after more than 50 years of service. Virtually all of its assets were taken over by the Manufacturers National Bank. At the time of its absorption by Manufacturers, the United Savings Bank had resources of $53,355,000 and deposits in excess of $48,000,000. The Manufacturers National Bank made another important consolidation in 1955 when it took over the Industrial National Bank and its 16 branches on November 18. With this consolidation the resources of the Manufacturers National Bank stood at $831,674,958, making it the city's third largest bank behind the National Bank of Detroit with resources of $2,012,453,994 and The Detroit Bank with resources of $839,184,744.

In addition to the take-over of the Industrial National by the Manufacturers National, the year 1955 marked one other major change in Detroit's banking community. This came about when the Michigan Bank was converted from an industrial bank into a state bank.

By 1955 The Detroit Bank had grown to be the 25th largest bank in the United States. With 42 offices it was one of the leading commercial and savings banks in the country and was providing a wide range of banking services to the citizens of Detroit. The bank was lacking in one significant area—it did not have a full-fledged trust department. For several years the bank had provided some minimal trust services but these were a very small part of the bank's total operation.

It was felt by Chairman Dodge that if The Detroit Bank was to continue to grow and effectively compete for Detroit's banking business, it would have to provide a complete range of trust services. At this time, the Detroit Trust Company had the largest personal trust operation in Michigan. With a long history of cooperation between the two institutions, a merger between The Detroit Bank and the Detroit Trust Company seemed to be a logical consideration.*

As early as January 1955, the idea of a merger was seriously discussed by the directors of The Detroit Bank. The directors of the Detroit Trust Company had been approached and the idea of a merger was warmly received. Following these preliminary meetings, in-depth merger plans were prepared by the officers of the Detroit Bank under the close direction of President Raymond T. Perring.[2]

* For many years The Detroit Bank had referred customers seeking trust assistance to the Detroit Trust Company and Detroit Trust had reciprocated by referring banking customers to The Detroit Bank. In addition, three of The Detroit Bank's eleven directors, James McMillan, Herbert B. Trix, and Cleveland Thurber, were also at this time directors of the Detroit Trust Company.[3]

EIGHT-DAY HOLIDAY FOR ALL BANKS IN MICHIGAN

  **EXTRA**

33D YEAR, NO. 137   DETROIT, MICHIGAN, TUESDAY, FEBRUARY 14, 1933   24 PAGES   THREE CENTS

Proclamation Closing Banks to Protect State

Whereas, in view of the acute financial emergency now existing in the city of Detroit and throughout the state of Michigan, I deem it necessary in the public interest and for the preservation of the public peace, health and safety, and for the equal safeguarding without preference of the rights of all depositors in the banks and trust companies of this state and at the request of the Michigan Bankers' Association and the Detroit Clearing House and after consultation with the banking authorities, both national and state, with representatives of the United States Treasury Department, the Banking Department of the State of Michigan, the Federal Reserve Bank, the Reconstruction Finance Corporation, and with the United States Secretary of Commerce, I hereby proclaim the days from Tuesday, February 14th, 1933, to Tuesday, February 21st, 1933, both dates inclusive, to be public holidays during which time all banks, trust companies and other financial institutions conducting a banking or trust business within the state of Michigan shall not be opened for the transaction of banking or trust business, the same to be recognized, classed and treated and have the same effect in respect to such banks, trust companies and other financial institutions as other legal holidays under the laws of this state, provided that it shall not affect the making or execution of agreements or instruments in writing or interfere with judicial proceedings. Dated this 14th day of February, 1933, 1:32 a. m.

WILLIAM A. COMSTOCK, Governor of the State of Michigan.

ERNIE SCHAAF SUCCUMBS TO BRAIN OPERATION AFTER KNOCKOUT

NEW YORK, Feb. 14.—Ernie Schaaf, Boston boxer knocked unconscious in his bout with Primo Carnera Friday night, died at Polyclinic Hospital at 4:20 o'clock this morning.

Mortgage Holiday Asked in Nebraska

LINCOLN, Neb., Feb. 14.— Charles W. Bryan today issued an "emergency" proclamation, in which he asked farm and home mortgage holders to re-record all foreclosures until Congress the state Legislature send a board of conciliation can act.

Banking Holiday Here Ties Up 720 Million

Funds on deposit in Detroit banks, according to statements of December 31, 1933, amount:

First National Bank—	
Detroit	$291,517,287
Guardian National Bank of Commerce	
Detroit	$62,971,363
Detroit Savings Bank	$61,971,669
Commonwealth Commercial State Bank	$15,603,368
United Savings Bank	$11,655,804
Industrial Morris Plan Bank	$5,069,553
Union Guardian Trust Company	$37,110,563
Peoples Wayne County Bank	$72,156,061
Equitable Trust Company	$57,881,667
$675,887,587	

War Supply Bill Hiked $24,000,000

WASHINGTON, Feb. 14.—The War Department supply bill, carrying a total of $578,000,000 in appropriations for the next fiscal operations for the next fiscal year— $24,000,000 more than the House bill was approved by the Senate. An amendment by Senator Couzens, appropriating $50,000,000 for the care of homeless youths was rescinded.

Prisoner Is Slain By Fellow Convict

HUNTSVILLE, Tex., Feb. 14.— Clyde Thompson, who admittedly killed two boys in Eastland County in 1928 "for no reason" but whose death sentence was commuted to life imprisonment, today was listed by state prison officials as the slayer of a third man, this a fellow convict.

Utility Chief Took Life, Coroner Says

CHARLOTTE, N. C., Feb. 14.— Death of Roy L. Peterman, vice-president of the Southern Public Utilities Co. was pronounced a suicide by a coroner's jury. Peterman was found shot to death in his office Monday night.

Lay $230,000 Theft To High School Boy

OMAHA, Neb., Feb. 14—Raymond F. Beamer, 21, high school student, was to be returned to Blair today to answer charges of stealing $230,000 worth of state bonds.

STATEMENTS BY OFFICIALS

GOVERNOR COMSTOCK

"At 5 p. m. Monday, February 13, I was requested by telephone to reach Detroit from Lansing at the earliest possible moment to take part in an important conference relative to the general banking situation. This conference was precipitated by an unforeseen and acute situation which had suddenly arisen in the affairs of one of our leading financial institutions, the Union Guardian Trust Company.

"It was the consensus of opinion after long conference by those present that the difficulties might be ironed out provided time could be had for negotiations. As matters stood it would have been necessary to close the doors of the institution involved on the morning of February 14th, which would likely bring in its train disaster to many others of our banking institutions in Michigan.

Crisis Caused by Threatened Withdrawals and Frozen Assets

"The crisis was caused by the inability to realize immediately upon the assets of the institution to meet threatened withdrawals. For the protection of smaller depositors in our institutions and to prevent the withdrawal of large sums from the state of Michigan it was deemed wise to declare a banking holiday for a period sufficiently long to allow the situation to be cleared up.

"The conference was participated in by representatives of all clearing house banks of Detroit, representatives of the Michigan Bankers Association, Secretary of Commerce of the United States Roy D. Chapin, Undersecretary of the United States Treasury Arthur A. Ballantine, the deputy governor of the Federal Reserve Bank for the seventh district, the chief national bank examiner for the seventh district, representatives of the Reconstruction Finance Corporation and the Michigan Banking Commission.

"I am convinced that the action taken is in the best interest of the people of this state and especially the smaller depositors in our banking institutions."

Gives Detroit Agencies Time To Work Out Stabilizing Plans

ROY D. CHAPIN
Secretary of Commerce

"After discussion of the Detroit banking situation with the various authorities in Washington, the undersecretary of the Treasury, Arthur A. Ballantine, and I came to Detroit Saturday to co-operate with the bankers here. Certain conditions had developed in which Detroit bankers demand assistance of federal agencies necessary. The requirements as well as the time involved to arrange all the details, when were changing rapidly, made it seem wise to the bankers and to us that a public holiday be requested of Governor Comstock. He has seen fit to declare this and during its period an opportunity is provided to work out plans which we hope will stabilize the entire Michigan situation."

Under Secretary of Treasury Pledges Fullest Aid of U. S.

ARTHUR A. BALLANTINE
Under-Secretary of the Treasury

"From close contact during some days with phases of the banking situation existing in this state I believe that Governor Comstock acted very wisely in making his declaration of public holidays. All agencies of the federal government touching the banking field have been giving closest attention and fullest support to these state problems. The time available proved to be too short for final solutions, but further time and effort should be productive of constructive results. The governor's action gives opportunity for this."

All Detroit Banks and Trust Companies to Close for Holiday

"In accordance with the proclamation of Governor Comstock, declaring a bank holiday during the period from Feb. 14, 1933, to Feb. 21, 1933, and believing it to be in the best interests of the financial and business institutions of the state of Michigan, all Detroit banks and trust companies will not be open for business until termination of the holiday proclaimed by the governor."

This statement was made by Detroit banks and trust companies, and also by the Michigan Bankers Association for the banks and trust companies throughout the state.

Appeal From Detroit Bankers For Eight-Day Breathing Spell

"To his excellency, the governor of the state of Michigan:

"In view of the acute financial emergency now existing in the city of Detroit and throughout the state of Michigan, we

(Continued on Next Page, Col. 5)

UNION GUARDIAN TRUST CO. DIFFICULTY CAUSES ORDER; BRINGING U. S. AID

Governor William A. Comstock at 3 o'clock this morning issued a proclamation closing all banks, trust companies and all other financial institutions in Michigan for an eight-day period from February 14 to February 21 inclusive.

This action, ties up for at least a week, $650,523,979 in deposits in Detroit banks alone. In addition, $71,567,808 of trust deposits are impounded.

About 500 banks and trust companies are affected by the bank holiday.

Governor Comstock, in a signed statement, announced the cause of the bank holiday in Michigan was due to difficulties in which the Union Guardian Trust Company found itself.

"It was the consensus of opinion," the governor asserted, "that the difficulties might be ironed out, provided time could be had for negotiations."

The governor's statement said the Union Guardian Trust Company would have had to close its doors today, and it was in fear this step would cause disaster to other banking

(Continued on Next Page, Col. 1)

Detroit Times, Tuesday, February 14, 1933, City Edition—Extra. Courtesy of author.

TO THE CUSTOMERS OF THE DETROIT SAVINGS BANK:

Having been given a license by the Treasury Department of the United States, effective Tuesday morning, March 14, 1933, to resume normal relations with our depositors, your bank will on that day reopen for business at the usual opening hour, on the following basis:

The Commercial Department will resume and carry on all of your normal commercial business. We will accept your deposits, including checks on other banks subject only to final payment; do your normal checking and credit business; and endeavor in all ways to give you the service to which you are accustomed and entitled, and for which you have selected this bank (of course, no checks on Michigan banks dated prior to February 23, 1933, can be accepted for any purpose). This department is subject to two restrictions which have been continued in force by the President:

1. We are prohibited from disbursing any gold or gold certificates; and
2. We are prohibited from allowing any withdrawals in cash for hoarding.

Until the new plan which has been so vigorously and constructively undertaken by President Roosevelt and the Federal Government shall become more completely operative, we propose to operate our Savings Department under the same limitations which were effective before the President's proclamation. This confines disbursements in this department to cases of real necessity only. New deposits will be accepted in this department on a safekeeping basis only, and will continually be held available in cash or Federal Reserve funds, but with the understanding that they will be added to your regular savings account as soon as this department resumes entirely normal business.

In view of the series of bank holidays which have undoubtedly caused a congestion in business, we sincerely request your continued cooperation and your tolerance if there shall be delay in the transaction of your business or if you should suffer annoyance from circumstances of any kind which may appear avoidable. Please remember that the officers and employees of your bank are doing their utmost to take care of an unusual number of customers, and to handle an almost unprecedented amount of business.

We again wish to express our gratitude and appreciation to you for your patience.

THE DETROIT SAVINGS BANK

GRISWOLD AT STATE STREET

27 BRANCHES THROUGHOUT THE CITY

Detroit Savings Bank reopening announcement, *Detroit Free Press*, Tuesday, March 14, 1933. Courtesy of the Burton Historical Collection, Detroit Public Library.

City of Detroit scrip. With its treasury empty, the city was forced to issue eight million dollars of scrip in April 1933 to pay municipal employees. Courtesy of Ronald G. Williams.

Walter L. Dunham, president of the Detroit Savings Bank, 1927–33. Reprinted from *The Detroiter*, vol. 13, May 1, 1922, p. 8.

Charles H. Hewitt, president of The Detroit Bank and Trust Company, 1963–66. Courtesy of Detroit Bank and Trust.

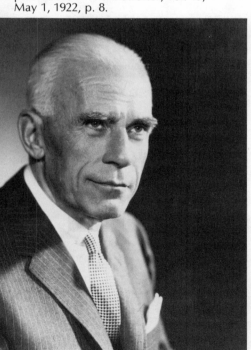

Raymond T. Perring, president of The Detroit Bank, and The Detroit Bank and Trust Company, 1952–63. Chairman of the board of The Detroit Bank and Trust Company, 1963 to date. Courtesy of Detroit Bank and Trust.

Joseph M. Dodge, president of the Detroit Savings Bank, and The Detroit Bank, 1933–52. Chairman of the board of The Detroit Bank, and The Detroit Bank and Trust Company, 1954–63. Courtesy of Detroit Bank and Trust.

Koichiro Asakai, Japanese Ambassador to the United States, presenting the Grand Cordon of the First Class Order of the Rising Sun to Joseph M. Dodge, 1962. This is the highest award that a non-Japanese national can receive. Courtesy of Detroit Bank and Trust.

C. Boyd Stockmeyer, president of The Detroit Bank and Trust Company, 1966 to date. Courtesy of Detroit Bank and Trust.

William B. Hall (at far left), senior vice-president (later executive vice-president and director), Detroit Bank and Trust, talks with Dr. Arnold Pilling (center), Wayne State University archeologist, while his associates examine the area where the remains of Fort Lernoult were found. Courtesy of Detroit Bank and Trust.

Remodeling of old Detroit Trust Company Building, in 1964. Courtesy of Detroit Bank and Trust.

Detroit Bank and Trust main office. Located at Fort Street and Washington Boulevard in the heart of Detroit's financial district, this building was opened in 1964. Courtesy of Detroit Bank and Trust.

For more than forty years, the Indian head has been the logo of The Detroit Bank, and The Detroit Bank and Trust Company. Courtesy of Detroit Bank and Trust.

Detroit Bank and Trust, branch no. 84, Fourteen Mile–Farmington Road. Located in West Bloomfield Township, this branch was opened in 1973. Courtesy of Detroit Bank and Trust.

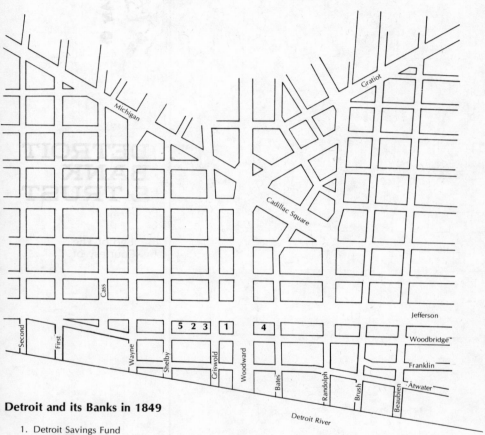

Detroit and its Banks in 1849

1. Detroit Savings Fund
   Institute.
2. Farmers and Mechanics'
   Bank of Michigan.
3. Michigan Insurance
   Company Bank.
4. Michigan State Bank.
5. Peninsular Bank.

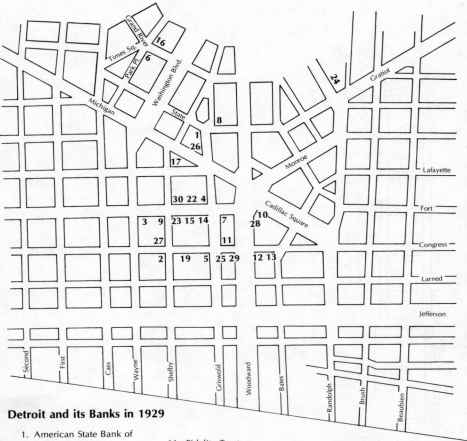

Detroit and its Banks in 1929

1. American State Bank of Detroit (1906).
2. Bankers Trust Company of Detroit (1917).
3. Bank of Detroit (1916).
4. Bank of Michigan (1884). (formerly the Dimes Savings Bank).
5. Central Trust Company of Detroit (1929).
6. City Industrial Bank (1927).
7. Commonwealth Commercial State Bank (1916).
8. Detroit Savings Bank (1849).
9. Detroit and Security Trust Company (1900) (formerly Detroit Trust Co.).
10. Equitable Trust Company (1926).
11. Fidelity Trust Company (1923).
12. Guaranty State Bank (1927).
13. Guaranty Trust Company of Detroit (1916).
14. Guardian Detroit Bank (1927).
15. Guardian Trust Company of Detroit (1924).
16. Industrial Morris Plan Bank (1917).
17. Metropolitan Industrial Bank (1928).
18. Metropolitan Trust Company (1925).*
19. Michigan Industrial Bank (1926).
20. Michigan State Bank of Detroit (1916).*
21. Northwestern State Bank (1915).*
22. Peninsular State Bank (1887).
23. Peoples Wayne County Bank (1928).
24. Standard Trust Company (1924).
25. Union Trust Company (1890).
26. United Savings Bank of Detroit (1901).
27. United States Trust Company (1925).
28. First National Bank in Detroit (1922).
29. National Bank of Commerce (1907).
30. Detroit Branch, Federal Reserve Bank of Chicago (1918).

*Bank is located outside downtown area.

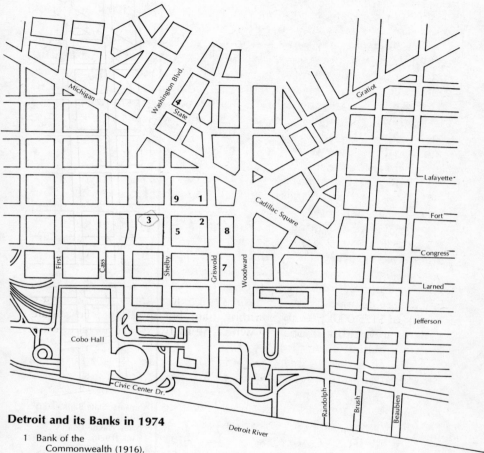

Detroit and its Banks in 1974

1. Bank of the
   Commonwealth (1916).
2. City National Bank (1949).
3. Detroit Bank and Trust
   Company (1849).
4. First Independence
   National Bank (1970).
5. Manufacturers National
   Bank (1933).
6. Merchants Bank (1928).*
7. Michigan National Bank
   (1926).
8. National Bank of
   Detroit (1933).
9. Detroit Branch, Federal
   Reserve Bank of
   Chicago (1918).

*Bank is located outside downtown area.

The first preliminary step of the merger occurred on August 1, 1955, when the Detroit Trust Company merged with the Wabeek State Bank under the name of the Detroit Wabeek Bank and Trust Company. Now a merger with the new Detroit Wabeek Bank and Trust would not only provide The Detroit Bank with a strong and established trust operation, it would also allow the bank to expand into Detroit's growing northern suburban communities of Birmingham and Ferndale. However, if The Detroit Bank was going to continue to operate the two Wabeek branch offices in Birmingham and Ferndale, it would also have to acquire, as required by state banking law, the other two local banks then in operation in these communities. They were the Birmingham National Bank and the Ferndale National Bank.

The Birmingham National Bank had been chartered June 15, 1933. It first opened for business on July 15 in offices on Woodward at Hamilton in the center of Birmingham. The bank's original capitalization was $100,000. During the following 22 years, the bank grew with the unprecedented population increase of the entire Birmingham-Bloomfield Hills area. Due to the rapid expansion, a branch office was opened in November 1954, on Woodward Avenue at 14 Mile Road. The Ferndale National Bank received its charter on January 23, 1945 and began operations the following November 15 with a capitalization of $175,000. Like the Birmingham National, the Ferndale National Bank grew proportionately with the active industrial and residential area in which it was located.[4]

While the merger plans were made as quietly as possible, a consolidation of this size could not be kept under cover for long. On November 15, 1955, the *Detroit Times* published an article stating that "the long rumored merger" between The Detroit Bank and the Detroit Wabeek Bank and Trust Company would take place within the next ten days to two weeks.[5] Although much of the information in the *Times* article was correct, the announcement was premature. There was still a considerable amount of work to be done before the consolidation could be completed.

The force behind this merger was President Raymond T. Perring. Through his strong leadership, the project was carried forward and the mountain of details attended to. Perring was faced with seemingly endless hours of meetings and conferences. It was his responsibility to bring together the various parts and pieces of this very complicated undertaking.

212

Finally, by the spring of 1956, the plans for the merger were completed. On June 11, 1956, the State Banking Department approved the consolidation.[6] That same day, the directors of the four banks voted to recommend approval of the merger to their respective stockholders. These recommendations were to be presented at special stockholders' meetings scheduled for mid-August, with the merger taking effect the first of September.

On the following day, June 12, a press conference was called at the prestigious Detroit Athletic Club to officially announce the impending merger. The small gathering of newsmen and bankers assembled in one of the DAC's decorous second-floor meeting rooms. The announcement was jointly made by Joseph M. Dodge, board chairman of The Detroit Bank; Selden B. Daume, president of the Detroit Wabeek Bank and Trust Company; and Herbert H. Gardner, president of the Birmingham National and Ferndale National banks. In less than two minutes the group was informed by Chairman Dodge that the majorities of the boards of directors of the four banks had agreed to merge.[7] Thus, except for the formalities of approval by the stockholders, The Detroit Bank, the Detroit Wabeek Bank and Trust Company, the Birmingham National Bank, and the Ferndale National Bank had pooled their resources to become a new giant on the Detroit financial scene—The Detroit Bank and Trust Company.

Joseph Dodge stated that the merger was the natural result of the growing community of interest between Detroit and its suburbs and was in line with the trend toward the creation of metropolitan authorities to resolve mutual problems. He also cited the spreading of industry to outlying areas and their need for larger banking facilities.[8]

The resources of the new Detroit Bank and Trust Company were to be in excess of one billion dollars, making the merger the largest corporate consolidation ever arranged in Michigan. Contributing to the resources of this billion-dollar bank were The Detroit Bank's $839,319,000; Detroit Wabeek's $187,387,000; Birmingham National's $40,450,000; and Ferndale National's $18,181,000. This merger would now make Detroit the third city in the nation to have two or more billion-dollar banks. New York and Chicago were the only other cities of that rank.[9]

At the press conference, Dodge introduced the eight principal officers of the new bank: Joseph M. Dodge, board chairman; Selden

213

B. Daume, vice-chairman of the board; Raymond T. Perring, president and director; Charles H. Hewitt, executive vice-president and director; Herbert H. Gardner, senior vice-president and director; Milton J. Drake, senior vice-president; Clarence J. Huddleston, senior vice-president; and William J. Thomas, senior vice-president.

In addition to introducing the bank's principal officers, Chairman of the Board Joseph M. Dodge announced to the assembled newsmen that the bank's board would now be comprised of 20 members. The new board was to include all of The Detroit Bank's 11 directors, including Chairman Dodge, President Perring, and Executive Vice-President Hewitt. Added to this number were Vice-Chairman Daume, and Senior Vice-President Gardner. The remaining seven directors were all former board members of the Detroit Wabeek Bank and Trust Company.

The merger that joined the Detroit Wabeek Bank and Trust Company, the Birmingham National Bank, and the Ferndale National Bank with The Detroit Bank produced not only a bank with greater resources but a bank with an expanded branch system. As a result of the merger, 10 branch offices were added to The Detroit Bank's 41. Branch number 42 was assigned to the Detroit Wabeek's main office building on West Fort Street at the corner of Shelby. Prior to the Wabeek State Bank merger in 1955, the building had housed the offices of the Detroit Trust Company. Opened in 1915, the building was designed by Albert Kahn and built especially for the Detroit Trust Company. Originally it occupied 40 feet on the southwest corner of Fort and Shelby. In 1926, the building was extended to a frontage of 140 feet on Fort Street and took the form familiar to Detroiters today.[10]

On August 21, 1956, a special stockholders' meeting of The Detroit Bank was held and the board of directors' merger recommendation was approved.[11] Along with this proposal, the stockholders approved the change of the bank's name to The Detroit Bank and Trust Company and voted to increase the bank's capital stock from $12,375,000 to $18,378,500.*

On September 4, an organizational meeting of the board of

* The merger was effected through a share-for-share exchange of stock in The Detroit Bank and Trust Company with that in The Detroit Bank, the Detroit Wabeek, and the Birmingham National, and nine-tenths of a share for each share in the Ferndale National.[12]

directors of what became The Detroit Bank and Trust Company was held. The bank's principal officers were elected and a new set of by-laws was approved. In addition, the directors appointed a Birmingham Advisory Board and a Ferndale Advisory Board. They felt that these men, who were formerly the directors of the Birmingham and the Ferndale National banks, would bring to the new bank their valuable knowledge of and experience in their communities. With the conclusion of this organizational meeting, The Detroit Bank and Trust Company was finally launched.[13]

By the end of 1956, the resources of The Detroit Bank and Trust Company stood at $1,024,282,384, with demand deposits of $533,993,311, and savings and time deposits of $416,880,951.[14] At the annual meeting held January 15, 1957, Chairman of the Board Joseph Dodge reported to the stockholders on the progress of the bank following the merger. He concluded his remarks by stating:

> Deposits, resources, and capital funds of the bank were increased as a result of the merger, but the principal objectives were to broaden and diversify services, and to extend operations into territories not already covered. The institutions complemented one another admirably and their consolidation involved a minimum of overlapping and duplication. While the full benefits of such a merger are realized only over a period of time . . . , The Detroit Bank and Trust Company with its well-rounded services and enlarged scope of operation has unquestionably improved its competitive position.[15]

It was with this positive attitude and forward-looking leadership that the merger had been undertaken and completed. The directors and officers of The Detroit Bank and Trust Company were now to turn their attention to the decade of the 1960s.

BRANCHES, BRANCHES EVERYWHERE

Generally, the decade of the 1950s was a period of prosperity for Detroit. However, the country suffered a sharp recession, which started during the latter part of 1957 and continued for about a year. The recession—the third economic adjustment in the past ten years—while more severe than the others, was also shorter in duration. To a large extent, the business decline was in the area of inventories and durable goods. Inventory liquidation was particularly sharp in the first half of 1958. Business expenditures for plant

215

equipment, which had been running at boom levels, also dropped at this time. Consumers reduced their purchases of durable goods, such as automobiles and appliances, but maintained their buying of non-durable goods and services.

The city of Detroit, a producer principally of durable goods, was one of the areas hardest hit by the recession. With automobile production off 30 percent to the lowest level in ten years, Detroit's economy suffered heavily. Local figures on unemployment, payrolls, retail sales, housing starts, electric power consumption, bank deposits and loans—all compared unfavorably with national statistics. Employment in Michigan auto plants, for example, which stood at 503,000 in 1953, dropped to 293,000 in 1958.[16]

The statements of The Detroit Bank and Trust Company reflected the downswing in the city's economy. Resources, which had stood at a high of $1,024,282,000 in 1956, fell to $954,940,000 by the end of 1958. During the same period, deposits dropped from $950,874,000 to $868,916,000; and loans dropped from $374,852,000 to $336,305,000.[17]

Indications that Detroit was in for a period of financial difficulty were evident early in 1957. At that time, Mayor Albert E. Cobo, who was in the last year of his second four-year term and who had been one of the city's most progressive mayors, was preparing his budget for the coming fiscal year. Cobo was having serious problems in balancing this budget and was faced with a $17,000,000 deficit. The spiral of inflation in costs and pay raises, higher welfare relief costs due to unemployment, and reduced sales tax revenues, all spelled trouble. In an effort to help solve this problem, Mayor Cobo turned to Detroit Bank and Trust Chairman Joseph M. Dodge. Cobo asked Dodge to form an advisory committee on taxation and finances to study the city's current financial situation and the impact of local taxes on the city's economic future.[18] Speaking of Dodge, Cobo said:

> He is the logical person to help us. He is a man of vast experience in finance and government with a warm love for his city and he can bring us facts and advice which will shape future fiscal policies.[19]

In outlining the functions of the proposed committee, Cobo stated:

> What we must determine is how the mounting tax rates of schools, county, and state are affecting industry and business. Are they being driven out of the city and state to cities with more favorable tax rates? How can we stop that, keep what we have and attract new industry and business? [20]

216

Dodge willingly accepted Cobo's request and in his characteristic, hard-driving style, set to work immediately. He broke his committee down into six subcommittees or task forces. Each task force was assigned a specific major area to study. This permitted a rather large group of participants, working concurrently, to concentrate their efforts and produce a series of objective, analytical reports that in combination would give broad coverage to the assignment. The six task forces were to study (1) pensions, (2) capital expenditures and debt, (3) assessment practices, (4) city-county government, (5) revenue sources, and (6) trends in operating expenditures. To coordinate the activities of these six task forces, Dodge established a Technical Committee and appointed George D. Bailey as its chairman. Bailey was a senior partner of the accounting firm of Touche, Niven, Bailey and Smart [currently, the firm is known as Touche Ross and Company].[21]

Dodge's committee worked zealously for almost a year. Unfortunately, Mayor Cobo never received its detailed and accomplished report. The mayor died of a heart attack on September 12, 1957. Louis C. Miriani, Common Council president, succeeded him. The Dodge Report, as it later became known, was sent to Miriani in late November, and was made public December 15, 1957.[22]

While some general principles which might serve as guides to further action were cited, and certain areas that called for future study were noted, the Dodge Report concentrated on the development of a suitable factual basis for the formulation of continuing sound fiscal policies. The report disclosed five major fiscal problems that would have to be dealt with effectively to keep the city financially stable and able to meet its future community responsibilities. These problems were: (1) the sharp and continuing upward trend of operating expenditures; (2) the partial abandonment of pay-as-you-go capital financing; (3) the large unfunded liability in the retirement systems; (4) the inequalities in property assessments; and (5) the near exhaustion of available revenues from present sources.[23]

As direction, the report pointed out four courses of action, no one of which would produce over-night results, but which had long-range potentialities for substantial savings. These included: (1) emphasis on the best methods of expenditure management and control; (2) more professional attention and study to the problems of forward capital budgeting; (3) the advantages of an opportunity to return to a pay-as-you-go basis within a few years for the city's

normal program of capital improvement; and (4) eliminating duplica-
tion and overlapping in city-county functions.[24]

In conclusion, the report stated that there was no evidence that
the upward trend of expenditures was abating. It stated, in fact, that
further study might determine a higher level of expenditures to be
necessary. Thus, the Dodge Committee felt that the city faced a
potentially increasing gap between revenues and expenditures. The
report suggested several courses of action that might be implemented to help meet this situation. These included: (1) tightening
control of expenditures; (2) transferring certain functions to the
county or state; (3) increasing the productivity of the existing
revenue system; and (4) developing new sources of revenue. The
nature of these alternatives indicated that emergency action was to
be avoided. However, "If they can be weighted, related, and
considered together for the purpose of arriving at objectives and
decisions, it may be found that a judicious use of all of them will
provide the soundest base for Detroit's financial future." [25]

The final report that the 52-member Dodge Committee turned
over to Mayor Miriani was 472 pages long, bound in 7 volumes, and
weighed over 5 pounds.[26] Some of the committee's recommendations were immediately put into effect, others were instituted a short
time later, while still others were never implemented. Generally, the
Dodge Report was enthusiastically received and the implementation
of many of its recommendations went a long way in holding the line
on, if not completely solving, Detroit's financial problems.[27]

Several years later when the city was again facing severe financial
problems, an editorial was published in the *Detroit Free Press* which
recalled the work of the Dodge Committee. It read in part:

> The City's entire fiscal situation was thoroughly reviewed several
> years ago by the Dodge Committee, and sound recommendations
> were made at that time, including steps to acquire new revenue
> sources.
> It might be wise to bring it out of whatever pigeon hole it
> languishes in, and give it a re-study.
> It might reveal ways and means for climbing out of some of the
> pitfalls into which Detroit has been pushed or permitted to fall.[28]

The recession of 1957–58 was in a large part caused by a drop in
automobile production and resulting unemployment, at least in the
Detroit area. In general, however, the automobile industry outdid
itself in the 1950s and 1960s. In 1955 a new all-time high of 9,169,292
vehicles were manufactured. This figure was not reached again until

1964 when 7,751,822 cars and 1,540,453 motor trucks and buses were produced. Then, in 1965, the magical ten-million figure was broken for the first time, as 11,057,366 units rolled off the assembly lines.[29]

There were many changes in the industry in a decade and a half. Nash, a Wisconsin-based company, became American Motors and absorbed the Hudson Motor Car Company in 1954. Both Nash and Hudson were discontinued, and American Motors concentrated on Ramblers. In 1954 the venerable Packard was taken over by Indiana-based Studebaker; the Detroit Packard plant was closed in 1956, and the last Packard was built in 1958. Then in 1963 Studebaker gave up, as far as United States production was concerned, and built cars only in Canada. A new effort to enter the field was made in 1947 when the Kaiser-Frazer line was introduced. That company merged with Toledo's Willys in 1953 and then ceased passenger car production in 1955, limiting itself thereafter to trucks and Jeeps. Another attempt in 1947 to establish a company producing a car of radical design, the Tucker, failed before it could get into actual production. By 1965 the auto manufacturers of passenger cars were down to the Big Three and the much smaller American Motors. In 1967 General Motors turned out its one-hundred-millionth unit, a Chevrolet, and a few days later Ford passed the seventy-million mark.

Largely as a result of the expansion of the auto industry, the growth of population in Detroit and Michigan which had started during the war years, continued at a rapid rate in the late forties and early fifties. By 1950 Michigan's population stood at 6,371,766, while Detroit's reached an all-time high of 1,849,568. During the next ten years, the population of Michigan continued to increase to 7,823,194, a gain of nearly 23 percent, greater than that of any other state in this part of the country. On the other hand, Detroit's population decreased, slipping to 1,678,613. A large part of this loss can be attributed to the move to suburbia by the city's white middle class. For while Detroit's population decreased 170,000, the three-county metropolitan area population increased by more than 750,000 between 1950 and 1960.

It was into these fast growing suburban areas that The Detroit Bank and Trust Company expanded its branch operations in the decade following 1956. During this ten-year-period, the bank opened 20 new branch offices. From 1957 through 1960, the bank established branches in Clarenceville, Franklin Village, Nankin Township [present-day Westland], Lake Point Village, Shelby Township, Birmingham, and Dearborn Township.

In early 1961, the bank announced a million-dollar branch office expansion and remodeling program. The year-long program involved customer service additions to ten banking offices throughout the bank's three-county branch system. Improvements ranged in size from a dramatic, contemporary $300,000 motor bank in Birmingham to new parking lots and night depository chutes. In 1960 the bank had also built or done remodeling work at six branch sites, representing an additional investment of over $500,000.[30]

During the next two years, three more branches were opened in the suburban communities of Royal Oak Township, Redford Township, and Sterling Township.[31] Branch 59 at Greenfield and Ten Mile in Royal Oak Township was typical of the new branches that the bank was opening. Originally opened in temporary quarters in July 1962, the branch's permanent office was completed in October 1963. Its contemporary design departed significantly from the conventional conception of bank offices. A dramatic effect was created by the use of masses of concrete, glass, and brick as basic materials. The architect described the building in these words:

> Basically the building is in a white motif to preserve the definition of the structural form, both on the outside and the inside.
> Bright and harmonious colors are used whenever accents of color are required to bring forth the importance of various details.
> The main public area consists of a pure white terrazzo floor with white marble chip aggregate column covers. Warmth is added in this area by the use of wood paneling on the teller cages, also with accent spots of deep cadmium orange over the drive-in windows.[32]

The bank continued its branch expansion by opening offices in Orchard Lake, Farmington Township, Sterling Township [present-day Sterling Heights], Clinton Township, and Plymouth Township. Thus by the end of 1966, the bank's branch system had grown to 71 offices located in Detroit and 13 suburban communities.

During this period of branch growth, there were several key changes of the bank's principal officers. On May 5, 1960, Vice-President William B. Hall was named a senior vice-president. In December 1961, Senior Vice-President and Director Herbert B. Gardner retired from his position as senior vice-president though he continued to serve as a director of the bank. The following year Vice-Chairman of the Board Selden B. Daume retired, though he too continued to serve as a director.

On January 15, 1963, Joseph M. Dodge stepped down as chairman and chief executive officer of The Detroit Bank and Trust Company.[33]

When Dodge had become president of the bank in December 1933, there were just over $60,000,000 in resources, 27 branches, and 16 officers. His contribution to the welfare of the institution can best be attested by the fact that when he retired just over 29 years later, there were resources of nearly $1,100,000,000, 59 branches, and 143 officers.[34] During this period, he stimulated and encouraged his associates and set forth the sound fundamental policies which guided the bank's growth and development into one of the nation's leading banking institutions. Dodge continued as a director of and management consultant to the bank and was elected to the position of honorary chairman.

Upon Joseph Dodge's retirement, the directors elected President Raymond T. Perring as chairman and chief executive officer, and Executive Vice-President Charles H. Hewitt as president and chief administrative officer. Perring was a worthy successor to Dodge, having begun his career with the bank in 1928 and serving as president since 1952. The final changes during this period came in September 1964, when senior vice-presidents Milton J. Drake and William B. Hall were named executive vice-presidents.

As chairman and chief executive officer, Raymond T. Perring was to give the bank leadership in a new direction. While Joseph M. Dodge had been a leader in local, national and international banking, and financial affairs, Perring was to be active in the city's civic and cultural life, helping to solve the many problems that faced Detroit and its citizens. This was a direction that the bank was to take into the sixties and seventies. Typical of Perring's involvement were his serving as a director of Detroit Renaissance; treasurer and trustee of the McGregor Fund; trustee and secretary-treasurer of New Detroit, Inc.; vice-president and director of the Detroit Symphony Orchestra, and vice-chairman for the Michigan chapter of the United Negro College Fund. Following Perring's lead, many of the bank's staff also became involved in Detroit's civic and cultural life, helping to make the city a better place for its people.

The years following the bank's merger witnessed a number of changes on the board of directors. In October 1962, Director Frank D. Eaman died and Director Herbert B. Gardner retired. Gardner continued to serve on the Birmingham and Ferndale Advisory Boards. These two vacancies were filled by the election of Frank A. Colombo and Roblee B. Martin. Colombo was executive vice-president and general manager of the J. L. Hudson Company, Detroit's world famous department store. Among his many civic responsibilities,

Colombo served as president of the Detroit Convention Bureau, chairman of the Greater Detroit Board of Commerce, president of the Central Business District Association, and as a trustee for Grace Hospital.

At the annual meeting held January 21, 1964, Selden B. Daume retired from the board. Daume had been vice-chairman of the board from 1956 to 1962. When he retired from active service in October 1962, he concluded a career spanning 35 years, nearly all of which was devoted to the trust business.

The late fifties and early sixties were a period of growth and expansion for The Detroit Bank and Trust Company—growth in terms of dollars; expansion in terms of physical plant and services. When Joseph Dodge stepped down, the bank's management assumed new leadership as Raymond Perring took control as chief executive officer.

The modern age of computers also came to the bank in the early sixties. The processing of checks, the centralization of record keeping, and demand deposit accounting, among other operations, were now all performed by new automatic electronic equipment. This sophisticated machinery provided increased operating efficiency and enhanced service to the bank's customers.[35] In addition to the expansion of the branch system into Detroit's growing suburban areas, plans were developed for the construction of a magnificent new main office building.

FORT AT WASHINGTON

When The Detroit Bank and Trust Company merger was completed in 1956, it was obvious that the Griswold-State main office would not be able to house the new bank. The 12 floors of the old Detroit Savings Bank Building were filled to overflowing; there was just no further room in which to expand. By 1956 several departments had been forced to move to a scattered half dozen downtown locations because of space limitations. With staff needs mounting, and with demands for suitable space for automated banking machines as well as for greatly enlarged banking volume and potential, it was decided that a new central headquarters building should be constructed.

To prepare recommendations for the board, a building committee comprising Directors Dodge, Daume, Perring, Green, Thurber, Trix, and Yaw was appointed in January 1957. They immediately began to search for an architect.[36]

Fortunately for the bank, a site for a new building was readily available. The property was on the southeast corner of Fort and Washington adjacent to the former Detroit Trust Company Building. A prime site from a real estate standpoint, although used as a parking lot in recent years, it was now owned by the bank, having previously been owned by the Detroit Trust Company prior to the merger.

On March 26, 1957, the board of directors approved a contract with the locally based architectural firm of Harley, Ellington and Day. The following November, the go-ahead was given to the architects to develop plans for a new bank building, which was to be nine stories plus two penthouse floors in height.[37] Planning was well underway when Vincent J. Peters, vice-president of Cushman and Wakefield, Inc., a leading New York office leasing and management firm, visited Detroit and heard about the project through a friend. The time was September 1960.

Peters was surprised to learn that no major building had been erected for general office rental in Detroit's downtown area in over 30 years. Returning to New York, he could not shake the idea that an opportunity existed in Detroit if creative, modern-day real estate thought could be applied. He formulated some ideas and returned to Detroit in November with two proposals for consideration by the bank's principal officers.[38]

One proposal was that the bank erect a larger building and devote part of it to rental space as an investment. The other was a suggestion that the bank's land be sold or leased to an outside owner who would erect a larger building and lease part of it back to the bank. The officers looked more favorably on the second plan, but only on condition that a compatible ownership that would retain long-term possession could be found.

Peters returned to New York with permission to seek insurance company backing for such a project. Although several were contacted, all turned the proposal down because of preoccupation with other major projects at the time. Persisting, Peters persuaded the bank's officers to meet with a private investment builder instead.

Sam Minskoff and Sons, builder-owner of many office properties in New York, was approached in May 1961. Expressing immediate interest, the Minskoffs worked with Peters in drawing up a proposal which was submitted to the bank's officials later that month. Negotiations and paperwork from this point on took less than three

223

months, and the final proposal was presented to the directors at a special board meeting on July 18. Following considerable discussion, the directors approved the revised plans; and a news conference was held on July 21 to officially announce the new building plan.[39]

The revised plan called for the bank to sell the land to the Minskoffs and sign a lease for seven floors of the proposed 26-story building. The builder-owner guaranteed not to sell the building for 30 years without prior bank approval and, at the end of that time, to give the bank the option to buy. Options on additional space for expansion were given to the bank in addition to the right of first refusal on any space vacated in the building. The bank was also protected with a voice in selection of the building design and materials. An interesting twist in the proceedings lay in the fact that the bank underwrote financing of both temporary construction and permanent mortgages. Harley, Ellington, Cowin and Stirton (Harley, Ellington and Day had adopted a new name in 1961; today their name is Harley Ellington-Pierce Yee and Associates) immediately went to work to expand their original design.

A New Home

On November 28, 1961, ground was broken for The Detroit Bank and Trust Company Building, as the new structure was to be named, and construction of the bank's eighth home office was begun.[40]

When the contractors began digging the foundation of the new building, they uncovered a number of interesting artifacts. The first was a bank vault which had seen service during the 1920s. Workmen who opened up a small section of blacktop for the groundbreaking ceremonies struck the top of the concrete vault, which had outlived by 30 years or so the bank for which it was originally built. Big and tough, the vault had been well planted when the main office of the old Bank of Detroit went up in 1921. When the building was razed in the early 1930s because of the merger with the Guardian Detroit Group, the vault was covered and its massive weight used for the foundation of the parking lot. The vault measured 80 by 12 feet, with walls 14 to 22 inches thick. The 12-inch roof had been built of I-beams, steel bars, and concrete. So well constructed was the vault that it took two 6,000 pound steel balls swinging from 80-foot tower cranes to demolish the old walls.[41] While the uncovering of this old vault was an interesting sidelight to Detroit's banking history, it could in no way compare to the major historical significance of the second finding.

A heavy spring downpour inundated the excavated area out of which the steel skeleton of the bank's new building was rising. When the sun emerged from behind the storm clouds, a strange post-like object was found projecting from the north wall of the huge hole which had been dug for the foundation of the building. A quick probing indicated that more lay behind the post.

All work in this area was stopped immediately and a call went out for Henry D. Brown, director of the Detroit Historical Museum. Within hours after the post was unearthed, Brown was at the site and tentatively authenticated the post as a portion of the old British stockade, Fort Lernoult. Positive confirmation came from Arnold Pilling, Wayne State University archeologist.

Further investigation by Pilling revealed that the post was one of a series attached to a crossbeam. A short distance away, Pilling's team of workers found another series of pickets, also a part of Fort Lernoult. Once the authenticity of the discovery was confirmed, news media were invited to the site, where Pilling explained that what had been uncovered was a section of the southwest bastion of the fort. Following an extensive study of historical records, it was discovered that it was at this very southwest bastion that Captain Moses Porter and his detachment of troops first raised the American flag over the village of Detroit on July 11, 1796.

Pilling described the finding as "the greatest discovery of this type in Detroit since 1891." [42] In that year, workmen constructing the first Federal Building had uncovered a large number of artifacts and remains.* Still later, laborers excavating the area for the foundation of the Detroit Trust Company Building had recovered additional items.

Valuable as these earlier findings were, they actually provided very little information about the fort. Archeology was an infant science then, and few records were kept of either discovery. Realizing that this current discovery provided a remarkable opportunity, the bank and Minskoff and Sons agreed to underwrite a program of reclaiming as many artifacts as possible from the area.

As a result of Pilling's research, a great deal of hitherto unknown or unproven information about Fort Lernoult was established: (1) the long-held belief that the center of the crossing of Fort and Shelby streets had been the center of the fort was finally confirmed now that the position of the southwest bastion was verified; (2) the many

* The first Federal Building occupied the same site as the present Federal Building, the north side of Fort Street across from the new Detroit Bank and Trust Building. [43]

conflicting descriptions of the fort were explained by the fact that it was almost continuously modified, sometimes to strengthen it, and other times to repair the damage wrought by an unsympathetic Mother Nature; (3) it was discovered that, although British in concept, the fort was quite French in construction. Villagers, who were forced by the British to aid in the building of the fort, had employed many French techniques, including the use of twig matting and mud mortar; and (4) bits of glassware, ceramics, animal bones and fruit pits, clearly identified by stratification by the archeological team, provided insight into the lives of both the British and American troops who had occupied the fort.[44]

Following the completion of Pilling's work, construction was resumed. Countless man-hours later, the building neared completion and the bank began occupying the first seven floors. The first major move began in September 1963, and it took 28 vans and 3000 man-hours to accomplish the transfer. A second move of comparable proportions took place in October 1964.* [45]

While the new building was nearing completion, and the first move was underway, the bank began a separate but related building project: the thorough renovation of the former Detroit Trust Company Building. The trust building handsomely complemented the main building and was linked to it by a three-story, glass-enclosed passageway. In the renovation process, the contractors virtually stripped the old building to the walls and then rebuilt to serve modern banking needs in such aspects as new reinforcings for floors which were to carry heavy automated equipment. Upon completion of the renovation, the old trust building became the principal customer banking lobby of the new man office, with related main office functions on its other four floors.[46]

On December 6, 1964, The Detroit Bank and Trust Company officially dedicated its new building. While the dedication ceremony was a gala affair, it was marked by a sad note. On Wednesday, December 2, the citizens of Detroit were saddened to learn of the death of Honorary Board Chairman Joseph M. Dodge. Dodge had been ill since September.

Joseph M. Dodge was a quiet, modest man who worked tirelessly and demanded excellence. Though reserved, there was a surge of

---

* With the opening of the new main office building, the office at Griswold and State was continued as a major downtown banking center and today houses the Time Credit (Consumer Loan), Mortgage, Training, and Trust Real Estate departments.[47]

warmth in him that friends said made him formal but not formidable. With his passing, Detroit, the nation, and the world lost a financial giant.

Of his many accomplishments, Dodge was probably best remembered for his work in Germany and Japan. In addition to his service under Presidents Truman and Eisenhower, Dodge also served President John F. Kennedy as treasurer of the Tractors for Freedom Committee, which tried to swap farm machinery for men captured in the abortive Bay of Pigs invasion.

In addition to his duties at the bank, Dodge had been chairman, member, trustee, or director of more than 40 civic, charitable, and business groups. He served as a director and member of the finance committee of the Chrysler Corporation, resigning in 1963 after 15 years on its board. Of the trophies and awards he received for his many public services, one he was particularly proud of came as the result of his service in Japan. For his three years' work there, the Emperor of Japan awarded him the Grand Cordon of the First Class Order of the Rising Sun in 1962.

Shortly after the dedication ceremonies of the new building, a descriptive article appeared in the *Detroit Free Press*. The article read in part:

> The Detroit Bank and Trust Company Building strikes a note of restrained dignity befitting a bank. Architects Harley, Ellington, Cowin and Stirton do not seem to have been concerned with acrophobia. Dark-tinted floor-to-ceiling windows are set in precast concrete frames. Projecting from the glass, these frames combine to form a grid pattern which gives the building its essential character. An arcade at the ground level and a crowning colonnade complete the composition. Following the recent trend, the building is set back from the street to provide space for a landscaped plaza.[48]

Following the opening of its new main office, The Detroit Bank and Trust Company continued to experience a period of growth which had begun after the 1958 recession. By the beginning of 1967, resources had grown from $954,940,000 (as of 1958) to $1,677,898,000. During this same period, commercial and consumer loans had increased from $336,305,000 to $592,626,500 and deposits had grown from $868,916,000 to $1,534,702,000.[49]

In 1968 the bank reached a milestone when its resources passed the two-billion-dollar mark. In its annual report to stockholders for 1968, the bank reported resources totaling $2,068,498,896 at year-end.[50] A portion of this growth came as a result of the bank's second merger which took place in 1967.

227

In the fall of 1966, the bank's principal officers were presented with a merger proposal by officials of the Commercial State Bank of Roseville.[51] The directors of the Roseville bank had been talking with a number of Detroit bankers about a merger following the recent death of the president and founder of the bank. John Huetteman, Sr., the former president, had also been the bank's major stockholder. Roseville is a suburban community northeast of Detroit. The Commercial State Bank of Roseville had been organized in March 1951, and served an area of approximately ten square miles. Operating three offices, the bank had deposits of nearly $25,000,000, and had a capitalization of $1,400,000. Roseville showed promise of continued growth and was in an area in which The Detroit Bank and Trust Company had not been permitted to open a branch office.[52]

At the board meeting of November 22, 1966, the subject of the merger was brought up. After lengthy discussion, Chairman Perring and the other senior officers were authorized to negotiate with the directors of the Roseville bank in an effort to develop a plan of stock acquisition and merger.[53]

In January 1967, the final merger plans were approved by the directors of The Detroit Bank and Trust Company. In March a special shareholders meeting was called and the merger was formally approved as was a capital stock increase. As required under the terms of the merger agreement, the bank's capital stock now stood at $21,789,660. On September 28, the Federal Reserve Board approved the merger effective as of the close of business October 31, 1967.[54]

As a result of this merger, The Detroit Bank and Trust Company acquired the three offices of the former Roseville bank, all three being located on Gratiot Avenue. In addition, the bank received permission from the State Banking Commission to open a fourth branch in Roseville. As was the case with the merger in 1956, the bank established an advisory board comprised of the acquired bank's directors. At the time of the merger, John Huetteman, Jr., chairman of the board of the Roseville bank, became a member of this advisory board.[55]

In addition to the branches acquired as a result of the Roseville merger, the bank opened seven more offices during 1967, 1968 and 1969. This brought to a total of 82 the number of branch offices operated by The Detroit Bank and Trust Company at the close of the 1960s. Another indicator of the growth that the bank was experiencing during this period was in the size of its staff. In 1960, the staff numbered 2,063; by the end of 1969, it had increased to 2,463.[56]

In 1967 the bank undertook another building project of a somewhat different nature from a banking office. On August 8 the bank and the 333 West Fort Corporation announced joint efforts to construct a nine-level parking garage to be located on Fort Street directly across Washington Boulevard from the bank's main office. Designed by Architect Louis Redstone, the garage was opened in May 1970, and included a ten-story office building constructed by the Detroit Mortgage & Realty Company.[57]

Another building project which the bank had undertaken was the construction of a new Purchasing Office Building which was completed in 1965. The Purchasing Department moved from its old Times Square offices, which it had occupied for nearly 20 years, on November 8. The new building was located on the city's near west side on Howard Street in the West Side Industrial Development area known for many years as the Corktown section of Detroit. Built at a cost of $100,000, the Purchasing Office Building is a truly modern service facility.[58]

Following the opening of the bank's new main office, there were a number of changes on the board of directors. At the annual meeting in January 1965, two new directors were elected to fill the vacancies caused by the deaths of Joseph M. Dodge and Calvin P. Bentley. William E. Grace, long active in the truck-trailer industry, was president and director of the Fruehauf Corporation, a position he had held since 1958. A director of the Truck-Trailer Manufacturers Association, he also served on the Advisory Board of the Business and Defense Administration of the United States Department of Commerce. Jason L. Honigman, senior partner, Honigman, Miller, Schwartz and Cohn, was one of Detroit's leading attorneys. For many years he had been active in the field of improvement in the laws of procedure. In addition to his duties at the bank, Honigman was chairman of the board and chief executive officer of Allied Supermarkets, Inc., and a director of Allied Industries, Inc.

In 1966 there were a series of major changes on the bank's management staff. Milton J. Drake, executive vice-president, died on January 9, 1966, bringing to an end a long career of distinguished and dedicated service to the bank and the banking fraternity. At the meeting held March 22, 1966 [beginning with 1966, the annual stockholders meeting was moved from January to the last Tuesday in March],[59] Charles H. Hewitt retired as president of The Detroit Bank and Trust Company. Ending almost 30 years of active service to the bank, Hewitt continued to serve in the capacity of director and consultant until he retired in March 1973.

Elected to succeed Hewitt as the bank's tenth president was C. Boyd Stockmeyer, formerly vice-president in charge of the Commercial Loan Department. Stockmeyer joined the bank in May 1941, as an analyst in the Credit Department. In 1946 he was appointed assistant cashier and a year later was made manager of the Credit Department. He transferred to the Commercial Loan Department in 1949, was promoted to assistant vice-president in 1951 and to vice-president in 1954. In September 1964, he became chief loan officer in charge of the Commercial Loan Department. His business and professional offices included the presidency of the Michigan Chapter of Robert Morris Associates; director, Michigan State Chamber of Commerce; and director, Detroit Clearing House Association. He was also an active participant in community affairs having served as president of the Wayne State University Alumni Association, and a director of the Wayne State Fund, the Detroit Area Council—Boy Scouts of America, New Detroit, Inc., the Police Athletic League, and the United Foundation.

Along with President Stockmeyer, two other directors were elected on March 22, 1966: Walter B. Ford II and William B. Hall. Hall had served as executive vice-president of the bank since 1964. He first joined the bank in 1936 as manager of the Monthly Payment Loan Department [now Time Credit]. He was appointed assistant cashier in 1940, assistant vice-president three years later and in 1947 was named vice-president. In 1960 he became a senior vice-president. Hall had served on a number of committees for both the American Bankers and Michigan Bankers Associations and as president of the Bank Public Relations and Marketing Association, the Detroit Chapter of the Public Relations Society of America, and the Detroit Chapter of the American Institute of Banking. An active civic leader, Hall served for several years as a member of the Board of Governors of Wayne State University.

Walter B. Ford II was chairman of the board and chief executive officer of Ford and Earl Design Associates, Inc. This is an industrial design firm specializing in space planning and interior design, graphic and exhibit design, product design and development. It was W. B. Ford Design that designed the interior of the bank's new main office complex.

On September 24, 1968, Edward J. Giblin, vice-president and treasurer of Ex-Cell-O Corporation, was elected a director of the bank. Giblin joined the accounting department of Ex-Cell-O in 1953. Following that time he served in a number of executive positions with Ex-Cell-O and was elected treasurer in 1960 and vice-president in 1965. Currently, he is that company's president.

During the following year, there were several additional changes on the bank's board of directors. At the annual meeting, Robert F. Roelofs and Arbie O. Thalacker were elected to the board. Roelofs was president and chief executive officer of Great Lakes Steel, a division of National Steel Corporation. Roelofs joined National Steel Corporation in 1961 after 20 years with United States Steel Corporation in various executive positions. Currently, Roelofs is executive vice-president of Imperial-Detroit Steel. Thalacker was president of Detrex Chemical Industries, Inc., a firm which manufactured specialty chemicals and machines for metal goods manufacturers and for the textile industry. He had previously served as a member of the bank's Oakland County Advisory Council and was a director of the Ferndale National Bank prior to its merger with The Detroit Bank in 1956.

At its November 25, 1969 meeting, the board of directors substantially expanded the bank's senior management team, electing two new executive vice-presidents and eight new senior vice-presidents. Rodkey Craighead and B. James Theodoroff were named executive vice-presidents. With his new position, Craighead assumed responsibility for the Commercial Loan, International, Marketing, Mortgage, and Time Credit departments. Craighead joined the bank in 1946, and prior to his appointment as executive vice-president was in charge of the Commercial Loan Department. Theodoroff had been with the bank since 1949 and continued as chief trust officer and officer-in-charge of the bank's trust operations.

The decade of the 1960s had been a prosperous one for The Detroit Bank and Trust Company. An important merger, continued branch expansion, and a fine new main office structure had all been completed during this period. The year 1969 ended with the bank's consolidated earnings reaching a new record high with income, before securities' gains or losses, increasing 27 percent over 1968, which had also been a record year. The bank also reached the end of the decade with resources at a record high of $2,156,176,725.[60]

TOMORROW

As The Detroit Bank and Trust Company entered the decade of the 1970s, it was faced, as was Detroit and the rest of the nation, with a series of domestic and international economic challenges. International banking conditions had had an increasingly important effect on The Detroit Bank and Trust Company since 1969, when the bank established its first foreign office. In January of that year, the bank formally opened a branch in London, England.

Assistant Vice-President Sydney E. Paulson was named officer-in-charge of the London branch in September 1968, shortly after approvals for the new office were received from federal and state regulatory agencies and appropriate British authorities. William F. Piper was named manager of the branch. Piper previously had been associated with Barclay's Bank, Ltd., and had served as a manager of a city branch of that bank. Initially, the London branch had opened for administrative work only in a small single room at 149 Leadenhall Street on October 3, 1968.[61] The branch was started with literally nothing, not even office furniture. In fact, the branch's first letter was written in longhand by Piper and taken by him to a friend at Barclay's to be typed.[62] On January 3, the bank moved into its permanent quarters up Leadenhall Street in the P and O Building in the heart of London's historic banking district. The branch's first check, dated February 4, 1969, was drawn on the branch itself for 79 pounds 4 shillings and 11 pence. In October 1970, the branch moved to larger quarters a few short blocks away on St. Helens near Leadenhall.[63]

Primarily, the opening of the London office was an extension of the bank's international activities and placed the bank in the largest international banking center in the world. The London office permitted the bank to expand its international activities and to shift some transactions from Detroit, where the demand for money had been extremely heavy, and where government guidelines had restricted growth in recent years.[64]

In August 1969, the bank announced it had received permission from the necessary state and federal agencies for the formation of a wholly-owned subsidiary to be known as Detroit Bank and Trust International.[65] This subsidiary, incorporated January 23, 1969, under section 25(a) of the Federal Reserve Act, enabled the bank to undertake certain overseas banking and financial activities which were not previously possible. Both the opening of the London office and the creation of Detroit Bank and Trust International underscored the growth which the bank's International Banking Department had achieved—a growth which continued into the 1970s. When the International Department was first organized in 1961, it was part of the Commercial Loan Department with a staff of three, two of whom were part-time. In 1963 the International Banking Department began full-time operations and by 1971, under the direction of Senior Vice-President Donald R. Mandich, had a staff in Detroit of over 50 with an additional 22 employees in the London office.[66]

The Detroit Bank and Trust Company continued to expand its domestic branch operations in the early 1970s; offices were opened in Bloomfield Township and West Bloomfield Township. In addition to opening these new branches, the bank became the first in the area to introduce a fully-automated teller machine, Ultra/Matic 24, capable of serving nearly 80 percent of a customer's personal banking needs on a 24-hour, seven-day-a-week basis. The first machine was installed in late November at the Woodward-Hamilton office in suburban Birmingham. This unique equipment was an experiment in electronic fund transfer systems and was installed to offer more convenient banking hours on an automated basis.[67]

While the bank was experiencing a growth of services and resources in the sixties and early seventies, there were also changes occurring to the other members of Detroit's banking community. On December 15, 1960, the City Bank adopted its present name of City National Bank of Detroit. This was followed in 1961 by the Michigan Bank converting to a national charter on August 1. In 1973, it adopted the name Michigan National Bank.

A major consolidation occurred in Detroit on October 12, 1966, when the Bank of the Commonwealth acquired the assets and liabilities of the Public Bank. Chartered on June 4, 1957, the Public Bank commenced business on December 19 with a capital stock of one million dollars. When the Public Bank was taken over by the Bank of the Commonwealth in 1966, it was operating nine branches and had assets of $140,000,000.

The next change came in 1970 when a group of Detroit's leading black businessmen established a new bank in the city, the First Independence National Bank. Founded as a commercial bank emphasizing service to Detroit's black community, the bank opened on May 14 with an initial capitalization of $1,500,000. The bank's offices were located in the Washington Boulevard Building; and by year-end, the bank had assets of over nine million dollars. Principal officers of the new bank were Chairman of the Board Waldo L. Cain and President and Chief Executive Officer David Harper.[68]

Thus, as Detroit entered the 1970s, its people, its industry, and its commerce were served by eight banking institutions. They included The Detroit Bank and Trust Company, Bank of the Commonwealth, City National Bank, First Independence National Bank, Manufacturers National Bank, Merchants Bank, Michigan Bank, and the National Bank of Detroit.

During the early 1970s, there were also a number of changes on the board of directors of The Detroit Bank and Trust Company and in its senior management. At its December 1970 meeting, the board of directors elected President C. Boyd Stockmeyer chief executive officer effective January 1, 1971. Raymond T. Perring continued his active service as chairman of the board although he asked to be relieved of the chief executive duties at year-end. This change had been preceded by the retirement of Executive Vice-President William B. Hall. Effective March 24, 1970, Hall's retirement came after 34 years with the bank. He continues his association with the bank, however, as a member of the board of directors and of the trust committee.

On December 28, 1971, Rodkey Craighead was elected to the bank's board. He had been elected executive vice-president of the bank in 1969 and directed the operations of the Commercial Loan, International Banking, Mortgage and Time Credit departments. He joined the bank in 1946 as a credit analyst. In 1956 he was promoted to assistant vice-president and in 1961 to vice-president. Six years later, Craighead was promoted to senior vice-president. Subsequent to his election to the board, Craighead managed both the Credit and Commercial Loan departments.

DETROITBANK Corporation

On March 27, 1973, a special stockholders meeting was held to consider a new direction for The Detroit Bank and Trust Company. At this meeting the directors recommended to the shareholders that they approve the formation of a bank holding company. After considerable discussion, the stockholders voted in favor of the board's recommendation, and the new holding company, DETROIT-BANK Corporation, was born. Under this proposal, The Detroit Bank and Trust Company became a wholly-owned subsidiary of the new holding company. Stock in the bank was exchanged tax-free on a share-for-share basis for the common stock of the holding company.

At this same meeting, the shareholders authorized a capital stock increase of 20,000 shares to 3,084,170 shares.[69]

Bank holding companies had developed into a large and expanding factor in commercial banking, particularly in the years since 1968. By 1973 they comprised a significant element of a vigorous and flexible banking system. A bank holding company, under federal law, is a corporation that controls one or more banks in the United States. In 1971, Michigan law was amended to allow corporations to own bank stock, which paved the way for establishment of bank holding companies in the state.[70]

At the beginning of 1972, there were an estimated 1,567 bank holding companies (with 2,469 affiliated banks and 9,692 branches) operating in all 50 states and the District of Columbia. The affiliated banks of bank holding companies, which included 72 of the nation's 100 largest banks, held an estimated $341,000,000,000 in deposits. By comparison, there then were 13,784 commercial banks in the entire United States with 22,888 branches and deposits of $538,000,000.[71] With the change in Michigan law, most of the larger banks in the state moved to form holding companies.

There were two compelling reasons for forming a holding company: (1) to take advantage of growth and profit opportunities in the expanding financial services industry, and (2) to meet increasing competition in the banking field by creation of a vehicle which would provide flexibility in establishing new services. Although The Detroit Bank and Trust Company offered a wide range of financial services, it could not, as appropriate opportunities arose, expand freely into the various types of financial services and into other geographic areas permitted to a bank holding company. The overall objective of such expansion was to develop an entity which was more useful to more people in more places.[72]

Activities in which a bank holding company may engage must meet two tests which were set down by Congress when the 1970 amendments to the Bank Holding Act were passed. The activity must be "so closely related to banking or managing or controlling banks as to be a proper incident thereto." And the activity "must reasonably be expected to produce benefits to the public . . . that outweigh possible adverse effects."[73]

In its interpretation of these amendments, the Federal Reserve Board had determined that a number of fields were available to bank holding companies, subject to certain limitations. These available fields became known as the "Fed's laundry list." In addition to owning one or more banks, holding companies could conduct the following types of operations: mortgage lending and servicing, commercial finance, consumer finance, credit cards, leasing personal property and equipment, factoring, trust functions, investment or financial advisor, data processing services, community welfare investments, and credit life, health, and accident insurance.[74]

These so called "bank-related" activities of a holding company could be conducted nationally across state lines or internationally, whereas the domestic banking activities of the bank or banks owned by a holding company had to be confined within a single state pursuant to that state's banking laws. The holding company could enter into these bank-related activities either directly or through newly formed subsidiaries or by acquisition of established companies. The holding company could also acquire other banks or establish *de novo* banks.[75]

It was the plan of senior management of The Detroit Bank and Trust Company that, in the foreseeable future, the bank would constitute the major portion of the revenues and earnings of DETROITBANK Corporation.[76] Accordingly, the bank would dominate the holding company structure. It is important to remember that one of the primary objectives of establishing and developing this new holding company was to strengthen The Detroit Bank and Trust Company.

March 5, 1974 commemorates the 125th anniversary of The Detroit Bank and Trust Company. During its long history, the bank has changed and grown as has the city of Detroit. The Detroit Bank and Trust Company of 1974 is as different from the Detroit Savings Fund Institute as is the giant, sprawling metropolitan industrial complex of present-day Detroit from the small, bustling riverfront community of 1849. Yet, many things are still the same. The concern that the bank has for the welfare of the people of the city of Detroit is as great today as it was 125 years ago. The bank is looking forward, confident that the qualities, implanted by Elon Farnsworth and the first trustees, which have enabled it to meet the challenges of the past, will continue to sustain it in the years ahead.

Under the guidance of newly-elected Chairman Stockmeyer and President Craighead, the directors and senior officers of The Detroit Bank and Trust Company are making plans and formulating ideas for the future. How these plans will be developed, what new ideas will be formulated, what new directions the bank will take are not known for certain today. Only tomorrow will tell.

appendices

AN ACT

To Incorporate the Detroit Savings Fund Institute.

SECTION 1. *Be it enacted by the Senate and House of Representatives of the State of Michigan,* That Elon Farnsworth, David Smart, John Palmer, Zina Pitcher, Charles Moran, Shubael Conant, B. B. Kercheval, Levi Cook, James A. Hicks, George M. Rich .and Gurdon Williams, and their successors, are constituted a body corporate and politic, by the name of the Detroit Savings Fund Institute.

SECTION 2. The real estate which it shall be lawful for said Corporation to take, hold and convey, shall be only—1st. Such as shall be necessary and convenient for an office or place for the transaction of its business. 2nd. Such as shall be mortgaged or otherwise conveyed to it as security for money loaned or some other indebtedness. 3rd. Such as shall be conveyed to it in payment of indebtedness, or which shall be purchased by it at sales under judgments or decrees recovered by, or belonging to said Corporation; and said Corporation shall not buy, sell, hold or trade in any goods or wares whatever: *Provided, however,* That this shall not be construed to apply to goods, or personal property which it may acquire as security for, or in payment of indebtedness to it, or which may be necessary or convenient for the transaction of its business.

SECTION 3. The business and property of said Corporation shall be managed by a Board of Trustees, eleven in number, and who shall at their first meeting, and as often thereafter as may be necessary, elect from their number a President and Vice President. The several persons named in the first section of this act shall be the first Trustees; and all vacancies in said Board shall be filled at the next regular meeting thereof, after such vacancy shall arise, and the person receiving a majority of the votes of the Trustees present shall be duly elected. Six Trustees shall constitute a quorum of said Board, for the transaction of all ordinary business.

SECTION 4. Said Corporation shall receive on deposit all such sums of money as shall from time to time be offered by tradesmen, mechanics, laborers, servants, minors, and others, for the purpose of being invested in any public stock, or upon bond and mortgage or other security, according to the provisions of this act. And such deposits shall be repaid to each depositor or his lawful representatives when required, at such times and

237

with such interest and under such regulations as the Board of Trustees shall from time to time prescribe; which regulations shall be printed and conspicuously posted in some place accessible and visible to all, in the business office of said Corporation; and no alteration which may at any time be made in such regulation, shall in any manner affect the rights of a depositor in respect to deposits made previous to said alteration.

SECTION 5. The Board of Trustees may invest deposits made with them, and profits accruing thereon, in any public stock of the United States, or of the State of Michigan, or upon bond secured by mortgage upon unincumbered real estate worth at least double the amount loaned, or upon any other security which shall be deemed by the Board to be amply sufficient: *Provided,* That no loan or investment shall be made on any class of securities not specifically mentioned above, except with the approval of at least five of the Trustees.

SECTION 6. No Trustee or officer of said Corporation shall directly or indirectly borrow any of the funds of said Corporation, or in any manner use any of said funds, except in the lawful business of said Corporation. All certificates or evidences of deposit made by the proper officers, shall be as effectual to bind the Corporation, as if made under the common seal thereof. But said Corporation shall not issue any bill or note to circulate as money. Any Trustee, officer or agent of said Company who shall use any of the funds except as in this act provided, or issue, or cause to be issued, any bill or note designed or intended to be circulated as money, shall be deemed guilty of a misdemeanor, and on conviction thereof, shall be punished by imprisonment in the State Prison not more than ten years, and by fine not exceeding ten thousand dollars, or both, in the discretion of the court.

SECTION 7. It shall be the duty of the Board of Trustees, from time to time, to regulate the rate of interest to be allowed to depositors, so that they shall receive a ratable proportion of all the profits of said Corporation, after deducting the necessary expenses: and they shall annually make a report to the Legislature of this State, on or before the first day of January, of all the funds and investments of the Corporation.

SECTION 8. A misnomer of said Corporation, in any deed, gift, grant or other instrument, contract or convayances [sic], shall not vitiate the same, if the Corporation shall be sufficiently described to declare the intention of the parties.

SECTION 9. When any deposit is made by a person being a minor, the said Corporation may pay to such depositor such sums as may be due to him, although he have no guardian: and the receipt or acquittance of such minor shall be in all respects valid in law.

SECTION 10. Said Corporation shall be subject to the provisions of chapter fifty-five, title ten, of the revised statutes of 1846. This act shall take effect from and after its passage, and the Legislature may at any time alter, amend or repeal the same.

L. CHAPMAN,
Speaker of the House of Representatives.
WM. M. FENTON, *President of the Senate.*

Approved, March 5, 1849.

STATE OF MICHIGAN, SS.—I hereby certify that the foregoing is a full, true and perfect copy of an original act of the Legislature of said State, on file and of record in my office, entitled "An act to incorporate the Detroit Savings Fund Institute," approved March 5th, 1849.

IN TESTIMONY WHEREOF, I have hereunto set my hand and affixed the Great Seal of the State of Michigan, this sixth day of March, in the year of our Lord one thousand eight hundred and forty-nine. GEO. W. PECK, *Sec'y of State.*

APPENDIX B

BY-LAWS

AND REGULATIONS
OF THE
DETROIT SAVINGS FUND INSTITUTE.

1.

Deposits of one dollar or any number of dollars may be received.

2.

The Institute will allow an interest of four per centum per annum on deposits, to be declared and paid as follows: On the second Wednesday in January in each year, there shall be declared and paid to each depositor, a dividend of two per cent on all sums of five dollars, which shall have been deposited by him for the space of six months next previous to the first day of that month; and in like manner on the second Wednesday of July in each year, there shall be declared and paid a dividend of two per cent on all sums above five dollars, which shall have been deposited for the space of six months next previous to the first day of that month; and on the above days respectively, there shall be declared and paid a dividend of one per cent on all sums above five dollars which shall have been deposited for the space of three months next previous to the first day of either of those months; but no interest will be paid on any deposits for a less term than three months, nor upon any fractional part of a dollar.

3.

No interest shall be paid on any sum withdrawn previous to the first day of January and July, for the period which may have elapsed since the last dividend.

4.

All dividends shall be added to the principal of the depositor, and shall be entitled to dividends as much as any original deposit of the date of the first day of January and July, as the case may be.

5.

There shall be appointed by the Board of Trustees, from their own number, a Secretary, who shall record the proceedings of the Board in a book kept by him for that purpose.

6.

The Board of Trustees shall annually appoint, from their own number, two persons, who with the President and Vice President shall constitute a finance committee, and who shall perform the duties of that committee until others are appointed in their place.

7.

It shall be the duty of the finance committee to see that all the moneys deposited in the Institution are properly invested in such public stocks, mortgages, or other securities as are authorized by the act of incorporation, except such sums as may be necessary for immediate use.

8.

Money deposited may be drawn out personally, or by the order in writing of the depositors (if the Institution have the signature of the party on their signature book,) or by letters of attorney duly authenticated, but no person shall receive any part of his principal or interest without producing the original book, that such payment may be entered therein. No money can be withdrawn except on the second Wednesday of each month, and one week's notice before the day of withdrawing must be given to the President, if the sum be less than two hundred dollars, but if the sum be more than two hundred dollars, then three month's notice shall be given; and no less sum than two dollars of the capital of any depositor shall be drawn, unless the sum in deposit be less than that amount. All moneys received shall be in specie, or in bills taken in deposit by the incorporated banks in the city of Detroit, and all payments shall be made in the same manner.

9.

All deposits shall, when received, be entered in the books of the Institute kept for that purpose, and shall also be entered in a book to be given and kept by each depositor, and all sums drawn by him shall be entered in his book, and said book shall be his voucher and evidence of his property in said Institute.

10.

As the officers of the Institute may be unable to identify every depositor transacting business at the office, the Institution will not be responsible for loss sustained, where a depositor has not given notice of his book being stolen or lost, if such book be paid in whole or in part on presentment.

11.

On making the first deposit, the depositor shall be required to subscribe and thereby signify his assent to the regulations and by-laws of the Institution.

12.

The finance committee are authorized to close the account, or refuse to receive the deposit of any individual whenever they may deem it expedient.

13.

The Board of Trustees may at any time make such other by-laws and regulations, or alter those made as they shall think proper; provided they be not contrary to the act of incorporation.

14.

The Trustees are at liberty to return the amount of all or any part of the deposits, whenever they think proper.

15.

All notices in relation to deposits and depositors, published by or under the direction of the Board, four weeks successively in one of the public newspapers printed in the city of Detroit, shall be deemed and taken as actual notice to each depositor.

16.

The office of this Institution shall be open for business, Mondays, Wednesdays and Fridays, except holidays, from the hours of ten, A.M., to one o'clock, P.M., and as a matter of favor, drafts may be made on each regular business day, but it is not intended hereby to repeal any part of the eighth article of these by-laws.

17.

At the expiration of any term of office of any officer of this Institution, he shall deliver to his successor, or to such person as shall be authorized by the Board of Trustees to receive the same, all accounts, books, papers and documents in his possession, belonging to the Institution, and shall account for and pay over all moneys in his hands, belonging to the Institution.

18.

The books of the Institution shall at all times be subject to the inspection of every member of the finance committee.

19.

The neglect to attend to the regular or called meetings of the Trustees, when personally notified on the part of any Trustee, unless satisfactory excuse is made at such meeting, shall be considered and held to be a resignation, and all vacancies thus occurring shall be filled at the next regular meeting of the board.

20.

At the end of every five years, the first to be computed from the second Wednesday in July, 1849, there shall be declared and paid a dividend of all the profits which may have accrued within the said five years, then remaining on hand, (after deducting the necessary expenses and the sums necessary to keep the capital sound,) to and among all those depositors whose deposits exceed the sum of five dollars, and which shall have remained in said Institute for the space of one year at least, next preceding the time of declaring said extra dividend, in proportion to the sums by them respectively deposited, and to the length of time during which said deposits have remained in said Institute; but in making said dividend, no regard shall be had to any fractional parts of a year, but each sum shall, for the purpose of the dividend, be referred to the second Wednesday of July next following the time in which it was deposited.

APPENDIX C

ARTICLES OF ASSOCIATION
OF
"THE DETROIT SAVINGS BANK"

To all to whom these Presents shall come: know ye:

That, whereas the Detroit Savings Fund Institute, a corporation organized and doing business under an Act of the Legislature of the State of Michigan approved March 5th, 1849, by resolution of its Board of Trustees, a copy of which resolution duly authenticated under the Seal of said Corporation is attached hereto, has determined to reorganize said Corporation under the provisions of "An Act to amend the General Banking Law entitled 'An Act to authorize the business of Banking' approved February 16th, 1857 and the acts amendatory thereto, so as to provide for the organization of Savings Banks,"—approved March 31st 1871.

Now, Therefore, In pursuance of the requirements and regulations of said Act, the undersigned do hereby certify,

First. That The Detroit Savings Fund Institute is so reorganized, and that the name of said Institute under such reorganization assumed to distinguish such association, and to be hereafter used in all its dealings is "The Detroit Savings Bank."

Second. That the place where the operations of *deposite,* investment, discount, and general business of said association as authorized by said act are to be carried on, is the City of Detroit, in the County of Wayne and State of Michigan, at which place such association will keep an office for the transaction of such business.

Third. The amount of the Capital Stock of the Detroit Savings Bank is the sum of Two Hundred Thousand Dollars—divided into Two Thousand Shares of One Hundred Dollars each.

Fourth. The names and places of residence of the several shareholders and the number of shares held and owned by each of them respectively, are as follows:

Elon Farnsworth	One hundred & fifty shares
Henry N. Walker	One hundred & fifty shares
Z. Pitcher	One hundred & fifty shares
Edward Lyon	One hundred & fifty shares
Samuel Lewis	One hundred & fifty shares
Henry P. Bridge	One hundred & fifty shares
Edmund Trowbridge	One hundred & fifty shares
Willard Parker	One hundred & fifty shares
Alex Lewis	One hundred & fifty shares
A. H. Adams	One hundred & fifty shares
Sidney D. Miller	One hundred & fifty shares
H. N. Walker, Trustee	Three hundred & fifty shares

All of said shareholders reside in the city of Detroit aforesaid.

Fifth. The period at which the corporate existence of said Detroit Savings Bank shall commence is the 18th day of July A.D., 1871; and said corporation shall continue for Thirty years from that date.

Sixth. The names and places of residence of the several Directors and officers, and the number of shares of the Capital Stock of the association owned and held by each of such directors and officers, are as follows:

Elon Farnsworth of Detroit, one hundred & fifty shares
Henry N. Walker of Detroit, one hundred & fifty shares
Samuel Lewis of Detroit, one hundred & fifty shares
Zina Pitcher of Detroit, one hundred & fifty shares
Edward Lyon of Detroit, one hundred & fifty shares
Henry P. Bridge of Detroit, one hundred & fifty shares
Edmund Trowbridge of Detroit, one hundred & fifty shares
Alexander Lewis of Detroit, one hundred & fifty shares
and Willard Parker of Detroit, one hundred & fifty shares.

Elon Farnsworth is to be the first President, and Henry N. Walker, the first Vice President.

Seventh. The business and property of such Detroit Savings Bank shall be managed by a Board of Directors of Nine Stockholders. The first Board of Directors shall be composed of the following named persons, Elon Farnsworth, Henry N. Walker, Samuel Lewis, Henry P. Bridge, Edward Lyon, Edmund Trowbridge, Zina Pitcher, Alexander Lewis & Willard Parker.

Eighth. The Associates under these articles hereby provide for the future increase of their Capital Stock to be made from time to time by a vote of a majority in interest of the entire stockholders—such increase not however to exceed in the aggregate the sum of Eight Hundred Thousand Dollars, nor so that the entire capital shall exceed the sum of One Million of Dollars.

In witness whereof, the several associates hereunder have hereto set their hands and seals this 18th day of July A.D. 1871.

Elon Farnsworth	(Seal)
Henry N. Walker	(Seal)
Z. Pitcher	(Seal)
Edward Lyon	(Seal)
Samuel Lewis	(Seal)
Henry P. Bridge	(Seal)
Edmund Trowbridge	(Seal)
Willard Parker	(Seal)
Alexander Lewis	(Seal)
A. H. Adams	(Seal)
Sidney D. Miller	(Seal)
H. N. Walker, Trustee	(Seal)

Copy of Resolution of the Trustees of the Detroit Savings Fund Institute.

"Resolved,—That the Detroit Savings Fund Institute be reorganized under the provisions of an Act entitled 'An Act to amend the General Banking Law, entitled An Act to authorize the business of Banking, approved February 16th, 1857, and the acts amendatory thereto so as to provide for the organization of Savings Banks,'—approved March 31st, 1871—That such reorganization be effected by filing Articles of Association as required by said Act—under which Articles the name of said reorganized corporation shall be 'The Detroit Savings Bank'—and, it shall be based upon a capital stock of Two Hundred Thousand Dollars with provisions allowing the increase thereof to an amount not exceeding one million of dollars."

I certify that the foregoing is a true copy of the Resolution of the Board of Trustees of The Detroit Savings Fund Institute adopted June 22d, 1871, and confirmed July 18th, 1871.

Witness my hand and the corporate seal of said Institute this 18th day of July 1871, at Detroit.

(Seal)   A. H. Adams, Cashier of the
                                    Detroit Savings Fund Institute.

State of Michigan ⎫
                  ⎬ ss.
County of Wayne   ⎭

On this 18th day of July A.D. 1871 before me, a Notary Public, personally came Elon Farnsworth, Henry N. Walker, Samuel Lewis, Zina

Pitcher, Henry P. Bridge, Edmund Trowbridge, Edward Lyon, Alexander Lewis, Willard Parker, Alexander H. Adams & Sidney D. Miller known to me to be the same persons subscribing the foregoing Articles of Association and severally acknowledged that they executed the foregoing instrument for the uses & purposes therein set forth.

John Weber
Notary Public, Wayne Co., Mich.

Appendix D
Detroit Bank and Trust merger history, March 1849–March 1974

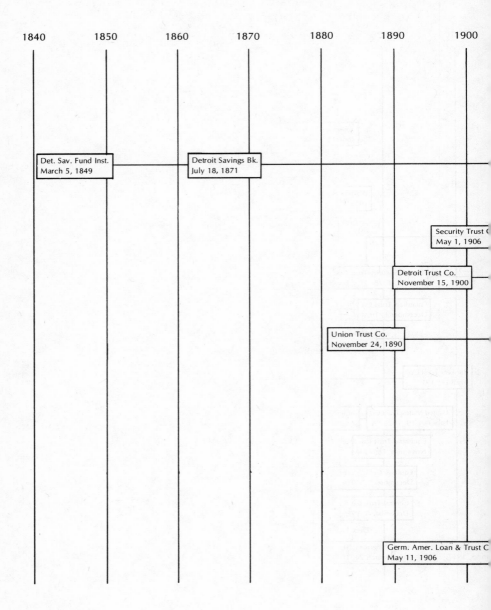

1840   1850   1860   1870   1880   1890   1900

Det. Sav. Fund Inst.
March 5, 1849

Detroit Savings Bk.
July 18, 1871

Security Trust (
May 1, 1906

Detroit Trust Co.
November 15, 1900

Union Trust Co.
November 24, 1890

Germ. Amer. Loan & Trust C
May 11, 1906

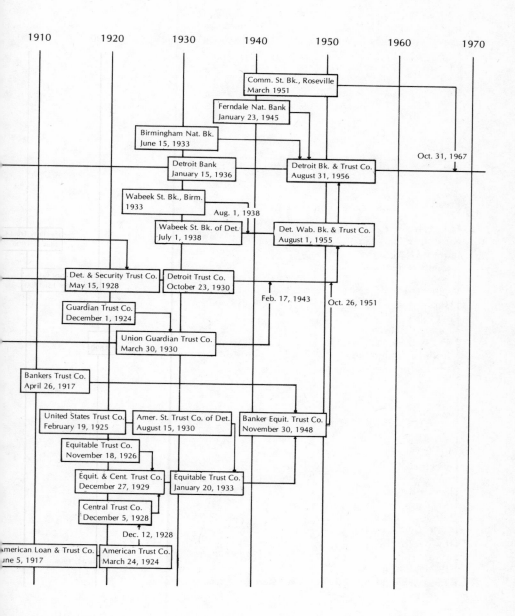

Chairmen of the Board

DeWitt C. Delamater	1919–1925
John M. Dwyer	1927–1934
Joseph M. Dodge	1952–1953
Cleveland Thurber (acting)	1953–1954
Joseph M. Dodge	1954–1963
† Raymond T. Perring	1963–1974
† C. Boyd Stockmeyer	1974–

APPENDIX F

Presidents

Elon Farnsworth	1849–1877
Alexander H. Adams	1878–1883
Sidney D. Miller	1884–1904
DeWitt C. Delamater	1904–1919
George S. Baker	1919–1927
Walter L. Dunham	1927–1933
Joseph M. Dodge	1933–1952
Raymond T. Perring	1952–1963
Charles H. Hewitt	1963–1966
† C. Boyd Stockmeyer	1966–1974
† Rodkey Craighead	1974–

APPENDIX G

Directors

Elon Farnsworth	1849–77 *
Shubael Conant	1849–67 *
Levi Cook	1849–66 *
James A. Hicks	1849–54 *
Benjamin B. Kercheval	1849–55 *

* Died in office.

† These senior management changes were made effective January 1, 1974.

Charles Moran	1849
John Palmer	1849–71 *
Dr. Zina Pitcher	1849–72 *
George M. Rich	1849–71
David Smart	1849–56 *
Gurdon Williams	1849
Henry N. Walker	1849–81
Samuel Lewis	1849–78
Henry P. Baldwin	1855–63
Edward Lyon	1855–84 *
Henry Ledyard	1856–62
Henry P. Bridge	1864–75
Edmund Trowbridge	1864–73 *
Alexander Lewis	1868–76
Willard Parker	1868–74
Alexander Adams	1871, 1875–83 *
Sidney D. Miller	1871, 1882–1904 *
Peter Henkel	1872–75
George Hendrie	1873–1913 *
George Jerome	1874–97 *
Simon Mandelbaum	1875–76 *
Thomas Ferguson	1876–92 *
Frederick B. Sibley	1877–1907 *
James McMillan	1877–1902 *
William K. Muir	1879–92 *
Alexander Chapoton, Sr.	1884–93 *
James E. Pittman	1884–1901 *
William K. Anderson	1892–1909 *
Charles A. Dean, Sr.	1892–1926 *
Dr. Edmond A. Chapoton	1893–1915 *
DeWitt C. Delamater	1897–1925 *
James H. Muir	1902–06 *
Philip H. McMillan	1902–19 *
Sidney T. Miller, Sr.	1904–40 *
Strathearn Hendrie	1905–16 *
Arthur M. Parker	1906–14 *
John M. Dwyer	1906–34
Paul F. Bagley	1909–31 *
David S. Carter	1913–48 *
Robert Henkel	1913–30 *
Jerome H. Remick	1913–31 *
Francis Palms	1915–29
Frederick T. Ducharme	1915–44 *
George T. Hendrie	1916–33
George S. Baker	1919–27 *
James T. McMillan	1920–46 *
Ralph N. Stoepel	1920–33
David M. Whitney	1920–27
Sidney T. Miller, Jr.	1925–36 *

James H. Doherty	1925–38 *
Charles A. Dean, Jr.	1926–55 *
Walter L. Dunham	1927–33
Edward D. Stair	1928–33
Charles H. Roehm	1928–38 *
Edward S. Evans	1930–33
Edward E. MacCrone	1930–33
Claude M. Harmon	1931–51 *
Nathan I. Viger	1932–43, 1947–54
Dr. Thaddeus Walker	1932–39 *
Joseph M. Dodge	1933–53, 1954–64 *
Frank W. Hubbard	1934–43 *
Herbert B. Trix	1934–
Ferris D. Stone	1938–45 *
H. Lynn Pierson	1944–
Ralph Hubbard	1945–56 *
C. David Widman	1945–64 *
Cleveland Thurber	1945–
James McMillan	1946–
H. Gray Muzzy	1947–69 *
George W. Mason	1950–54 *
Walter L. Cisler	1951–
Raymond T. Perring	1952–
Charles H. Hewitt	1953–73
Selden B. Daume	1956–64
Herbert A. Gardner	1956–62
Calvin P. Bentley	1956–64 *
Willard M. Cornelius	1956–57 *
Frank D. Eaman	1956–62 *
William A. Fisher	1956–69 *
Leslie H. Green	1956–73
Frederich C. Matthaei	1956–69
William R. Yaw	1956–
William C. Newberg	1957–60
Louis A. Fisher	1959–
Paul H. Carnahan	1961–65 *
Frank A. Colombo	1962–
Roblee B. Martin	1962–72
James O. Wright	1964–73
William E. Grace	1965–
Jason L. Honigman	1965–
C. Boyd Stockmeyer	1966–
Walter B. Ford II	1966–
William B. Hall	1966–
C. D. Smith	1968–70
Edward J. Giblin	1968–
Robert F. Roelofs	1969–
Arbie O. Thalacker	1969–
Kenneth J. Whalen	1969–73

Paul S. Mirabito	1971–
Rodkey Craighead	1971–
E. Joseph Moore	1972–
W. Warren Shelden	1973–
E. A. Cafiero	1973–

APPENDIX H

Detroit Bank and Trust offices as of January 1, 1974*

Downtown Offices
G Griswold at State[1,2,4]
36 David Whitney Building[1,4]
42 Fort at Washington[1,2]
44 Ford Building[2]

East Side Offices
10 Boulevard–St. Antoine
11 Canfield–Russell
39 Eight Mile–Dresden[1,2,3]
30 Gratiot–Eastwood [1]
 8 Gratiot–Mack
31 Gratiot–Outer Drive[1]
23 Gratiot–Westphalia
26 Harper–Chalmers[1]
65 Jefferson–Chene[1]
 5 Jefferson–Hillger[1]
27 Jefferson–Piper[1]
22 John R–Nevada[1]
12 Kercheval–Van Dyke[1,3]
 1 Lafayette–Beaubien[1,2]
21 Mack–Chalmers
34 Mack–Hillcrest[1,2,3]
 7 Medical Center[1,2,4]
73 Morang–Duchess[1,2,3]
38 Mound Road–Eight Mile[1,2,3,4]
13 Oakland–Woodland
28 Van Dyke–Malvern[1,2]
 3 Woodward–Milwaukee[1,2]

West Side Offices
 9 Boulevard–Twelfth
25 Fenkell–Fairfield[1,3]
43 Fisher Building[1,2,4]
14 Fort–Campbell[1,3]
69 Fort–Green[1,2]
48 Grand River–Forrer[1,2,3]
16 Grand River–Joy Road[1,2]
24 Grand River–Meyers Road[1]
29 Grand River–Redford[1,2]
19 Grand River–Trumbull[1]
17 Hamilton–Collingwood
15 Linwood–Joy Road[1]
33 Livernois–Clarita[1,2]
72 McNichols–Meyers[1,2,3]
41 McNichols–Oakfield[1,2,3]
47 McNichols–San Juan[1,2]
 6 Michigan–Twenty Fourth
32 Plymouth Road–
     Mansfield [1,2,3]
62 Seven Mile–Telegraph[1,2,3]
 2 Vernor–Junction[1,2]
35 Warren–Greenfield [1,2]
18 Warren–Junction [1]

Suburban Offices

AVON TOWNSHIP
82 Rochester Road–Avon[1,2,3]

* In addition to the offices in the Detroit metropolitan area, the bank maintains a branch office in London, England.

Key: [1] Night Depositories; [2] Safe Deposit Vaults; [3] Drive-in Windows; [4] Walk-up Windows; [5] Ultra/Matic 24 Service

Appendices

BIRMINGHAM
45 Wabeek Building[1,2]
50 Woodward–
   Fourteen Mile[1,2,3]
49 Woodward–Hamilton[1,2,5]
58 Woodward–Oakland[1,2,4]

BLOOMFIELD TOWNSHIP
83 Maple–Telegraph[1,2,3]

CLINTON TOWNSHIP
67 Garfield–
   Metropolitan Pky.[1,2,3]

DEARBORN HEIGHTS
55 Joy Road–
   Beech Daly Road [1,2,3]

FARMINGTON HILLS
52 Grand River–Middlebelt[1,2,3]
64 Twelve Mile–
   Orchard Lake Rd.[1,2,3]

FERNDALE
70 Nine Mile–Hilton[1,2,3]
46 Nine Mile–Woodward [1,2]
51 Woodward–Vester[1,2]

FRANKLIN
53 Franklin Village[1,2,3]

HARRISON TOWNSHIP
81 Jefferson–Shook[1,2,3]

PLYMOUTH TOWNSHIP
68 Ann Arbor Rd.–Lilley[1,2,3]
56 Lake Pointe Village[1,2,3]

REDFORD TOWNSHIP
60 Schoolcraft–Inkster[1,2,3]
40 Schoolcraft–Telegraph[1,2,3]

ROSEVILLE
76 Eastgate[1,2,3]
77 Gratiot–Martin[1,2,3]
79 Groesbeck–12 Mile[1,2,3]
78 Macomb Mall [1,2,3]

ROYAL OAK TOWNSHIP
59 Greenfield–Ten Mile[1,2,3]

SHELBY TOWNSHIP
57 Van Dyke–21 Mile Road [1,2,3]

SOUTHFIELD
37 Northland [1,2,3,5]

STERLING HEIGHTS
66 Fourteen–Mile–
   Dequindre[1,2,3]
75 Fourteen Mile–
   Mound Rd.[1,2,3]
61 Van Dyke–16 Mile Rd.[1,2,3]

TAYLOR
80 Southland [1,2,3]

WEST BLOOMFIELD TOWNSHIP
84 Fourteen Mile–
   Farmington Road [1,2,3]
74 Maple–
   Orchard Lake Road [1,2,3]

WESTLAND
54 Ann Arbor Trail–
   Merriman Road [1,2,3]
71 Newburgh–Palmer[1,2,3]
63 Wayne–Warren[1,2,3]

Key: [1] Night Depositories; [2] Safe Deposit Vaults; [3] Drive-in Windows; [4] Walk-up Windows; [5] Ultra/Matic 24 Service

Ed. Note: Branch 20 was permanently closed in 1970. Branch 4 is permanently closed.

Detroit Bank and Trust List of Officers and Departments
as of January 1, 1974

C. Boyd Stockmeyer
Chairman

Rodkey Craighead
President

Jerome R. Heyer
Executive Vice President, Operations

Donald R. Mandich
Executive Vice President, Loans

B. James Theodoroff
Executive Vice President, Trust

Loan Departments

COMMERCIAL LOANS
Albert W. Holcomb
Senior Vice President

NATIONAL DIVISION
Burt R. Shurly, Jr.
Senior Vice President

David C. Bird
Vice President

Charles F. Insley
Vice President

Roland C. Schroeder
Vice President

D. James Watson, Jr.
Vice President

Stephen M. Conway
Assistant Cashier

MICHIGAN DIVISION
Joseph F. Schadler
Vice President

Stuart G. Lucas
Vice President

Robert C. Robinson
Vice President

Peter E. Fisher
Assistant Vice President

C. Scott Thiss
Assistant Cashier

METROPOLITAN DIVISIONS
West Side
J. William Berns
Vice President

Thomas R. Johnson
Assistant Vice President

Thomas W. Radcliffe
Assistant Vice President

Ronald T. Oppat
Assistant Cashier

Kenneth J. Safran
Assistant Cashier

Walter E. Schemanske
Assistant Cashier

East Side
James R. Waterston
Vice President

James E. Tompkins
Assistant Vice President

Ronald C. Vogt
Assistant Cashier

Uptown
William J. Luke
Vice President

Joseph W. Clark
Vice President

David J. Scalise
Assistant Vice President

Macomb County
Carl A. Holth
Vice President

Joseph G. Horonzy
Assistant Cashier

Oakland County
Richard J. Thomas, Jr.
Vice President

Howard B. Gurney
Assistant Vice President

James B. Haeffner
Assistant Cashier

EQUIPMENT LEASING
Charles F. Barnes
Assistant Cashier

INTERNATIONAL BANKING
Frederick C. Hertel
Vice President

Sydney E. Paulson
Vice President

Fenton M. Remick
Vice President

Charles F. Turner
Vice President

Johann B. Wendt
Vice President

Lawrence N. David
Assistant Vice President

Thomas J. Hector
Assistant Vice President

James A. Mitchell
Assistant Vice President

Matthew J. Plawchan
Assistant Vice President

Michael L. Lauer
Assistant Cashier

Jerome T. Nosek
Assistant Cashier

Michael J. Schefke
Assistant Cashier

Fred A. Woolsey
Assistant Cashier

MORTGAGE LOANS
Richard J. Peters
Senior Vice President

Donald C. Layher
Vice President

Richard W. McEvilly
Vice President

Charles E. Chapman
Assistant Vice President

Frank G. Ebner
Assistant Vice President

Robert E. Perry
Assistant Vice President

Vincent J. Sirvaitis
Assistant Cashier

TIME CREDIT LOANS
Gerald E. Brielmaier
Senior Vice President

John J. Lund
Vice President

Harry S. Bruce
Assitant Vice President

James E. Doran
Assistant Vice President

Alfred V. Meyer
Assistant Vice President

Don L. Clark
Assistant Cashier

Robert B. Kipp
Assistant Cashier

Master Charge
Thomas W. Winn
Vice President

Donald G. Sutherland
Assistant Vice President

Robert W. Blehm
Assistant Cashier

Aram M. Gavoor
Assistant Cashier

LOAN CONTROL
Rollo G. A. Fisher
Vice President

Credit
George W. Lindenberg
Assistant Vice President

John D. Berkaw
Assistant Cashier

Discount
Michael L. Kenny
Assistant Vice President

Nicholas P. Bogaerts
Assistant Cashier

Accounts Financing
Henry J. Hajdas
Assistant Vice President

Administrative Departments

AUDITING
David J. Westhoff
Vice President & Auditor

William J. Kalmar
Assistant Cashier

Einar E. Martin
Assistant Cashier

BANK PROPERTIES
Andrew F. Butt
Vice President

BRANCH OFFICES ADMINISTRATION
Jack L. Talbot
Senior Vice President

Dean L. Forhan
Vice President
Stuart K. Wallhead
Vice President
Mark A. Benner
Assistant Vice President
Willard L. Oliver, Jr.
Assistant Vice President

COMMERCIAL BUSINESS
DEVELOPMENT
William J. Croul
Vice President
John S. Black
Assistant Vice President

CONTROLLER
Eugene A. Miller
Vice President & Controller
John Huta
Assistant Vice President
James E. Iseler
Assistant Vice President
Robert N. Olsen
Assistant Cashier

DATA PROCESSING
James B. Lyons
Vice President
William J. Dodd
Vice President
Mark E. Burgess
Assistant Vice President
J. Robert Foley
Assistant Vice President
Robert E. Lauzon
Assistant Vice President
Frederick M. DeWitt
Assistant Cashier

DISTRIBUTION AND TRANSIT
Douglas G. Chalou
Assistant Vice President
Edward A. Rock
Assistant Cashier

ECONOMICS DIVISION
Dr. Martha R. Seger
Vice President & Economist
HOLDING COMPANY PLANNING
Walter B. Fisher
Vice President

Stanley E. Rulapaugh
Assistant Cashier

MARKETING
Charles J. Snell
Vice President
Richard G. Williams
Vice President
Darwin D. Martin, Jr.
Assistant Vice President

OPERATIONS
Bruce R. Gibson
Vice President & Cashier
C. Duane Christie
Assistant Vice President
David A. Borrusch
Assistant Cashier
Robert E. Howe
Assistant Cashier
Purchasing
Ted B. Wahby
Assistant Vice President

PERSONNEL
David L. Conrad
Vice President
Thomas E. Cain
Assistant Cashier
Loretta C. Collins
Assistant Cashier
John D. Lewis
Assistant Cashier

Training
Clifford J. Rutz
Assistant Cashier

PUBLIC FUNDS
Wilson D. Tyler
Vice President
Eugene R. Norey
Assistant Vice President

Investment Departments
John B. Watkins
Senior Vice President

BANK INVESTMENT
John F. Boyd
Vice President

Government and Municipal Bonds

James C. Buysse
Assistant Vice President

Robert L. Kisiel
Assistant Cashier

Municipal Bond Trading and Underwriting

Wilfred J. Friday
Vice President

Frederick L. Davies
Assistant Cashier

Lawrence M. Kelly
Assistant Cashier

James M. Menard
Assistant Cashier

TRUST INVESTMENT

Portfolio Management—Personal

W. Howard T. Snyder
Vice President

Raymond C. Gunn
Vice President

Richard P. Chester
Assistant Trust Officer

John T. Kearns
Assistant Trust Officer

Kenneth H. Mortenson
Assistant Trust Officer

James A. Sansoterra
Assistant Trust Officer

Portfolio Management—Pension and Profit Sharing

William J. Barton, Jr.
Vice President

Richard F. Taylor
Vice President

Gerald R. Root
Trust Officer

Investment Research

Philip S. Dano
Vice President

John B. Fields
Assistant Trust Officer

Ann C. Jacobowitz
Assistant Trust Officer

Stephen McGratty
Assistant Trust Officer

Management Services

Vincent O. Enright, Jr.
Assistant Trust Officer

William Krantz
Assistant Trust Officer

Ervin J. Siuda
Assistant Trust Officer

Trust Departments
Cleveland Thurber, Jr.
Senior Vice President

PERSONAL TRUST
Cleveland Thurber, Jr.
Senior Vice President

Roger H. Fitch
Vice President

Allan J. Fletcher
Vice President

Jamil N. Khoury
Vice President

George W. Menold
Vice President

William A. Penner, Jr.
Vice President

Elmer L. Pfeifle, Jr.
Vice President

Donald R. Spencer
Vice President

John P. Worcester
Vice President

Robert S. Colladay
Trust Officer

Donald E. Draper
Trust Officer

Michael R. Dufour
Trust Officer

William M. Fury
Trust Officer

Sheldon F. Hall, Jr.
Trust Officer

William B. Matakas
Trust Officer

David A. McClenic,
Trust Officer

Bernard E. Stuart
Trust Officer

Boris A. Vasileff
Trust Officer

David E. Bryant
Assistant Trust Officer

Daniel L. Curry
Assistant Trust Officer

William D. Dahling
Assistant Trust Officer

Robert M. DeLonge
Assistant Trust Officer

David E. Engelbert
Assistant Trust Officer

Terry L. Netzloff
Assistant Trust Officer

Gary M. Schwind
Assistant Trust Officer

John B. Whitledge
Assistant Trust Officer

CORPORATE TRUST
Harry C. Pratt
Vice President

Robert R. Garey
Trust Officer

Lloyd H. Myas
Trust Officer

John E. Woodison
Trust Officer

Harry W. Marchand
Assistant Trust Officer

PENSION TRUST
Robert K. Smith
Vice President

William C. Hamming
Vice President

Robert C. Knudsen
Trust Officer

William R. McClelland
Trust Officer

William M. Fournier
Assistant Trust Officer

OPERATIONS
Lawrence B. Kingery
Vice President

John E. Dicker
Assistant Trust Officer

Edmond J. Montbleau
Assistant Trust Officer

TAX SERVICES
Andrew M. Savel
Vice President

Wilma H. Wackerle
Trust Officer

Arthur W. Mostek
Assistant Trust Officer

Margaret Paulton
Assistant Trust Officer

REAL ESTATE SERVICES
Gari W. Kersten
Vice President

Robert W. Reas
Trust Officer

Arthur Rettberg
Assistant Trust Officer

BUSINESS DEVELOPMENT
John E. Park
Vice President

Alvin J. Tobin
Vice President

Terrence E. Keating
Trust Officer

G. Ernest Pyle
Trust Officer

Irving Herman
Assistant Trust Officer

Douglas H. Mueller
Assistant Trust Officer

John D. Slocum
Assistant Trust Officer

Robert E. Vince
Assistant Trust Officer

notes

In the Notes the following abbreviations are used:
DSFI—Detroit Savings Fund Institute
DSB—Detroit Savings Bank
DB—The Detroit Bank
DBTC—The Detroit Bank and Trust Company
Teller—Employee magazine published by the Detroit Bank and Trust Company, volume I, 1934.
MPHC—*Michigan Pioneer and Historical Collections* (40 vols.; Lansing, 1877–1929).
AHC—Automotive History Collection, Detroit Public Library
BHC—Burton Historical Collection, Detroit Public Library
MHC—Michigan Historical Collections, University of Michigan

CHAPTER 1

1. Fred C. Hamil, *When Beaver was King* (Detroit, 1951), pp. 6–7; Alexander Henry, *Travels and Adventures in the Years 1760–76* (Chicago, 1921), pp. 15–16.
2. F. Clever Bald, *Detroit's First American Decade* (Ann Arbor, 1948), pp. 76–77.
3. Silas Farmer, *History of Detroit*, 3rd ed. (Detroit, 1890), p. 17.
4. Willis F. Dunbar, *Michigan: A History of the Wolverine State* (Grand Rapids, 1965), pp. 89–90.
5. Dunbar, p. 84; Hamil, p. 7.
6. Frank B. Woodford and Arthur M. Woodford, *All Our Yesterdays: A Brief History of Detroit* (Detroit, 1969), p. 36.
7. James Sullivan, ed., *Papers of Sir William Johnson* (14 vols.; Albany, 1921–65), 3:331 (hereafter referred to as *Johnson Papers*).
8. Howard H. Peckham, *Pontiac and the Indian Uprising* (Princeton, 1947), pp. 71, 85; *Johnson Papers*, 3:531–35; Sylvester K. Stevens and Donald H. Kent, eds., *Papers of Colonel Henry Bouquet* (17 vols.; Harrisburg, 1940–43), series 21646, p. 26.
9. Henry, p. 304.
10. Woodford and Woodford, *All Our Yesterdays*, p. 66.
11. Haldimand Papers, *MPHC*, 9 (1886): 456.

12. Philip P. Mason, *Detroit, Fort Lernoult and the American Revolution* (Detroit, 1964), unpaged.
13. Woodford and Woodford, *All Our Yesterdays*, p. 73.
14. Bald, *Detroit's First American Decade*, pp. 78–79; Hamil, pp. 16–17; Ida A. Johnson, *Michigan Fur Trade* (Lansing, 1919), pp. 66–67.
15. Bald, *Detroit's First American Decade*, p. 81.
16. *Ibid.*, p. 83.
17. Farmer, p. 846.
18. Margaret G. Myers, *Financial History of the United States* (New York, 1970), p. 3; Farmer, p. 846.
19. Simon L. Adler, "Money and Money Units in the American Colonies," *Rochester Historical Society Publications*, 8 (1929): 145; Jackson T. Main, *The Social Structure of Revolutionary America* (Princeton, 1965), pp. 9, 289–90.
20. Bald, *Detroit's First American Decade*, p. 82.
21. Frank B. Woodford, *Mr. Jefferson's Disciple; A Life of Justice Woodward* (East Lansing, 1953), pp. 40–41, 47.
22. Harold Bowen, *State Bank Notes of Michigan* (Detroit, 1956), pp. 79, 164; Clarence M. Burton, ed., *City of Detroit Michigan* (5 vols.; Detroit, 1922), 2:622–27; Farmer, pp. 854–58; Woodford, *Mr. Jefferson's Disciple*, pp. 55–59; W. L. Jenks, *The First Bank in Michigan* (Port Huron, 1916), unpaged; *Laws of the Territory of Michigan* (4 vols.; Lansing, 1871–84), 4:7–9.
23. Hamil, pp. 19–20; Johnson, pp. 146, 153, 177; North American Fur Trade Conference, 1965, *Aspects of the Fur Trade* (St. Paul, 1967), p. 71.

CHAPTER 2

1. Floyd R. Dain, *Every House a Frontier: Detroit's Economic Progress, 1815–1825* (Detroit, 1956), pp. 13, 133–34, 143.
2. *Ibid.*, pp. 103–4.
3. *Detroit Gazette*, September 10, 1819; October 22, 1819.
4. Dain, p. 106.
5. Farmer, *History of Detroit*, p. 847.
6. Frank B. Woodford and Albert Hyma, *Gabriel Richard, Frontier Ambassador* (Detroit, 1958), p. 110; *Detroit Gazette*, August 18, 1818.
7. Crandall Melvin, Sr., *A History of the Merchants National Bank and Trust Company of Syracuse, New York* (Syracuse, 1969), p. 35.
8. Dain, p. 102.
9. *Ibid.*, p. 103.
10. *Detroit Gazette*, August 24, 1821.
11. Dain, p. 16.
12. Friend Palmer, "The Old Bank of Michigan," *MPHC*, 30 (1906): 410–23; *Laws of the Territory of Michigan*, 1:438–47.
13. Dain, pp. 112–13.
14. Palmer, pp. 412, 415.
15. Farmer, p. 859; *Laws of the Territory of Michigan*, 3:866–67, 1299.

16. Milo M. Quaife and Sidney Glazer, *Michigan* (New York, 1948), p. 153.
17. John B. Mansfield, *History of the Great Lakes* (2 vols.; Chicago, 1894), 1:792,858.
18. F. Clever Bald, *Michigan in Four Centuries* (New York, 1961), pp. 154–55.
19. Dunbar, *Michigan*, pp. 245–46.
20. Frank B. Woodford, *Yankees in Wonderland* (Detroit, 1951), p. 17.
21. *Detroit Gazette*, December 5, 1825.
22. Woodford, *Yankees in Wonderland*, p. 23.
23. *Ibid.*, p. 14.
24. Dunbar, *Michigan*, p. 328.
25. *Laws of the Territory of Michigan*, 2:333–39.
26. Jack F. Kilfoil, *C. C. Trowbridge, Detroit Banker and Michigan Land Speculator, 1820–1845* (Ann Arbor, 1970), p. 53.
27. Farmer, pp. 860–61; *Laws of the Territory of Michigan*, 2:753–58.
28. Farmer, pp. 862–63; *Laws of the Territory of Michigan*, 3:1308–12.
29. Farmer, pp. 863–64; *Laws of the Territory of Michigan*, 3:1397–1403.
30. Bald, *Michigan in Four Centuries*, pp. 206–7.
31. Dunbar, *Michigan*, p. 323.
32. Myers, *Financial History*, p. 93; Edward G. Bourne, *The Surplus Revenue of 1837* (New York, 1885), p. 35; Kilfoil, p. 186.
33. John Sperling, *Great Depressions* (Glenview, Illinois, 1966), p. 24.
34. Bald, *Michigan in Four Centuries*, p. 206; Myers, p. 95.
35. Bourne, pp. 35, 40.
36. Bourne, p. 76; Myers, p. 96.
37. Alpheus Felch, "Early Banks and Banking in Michigan," *MPHC*, 2 (1880): 111–24.
38. *Laws of the Territory of Michigan*, 3:1299.
39. *Acts of the Legislature of the State of Michigan passed at the annual session of 1837* (Detroit, 1837), Act No. 47, pp. 76–88.
40. Felch, p. 115.
41. Sperling, pp. 32–33.
42. *Detroit Daily Advertiser*, May 18, 1837.
43. *Acts of the Legislature of the State of Michigan passed at the special session of 1837* (Detroit, 1837), Act No. 9, pp. 311–14.
44. Felch, pp. 111–24; Henry M. Utley, "The Wild Cat Banking System of Michigan," *MPHC*, 5 (1884): 209–22; Bowen, *State Bank Notes of Michigan*, p. 23.
45. Felch, p. 122; Utley, p. 217.
46. Utley, p. 217.
47. Silas Beebe, "A Trip from Utica, New York, to Ingham County, Michigan," *MPHC*, 1 (1877): 190.
48. Utley, p. 222.
49. Bowen, *State Bank Notes of Michigan*, p. 1.
50. Bald, *Michigan in Four Centuries*, pp. 214–15, 221–22; W. L. Jenks, "Michigan's Five Million Dollar Loan," *Michigan History*, 15 (1931): 575–634.
51. Beebe, p. 191.
52. Felch, p. 123.
53. *Acts of the Legislature of the State of Michigan passed at the annual*

session of 1839 (Detroit, 1839), Act No. 37, pp. 37–64; Act No. 112, p. 207.
54. George B. Catlin, *The Story of Detroit* (Detroit, 1926), p. 312; Dunbar, *Michigan*, p. 342; Kilfoil, p. 220.
55. Myers, p. 99. This letter is in the Phelps Dodge Papers, Manuscripts Division of the New York Public Library.
56. T. H. Hinchman, *Banks and Banking in Michigan* (Detroit, 1887), pp. 30, 33, 37–38.
57. Kilfoil, p. 234.
58. Kilfoil, p. 266; Palmer, pp. 410–23.
59. Frank B. Woodford, *Lewis Cass—the Last Jeffersonian* (New Brunswick, N.J., 1950), p. 219.
60. Farmer, p. 864.
61. Kilfoil, p. 250; Michigan State Bank, *Directors' Minutes*, June 9, 1845.
62. Farmer, pp. 862–63.

CHAPTER 3

1. The major portion of the material in this section was gathered from the following: Clarence M. Burton, *History of Detroit: 1780–1850: Financial and Commercial* (Detroit, 1917); George B. Catlin, *The Story of Detroit* (Detroit, 1926); Silas Farmer, *History of Detroit*, 3rd ed. (Detroit, 1890); Frank B. Woodford and Arthur M. Woodford, *All Our Yesterdays* (Detroit, 1969); Rae Rips, ed., *Detroit in its World Setting* (Detroit, 1953); *Detroit Daily Advertiser and City Directory for the year 1850* (Detroit, 1850).
2. U.S., Census Office, Seventh Census, 1850. *Digest of the Statistics of Manufacturers* (Washington, 1859), p. 143.
3. *Shove's Business Advertiser and Detroit City Directory, 1852–53* (Detroit, 1853), p. 10.
4. Letter from DeWitt Clinton to Lewis Cass, September 17, 1824, Farnsworth Papers, BHC.
5. Alpheus Felch, "Michigan Court of Chancery," *MPHC*, 21 (1894): 328.
6. *Detroit Daily Advertiser*, February 1, 1849; February 11, 1849; *Acts of the Legislature of the State of Michigan passed at the annual session of 1849* (Lansing, 1849), Act No. 61, pp. 52–54.
7. *Ibid.*, sec. 4, p. 53.
8. *Ibid.*, sec. 6, p. 54.
9. *Ibid.*, sec. 5, p. 53.
10. DSFI, *Directors' Minutes*, March, 1849, p. 1. Hereafter referred to as *Minutes*.
11. Biographical sketch, Walker Papers, MHC.
12. DSFI, *Ledger, 1849–1851*, p. 106.
13. George B. Catlin, *A Brief History of Detroit in the Golden Days of '49* (Detroit, 1921), p. 6.
14. *Minutes*, May 9, 1849.
15. DSFI, *By-Laws and Regulations*, May 9, 1849, sec. 6, sec. 7.
16. *Minutes*, May 9, 1849.

17. Milo M. Quaife, "The Story of Mariners Church," *Michigan History*, 29 (1945): 37.
18. *Detroit Daily Advertiser*, December 22, 1849.
19. Quaife, "The Story of Mariners Church," pp. 35–36.
20. *Ibid.*
21. *Detroit Free Press*, April 10, 1849; *Detroit Daily Advertiser*, December 22, 1849.
22. Woodford and Woodford, *All Our Yesterdays*, p. 375.
23. *Detroit Free Press*, October 24, 1849; *Detroit Daily Advertiser and City Directory, 1850*, p. 4.
24. *Detroit Daily Advertiser and City Directory for the year 1850* (Detroit, 1850), pp. 57, 62, 179.
25. DSFI, *Ledger, 1849–51*, p. 53.
26. *Ibid.*
27. *Detroit Free Press*, July 2, 1851.
28. *Detroit Free Press*, December 2, 1883; *Detroit Post and Tribune*, December 2, 1883.
29. Michigan State Bank, *Directors' Minutes*, September 25, 1854.
30. *Minutes*, April 30, 1855.
31. *Teller*, 2 (September, 1935): 6.
32. Myers, *Financial History*, p. 126.
33. *Ibid.*
34. George W. VanVleck, *The Panic of 1857* (New York, 1943), pp. 91–92.
35. Michigan State Bank, *Directors' Minutes*, June 29, 1857; February 20, 1858.
36. Farmer, *History of Detroit*, p. 866.
37. Letter from Elon Farnsworth to the Board of Trustees, February, 1870. In the files of the Cashier's Office DBTC.
38. Biographical sketch, Farnsworth Papers, MHC.
39. Undated newspaper clipping, Walker Papers, MHC.
40. Biographical sketch, Walker Papers, MHC.
41. *Minutes*, January 13, 1857; January 19, 1857.
42. *Minutes*, November 3, 1859.
43. *Minutes*, November 7, 1859.
44. *Ibid.*
45. *Minutes*, November 7, 1859; June 27, 1870.
46. Teller, 2 (September, 1935): 6.
47. Farmer, p. 311.
48. Myers, pp. 163–65.
49. *Teller*, 2 (September, 1935): 6.
50. *Minutes*, February 13, 1866.
51. *Minutes*, July, 1861; July 1, 1863; December 29, 1864.

CHAPTER 4

1. Dunbar, *Michigan*, p. 458.
2. *Ibid.*, p. 459.
3. *Ibid.*

4. William L. Weber, "Discovery and Development of the Salt Interest in the Saginaw Valley," *MPHC*, 4 (1881): 13–23.
5. Bald, *Michigan in Four Centuries*, p. 298.
6. Bald, *Michigan in Four Centuries*, p. 298; Catlin, *The Story of Detroit*, pp. 658–63; Dunbar, *Michigan*, pp. 483–84.
7. Sidney Glazer, "The Beginnings of the Economic Revolution in Michigan," *Michigan History*, 34 (1950): 14.
8. U.S., Census Office, Tenth Census, 1880, *Report on the Manufacturers of the United States* (Washington, 1883), pp. 282, 409.
9. Bald, *Michigan in Four Centuries*, p. 255.
10. *Acts of the Legislature of the State of Michigan passed at the regular session of 1857* (Lansing, 1857), Act No. 135, pp. 362–80.
11. *Ibid.,* sec. 21; sec. 22; sec. 39.
12. Willis F. Dunbar, *Michigan Through the Centuries* (2 vols.; New York, 1955), 2:230.
13. *Minutes*, April 20, 1870.
14. Letter from Elon Farnsworth to the Board of Trustees, February, 1870. In the files of the Cashier's Office DBTC.
15. *Acts of the Legislature of the State of Michigan passed at the regular session of 1871* (3 vols.; Lansing, 1871), 1: Act No. 74, pp. 93–8.
16. *Minutes*, June 22, 1871.
17. *Minutes*, July 18, 1871; July 22, 1871.
18. *Minutes*, July 22, 1871.
19. *Minutes*, November 14, 1872.
20. *Ibid.*
21. *Acts of the Legislature of the State of Michigan passed at the regular session of 1871*, (3 vols.; Lansing, 1871), 1: Act No. 58, pp. 70–74.
22. Hinchman, *Banks and Banking*, p. 99; Farmer, *History of Detroit*, p. 870.
23. James VanHorne, "Michigan Banking in Retrospect," *Michigan Economic Record*, 6 (December, 1964): 3–6.
24. *Teller*, 2 (September, 1935): 6.
25. *Minutes*, April 9, 1874.
26. *Minutes*, March 29, 1877.
27. Unidentified and undated newspaper article, Felch Papers, MHC, ca. 1877.
28. *Minutes*, January 17, 1878.
29. *Minutes*, February 28, 1878.
30. *Minutes*, March 6, 1878.
31. *Agency Book*, p. 160, Miller Papers, BHC.
32. *Detroit Free Press*, December 19, 1878.
33. Biographical sketch, Walker Papers, MHC; *Minutes*, June 27, 1881.
34. *Public Acts of the Legislature of the State of Michigan passed at the regular session of 1881* (Lansing, 1881), Act No. 248, p. 338.
35. *Minutes*, May 1, 1882.
36. J. W. Weeks, *Detroit City Directory for 1883* (Detroit, 1883), p. 14.
37. Hinchman, pp. 142–43; Detroit Clearing House Association, *Constitution* (Detroit, 1883), unpaged.
38. J. W. Weeks, *Detroit City Directory for 1884* (Detroit, 1884), p. 21.
39. *Encyclopedia of the Social Sciences* (15 vols.; New York, 1935), 3:546.
40. *Minutes*, December 1, 1883.

41. *Detroit Post and Tribune*, December 2, 1883.
42. *Minutes*, December 18, 1883.
43. *Minutes*, July 1, 1884.
44. *Minutes*, July 1, 1888.
45. *Minutes*, February 21, 1888.
46. *Teller*, 2 (September, 1935): 6.
47. Dunbar, *Michigan Through the Centuries*, 2:231.
48. *Public Acts of the Legislature of the State of Michigan passed at the regular session of 1887* (Lansing, 1887), Act No. 205, pp. 225–42.
49. R. L. Polk, *Detroit City Directory for 1890* (Detroit, 1890), pp. 12–13; R. L. Polk, *Detroit City Directory for 1891* (Detroit, 1891), pp. 43–44.
50. *Minutes*, February 8, 1887.
51. Myers, *Financial History*, p. 214, 216; Sperling, *Great Depressions*, pp. 57–8; Robert Sobel, *Panic on Wall Street* (New York, 1968), pp. 230–73.
52. Dunbar, *Michigan Through the Centuries*, 2:232–33; Quaife and Glazer, *Michigan*, pp. 278–79; *Minutes*, May 31, 1893.
53. *Teller*, 2 (September, 1935): 6.
54. *Minutes*, July 18, 1893; August 12, 1893.
55. *Minutes*, August 22, 1893.
56. *Teller*, 2 (September, 1935): 6.
57. *Minutes*, October 6, 1885.
58. *Minutes*, December 13, 1899; January 18, 1900; March 20, 1900.
59. *Minutes*, June 10, 1901.
60. *Minutes*, June 18, 1901.
61. *Minutes*, April 6, 1904.

CHAPTER 5

1. Frank Donovan, *Wheels for a Nation* (New York, 1965), p. 54.
2. Merrill Denison, *The Power to Go* (Garden City, 1956), pp. 103–4.
3. *Ibid.*, p. 110.
4. Philip H. Smith, *Wheels Within Wheels* (New York, 1970), p. 24.
5. Donovan, pp. 51–61; John B. Rae, *The American Automobile* (Chicago, 1965), pp. 25–26.
6. W. Hawkins Ferry, *The Buildings of Detroit* (Detroit, 1968), pp. 183, 186, 189.
7. Donovan, pp. 142–45.
8. Rae, pp. 62–63.
9. Denison, pp. 156–64.
10. Ferry, pp. 180–81.
11. Automobile Manufacturers Association, *Automobiles of America* (3rd ed., Detroit, 1970), pp. 195–96, 210.
12. Statistics Folder, Vertical File, AHC.
13. Denison, pp. 65–76.
14. Sidney D. Miller, *Reading Room File*, BHC.
15. *Minutes*, July 12, 1887.
16. *Minutes*, June 17, 1890; "Plan for Savings in Small Sums (5, 10, 25, and 50

cents) adopted in June, 1890 by the Detroit Savings Bank." DBTC, *Excerpts and Miscellaneous File*, BHC.

17. *Ibid.*
18. *Minutes*, March 17, 1903.
19. R. L. Polk, *Detroit City Directory for 1889* (Detroit, 1889), p. 709.
20. *Minutes*, November 17, 1903; November 19, 1903; November 24, 1903.
21. *Minutes*, June 9, 1904; June 24, 1904.
22. *Teller*, 2 (September, 1935): 2–3; *Detroit News Tribune*, October 2, 1904.
23. R. L. Polk, *Detroit City Directory for 1904* (Detroit, 1904), p. 2701.
24. R. L. Polk, *Detroit City Directory for 1903* (Detroit, 1903), p. 43; *Detroit City Directory for 1929–1930* (Detroit, 1930), p. 35.
25. *Teller*, 7 (December, 1940): 22.
26. *Teller*, 2 (October, 1935): 2.
27. *Minutes*, December 8, 1908; April 20, 1909; April 7, 1914; July 16, 1915.
28. *Teller*, 2 (December, 1935): 2.
29. R. L. Polk, *Detroit City Directory, 1920–21* (Detroit, 1921), p. 50.
30. *Minutes*, December 29, 1882.
31. Wages and prices in 1882 from *Michigan and its Resources*, a pamphlet issued to interest immigrants in settling in Michigan; Bald, *Michigan in Four Centuries*, p. 295.
32. *Minutes*, December 19, 1899; January 9, 1917; January 14, 1930.
33. *Teller*, 2 (September, 1935): 6.
34. *Minutes*, February 3, 1905.
35. *Minutes*, February 10, 1905; January 9, 1906.
36. Penobscot Building, *Excerpts and Miscellaneous File*, BHC.
37. Penobscot Building, *Excerpts and Miscellaneous File*, BHC.
38. *Minutes*, February 27, 1906.
39. DeWitt Delamater, *Scrapbook*, 2 vols., 1: 32, BHC.
40. *Teller*, 8 (March, 1942): 7.
41. *Minutes*, January 14, 1908; April 5, 1910; May 17, 1910; October 25, 1910; July 25, 1911; April 2, 1912; May 27, 1913.
42. *Teller*, 2 (September, 1935): 6.
43. *Ibid.*
44. *Minutes*, October 2, 1913.
45. Delamater, *Scrapbook*, 1:40.
46. *Teller*, 2 (September, 1935): 6.
47. Robin Hood Flour Mill, *Excerpts and Miscellaneous File*, BHC; *Detroit News*, July 18, 1973.
48. *Minutes*, October 16, 1917; October 23, 1917.
49. *Minutes*, October 13, 1914.
50. *Minutes*, May 26, 1917; June 5, 1917; *Teller*, 8 (April, 1942): 13–14, 17.
51. *Minutes*, June 5, 1917.
52. *Teller*, 8 (April, 1942): 17.
53. *Minutes*, December 12, 1917.
54. Michigan State Banking Department, *Annual Report of the Commissioner, 1914* (Lansing, 1915), p. 133; *Annual Report of the Commissioner, 1918*, p. 146; *Annual Report of the Commissioner, 1919*, p. 156.
55. *Minutes*, October 31, 1919.
56. *Minutes*, January 13, 1920.
57. *Minutes*, June 27, 1920.

58. DSB, "Condensed Statement of Condition," February, 1921; "Condensed Statement of Condition," March, 1922; "Condensed Statement of Condition," October, 1922.
59. *Automobiles of America*, pp. 263–64.
60. Woodford and Woodford, *All Our Yesterdays*, p. 275.
61. *Minutes*, January 29, 1920; February 26, 1920.
62. *Minutes*, January 16, 1912; February 29, 1912.
63. *Minutes*, September 14, 1915.
64. "Facts in Connection with the Purchase of the Detroit Savings Bank Building as related by Sidney T. Miller." Typewritten paper, unpaged, in the files of the Cashier's Office, DBTC. Herafter referred to as the "Miller Paper."
65. *Minutes*, November 3, 1915; "Miller Paper."
66. *Minutes*, July 17, 1918.
67. *Minutes*, January 29, 1919.
68. *Minutes*, April 12, 1921; May 31, 1921.
69. *Minutes*, April 3, 1920.
70. "Miller Paper."
71. *Minutes*, January 11, 1921.
72. Michigan State Banking Department, *Annual Report of the Commissioner, 1922* (Lansing, 1923), p. 87; *Annual Report of the Commissioner, 1929*, p. 97.
73. *Minutes*, 1922–29, various pages.
74. *Teller*, 2 (August, 1935): 2.
75. *Minutes*, September 20, 1927.
76. *Minutes*, November 1, 1927.
77. DSB, "Annual Statement to Stockholders," December 31, 1928.

CHAPTER 6

1. U.S., Department of Commerce, Bureau of the Census, *Biennial Census of Manufacturers, 1927* (Washington, 1930), pp. 1437–38.
2. U.S., Department of Commerce, Bureau of the Census, *Fifteenth Census of the United States: Manufacturers, 1929* (3 vols.; Washington, 1933), 3:249–64.
3. *Automobiles of America*, pp. 263–64.
4. The major portion of the data on Detroit banks for this chapter was obtained from: Walter L. Dunham, *Banking and Industry in Michigan* (Detroit, 1929); Michigan State Banking Department, *Annual Reports of the Commissioner, 1914–1929*; D. Maitland Irwin, *A Chronology of Banking in Detroit, 1897–1957* (Bankers Club of Detroit, 1957); *Detroit City Directories, 1914–1929.*
5. U.S., Federal Reserve Board, *Bulletin*, 16 (1930): 777.
6. *Public Acts of the Legislature of the State of Michigan passed at the regular session of 1917* (Lansing, 1917), Act No. 296, pp. 732–38.
7. Michigan State Banking Department, *Annual Report of the Commissioner, 1910* (Lansing, 1911), various pages; *Annual Report of the*

Commissioner, 1920, various pages; Dunbar, *Michigan Through the Centuries,* 2:234.

8. G. Walter Woodworth, *The Detroit Money Market, 1934–1955* (Ann Arbor, 1956), pp. 25–26.
9. *Public Acts of the Legislature of the State of Michigan passed at the regular session of 1929* (Lansing, 1929), Act No. 66, pp. 108–50.
10. Patricia O'Donnell McKenzie, *Some Aspects of the Detroit Bank Crisis of 1933* (Ann Arbor, 1963), pp. 14–15.
11. Howard R. Neville, *The Detroit Banking Collapse of 1933* (East Lansing, 1960), pp. 11–13.
12. *Ibid.,* pp. 13–17.
13. G. Walter Woodworth, "The Detroit Money Market," *Michigan Business Studies,* 5 (1932): 245.
14. McKenzie, p. 127.
15. Bald, *Michigan in Four Centuries,* pp. 406–7.
16. James T. Adams, *Dictionary of American History* (6 vols.; New York, 1940), 1:157.
17. *Minutes,* March 17, 1931.
18. Rev. Charles E. Coughlin, *The New Deal in Money* (Royal Oak, Michigan, 1933), pp. 28–30.
19. McKenzie, p. 158.
20. Neville, p. 51.
21. Frank B. Woodford, *Alex J. Groesbeck: Portrait of a Public Man* (Detroit, 1962), p. 276.
22. *Ibid.*
23. Neville, p. 54.
24. Woodford, *Alex J. Groesbeck,* p. 277.
25. *Detroit Free Press,* February 14, 1933.
26. *Detroit Free Press,* February 15, 1933.
27. *Detroit Free Press,* February 17, 1933.
28. *Detroit Free Press,* February 18, 1933.
29. McKenzie, pp. 162–63.
30. *Ibid.,* p. 165.
31. *Detroit Free Press,* February 21, 1933.
32. *Detroit Free Press,* February 22, 1933.
33. McKenzie, pp. 166, 167.
34. *Detroit Free Press,* February 27, 1933.
35. *Minutes,* February 14–28, 1933; *Teller,* 2 (November, 1935): 8; *Detroit News,* March 18, 1949; Interview with Raymond T. Perring, March 15, 1973.
36. *Detroit Free Press,* February 28, 1933.
37. Cited above, note 35.
38. McKenzie, p. 168; *Detroit Free Press,* March 1, 1933.
39. *Detroit Free Press,* February 28, 1933.
40. Neville, p. 57.
41. McKenzie, p. 172.
42. Dunbar, *Michigan Through the Centuries,* 2:237.
43. *Ibid.,* p. 238.
44. *Detroit News,* March 14, 1933; March 16, 1933.
45. *Detroit News,* March 13, 1933.

46. Woodford, *Alex J. Groesbeck*, p. 278.
47. Jesse H. Jones, *Fifty Billion Dollars* (New York, 1951), p. 67.
48. Michigan State Banking Department, *Annual Report of the Commissioner, 1949* (Lansing, 1950), p. 10.
49. Michigan State Banking Department, *Annual Report of the Commissioner, 1933* (Lansing, 1934), p. xi.
50. McKenzie, p. 173.
51. Jones, p. 68.
52. Michigan State Banking Department, *Annual Report of the Commissioner, 1933* (Lansing, 1934), p. xi.
53. McKenzie, p. 173.
54. Woodford and Woodford, *All Our Yesterdays*, p. 313.
55. Michigan State Banking Department, *Annual Report of the Commissioner, 1933* (Lansing, 1934), pp. 55–60, 203–204.
56. Michigan State Banking Department, *Annual Report of the Commissioner, 1932* (Lansing, 1933), p. 69; *Annual Report of the Commissioner, 1933*, p. 57.
57. *Minutes*, November, 1933.
58. *Teller*, 2 (November, 1935): 8.
59. *Minutes*, October 31, 1933; November 7, 1933.
60. *Detroit News*, October 31, 1933; *Detroit Free Press*, November 1, 1933.
61. *Minutes*, November 7, 1933.

CHAPTER 7

1. Letter from Joseph M. Dodge to Mrs. Dodge, ca. 1916; and *Bay City Times Tribune*, August 5, 1916, Bank Examiner Box, Dodge Papers, BHC.
2. Letter from Joseph M. Dodge to F. W. Merrick, December 5, 1916, Bank Examiner Box, Dodge Papers, BHC.
3. Letters from Joseph M. Dodge to Thomas Doyle, December 30, 1930, December 2, 1931, December 5, 1931, Doyle Auto Agency Box, Dodge Papers, BHC.
4. Letter from Joseph M. Dodge to Thomas Doyle, August 6, 1932, Doyle Auto Agency Box, Dodge Papers, BHC.
5. Biographical sketch, Biography Box, Dodge Papers, BHC.
6. Biographical sketch, Biography Box, Dodge Papers, BHC.
7. *Fortune*, March, 1953, p. 142.
8. *Minutes*, December 19, 1933; December 21, 1933.
9. *Minutes*, February 20, 1934; February 27, 1934; March 27, 1934; April 10, 1934.
10. *Minutes*, October 10, 1934.
11. *Minutes*, March 13, 1934; *Teller*, 1 (December, 1934): 4.
12. *Minutes*, July 3, 1934.
13. *Minutes*, August 7, 1934.
14. DSB, "Condensed Statement of Condition," 1933, 1934.
15. *Minutes*, January 3, 1935.
16. *Detroit Free Press*, January 20, 1935; *Minutes*, January 22, 1935.
17. *Minutes*, March 5, 1935; *Teller*, 1 (March, 1935): 10.
18. *Minutes*, August 13, 1935.

19. *Minutes*, July 18, 1939.
20. *Minutes*, April 9, 1935; DSB, "Condensed Statement of Condition," 1935.
21. *Minutes*, January 14, 1936.
22. *Minutes*, July 23, 1935; July 30, 1935.
23. *Teller*, 2 (January, 1936): 3.
24. *Minutes*, July 23, 1935; July 30, 1935; December 17, 1935.
25. *Teller*, 2 (January, 1936): 3.
26. *Minutes*, April 14, 1936.
27. *Teller*, 3 (August, 1936): 5.
28. *Teller*, 3 (October, 1936): 2–4, 11.
29. *Teller*, 4 (December, 1937): 3–5, 11.
30. *Minutes*, December 4, 1934; August 31, 1937; January 18, 1938.
31. *Public and Local Acts of the Legislature of the State of Michigan passed at the regular and extra sessions of 1937* (Lansing, 1937), Act No. 341, pp. 702–806.
32. *Minutes*, August 17, 1937.
33. *Automobiles of America*, p. 263.
34. *Minutes*, January 25, 1938.
35. DB, "Condensed Statement of Condition," 1938, 1939.
36. *Minutes*, January 10, 1939.
37. *Minutes*, May 28, 1940.
38. Michigan State Banking Department, *Annual Report of the Commissioner, 1930* (Lansing, 1931), pp. xxx–xxxv; *Annual Report of the Commissioner, 1940*, pp. 6–12.
39. *Teller*, 7 (January, 1941): 3.
40. *Ibid.*, p. 5.
41. Woodford and Woodford, *All Our Yesterdays*, p. 336.
42. Dunbar, *Michigan*, p. 575.
43. *Automobiles of America*, pp. 109, 113.
44. *Teller*, 10 (April, 1944): 2.
45. *Teller*, 10 (April, 1944): 2–6; *Automobiles of America*, pp. 102–14; Dunbar, *Michigan*, p. 575.
46. *Minutes*, June 17, 1941; December 2, 1941.
47. *Teller*, 8 (January, 1942): 18.
48. *Teller*, 12 (January, 1946): 6.
49. DB, "Statement of Condition," 1943.
50. *Ibid.*
51. *Public and Local Acts of the Legislature of the State of Michigan passed at the regular session of 1943* (Lansing, 1943), Act No. 82, pp. 107–8.
52. Biographical sketch, Biography Box, Dodge Papers, BHC.
53. *Minutes*, September 2, 1943; *Teller*, 11 (September, 1944): 2–3.
54. *Minutes*, February 16, 1943.
55. *Teller*, 11 (March, 1945): 4.
56. *Fortune*, March, 1953, p. 144.
57. DB, "Statement of Condition," 1940, 1945.
58. *Ibid.*
59. Introduction to Finding Aid, Dodge Papers, BHC.
60. *Teller*, 13 (July, 1946): 6.
61. Biographical sketch, Biography Box, Dodge Papers, BHC.
62. *Detroit News*, December 3, 1964.

63. *Time*, January 24, 1955, p. 13.
64. *Detroit News*, May 10, 1951.
65. *Fortune*, March, 1953, p. 138.
66. Introduction to Finding Aid, Dodge Papers, BHC.
67. *Teller*, 17 (October, 1950): 2–3.
68. *Ibid.*
69. Dunbar, *Michigan*, p. 575.
70. *Minutes*, December 17, 1946; April 22, 1947; June 24, 1947; April 13, 1948.
71. *Minutes*, February 4, 1947; December 31, 1946; September 16, 1947.
72. DB, "Statement of Condition," 1945; DB, *Annual Report, 1949.*
73. *Minutes*, January 9, 1951.
74. Biographical sketch, Biography Box, Dodge Papers, BHC.
75. *Minutes*, December 30, 1952.
76. *Minutes*, January 15, 1953.
77. *Teller*, 20 (April, 1954): 6.
78. *Teller*, 15 (May, 1949): 4; DB, *Annual Report, 1951*; DB, *Annual Report, 1956.*
79. *Teller*, 19 (May, 1953): 3; 20 (April, 1954): 4.
80. DB, "Statement of Condition," 1941; DB, *Annual Report, 1955.*
81. DB, "Statement of Condition," 1945; DB, *Annual Report, 1955.*
82. DB, "Statment of Condition," 1946; DB, *Annual Report, 1955; Minutes*, December 18, 1951; April 29, 1952.

CHAPTER 8

1. Michigan State Banking Department, *Annual Report of the Commissioner, 1933* (Lansing, 1934), pp. 55–60, 203–204; Irwin, *A Chronology of Banking.*
2. *Minutes*, January 29, 1955.
3. Interview with Raymond T. Perring, March 15, 1973.
4. *Teller*, 23 (July-August, 1956): 3.
5. *Detroit Times*, November 15, 1955.
6. *Minutes*, June 12, 1956.
7. *Teller*, 23 (July-August, 1956): 3.
8. *Detroit News*, June 13, 1956.
9. *Detroit Free Press*, June 13, 1956.
10. Ferry, *Buildings of Detroit*, p. 226.
11. *Minutes*, August 21, 1956.
12. *Detroit News*, June 13, 1956.
13. *Minutes*, September 4, 1956.
14. DBTC, *Annual Report, 1956.*
15. *Ibid.*
16. DBTC, *Annual Report, 1958*; Dunbar, *Michigan*, p. 577.
17. DBTC, *Annual Report, 1956; Annual Report, 1958.*
18. *Detroit Free Press*, January 30, 1957; *Detroit Times*, January 30, 1957; *Detroit News*, March 30, 1962.
19. *Detroit News*, January 30, 1957.

20. *Ibid.*
21. Letter from Joseph M. Dodge to Mayor Louis C. Miriani, November 15, 1957, Detroit and Michigan Finances, Box 1, Dodge Papers, BHC; *Detroit News*, March 30, 1962.
22. *Ibid.*
23. Letter from Joseph M. Dodge to Mayor Louis C. Miriani, November 15, 1957, Detroit and Michigan Finances, Box 1, Dodge Papers, BHC.
24. *Ibid.*
25. *Ibid.*
26. Unidentified and undated collection of newspaper articles collectively titled "Dodge Report," Detroit and Michigan Finances, Box 1, Dodge Papers, BHC, ca. 1958.
27. Undated *Free Press* clipping, Detroit and Michigan Finances, Box 1, Dodge Papers, BHC, ca. 1958.
28. *Detroit Free Press*, July 12, 1961.
29. *Automobiles of America*, p. 264.
30. *Teller*, 27 (April, 1961): 3–4.
31. *Teller*, 29 (July-August, 1962): 3; *Teller*, 29 (March, 1963): 7.
32. *Teller*, 30 (November, 1963): 3.
33. *Minutes*, January 15, 1963.
34. DBTC, *Annual Report, 1963.*
35. DBTC, *Annual Report, 1961; Annual Report, 1962.*
36. *Minutes*, January 15, 1957.
37. *Minutes*, March 26, 1957.
38. *Teller*, 31 (December, 1964): 23.
39. *Minutes*, July 18, 1961.
40. *Teller*, 28 (December, 1961): 3.
41. *Ibid.*
42. *Teller*, 31 (December, 1964): 29.
43. R. L. Polk, *Detroit City Directory, 1932/33* (Detroit, 1933), p. 33.
44. *Teller*, 28 (May, 1962): 11; 29 (June, 1962): 3; 31 (December, 1964): 30.
45. *Teller*, 30 (October, 1963): 10; 31 (December, 1964): 11.
46. *Teller*, 31 (December, 1964): 24.
47. *Teller*, 32 (May, 1966): 3.
48. *Detroit Free Press*, February 3, 1965.
49. DBTC, *Annual Report, 1958; Annual Report, 1966.*
50. DBTC, *Annual Report, 1968.*
51. *Minutes*, November 22, 1966.
52. *Teller*, 34 (November, 1967): 3.
53. *Minutes*, November 22, 1966.
54. *Minutes*, January 24, 1967; March 28, 1967; October 24, 1967.
55. *Teller*, 34 (November, 1967): 3.
56. DBTC, *Annual Report, 1960; Annual Report, 1969.*
57. DBTC, *Annual Report, 1967; Annual Report, 1970; Minutes*, May 23, 1967.
58. *Teller*, 32 (November, 1965): 3.
59. *Minutes*, October 26, 1956.
60. DBTC, *Annual Report, 1969.*
61. *Teller*, 35 (February, 1969): 3.
62. Interview, William F. Piper.
63. *Teller*, 35 (February, 1969): 3.

64. DBTC, *Annual Report, 1969.*
65. *Ibid.*
66. DBTC, *Annual Report, 1971.*
67. DBTC, *Annual Report, 1972.*
68. "First Independence National: Michigan's Only Minority Bank Growing at Impressive Rate," *Michigan Tradesman,* 89 (February, 1972): 4–5.
69. *Minutes,* March 27, 1973.
70. *Public and Local Acts of the Legislature of the State of Michigan passed at the regular session of 1971,* (Lansing, 1971), Act No. 2, pp. 7–9.
71. *Teller,* 39 (November, 1972): 9.
72. *Minutes,* October 24, 1972.
73. Association of Registered Bank Holding Companies, *The Bank Holding Company: Its History and Significance in Modern America* (Washington, 1972), pp. 8–9.
74. *Teller,* 39 (April, 1973): 12.
75. *Ibid.,* p. 13.
76. DBTC, "Notice of Special Meeting of Stockholders, March 27, 1973."

bibliography

Papers and Unpublished Documents

Delamater, DeWitt. *Scrapbook.* 2 vols. Burton Historical Collection, Detroit Public Library.

Detroit Savings Fund Institute. *Ledger, 1849–1851.*

Detroit Savings Fund Institute. *Trustees Minutes, 1849–1871.*

Detroit Savings Bank. *Directors Minutes, 1871–1936.*

Detroit Bank. *Directors Minutes, 1936–1956.*

Detroit Bank and Trust Company. *Directors Minutes, 1956 to date.*

Dodge, Joseph M. *Papers.* Burton Historical Collection, Detroit Public Library.

Farnsworth, Elon. *Papers.* Burton Historical Collection, Detroit Public Library.

Farnsworth, Elon. *Papers.* Michigan Historical Collections, University of Michigan.

Felch, Alpheus. *Papers.* Michigan Historical Collections, University of Michigan.

Koska, Leslie. "Purchasing Power of the Dollar." 1970. Unpublished statistics, Detroit Branch, Federal Reserve Bank of Chicago.

Michigan State Bank. *Directors Minutes, 1835–1855.* Minutes Book is in the possession of the cashier, Detroit Bank and Trust Company.

Miller, Sidney D. *Papers.* Burton Historical Collection, Detroit Public Library.

Miller, Sidney T. "Facts in connection with the purchase of the Detroit Savings Bank Building as related by Sidney T. Miller." ca. 1930. Unpublished typewritten paper in the possession of the cashier, Detroit Bank and Trust Company.

Walker, Henry N. *Papers.* Michigan Historical Collections, Univeristy of Michigan.

Public Documents

Federal Reserve Bulletin. V. 14, 1930. Washington, D.C.: U.S. Government Printing Office.

Michigan. *Laws of the Territory of Michigan.* Lansing: W. S. George, printer, 1871–84. 4 vols.

Bibliography

Michigan. *Laws in Relation to Banking Associations in the State of Michigan, Passed at the Session of 1837.* Detroit: John S. Bagg, printer, 1837.

Michigan. *Laws in Relation to Banking Associations in the State of Michigan, Passed at the Adjourned Session of the Legislature for 1837.* Detroit: John S. Bagg, printer, 1837.

Michigan. *Michigan Public and Local Acts.* Detroit and Lansing: various publishers, 1838 to date.

Michigan. *General Banking Law of the State of Michigan. Sections Relating Wholly to the Issue of Circulating Notes Being Omitted.* Lansing: W. S. George, 1885.

Michigan Banking Commission. *Annual Report.* Lansing: various publishers, 1838 to date.

U.S., Bureau of the Census. *Historical Statistics of the United States, Colonial Times to 1957.* Washington, D.C.: U.S. Government Printing Office, 1960.

U.S., Census Office. *10th Census, 1880. Report of the Manufacturers of the United States.* Washington, D.C.: U.S. Government Printing Office, 1883.

U.S., Census Office. *7th Census, 1850. Digest of the Statistics of Manufacturers . . .* Washington, D.C.: U.S. Government Printing Office, 1859.

Books

Association of Registered Bank Holding Companies. *The Bank Company: Its History and Significance in Modern America.* Washington, D.C.: ARBHC, 1972.

Automobile Manufacturers Association, Inc. *Automobiles of America.* 3rd ed, rev. Detroit: Wayne State University Press, 1970.

Bald, F. Clever. *Detroit's First American Decade.* Ann Arbor: University of Michigan Press, 1948.

―――. *Michigan in Four Centuries.* Rev. ed. New York: Harper & Brothers, 1961.

Barnard, Harry. *Independent Man: The Life of Senator James Couzens.* New York: Scribner's, 1958.

Bingay, Malcolm. *Detroit: Its My Home Town.* New York: Bobbs-Merril, 1946.

The Papers of Col. Henry Bouquet. Sylvester K. Stevens and Donald H. Kent, editors. 17 vols. Harrisburg: Pennsylvania Historical Commission, 1940–43.

Bourne, Edward G. *The Surplus Revenue of 1837.* New York: Putnam, 1885.

Bowen, Harold L. *Early Michigan Script.* no pub. cited, ca. 1969.

―――. *State Bank Notes of Michigan.* Detroit: Havelt Advertising Services, 1956.

Bremer, Cornelius D. *American Bank Failures.* New York: AMS Press, 1968.

Burton, Clarence M. *The City of Detroit Michigan.* 5 vols. Detroit: Clarke Publishing Co., 1922.

―――. *History of Detroit: 1780 to 1850: Financial and Commercial.* Detroit: Report of the Historiographer, 1917.

―――. *History of Wayne County and the City of Detroit.* 5 vols. Chicago: Clarke Publishing Co., 1930.

Catlin, George B. *A Brief History of Detroit in the Golden Days of '49.* Detroit: Detroit Savings Bank, 1921.

————. *The Story of Detroit*. Detroit: The Detroit News, 1926.

Colt, C. C. and N. S. Keith. *A History of the Banking Crisis*. New York: Greenberg Publisher, Inc., 1933.

Coughlin, Rev. Charles E. *The New Deal in Money*. Royal Oak, Michigan: Radio League of the Little Flower, 1933.

Dain, Floyd R. *Every House a Frontier: Detroit's Economic Progress, 1815–1825*. Detroit: Wayne [State] University Press, 1956.

Denison, Merrill. *The Power to Go*. Garden City, N.Y.: Doubleday, 1956.

Detroit. *City Directory*. Detroit: various publishers, 1837 to date.

Detroit Clearing House Association. *Constitution*. Detroit: John F. Eby & Co., 1883.

Detroit Savings Bank. *Plan for Savings in Small Sums (5, 10, 25 and 50 cents) adopted in June, 1890 by the Detroit Savings Bank*. Detroit, 1890.

Dictionary of American History. James T. Adams, editor in chief. 6 vols. New York: Scribner's, 1940.

Donovan, Frank. *Wheels for a Nation*. New York: Crowell, 1965.

Dunbar, Willis F. *Michigan: A History of the Wolverine State*. Grand Rapids, Mich.: Eerdmans Publishing Co., 1965.

————. *Michigan Through the Centuries*. 2 vols. New York: Lewis Historical Publishing Co., 1955.

Dunham, Walter L. *Banking and Industry in Michigan*. Detroit: Madeira Publishing Co., 1929.

Encyclopedia Americana. 30 vols. New York: Americana Corp., 1973.

Encyclopaedia Britannica. 23 vols. Chicago: Encyclopaedia Britannica, 1973.

Encyclopedia of the Social Sciences. 15 vols. New York: Macmillan, 1930–35.

Farmer, Silas. *History of Detroit and Wayne County and Early Michigan*. 3rd ed. Detroit: Farmer & Co., 1890.

Ferry, W. Hawkins. *The Buildings of Detroit*. Detroit: Wayne State University Press, 1968.

Galbraith, John K. *The Great Crash, 1929*. Boston: Houghton Mifflin, 1954.

Gibbons, James S. *The Banks of New York . . . and the Panic of 1857*. New York: Appleton, 1859.

Hamil, Fred C. *When Beaver was King*. Detroit's 250th Birthday Festival. Historical Booklets, v. 8, ed. by Joe L. Norris. Detroit: Wayne [State] University Press, 1951.

Hammond, Bray. *Banks and Politics in America from the Revolution to the Civil War*. Princeton: Princeton University Press, 1957.

Henry, Alexander. *Alexander Henry's Travels and Adventures in the Years 1760–76*. Edited with historical introduction and notes by Milo M. Quaife. Chicago: R.R. Donnelley, 1921.

Hildreth, R. *Banks, Banking, and Paper Currencies*. New York: Greenwood Press, 1968. Originally published in 1840.

Hinchman, T.H. *Banks and Banking in Michigan*. Detroit: Wm. Graham, printer, 1887.

Irwin, D. Maitland. *A Chronology of Banking in Detroit, 1897–1957*. Detroit: Bankers Club of Detroit, 1957. Chart published in celebration of the 50th anniversary of the Bankers Club of Detroit.

Jenks, William L. *The First Bank in Michigan*. Port Huron, Mich.: First National Exchange Bank, 1916.

Bibliography

Johnson, Ida A. *The Michigan Fur Trade*. Lansing: Michigan Historical Commission, 1919.

The Papers of Sir William Johnson. Sullivan, Flick, and Lauber editors. 14 vols. Albany: University of the State of New York, 1921–65.

Jones, Jesse H. with Edward Angly. *Fifty Billion Dollars*. New York: Macmillan, 1951.

Kilfoil, Jack F. "C.C. Trowbridge, Detroit Banker and Michigan Land Speculator, 1820–1845." Ph.D. dissertation, Claremont Graduate School, 1970.

Lanier, Henry W. *A Century of Banking in New York: 1822–1922*. New York: Gilliss Press, 1922.

Lanzillotti, Robert F. *Banking Structure in Michigan: 1945–1963*. Michigan State University, Bureau of Business and Economic Research, 1966.

McKenzie, Patricia O. "Some Aspects of the Detroit Bank Crisis of 1933." Ph.D. dissertation, Wayne State University, 1963.

Main, Jackson T. *The Social Structure of Revolutionary America*. Princeton: Princeton University Press, 1965.

Mansfield, John B. *History of the Great Lakes*. 2 vols. Chicago: Beers & Co., 1894.

Mason, Philip P. *Detroit, Fort Lernoult, and the American Revolution*. Detroit: Wayne State University Press, 1964.

Melvin, Crandall. *A History of the Merchants National Bank and Trust Company of Syracuse, New York*. Syracuse: Syracuse University Press, 1969.

Myers, Margaret G. *A Financial History of the United States*. New York: Columbia University Press, 1970.

National Cash Register Company. *Financial Terminology*. Dayton, Ohio: National Cash Register Company, 1970.

Neville, Howard R.. "The Detroit Banking Collapse of 1933." Occasional paper no. 2. Bureau of Business and Economic Research. College of Business and Public Service. Michigan State University, East Lansing, 1960.

North American Fur Trade Conference, 1965. Selected Papers. *Aspects of the Fur Trade*. St. Paul: Minnesota Historical Society, 1967.

Peckham, Howard H. *Pontiac and the Indian Uprising*. Princeton: Princeton Univeristy Press, 1947.

Quaife, Milo M. and Sidney Glazer. *Michigan*. New York: Prentice-Hall, Inc., 1948.

Rae, John B. *The American Automobile*. Chicago: University of Chicago Press, 1965.

Rips, Rae E. ed. *Detroit in its World Setting: A 250-Year Chronology, 1701–1951*. Detroit: Detroit Public Library, 1953.

Rodkey, Robert G. *State Bank Failures in Michigan*. Ann Arbor, University of Michigan, Bureau of Business Research, 1935.

Smith, Philip H. *Wheels Within Wheels*. 2nd ed. rev. New York: Funk & Wagnalls, 1970.

Sobel, Robert. *Panic on Wall Street: A History of America's Financial Disasters*. New York: Macmillan, 1968.

Sperling, John. *Great Depressions: 1837–1844, 1893–1898, 1929–1939*. Glenview, Ill.: Scott, Foresman & Co., 1966.

278

VanVleck, George W. *The Panic of 1857.* New York: Columbia University Press, 1943.

Wendell, Emory. *History of Banking . . . and Banks and Bankers in Michigan . . .* Detroit: Winn & Hammond, ca. 1905.

Woodford, Frank B. *Alex J. Groesbeck: Portrait of a Public Man.* Detroit: Wayne State University Press, 1962.

————. *Lewis Cass—the Last Jeffersonian.* New Brunswick, N.J.: Rutgers University Press, 1950.

————. *Mr. Jefferson's Disciple: A Life of Justice Woodward.* East Lansing, Michigan State College Press, 1953.

————. *Yankees in Wonderland.* Cass Lectureship Series. Detroit: Wayne [State] University Press, 1951.

Woodford, Frank B. and Albert Hyma. *Gabriel Richard, Frontier Ambassador.* Detroit: Wayne State University Press, 1958.

Woodford, Frank B. and Arthur M. Woodford. *All Our Yesterdays: A Brief History of Detroit.* Detroit: Wayne State University Press, 1969.

Woodworth, G. Walter. *The Detroit Money Market, 1934–1955.* Bureau of Business Research. Ann Arbor: University of Michigan, 1956.

Newspapers

Detroit Daily Advertiser.
Detroit Free Press.
Detroit Gazette.
Detroit News.
Detroit Post and Tribune.
Detroit Times.

Periodicals

Adler, Simon L. "Money and Money Units in the American Colonies," *Rochester Historical Society, Publications,* 8 (1929): 143–73.

Ballatine, A. A. "When All the Banks Closed," *Harvard Business Review,* 26 (1948): 129–43.

Beebe, Silas. "A Trip from Utica, New York, to Ingham County, Michigan," *MPHC.* 1 (1877): 187–92.

Cooley, Thomas M. "State Bank Issues," *Michigan Political Science Association Publications,* 1 (1893): 4–22.

Felch, Alpheus. "Early Banks and Banking in Michigan," *MPHC,* 2 (1880): 111–24.

————. "Michigan's Court of Chancery," *MPHC,* 21 (1894): 324–35.

"First Independence National: Michigan's Only Minority Bank Growing at Impressive Rate," *Michigan Tradesman,* 89 (1972): 4–5.

Glazer, Sidney. "The Beginnings of the Economic Revolution in Michigan," *Michigan History,* 34 (1950): 193–202.

Goodrich, Enos. "Pioneer Memories," *MPHC,* 26 (1896): 581–84.

Bibliography

Haldimand Papers. "Letters from Lt. Gov. Hamilton. Council Held at Detroit, June 29, 1778," *MPHC,* 9 (1886): 456.

Huggins, Andrew. "Exchange Bank of Shiawassee," *MPHC,* 28 (1900): 511–13.

Jenks, William L. "Michigan's Five Million Dollar Loan," *Michigan History,* 15 (1931): 575–634.

Palmer, Friend. "The Old Bank of Michigan," *MPHC,* 30 (1906): 410–23.

Piper, William F. "U.S. Bank in London Looks Across the Atlantic," *The Guardian,* (Banking Supplement), June 2, 1969.

Quaife, Milo M. "The Story of Mariners Church," *Michigan History,* 29 (1945): 31–43.

Reichert, Rudolph E. "As I Remember It—The Bank Holiday," *Washtenaw Impressions,* 14 (1959): 13–16.

Scheirber, Harry N. "George Bancroft and the Bank of Michigan, 1837–1841," *Michigan History,* 44 (1960): 82–90.

Shade, William G. "The Background of the Michigan Free Banking Law," *Michigan History,* 52 (1968): 229–344.

———. "Banks and Politics in Michigan, 1835–1845." *Michigan History,* 57 (1973): 28–68.

Teller, June 1934 to April 1973.

Utley, Henry M. "The Wild Cat Banking System of Michigan," *MPHC,* 5 (1884): 209–22.

Van Horne, James. "Michigan Banking in Retrospect," *Michigan Economic Record,* 6 (1964): 3–6.

Weber, William L. "Discovery and Development of the Salt Interest in the Saginaw Valley," *MPHC,* 4 (1881): 13–23.

Woodworth, G. Walter. "The Detroit Money Market," *Michigan Business Studies,* 5 (1932): 187–406.

index

Abbott, James, 27
Acme White Lead and Color Works, 100
Adams, Alexander H., 76, 80, 86, 92, 106, 107, 108, 111, 114, 115, 116, 135
Advisory Committee on Government Organization, 206
Agriculture, 18, 19, 81, 87, 119
Albany, N.Y., 40, 45, 72, 85, 99
Alexander's, John, Dry Goods Shop, 132
Alkali industry, 97
Allied Industries, Inc., 229
Allied Supermarkets, Inc., 229
American Bankers Assoc., 199–200, 230
American Car & Foundry Co., 97
American Exchange National Bank, 92, 104–5, 154
American Exchange National Bank of New York, 120
American Fur Co., 42
American Institute of Banking, 230
American Loan and Trust Co., 155

American Motors Corp., 219
American Red Cross, 137
American State Bank of Detroit, 153, 164
American Trust Co., 155, 158
American Revolution, 23–25
Amherstburg, Canada, 26
Amoskeag Co., 66
Anderson, Col. John, 76
Anderson, Mrs. Julia, 43, 76, 77
Anderson, William K., 133, 139
Andrews' Railroad Hotel, 65
Antislavery movement, 72, 89
Argo (steamboat), 44
Arithmometer Co., 131
Askin, John, 27
Assembly-line production, 127
Assignment of Claims Act, 190
Association of Reserve City Bankers, 200, 200n
Astor, John J., 42
Atlantic (steamboat), 64
Auburn automobile, 147
Austria, 199

Automobile industry, 124–31, 143–44, 146–47, 152–53, 153n, 160, 162, 187, 190, 191–93, 202, 216, 218–19
Automobile parts and accessory companies, 95, 126, 130, 131
Automobile self-starter, 146
Automotive Council for War Production, 191

B-24 Liberator bombers, 191, 192
Bagley, John J., 99
Bagley, Paul F., 139
Bagley Land Co., 139
Bailey, George D., 217
Baker, George S., 145, 150
Baldwin, Henry P., 76, 80, 92, 101, 115
Ballantine, Arthur A., 166, 167
Ballantyne, John, 161
Baltimore, Md., 50
Bank Block, 105
Bank branch offices, 41, 51, 132–35, 158, 187, 206, 207, 214, 219–20, 228, 232–33
Bank Chambers, 111–13, 131–32, 135, 137, 149
Bank failures, 60–61, 83–84, 109, 119, 120, 163–64, 163n
Bank Holding Act, 235
Bank holiday (1933), 153, 168–73, 184
Bank Note Detector, 91
Bank of America (San Francisco), 202
Bank of Brest, 55
Bank of Detroit (1806), 31–32, 40, 41
Bank of Detroit (1916), 155, 160, 162, 180, 224
Bank of England, 53
Bank of Michigan (1817), 39–41, 46, 47, 48, 50, 51, 60–61
Bank of Michigan (1929), 158, 161
Bank of Michigan Building, 60, 68, 84, 104
Bank of St. Clair, 61
Bank of Sandstone, 54
Bank of Shiawassee, 55
Bank of the Commonwealth, 210, 233, 234
Bank of the River Raisin, 51

Bank of the United States, 49–50, 52, 53
Bank of the United States in Pennsylvania, 57–58, 60–61
Bank Public Relations and Marketing Assoc., 230
Bankers-Equitable Trust Co., 210
Bankers Trust Company of Detroit, 155, 176, 209, 210
Banking Act of 1935, 175
Barclay's Bank, Ltd. (England), 232
Barnum Wire and Iron Works, 99
Barron, John, 139n
Bates, Asher B., 74
Bates, Frederick, 29
Battle of Antietam, 88
Battle of Bull Run, 88
Battle of Fallen Timbers, 26
Battle of Gettysburg, 80
Bay City, Mich., 95
Bay of Pigs invasion, 227
Beaver hat, 14
Beebe, Silas, 58
Beilfield Tire Co., 149
Bentley, Calvin P., 229
Berry Brothers, 100
Bessemer process, 98
Bethel A.M.E. Church, 67
Biddle, Nicholas, 49
Biddle House, 65–66
Big Three auto companies, 129, 147, 219
Bird, Capt. Henry, 24–25
Birmingham, Mich., 210, 212, 219, 220, 233
Birmingham Advisory Board, 215, 221
Birmingham National Bank, 212, 213, 214, 214n, 215
Bissell, John H., 113
Black Rock, N.Y., 43
Black Swamp, 42, 42n
Blacks in Detroit, 66–67, 88–89, 233–34
Blacksmithing, 102, 130
Bloomfield Hills, Mich., 212
Bloomfield Township, Mich., 233
Blue Cloud (Sioux Indian chief), 203
Boiler manufacturing, 63, 97

Boot and shoe manufacturing, 63, 80, 100, 101, 102
Boss, Cyrus, 139n, 145
Boston, Mass., 40, 50, 70, 72, 90, 98, 120, 148
Bourgeois, 14–15
Bowman, Eustace C., 115, 132, 135
Boy Scouts of America, 230
Boydell Brothers, 100
Brass industry, 94, 95, 130
Brennan, John, 63
Breweries, 100, 102
Bridge, Henry P., 107, 108
Briggs Manufacturing Co., 131
Brink's, Inc., 202
Briscoe, Benjamin, 129
Briscoe Manufacturing Co., 126
Brock, Gen. Isaac, 33
Broderick, James, 169
Broderick Plan, 169
Brodhead, Daniel, 24
Bronson, Mich., 41
Brown, Henry D., 225
Brush automobile, 129
Buffalo, N.Y., 42, 43, 45, 46, 64, 66, 85
Buhl Block, 155
Buhl Stamping Co., 137
Buick, David D., 128
Buick automobile, 128, 129n
Buick Motors Co., 128, 129
Building and loan associations, 118, 176
Burroughs Adding Machine Co., 131
Burroughs Corp., 131
Butler, William A., 78
Butler, William B., 105
Butler, William B., and Co., 105
Butler Block, 105

Cadieux's General Store, 132
Cadillac, Antoine, 16–19
Cadillac automobile, 128, 129, 129n, 146
Cadillac Motor Car Co., 128, 134, 144
Cain, Waldo L., 234
Callian's Book and Stationery Shop, 132
Campbell, Capt. Donald, 21, 22
Campbell, James V., 76, 113

Canals, 44–45, 51, 56–58, 84–85, 95, 98
Capitol Building, Mich. (1824), 48–49, 67, 89
Carter, David S., 139
Cass, Lewis, 41–42, 44, 45, 48, 49, 61n, 67, 71, 94
Central Hanover Bank (New York), 172
Central Savings Bank, 153, 154, 157, 162, 179
Central Trust Co., 158
Center Line, Mich., 191
Chalmers automobile, 129
Chamber of Commerce Building, 147–48
Chapin, Roy D., 129–30, 166, 167
Charles Townsend (steamboat), 44
Charlevoix Rock Product Co., 180
Chase, Salmon P., 90
Chemical Bank (New York), 82
Chemicals industry, 100, 101, 131
Chevrolet automobile, 129, 147, 219
Chicago, Ill., 64, 65, 66, 85, 95, 154, 168, 195, 213
Chillicothe, Ohio, 40
Chipman, Henry, 76
Christ P.E. Church, 67, 116
Chrysler, Walter P., 129, 130
Chrysler Corp., 129, 147, 165, 175, 191, 192, 202, 227
Cincinnati, Ohio, 82, 184, 195
Cisler, Walker L., 203–4
Cities Service Co., 149
Citizens' Savings Bank, 145
City Bank (1872), 108, 110
City Bank (1949), 210–11, 233
City Hall (1835), 67–68; (1871), 120
City Industrial Bank, 158
City National Bank of Detroit, 233, 234
City Savings Bank, 118
Civil War, 87–93, 95, 96, 118
Clarenceville, Mich., 219
Clark family, 148
Clark, Fred, 125
Clark, Gen. George R., 24
Clay, Gen. Lucius, 198, 204
Clearing houses, 115–16, 115n, 119, 172

Cleland's, Henry, Drugstore, 132
Clermont (steamboat), 43
Cleveland, Grover, 119
Cleveland, Ohio, 64, 195
Clinton, DeWitt, 44, 71
Clinton Township, Mich., 220
Cobo, Albert E., 216–17
Colombo, Frank A., 221–22
Columbia automobile, 129
Commercial Milling Co., 140
Commercial National Bank, 154
Commercial State Bank of Roseville, 228
Commercial State Savings Bank, 148, 157
Commonwealth Bank, 210
Commonwealth-Commercial State Bank, 157, 168, 173, 176, 209, 210
Commonwealth Federal State Bank, 155, 157
Commonwealth Savings Bank, 155
Comstock, William A., 153, 167, 168, 170, 172, 173, 174
Conant, Shubael, 72, 75, 86
Congress Building, 156
Connolly, William, 173–74
Conscription of Industry Act, 190
Continental Bank of Detroit, 157
Cook, Levi, 72
Cooperage industry, 102
Copper and brass industry, 94, 95–96, 130
Copper mining, 61, 94, 95–96
Cord automobile, 147
Corktown, 229
Coughlin, Charles E., 164
Coureurs de bois, 14–15
Couzens, Frank, 210
Couzens, James S., 127, 165–66, 170, 210
Coxey, Jacob S., 119n
Coxey's Army, 119, 119n
Craighead, Rodkey, 231, 236
Crane & Company's Oriental Circus, 68
Credit unions, 176
Crimean War, 81, 85
Currency: beaver pelts, 22; deer skins, 22; furs, 22; card money, 27; earliest in Detroit, 27; wampum, 27; shinplasters, 37–38; cut money, 38–39
Cushman and Wakefield, Inc., 223
Cut money, 38–39
Czechoslovakia, 199

Daume, Selden B., 213, 214, 220, 222
David Whitney Building, 207
Davis, George S., 100–101
Davis, William, 97
Day, Augustus, 98
Dean, Charles A., 137, 148
Dearborn, Mich., 161
Dearborn State Bank, 175
Dearborn Township, Mich., 219
Dee, Edward J., 133, 134
Defense bonds, 193–94
Delamater, DeWitt C., 133, 136–37, 139, 140, 144–45, 149
Delamater Hardware Co., 137
Depression (1920–21), 145–46; (1930s), 152–53, 159, 163–67, 176, 189
Detrex Chemical Industries, Inc., 231
Detroit: founding, 13, 16–18; French influence, 18–20; fur trade, 18, 21–23, 27, 31, 32, 33, 34; ribbon farms, 19; British settlement, 21, 26; population, 21 (1760), 30 (1805), 42 (1814), 46 (1819), 46 (1830), 46 (1836), 46 (1840), 63 (1849), 46 (1850), 46, 102 (1860), 102 (1870), 102 (1880), 135 (1900), 135 (1910), 135 (1920), 219 (1950), 219 (1960); American occupation, 26–27; banking community, 27–28, 46–48, 61–62, 69, 83–84, 91–92, 104–5, 115, 118, 153–59, 176, 189, 209–11, 233–34; trading supplies, 27; fire, 29–30 (1805), 65–66 (1848); incorporated, 29; first bank, 31–32; surrender to British (1812), 33; cost of living, 35 (1814), 135–36 (1882); sound currency (1820s), 39–40; and steamboat, 43–46; and Erie Canal, 44–46; sale of public lands (1820), 44; territorial capital at, 48–49; price of

goods (1840s), 58; panic of 1857, 83 / 1873, 109–10 / 1893, 120; manufacturing during Civil War, 99–100; industrial production and manufacturing (1880), 102; first automobile, 124–25; as motor capital, 130–31; growth of area (1880–1900), 131; bank branches, 133, 133n (1903), 135 (1920), 133n (1929); first bank branch office, 133; bank holiday (1933), 153, 168–73, 184; scrip issue (1933), 176; "Arsenal of Democracy," 190; price controls and rationing, W.W. II, 194; recession of, 1957–58, 215–16, 218; Dodge Report, 216–18

Detroit & Cleveland Navigation Co., 123, 139, 145, 203

Detroit and Hamtramck Iron Co., 107, 110

Detroit & Milwaukee R.R., 74, 92, 107, 108, 113, 114, 116

Detroit & Pontiac R.R., 64–65, 74

Detroit & St. Joseph R.R., 65

Detroit and Security Trust Co., 158

Detroit Antislavery Society, 72

Detroit Athletic Club, 213

Detroit Automobile Co., 126, 128

Detroit Bank: 184–85, 187, 193–94, 195–97, 202–4, 205, 206–8, 209, 211–15, 211n, 214n, 231; name changed from Detroit Savings Bank, 184–85; main office modernization, 186, 206–7; staff, 186n (1934–37), 207 (1941–55); capital stock increases, 188, 197, 207; resources, 188 (1938–39), 197 (1940–45), 203 (1945–49), 207 (1945–55), 211 (1955), 213 (1956); and sale of savings bonds, 193–94; loans for producing war materials, 194; buys Times Square Building, 196; Detroit Savings Bank Building Co. dissolved, 196; 100th anniversary celebration, 203; expansion after W.W. II, 206–7; merger with Detroit Wabeek Bank and Trust Co., 211–15

Detroit Bank and Trust Co.: 211–15, 214n, 220–21, 227–28, 231, 232–33, 234–36; and Renaissance Center, 140n; formation of, 211–15; branches, 214, 219–20, 228, 232, 233; capital stock increases, 214, 228, 235; objectives, 215; resources, 215 (1956), 216 (1956–58), 227 (1958), 227 (1967), 231 (1969), over two billion dollars, 227; expansion program (1961), 220; Fort-Washington office, 222–27; services (1960s), 222; ruins of Fort Lernoult uncovered, 225–26; acquires Commercial State Bank of Roseville, 228; staff, 228; annual meeting date change, 229; builds garage with 333 W. Fort Corp., 229; new Purchasing Office Building, 229; international banking, 232–33; DETROITBANK Corp., 234–36

Detroit Bank and Trust Company Building, 222–27, 230

Detroit Bank and Trust International, 232–33

Detroit Bankers Co., 159, 161–62, 163, 173–74, 174n, 181

Detroit Bar Assoc., 188

Detroit Barrel Company, 140

Detroit Board of Commerce, 131, 143, 197, 203, 222

Detroit Board of Education, Committee on Library, 116

Detroit Board of Trade, 72, 99

Detroit Bridge & Iron Works, 99

Detroit Car & Manufacturing Co., 97

Detroit Car Works, 107, 110

Detroit Central Business District Assoc., 222

Detroit City Bank (1837), 59–60

Detroit City Bank (1872), 110

Detroit City Poor Commission, 120

Detroit City Railroad Co., 107, 108, 112, 116

Detroit Clearing House Assoc., 115–16, 119, 164, 166, 167, 169, 170, 177, 200, 230

Detroit Club, 167

Detroit College of Law, 145

Detroit Convention Bureau, 222

Detroit Creamery Co., 140, 149, 151
Detroit Edison Co., 125, 202, 204
Detroit Fire and Marine Insurance Co., 151
Detroit Free Press, 85, 114, 122, 139, 140, 150, 167
Detroit Harvester Co., 197, 202
Detroit Historical Museum, 225
Detroit Light Guard, 88
Detroit Mortgage & Realty Co., 229
Detroit National Bank, 115, 154
Detroit Opera House Building, 147, 148
Detroit Public Library, 49, 116, 137
Detroit Range Boiler Co., 139
Detroit Renaissance, 221
Detroit River, 97
Detroit River Savings Bank, 118
Detroit Safe Co., 99
Detroit Savings Bank: 108–9, 114–15, 116, 131, 136, 140, 142, 144–46, 150, 153, 158, 164, 166, 168, 169, 174n, 176–78, 180–82, 183, 205, 209; reorganized from Detroit Savings Fund Institute, 105–6; by-laws adopted (1871), 107; first directors, 107; hours, 107; resources, 107, 109 (1872), 110 (1876), 117 (1882–1888), 120 (1892–1893), 121 (1894–1898), 122 (1901), 137 (1904), 139 (1906), 140 (1913), 144 (1914–1919), 145–46, 149 (1920–1922), 158 (1928), 149, 151 (1929), 176 (1932–1933), 182 (1934), 184 (1935); and Panic of 1873, 110 / 1893, 120–21; staff, 110, 115, 135, 136, 138, 143, 182; move into Bank Chambers (1878), 111–13; annual stockholder meetings, 114; Miller study, 116–17; first commercial accounts, 117n; attendance of directors, 121; capital stock increases, 121, 140, 147, 181; commended by state banking commissioner (1901), 122; branches, 132–35, 148n, 158; move into Penobscot Building (1906), 137–38; safe deposit boxes, 138, 148, 149, 149n, 182; women employees, 138, 143; deposits reach ten million dollar level, 139, 139n; and Federal Reserve, 141–42; Liberty Bonds, W.W. I, 142–43; depository for U.S. Postal Savings deposits, 143, 182; as depository for public monies, 143, 182; manpower shortages, W.W. I, 143; growth during W.W. I, 144; and Depression of 1920–21, 145–46; move into Detroit Savings Bank Building (1921), 147–48; Safe Deposit Company, 149, 149n; depositors, 151, 177; and bank holiday, 170–71, 173, 176; and Reconstruction Finance Corp., 181; mortgages under National House Act (1935), 183; name changed to Detroit Bank, 184–85
Detroit Savings Bank Building (1921), 147–48, 206–7, 222, 226n
Detroit Savings Bank Building Co., 148n, 196
Detroit Savings Fund Institute: 77, 83, 88, 92, 101, 104, 107, 108, 236; incorporated, 69, 73; purpose, 69–70; first directors, 72; charter, 73; resources, 74, 79, 81, 84, 87, 92, 105; by-laws 75 (1849), 85–86 (1857); first officers, 75; hours (1849), 75, 78 / (1857), 86; and Mariners' Church, 75–78; regulations (1849), 75; expenses (1849–51), 78–79, 80; opens for business, 78; depositors, 79, 92; new office (1851), 79; first full-time cashier, 80; move into Michigan State Bank Building (1855), 80, 81; and Panic of 1857, 84; move into Lewis Building (1860), 86–87; staff, 86, 92; investments during Civil War, 92; reorganized as Detroit Savings Bank, 106–7
Detroit Savings Safe Deposit Co., 149
Detroit Shipbuilding Co., 122
Detroit State Bank (proposed), 185
Detroit Stock Exchange, 169
Detroit Stove Works, 99
Detroit Symphony Orchestra, 221
Detroit Trust Company, 137, 145, 149,

150, 151, 153, 158, 161, 173, 176, 197, 203, 209, 210, 211–12, 211n, 223
Detroit Trust Company Building, 214, 223, 225, 226
Detroit United Railways, 134
Detroit Wabeek Bank and Trust Co., 212–15, 214n
Detroit White Lead Works, 100
DETROITBANK Corp., 234–36
Dey, A. H., 92
Dime Savings Bank, 150, 153, 158
Dix-Vernor Branch Office, 134
Dodge, Horace and John, 126, 127, 130
Dodge, Joseph M.: 179–82, 183, 184, 187–88, 197, 198–202, 204, 205, 206, 211, 213, 214, 220–21, 222, 226–27, 229; President, Detroit Savings Bank, 177–78, 181; birth and early career, 179–81; banking philosophy, 181; recommends change of bank's name, 184–85; heads War Contracts Adjustment Board, 195–96; rebuilding Germany's economy, 198–99; rebuilding Japan's economy, 198, 200–2; awarded Medal of Merit, 199; heads U.S. Delegation, Four-Power Commission, 199; awarded Decoration for Exceptional Civilian Service, 201–2; director of Bureau of the Budget, 204, 205, 206; Chairman of the Board, Detroit Bank, 204, 205, 206; heads advisory committee on taxation and finances for City of Detroit, 216–18; death, 226–27; awarded Grand Cordon of the First Class Order of the Rising Sun, 227
Dodge automobile, 130
Dodge Brothers Co., 130, 146
Dodge Report, 216–18
Doherty, James H., 150, 188
Doolittle, James, 191
Douglas and Bowen, 113
Doyle, Edward H., 180n
Doyle, T. C., Agency, 180
Doyle, Thomas C., 180, 180n
Drake, Milton J., 214, 221, 229

Dresden, Germany, 199
Drug and pharmaceutical industry, 100, 102, 131
Dudgeon, Lewis and Graves, 75
Due bills, 28, 37–38, 39
Duffield, Dr. Samuel, 100–1
Dufrene's, George W., Grocery, 132
Dumfriesshire, Scotland, 70
Duncan, Henry, 70
Dunham, Walter L., 150, 166, 171, 177
Durant, William C., 128–29
Dwight, Henry, 40–41
Dwyer, Jeremiah, 99
Dwyer, John M., 139, 150, 177
Dwyer & Vhay, 139

Eagle boats, 144
Eaman, Frank D., 221
East Saginaw Salt Co., 96
Eaton, Theodore, 101
Eaton Manufacturing Co., 197
Edison Illuminating Co., 125
Eisenhower, Dwight D., 204, 205, 206, 227
Electric automobile, 130, 146
Enterprise (steamboat), 44
Equitable and Central Trust Co., 158–59
Equitable Trust Co., 158–59, 176, 209, 210
Erie Canal, 44–45, 56
Essex automobile, 147
Eureka Iron and Steel Works, 98, 107, 114, 116
Everett-Metzger-Flanders Co., 134
Ex-Cell-O Corp., 230–31
Exchange Bank of Shiawassee, 54

Fairview Village, 135
Farmers and Mechanics' Bank of Michigan, 47, 50, 51, 60, 61, 62, 69, 74n, 83–84
Farmers Loan and Trust Co. (New York), 120
Farmington Township, Mich., 220
Farnsworth, Caroline, 78
Farnsworth, Elon: 73–74, 75, 76, 77, 78, 80, 105, 236; birth and early career, 71; candidate for governor,

71; chancellor of Michigan, 71, 72; regent, University of Michigan, 71; state attorney general, 71; director, Michigan Central Railroad, 72; and rail connections to Detroit, 85; and Soo Canal, 85; and Civil War bounty committee, 88; and Detroit Savings Fund Inst., 75, 84, 105; president, Detroit Savings Bank, 107; death, 110–11
Farnsworth, Hannah Blake, 110
Farrand, Jacob, 100
Farrand, Williams and Co., 100
Farwell Building, 156
Federal Building (1860), 87, 88 / (1897), 225, 225n / (1934), 225n
Federal Deposit Insurance Act (1950), 175
Federal Deposit Insurance Corp., 175–76, 187
Federal Housing Authority, 183, 187
Federal Reserve Act, 141, 156, 232
Federal Reserve Bank of Chicago, 142, 156, 182, 184
Federal Reserve Bank of Chicago, Detroit Branch, 156, 156n, 197
Federal Reserve Bank of Minneapolis, 156n
Federal Reserve banks, 141, 156, 164, 175
Federal Reserve Board, 141, 169, 184, 200, 228, 235
Federal Reserve notes, 141
Federal Reserve System, 141, 156, 168, 172, 173, 198
Federal Reserve System, Ninth District (Minneapolis), 170
Federal Reserve System, Seventh District (Chicago), 167, 193
Federal State Bank, 153, 155
Felch, Adelphus, 72, 110
Ferguson, Thomas, 108, 111, 113, 114, 115, 121
Ferndale, Mich., 210, 212
Ferndale Advisory Board, 215, 221
Ferndale National Bank, 212, 213, 214, 214n, 215, 231
Ferry, D. M., & Co., 102
Ferry, Dexter M., 101–2
Ferry, Morse Seed Co., 102, 203
Fidelity Bank and Trust Co., 163
Fidelity Trust Co., 157
First and Old Detroit National Bank (1914), 154
First Baptist Church, 66
First Independence National Bank, 233–34
First Michigan Infantry, 88
First National Bank Building, 154
First National Bank—Detroit (1922), 150, 154, 158, 161, 162, 164, 165, 168, 170, 171, 172, 173, 174, 175n, 180–81
First National Bank of Chicago, 193
First National Bank of Detroit (1863), 91–92, 104, 115, 154
First Presbyterian Church, 66, 67
First State Bank of Detroit, 155, 157
Fish, Job, 43
Fisher Body Corp., 134
Fisher Brothers, 126
Fisher Building, 134, 210
Fitzgerald, Frank D., 183
Five-dollars-a-day, 127–28
Five million dollar loan, 57–58, 60–61, 103
Flanagan, William, 31
Flanders automobile, 129
Fleming, Wilson, 177
Flint, Mich., 49, 129, 191
Ford, Edsel, 165, 170, 171, 175
Ford, Henry, 125, 126–28, 128–29, 143, 150, 165, 166, 170, 171, 175
Ford, Walter B., II, 230
Ford and Earl Design Associates, Inc., 230
Ford automobile, 129n
Ford Motor Co., 126–28, 130, 134, 144, 147, 150, 165, 166, 191, 192, 219
Fort de Buade, 14, 16
Fort Detroit, 21, 25
Fort Lernoult, 24–25, 225–26
Fort Malden, 26, 33, 34
Fort Pontchartrain, 17–18, 21
Fort St. Joseph (Port Huron), 14, 23
Fort Shelby, 25
Fort Wayne (Detroit), 88, 89
Foundries, 63, 97, 130

Foundry and machine shop products, 97, 102, 130
Franklin automobile, 147
Franklin Village, Mich., 219
Fraser, Alexander D., 76
Freeman—Delamater & Co., 136
French and Indian War, 20
Frontenac, Count, 15–16
Freuhauf Corp., 202, 229
Fur trade, American, 27, 31, 32, 33, 34, 35–36, 42; British, 21–23, 27; French, 13–16, 27
Fur trade canoes, 15
Fur trading posts, 21, 27
Furniture industry, 95, 100
Fyfe, Richard, 101

Gale Manufacturing Co., 139
Gardner, Herbert H., 213, 214, 220, 221
Gardner, Miles T., 102
Gasoline powered automobile, 130, 146
General Banking Law Amendment of 1871, 105–6, 106n, 108, 118
General Banking Law of 1837, 52–53, 56, 58–59, 103, 104; 1857, 104, 105–6; 1888, 118, 159; 1929, 159
General Motors Building, 134
General Motors Co., 128–29
General Motors Corp., 128, 130, 147, 165, 174–75, 191, 192, 194, 202, 219
Geneva, N.Y., 40
German American Bank, 108, 153, 155
Germany, 198–99, 204, 227
Giblin, Edward J., 230–31
Gladwin, Maj. Henry, 23
Gladwin Farm and Cattle Co., 149
Glass manufacture, 97
Goodrich, Mich., 55
Grace, William E., 229
Grace Hospital, 222
Graham-Paige Plant, 191
Grand Rapids, Mich., 56
Grand River—Joy Road Branch Office, 149n
Grand River—Warren Branch Office, 134

Grand Trunk Western R.R., 65
Gratiot—St. Antoine Branch Office, 133–34
Gray, John S., 126
Gray Marine Motors Co., 194
Great Lakes Steel Corp., 231
Great Western R.R., 85
Green, Leslie H., 222
Greenbacks, 90
Greenfield—Ten Mile Branch Office, 220
Greiner's, Michael, General Store, 132
Gresham's Law, 90
Griffin, John, 29
Griswold, George R., 73
Griswold, Stanley, 29
Griswold Building, 207
Griswold—First State Bank, 157, 158, 162
Griswold National Bank, 157
Groesbeck, Alex J., 173–74
Grosse Ile, Mich., 17
Grosse Pointe, Mich., 126
Grosse Pointe Bank, 139–40
Group banking, 159–63, 173–74
Guaranty State Bank, 157
Guaranty Trust Building, 157
Guaranty Trust Company of Detroit, 155, 157, 163
Guardian Bank of Dearborn, 175
Guardian Building, 157
Guardian Detroit Bank, 157, 160, 162
Guardian Detroit Co., 160
Guardian Detroit Group, Inc., 160–61
Guardian Detroit Trust Co., 160
Guardian Detroit Union Group, Inc., 159–61, 162, 163, 165, 166, 167, 173–74, 224
Guardian National Bank of Commerce, 166, 168, 170, 173, 174, 175n, 181
Guardian Trust Co., 157
Guardian Union National Bank of Commerce, 165

Haass, Julius H., 161
Habitants, 15, 19–20
Hall, William B., 220, 221, 230, 234

Hamburg, Germany, 70
Hamilton, Henry, 23–24
Hammond, George H., 98
Hammond Building, 155
Hammond-Standish Co., 98
Hamtramck, Mich., 85, 130
Harley, Ellington and Day, 223, 224
Harley, Ellington, Cowin and Stirton, 224, 227
Harley Ellington–Pierce Yee and Assoc., 224
Harmon, Claude M., 204
Harper, David, 234
Harper Hospital, 188
Hargreaves Manufacturing Co., 107
Harrison, William H., 33
Hastings, Eurotas P., 41
Hayes, Frederick W., 115
Hendrie, George, 108, 113, 114, 139
Hendrie, Strathearn, 139
Hendrie and Co., 108
Henkel, Robert, 139, 140, 140n
Henry Clay (steamboat), 44
Henry Ford Automobile Co., 126
Hewitt, Charles H., 195, 204, 205–6, 214, 221, 229–30
Hiawatha Tobacco, 99
Hicks, James A., 72, 76, 77, 80
Highland Park, Mich., 127, 161, 163
Highland Park Ford Plant, 127–28, 144
Highland Park State Bank, 150, 155, 175
Highland Park State Bank of Detroit, 155, 180
Hillsdale College, 188
Hodge's Notions, 132
Holding companies, 159–63, 173–74, 234–36
Hollis, R. T., & Co., 179
Home Savings Bank, 133, 154
Homestead Act (1862), 87
Honigman, Jason L., 229
Honigman, Miller, Schwartz and Cohn, 229
Hoop skirt manufacturing, 102
Hoover, Herbert, 165, 169
Houghton, Douglass, 94, 96
Howard, Charles, 74n
Hubbard, Frank W., 197

Huddleston, Clarence J., 214
Hudson, J. L., Co., 202, 206, 221
Hudson, Joseph L., 130
Hudson automobile, 219
Hudson Motor Car Co., 129–30, 147, 191, 192, 203, 219
Hudson Motor Car Co., naval gun arsenal, 191
Huetteman, John, Sr., 228
Huetteman, John, Jr., 228
Hull, William, 29, 31, 32, 33
Huntington, Samuel, 29
Hupp automobile, 129
Hurons (Indian tribe), 18
Hydraulic Iron Works, 99
Illinois Central R.R., 81–82
Imperial-Detroit Steel Corp., 231
Indians, 14–16, 17, 18, 21–24, 26, 28, 33, 34, 42, 44, 68, 203; see also names of tribes
Industrial banks, 153, 155–56, 157–58, 176, 187, 209
Industrial Morris Plan Bank of Detroit, 150, 155–56, 168, 173, 176, 209, 210
Industrial National Bank, 210, 211
Insurance company banks, 47, 51
Internal improvements, 51, 56–58, 60–61, 80, 103
International Bank for Reconstruction and Development, 206
International banking, 232–33
International Monetary Fund, 206
Ionia, Mich., 49
Iron Brigade, 88
Iron mining, 61, 94–95, 96
Iron and steel industry, 95, 98, 102, 130
Iroquois (Indian tribe), 14, 17
Istanbul, Turkey, 206

Jackson, Andrew, 49–50, 52, 53, 103
Jackson, Mich., 161, 179
Jackson County Bank, 54
Japan, 198, 200–2, 227
Jay, John, 26
Jeep, 193, 219
Jefferson—Hilger Branch Office, 135
Jerome, George, 108, 114

Johnson, H. R., 67
Johnson, Sir William, 21–22
Johnson's Hotel, 65, 67
Jones, Jessie H., 174n
Joy, Henry B., 129
Joy, James F., 85
Judge's Cigar Store, 132
Judson, George B., 210

Kahn, Albert, 127, 129, 133, 134, 148, 214
Kaiser-Frazer Corp., 219
Kalamazoo, Mich., 41, 49, 65
Kanady & Taylor, 108
Kanter, Edward, 108
Kanzler, Ernest, 166
Kast, Edward, 134
Keller, K. T., 129
Kelsey-Hayes Corp., 131
Kelsey Wheel Co., 131
Kennedy, John F., 227
Kercheval, Benjamin B., 72, 74n, 80
Kettering, Charles F., 146
Keyes, Paul C., 173n
King, Charles B., 124–25, 130
King, James W., 59
King, R. W., and Co., 64
Knickerbocker Trust Co. (New York), 141
Knudsen, William S., 191
Krit automobile, 130

Labor unions, 83
Laing and Fleming's Drug Store, 132
Lake Point Village, Mich., 219
Lake St. Clair, 49, 126
Lansing, Mich., 125, 170, 173
Larned-Carter Co., 139
Lauer, John, 124
Lawton, Frederick J., 204
Ledyard, Henry, 86
Leipzig, Germany, 199
Leland, Henry M., 126, 128, 144
Leland, Wilfred, 144
Leland & Faulconer Manufacturing Co., 126, 128
Lenawee County Bank, 54
Lend-Lease Act, 190
Leonard Thrift Bank, 173, 176

Lernoult, Capt. Richard B., 24–25
Leyburn, Alfred P., 167
Lewis, Alexander, 107
Lewis, Gleason, 77, 77n
Lewis, Samuel, 75, 86, 107, 112, 114
Liberty aircraft engines, 144
Liberty automobile, 130
Liberty Loan Committees, 142–43
Liberty Loans, World War I, 142–43
Lincoln, Abraham, 88
Lincoln Motor Co., 144
Lloyd, Gordon W., 112n
Lloyd and Pearce, 112
Logging engine manufacturing, 94
London, England, 115n, 199, 232–33
London Branch Office, 232–33
London Clearing House, 115n
Longley, Clifford, 166
Lord, Robert O., 166
Louis XIV, 16
Lumbering, 61, 82, 95, 96, 97, 130
Lyon, Edward, 80, 86, 107, 111, 114
Lyster, William, 86

MacArthur, Gen. Douglas, 200, 201
McCloskey, James, 39–40
McCord Manufacturing Co., 131
McCord Radiator Co., 150
McGraw Building, 154
McGregor Fund, 221
Machine shops, 102
McKee, John K., 167
McMillan, James, (1838–1902), 111, 114, 122, 145
McMillan, James, (1911–   ), 203, 211n
McMillan, James T., (1885–1946), 145, 203
McMillan, Philip H., 122–23, 133, 148
Macomb, William, 27
Macomb County Advisory Board, 228
Malcomson, Alexander Y., 126
Maltz, George L., 122
Mandich, Donald R., 233
Manning, Randolph, 72
Manufacturers National Bank (proposed), 170
Manufacturers National Bank of Detroit, 174–75, 176, 209, 211, 234

Manufacturing, 63–64, 64n, 81, 87, 94, 97–103, 109, 130–31, 138–39, 152–53; see also specific industries
Marine equipment industry, 131
Marine gasoline engine industry, 130
Mariners' P. E. Church, 43, 66, 75–78, 80, 87, 203
Marschner, Adolph F., 173–74
Marshall, Geroge C., 199
Martin, Roblee B., 221
Mason, John T., 49
Mason and Rice, 113
Maxwell, Jonathan, 129
Maxwell automobile, 129
May, John, 27
Mayflower (steamboat), 64
Mayflower Tobacco, 99
Meat packing industry, 98, 102
Mechanics' Bank, 105
Merchants and Manufacturers Bank, 105
Merchants' and Manufacturers' Exchange, 137
Merchants and Manufacturers' National Bank, 115
Merchants' and Mechanics' Bank of Michigan, 46–47
Merchants Bank of Detroit, 176, 209, 234
Merchant's National Bank, 154–55, 158
Merrell & Ferguson, 108, 113
Metropolitan Industrial Bank, 158
Metropolitan State Bank, 155
Metropolitan Trust Co., 163
Metzger automobile, 129
Mexican War, 81
Miamis (Indian tribe), 18
Michigan, bank failures (1929–32), 163n
Michigan, banking community (1837), 51, 61; (1871–1888), 118; (1910–20), 156; (1930), 189; (1940), 189
Michigan, banking holiday (1933), 153, 168–73, 184
Michigan, banking laws, 52–53, 58–59, 103–4, 105–6, 106n, 108, 109, 114, 118, 121, 155–56, 159, 173, 186–87, 194–95, 235
Michigan, constitution of 1850, 103
Michigan, manufacturing stimulated by Civil War, 99
Michigan, Governor Comstock's proclamation, 153, 167, 174
Michigan, Panic of 1857, 82–83
Michigan, population, 42, 219
Michigan, public land sales, 44, 49
Michigan, state banking dept., 118, 163, 167, 179–80, 182, 184, 195, 205, 213, 228
Michigan, state banking commissioner, 52, 54–55, 58, 104, 118, 167, 171, 173, 174, 180n, 205
Michigan (steamboat), 44
Michigan Bank, 211, 233, 234
Michigan Bankers Assoc., 118, 150, 167, 177, 200, 230
Michigan Car Co., 97, 99, 111
Michigan Central R.R., 56, 57, 64, 65, 74, 80, 84, 85, 105, 121
Michigan Clearing House Assoc., 171
Michigan Copper and Brass Co., 139
Michigan Exchange, 65, 80
Michigan Financial Institutions Act (1937), 186–87
Michigan Industrial Bank, 157–58, 160, 209–10, 211
Michigan Insurance Company Bank, 47, 61, 62, 69, 74, 84, 92
Michigan Iron Foundry, 63
Michigan National Bank, 233
Michigan National Guard, 88
Michigan Northern R.R., 56, 57
Michigan-Peninsular Car Co., 121
Michigan Savings Bank, 154
Michigan Securities Commission, 179
Michigan Southern R.R., 56, 57
Michigan State Bank, 47, 51, 60, 61, 69, 80, 81, 83, 86
Michigan State Bank Building, 80, 81
Michigan State Bank of Detroit, 155, 163
Michigan State Chamber of Commerce, 230

Michigan State Fair, 69
Michigan State Fair Grounds, 69, 88
Michigan Stove Co., 99
Michilimackinac, 16
Miller, Canfield, Paddock and Stone, 137, 188, 197
Miller, Charles, 165
Miller, George, 99
Miller, Sidney D., 105, 106, 111–13, 114, 116, 118n, 120, 121, 122, 123, 131, 133, 136, 188
Miller, Sidney T., 137, 148, 149, 188–89, 196–97
Miller, Sidney T., Jr., 149, 170–71, 185–86
Milwaukee, Wis., 64
Mining, 94–95, 96–97, 130
Miriani, Louis C., 217–18
Model A Ford, 147
Model T Ford, 127, 129, 147
Monroe, Senator, 118n
Monroe, James, 43
Monroe, Mich., 49, 56
Montgomery Ward department store, 202
Montreal, Canada, 15, 20, 26
Moran, Charles, 72, 75
Morgan, J. P., and Co., 141
Morris Canal and Banking Co., 57–58, 60–61
Morse, Dr. Jedediah, 42–43
Mt. Clemens, Mich., 56, 135
Muir, William K., 114, 133
Murray Manufacturing Co., 131
Muskegon, Mich., 95
Mutual Life Insurance Company of New York, 108, 113
Mutual savings banks, 176, 184

Nankin Township, Mich., 219
Nash automobile, 219
Nash-Kelvinator Corp., 194
Nash Motor Car Co., 192, 219
National Bank of Commerce of Detroit, 154, 158, 162
National Bank of Detroit, 174–75, 176, 177, 181, 193, 209, 211, 234
National Banking Act (1863), 83, 90–91, 92

National banking system, 90–92, 109, 141
National banks, 91–92, 118, 141, 142, 154–55, 156, 170, 174, 176, 189, 209, 233–34
National Citizens Bank (New York), 120
National Cordage Co., 119
National Hotel, 65
National Housing Act, 183, 187
National Insurance Bank, 92
National Monetary Commission, 141
National Security Council, 204, 206
National Steel Corp., 231
New Buffalo, Mich., 56
New Center area, 134
New Detroit, Inc., 221, 230
New Orleans, La., 16
New York, N.Y., 45, 46, 50, 53, 72, 82, 85, 90, 115, 119, 120, 141, 154, 168, 213, 223
New York and Harlem R.R., 81
New York Central Park Authority, 107
New York Central Park Co., 92
New York Central R.R., 85
New York Clearing House, 115, 115n
New York, New Haven and Hartford R.R., 81
New York Stock Exchange, 109, 141, 145, 151
Newberry, John, 111
Newberry, Oliver, 44, 55
Newberry, Truman H., 129
Newberry and McMillan, 111
Newberry and McMillan Building, 116
Niagara (steamboat), 44
Niagara River, 85
Niles, Mich., 14
Northland Branch Office, 207
Northland Center, 207
Northwest Ordinance, 25
Northwestern State Bank, 163
Norwalk, Ohio, 126

Oakland & Ottawa R.R., 74
Oakland automobile, 129
Oakland County Advisory Board, 231

Ocean (steamboat), 64
Office of Production Management, 191
Ohio Life Insurance and Trust Co., 82
Old Detroit National Bank, 154, 155
Oldfield, Barney, 126
Olds, Ransom E., 125–26, 129
Olds Motor Works, 125–26, 130
Oldsmobile automobile, 125–26, 129, 129n
Orchard Lake, Mich., 220
Ottawas (Indian tribe), 18, 23

P and O Building, 232
Pace, Frank, Jr., 201
Packard automobile, 129, 147
Packard Motor Car Co., 122, 129, 139, 144, 145, 192, 194, 203, 219
Paige automobile, 129
Paige-Detroit automobile, 147
Paige Motor Car Co., 140, 151
Paint and varnish industry, 100, 102, 130
Palmer, John, 72, 86, 106
Palmer, Mason, 76
Panic of 1837, 44, 56–61, 71; 1857, 81–84, 105, 114; 1873, 109–10, 111, 114; 1893, 119–21; 1907, 140–41
Paper money, 28, 32, 36–38, 50, 53, 54–55, 58, 90–91, 103
Parke, Harvey C., 100–1
Parke, Davis & Co., 100–1, 140, 197, 203
Parker, Arthur M., 139
Parker, Willard, 107
Parsons, Philo, 91–92
Paton, Kenneth, 139n
Patterson, B. K., 167
Patterson, Robert, 196n
Paulson, Sydney E., 232–33
Peacock (steamboat), 44
Pearce, John, 112n
Peninsular Bank, 69, 74n, 83, 84, 104
Peninsular Car Works, 97
Peninsular Savings Bank, 139
Peninsular State Bank, 153, 158, 161
Peninsular Stove Co., 99, 149
Penobscot Building, 137–38, 137n, 147, 148, 149, 211

People's National Bank (proposed), 170
People's Savings Bank, 108, 109
People's State Bank, 153, 158
People's Wayne County Bank, 158, 161, 164
People's Wayne County Bank of Dearborn, 175
People's Wayne County Bank of Highland Park, 175
Perring, Raymond T., 195, 204–5, 212–13, 214, 221, 222, 228, 234, 236
Pet banks, 50
Peters, Vincent J., 223
Petz, Joseph A., 133
Philadelphia, Pa., 50, 70, 90
Philadelphia & Reading R.R., 119
Philadelphia Savings Fund Society, 70
Pierson, H. Lynn, 197
Pilling, Arnold, 225–26
Pingree, Hazen S., 101, 120
Ping's Potato Patches, 120
Piper, William F., 232
Pitcher, J. W., 92
Pitcher, Dr. Zina, 72, 75, 107, 108
Pittsburgh, Pa., 95
Plymouth Township, Mich., 220
Police Athletic League, 230
Pontchartrain, Count, 17
Pontchartrain Hotel (1907), 154
Pontiac (Ottawa Indian chief), 23, 28
Pontiac, Mich., 129
Pontiac automobile, 129
Pontiac's War, 23
Port Huron, Mich., 14, 56, 161
Porter, George B., 49
Porter, Capt. Moses, 26, 225
Post Office, 1849, 77, 77n; 1860, 77, 87, 88
Potawatomis (Indian tribe), 18
Pratt and Whitney aircraft engines, 192
Procter, Gen. Henry, 33
Procter and Gamble Co., 184–85
Provident Institution for Savings (Boston), 70
Provident Loan and Savings Society of Detroit, 197

PT boats, 192
Public Bank, 233
Public Relations Society of America, 230
Pullman, George, 97
Pullman sleeping car, 97
Purchasing Office Building, 229

Quebec, Canada, 15, 20

Race riot (1863), 88–89
Rackham, Horace H., 126
Railroad company banks, 51
Railroad equipment industry, 97–98, 102, 131
Railroads, 51, 56–58, 64–65, 74, 81–82, 85, 97–98, 109, 202
Rambler automobile, 219
Ransom, Epaphroditus, 69
Recession of 1957–58, 215–16, 218
Reconstruction Finance Corp., 163, 165–66, 167, 170, 172, 174–75, 175n, 181, 184, 186, 197, 205
Redford Township, Mich., 220
Redstone, Louis, 229
Refrigerator railroad car, 98
Regal Motor Car Corp., 134
Remick, J. H., Co., 140
Remick, Jerome H., 139, 140
Renaissance Center, 140n
Ribbon farms, 19
Rich, George M., 72, 106
Richard, Gabriel, 37–38, 48
Rickenbacker automobile, 130
Ridgeway, Gen. Matthew, 201
Robert Morris Associates, 205, 230
Robin Hood Flour Mill Co., 140n
Rock salt, 97
Roehm, Charles H., 188
Roelofs, Robert F., 231
Rolls-Royce aircraft engines, 192
Roosevelt, Franklin D., 172, 189, 190
Roseville, Mich., 228
Rouge Ford Plant, 144, 193
Rowe and Co., 64
Royal Oak Township, Mich., 220
Rueff, Jacques, 199

Russel, Dr. George B., 97
Russia, 199
Ruthwell Parish, 70

Saddlery and harness manufacturing, 102
Safe and vault manufacturing, 102
Safe Deposit Co., 109
Safety deposit boxes, 109, 138, 149, 149n
Safety fund system, 52–53
Safford, Charles H., 92
Saginaw, Mich., 61, 95, 96
Saginaw River, 85
Ste. Anne's R. C. Church, 18, 18n, 37–38, 66
St. Clair River, 97
St. Ignace, Mich., 14, 16
St. Joseph, Mich., 14, 47
St. Louis, Mo., 16, 131
St. Mary's Falls Ship Canal Co., 84–85
St. Mary's River Canal, 56, 57, 84–85, 95, 98
St. Paul's P. E. Church, 66
SS. Peter and Paul R. C. Church, 66
Salt mining and production, 96–97, 131
Sam Minskoff and Sons, 223–24, 225
Sault Ste. Marie, Mich., 14; see also Soo Canal
Savings and loan assoc., 118, 176
Savings banks, 70, 105–6, 176, 184
Savings bonds, 193–94
Sawmills, 63, 85, 95, 97
Saxon automobile, 130
Schram, B. C., 173n
Scotch Store, 64
Scotten, Daniel and Oren, 99
Scott's, John, General Store, 132
Sears, Roebuck and Co. department store, 202
Second Baptist Church, 66–67
Second National Bank, 92, 104, 154
Second United States Bank, Cincinnati Branch, 80
Security Trust Co., 153, 158
Seed industry, 101–2
Senate Committee on Banking and Currency, 165

Seymour Finney's Temperance House, 89
Shelby Township, Mich., 219
Shipbuilding industry, 63, 94, 95, 97, 100, 102, 131
Shipping, 64, 130
Shinplasters, 37–38, 37n
Shoe and boot manufacturing, 63, 80, 100, 101, 102
Sibley, F. B., & Co., 108
Sibley, Fred T., 113
Sibley, Frederick B., 108, 114, 137
Sibley, Solomon, 48, 71, 108
Sibley, Mrs. Solomon, 66
Silberman and Hersch Co., 64
Singapore, Mich., 55
Smart, David, 72, 86
Smith, Charles A., 101
Smith, Samuel L., 125
Smith's, William, Barbershop, 132
Soda ash, 97
Somervell, Lt. Gen. Brehon B., 192
Soo Canal, 56, 57, 84–85, 95, 98
Southfield, Mich., 207
Specie Circular of 1836, 53–54
Spindletop, 130
Springwells, 63
Stair, Edward D., 150–51, 174n
Standard Accident Insurance Co., 179, 197
Standard Trust Co., 157, 163
State Bank of Indiana, 59
State Bank of Michigan (1839), 59
State Bank of Michigan (1859), 92
State banks, 50, 51–56, 61, 81, 90–91, 104, 118, 141, 142, 154–55, 157–59, 163, 170, 173, 174, 176, 187, 189, 209, 233–34
State Savings Bank of Ann Arbor, 205
Steam automobile, 130
Steamboats, 43–44, 85
Stearns, Frederick, 100
Steel production, 98, 102
Sterling Heights, Mich., 220
Sterling Township, Mich., 220
Stevens, Eugene, 182
Stimson, Henry L., 195, 196n
Stockmarket crash (1929), 151, 152, 153n, 180

Stockmeyer, C. Boyd, 230, 234, 236
Stoepel, Ralph N., 145
Stone, Ferris D., 188, 197
Stove industry, 99, 131
Streetcars, 108
Studebaker automobile, 147
Studebaker Corp., 192, 219
Superior (steamboat), 44
Surplus Distribution of 1837, 50–51, 53
Swift and Co., 202

Tanks, production in Detroit, 144, 192, 193
Taylor, Charlotte, 43, 76
Taylor, Malcolm C., 167
Telegraph, 66
Ten Thousand Acre Tract, 30, 38
Thalacker, Arbie O., 231
Theodoroff, B. James, 231
Thomas, William J., 214
333 West Fort Corp., 229
Thurber, Cleveland, 197, 205, 211n, 222
Times Square Purchasing Office Building, 196, 229
Tin Lizzie, see Model T. Ford
Tobacco industry, 63, 99, 102
Tokyo, Japan, 200–1
Toledo, Ohio, 193, 219
Tonty, Alphonse de, 18
Toronto, Canada, 85, 121
Touche, Niven, Bailey and Smart, 217
Touche Ross and Co., 217
Tractors for Freedom Committee, 227
Trix, Herbert B., 211n, 222
Trowbridge, Charles C., 41, 45, 62, 76, 113
Trowbridge, Edmund, 107
Troy, N.Y., 45, 99
Truck-Trailer Manufacturers Assoc., 229
Truman, Harry S., 199, 200, 204, 227
Trust companies, 109, 141, 153, 155, 156, 157, 158, 159, 163, 174, 176, 187, 189, 209
Tucker automobile, 219
24th Michigan Infantry, 88

Ultra/Matic 24, 233
Underground Railroad, 89
Union Building Co., 160
Union Commerce Corp., 160, 161
Union Commerce Investment Co., 160
Union Co., 160
Union Guardian Trust Co., 165, 166, 167, 209, 210
Union Pacific R.R., 202
Union Title and Guaranty Co., 160
Union Trust Building, 157
Union Trust Co., 139, 153, 160, 205
Uniroyal Tire Plant, 125
United Foundation, 230
United Negro College Fund, 221
United Savings Bank of Detroit, 153, 168, 173, 176, 209, 211
U.S. Customs House, 68
U.S. Land Office, 68
U.S. Military Assistance Program, 206
U.S. National Defense Council, 191
U.S. Postal Savings System, 143, 163
U.S. Radiator Corp., 137
U.S. Steel Corp., 231
United States Trust Co., 157
University of Detroit, 203
University of Michigan, 71, 72, 145, 205

Van Buren, Martin, 51
Vandenberg, Arthur H., 165
Vernor, James, 101
Vernor-Junction Branch Office, 134
Vernor's Ginger Ale, 101
Veterans' Memorial Building, 17
Victory Loan (1918), 142–43
Victory War Loan (1945), 194
Viger, Nathan I., 197
Vincent, Jesse G., 144
Voyageurs, 15, 17

Wabeek State Bank, Birmingham, 210
Wabeek State Bank of Detroit, 210, 212
Wagon and carriage industry, 95, 130
Walk-in-the-Water (steamboat), 43, 76

Walker, Henry N., 73, 74, 74n, 75, 84, 85, 107, 110, 111, 114
Walker, William, 78
Wampum money, 28
War Contracts Price Adjustment Board, 195–96, 196n
War loan drives, World War II, 193–94
War of 1812, 33–34
Ward, Eber Brock, 98, 107
Warner-Lambert Corp., 101
Warren, Mich., 191
Warren, Ohio, 129
Washington Boulevard Building, 233–34
Washington Trust Company (New York), 120
Washtenaw County, Mich., 55
Wayne, Gen. Anthony, 26
Wayne County Building (1844), 67
Wayne County & Home Savings Bank, 153, 154, 158
Wayne County Savings Bank, 108–9, 154
Wayne State University, 205, 225, 230
Webster, Daniel, 74
West Bloomfield Township, Mich., 233
West Side Industrial Development Area, 229
Westinghouse Electric and Manufacturing Co., 141
Westland, Mich., 219
Whippet tanks, 144
Whitney, David M., 145
Whitney Realty Company, Ltd., 197
Wholesale and retail trade, 63–64
Wildcat banks, 54–56, 58–60, 61
William Penn (steamboat), 44
Williams, Gurdon, 72, 74
Williams, John R., 39, 40–41, 47, 48
Willow Run Plant, 191, 192
Willys Motor Corp., 193, 219
Wilson, Woodrow, 142
Windsor, Canada, 85, 126
Witherell, James, 35
Woodbridge, William, 48, 71
Woodward, Augustus B., 29, 30n, 31–32, 37

Woodward-Hamilton Branch Office, 233
Woodward Plan, 30, 30n, 48
Woodward-Milwaukee Branch Office, 134, 149n
Woodworking industry, 95, 100
World War I, 135, 137, 141, 142–44, 146, 146n, 152, 190, 198
World War II, 135, 146n, 189–96, 197–98
Wright Cyclone aircraft engines, 192

Wyandotte, Mich., 97, 98
Wyandotte Rolling Mill, 107
Wyandotte Savings Bank, 137, 149

Yaw, William R., 223
Yoshida, Shigeru, 202
Ypsilanti, Mich., 66, 89

Zeder, James M., 129
Zeigler, Charles G., 92

Arthur M. Woodford, a native Detroiter, is currently director of personnel and labor relations, Detroit Public Library. He received a degree in Civil Engineering from the University of Wisconsin in 1960, a B.A. degree from Wayne State University in 1963, and an A.M.L.S. in Library Science from the University of Michigan in 1964. He is co-author with Frank B. Woodford of *All Our Yesterdays: A Brief History of Detroit* (Detroit: Wayne State University Press, 1969).

The manuscript was prepared for publication by Alice Nigoghosian. The book was designed by Don Ross. The type face for the text is Optima designed by Hermann Zapf in 1960, and the display face is Thorne Shaded designed for the Stephenson Blake Foundry about 1820.

The text is printed on Nashoba text paper and the book is bound in Columbia Mills' Bayside Vellum cloth for the spine and back, and the front panel is Fictionette Natural Finish cloth over binders boards. Manufactured in the United States of America.